A Guide to 85 Tests for Special Education

Carolyn Compton, Ph.D.
Educational Director
Children's Health Council
Palo Alto, California

New Edition

Fearon Education
Belmont, California

Contributing Authors

Joan Bisagno
M.S., Learning Disability Specialist

Polly Bredt
M.A., C.C.C., Speech and Language Pathologist

Barbara Fourt
OTR, Registered Occupational Therapist

Beth Harper
OTR, Registered Occupational Therapist

Marsha Silver
M.S., C.C.C., Speech and Language Pathologist

Karen Travis
M.S., C.C.C., Speech and Language Pathologist and
Lawyer

ISBN 0-8224-3585-3
Printed in the United States of America
1. 9 8 7 6 5 4 3 2 1

Contents

Alphabetical Listing of Tests

Acknowledgments

Grateful acknowledgement is made to the following authors and publishers for their permission to reprint copyrighted sample test materials and illustrative matter.

SAMUEL A. KIRK, JAMES J. MCCARTHY, and WINIFRED D. KIRK, for illustrations from *The Illinois Test of Psycholinguistic Abilities*. Copyright © 1968 by Board of Trustees of the University of Illinois. University of Illinois Press, Urbana.

M. FROSTIG, for illustrations from *The Developmental Test of Visual Perception*, Palo Alto, CA: Consulting Psychologists Press, Inc., 1966.

THE PSYCHOLOGICAL CORPORATION, for illustrations from the standardization edition of the *Basic Achievement Skills Individual Screener*. Copyright © 1983 by The Psychological Corporation, San Antonio, TX. Reproduced by permission. All rights reserved.

ALBERT H. BRIGANCE, for illustrations from *Brigance® Diagnostic Inventories*. North Billerica, MA: Curriculum Associates, Inc., 1976, 1978, 1981, 1983. By permission of the author and publisher.

PHYLLIS L. NEWCOMER and DOLORES CURTIS, for illustrations from *Diagnostic Achievement Battery*. Austin, TX: Pro-Ed, 1984.

DONALD D. HAMMILL and STEPHEN C. LARSEN, for illustrations from *Test of Written Language*. Austin, TX: Pro-Ed, 1983.

CURRICULUM ASSOCIATES, INC., for illustrations from *Enright® Diagnostic Inventory of Basic Arithmetic Skills*. North Billerica, MA: Curriculum Associates, Inc., © 1983. Reproduced by permission.

BETH SLINGERLAND, for illustrations from *Slingerland Pre-Reading Screening Procedures*. Cambridge, MA: Educators Publishing Service, Inc., 1977.

KEITH E. BEERY and NORMAN A. BUKTENICA, for illustrations from *Beery-Buktenica Developmental Test of Visual-Motor Integration*. Copyright © 1967 by Keith E. Beery and Norman A. Buktenica. Used by permission of Modern Curriculum Press, Cleveland.

RONALD P. COLARUSSO and DONALD D. HAMMILL, for illustrations from *Motor-Free Visual Perception Test*. Novato, CA: Academic Therapy Publications, 1972. By permission of the authors and publisher.

DOROTHY TYACK AND ROBERT GOTTSLEBEN, for illustrations from *Language Sampling, Analysis, and Training*. Palo Alto, CA: Consulting Psychologists Press, Inc., 1977.

ELIZABETH CARROW-WOOLFOLK, for illustrations from *Test for Auditory Comprehension of Language—Revised*. Allen, TX: DLM Teaching Resources, 1985.

DONALD D. HAMMILL, VIRGINA L. BROWN, STEPHEN C. LARSEN, and J. LEE WEIDERHOLT, for illustrations from *Test of Adolescent Language*. Austin, TX: Pro-Ed, 1987.

DONALD D. HAMMILL, for illustrations from *Detroit Test of Learning Aptitude—Revised*, Austin, TX: Pro-Ed, 1985.

AMERICAN GUIDANCE SERVICE, for photograph and illustration used in review of *Kaufman Assessment Battery for Children*, © 1983 by Alan S. Kaufman and Nadeen L. Kaufman. Reprinted by permission of American Guidance Service, Circle Pines, MN.

THE PSYCHOLOGICAL CORPORATION, for illustrations from the *System of Multicultural Pluristic Assessment* Copyright © 1977, 1979 by The Psychological Corporation, San Antonio, TX. Reproduced by permission. All rights reserved.

D. WECHSLER, for illustrations from the *Wechsler Intelligence Scales for Children—Revised*. Copyright © 1974 by The Psychological Corporation, San Antonio, TX. Reproduced by permission. All rights reserved.

Preface

A *Guide to 65 Tests for Special Education* was published in 1980. The revised edition, *A Guide to 75 Tests for Special Education,* published in 1984, included new tests in the field and documented several trends in assessment. These trends included a strong renewed interest in formal standardized tests, a decline in tests assessing "processing" or "modality strengths," attention to cost effectiveness in test administration and scoring, and the combining of aptitude and achievement tests in the same instrument, normed on the same population. Now, five years later, it is interesting to note the status of those trends.

The interest in formal standardized testing instruments is clearly the main focus in the field of special education assessment. Each state, in compliance with new regulations regarding P.L. 94-142 (the Education for All Handicapped Children Act), has developed eligibility criteria for determining which students will receive what kind and what amount of special education services. In most instances, the eligibility requirements are based upon standardized test scores. In some states, the standardized tests to be used are actually named in state regulations; they usually include tests of general intelligence, aptitude, and academic achievement, as well as oral language development. While professors, researchers, and teachers may continue to prefer criterion-referenced assessments which lead directly to instructional planning, the student must be declared eligible for special education based on performance on standardized tests. Standardized tests are, therefore, included in this volume.

The earlier decline in "process" or "modality" testing has reversed somewhat since the early part of the decade. Several of the new leaders in general intelligence and aptitude tests, such as the Kaufman Assessment Battery for Children (K-ABC) and the Detroit Tests of Learning Aptitude—Revised (DTLA-2), emphasize differences in processing styles among individual children. New and revised tests in the language field include subtests of auditory and visual processes. In addition, the eligibility criteria in some states for assistance as a student with specific learning disabilities depends upon the documentation of a "processing" disorder. As a result, the chapter on perception and memory has been reorganized in this edition, and five tests have been added.

Each school district must determine a cost-effective means of complying with the requirements of assessment in special education. Lengthy individual diagnostic procedures are prohibitive in terms of time and money, and new or revised testing instruments (as well as books on testing) are expensive. Group testing is not generally a viable alternative. Three options continue to be explored: 1) the use of paraprofessionals for test administration and scoring, with experienced clinicians interpreting and reporting the results; 2) the use of computer scoring and analysis procedures; and 3) the development of screening tests to identify students in need of further assessment. Short forms or screening tests are available for several of the tests reviewed in this volume. Computer programs for scoring and interpretation are listed where available.

The most obvious way to decrease the cost of the assessment process is to shorten it. Many districts do this by administering only those tests necessary to establish eligibility for special education services. These tests may or may not be good tools for diagnosing a student's disabilities. The same tests are sometimes repeated the following year to measure progress; and there may be little awareness of whether the instruments were even designed to measure progress. The lengthy battery of diagnostic tests designed to tease out the details of a student's learning difficulties is becoming increasingly rare in public school special education programs. Such testing is more likely to occur in research projects or in private or hospital clinics, with private practioners.

In *75 Tests,* it was noted that the cominbing of aptitude and achievement measures in the same instrument was a growing trend. This organization is seen in two very popular tests for special education, the Woodcock-Johnson Psycho-Education Battery (WJPEB) and the Kaufman Assessment Battery for Children (K-ABC). While this particular combination is not noted in other tests, it is clear that batteries of tests which allow comparison between several aspects of a student's functioning are very popular. This trend is seen in new tests in language (CELF-R, TOAL-2, TOLD-P, TOLD-1), academics (WRAT-R, BASIS, NEAT, DAB), and intellectual functioning (DTLA-2, DTLA-P). Perhaps this trend relates to the need for cost-efficient assessment procedures. One examiner giving a wide-range battery saves time and money.

A Guide to 85 Tests for Special Education has, as did its predecessors, three functions: to enable the teacher to understand and interpret test performance based on knowledge of the test's format, strengths, and limitations; to help the special education teacher, psychologist, or administrator plan a testing program by providing basic information about the major tests available in each skill area; and to provide a means for improved communication among teachers, diagnosticians, and parents about the purposes, procedures, and results of testing.

85 Tests should be of help to teachers and diagnosticians who need to interpret reports on students completed by other examiners. The tests are grouped according to skills and to the purposes of the test authors. Information is given to allow education professionals to find out what a test measures, how the test measures it, and what the test scores mean.

85 Tests is also intended to be a selection guide. No book of tests is ever complete, and this volume should certainly not be considered unabridged. Tests have been selected because of their wide usage or their unique strengths with a special population. Enough information is given in each test review to enable professionals to compare several tests in a given skill area and to determine which are the most useful and appropriate.

The third function of *85 Tests* is to improve communication between the people giving the tests, the people using the test results, the parents of students, and, when appropriate, the students themselves. A glossary of testing terms is provided to increase knowledge of test terminology.

85 Tests is organized somewhat differently from its predecessors. Following an overview of assessment procedures in the introduction and a section titled Grandaddies, which describes five of the veteran testing instruments, the test reviews are organized into six chapters.

Chapter One: Academic Tests contains the reviews of tests of reading, writing, spelling, and mathematics.

Chapter Two: Perception, Memory, and Visual-Motor Tests includes reviews of tests which assess visual and auditory perception, memory, and drawing skills.

Chapter Three: Speech and Language Tests contains assessments for oral language, both receptive and expressive.

Chapter Four: Bilingual Assessments includes brief reviews of assessment instruments for Spanish-speaking children.

Chapter Five: Gross and Fine Motor Tests reviews measures of gross and fine motor skills.

Chapter Six: General Intelligence and Developmental Scales includes a variety of instruments applicable to a wide age range of children, adolescents, and adults.

In *65 Tests* and *75 Tests* a separate section was provided for preschool and kindergarten tests. In this volume, such tests have been incorporated into other chapters. Within each chapter, tests are organized into sections and then alphabetized within each section to facilitate their location.

This book is written by clinicians. Over the years, colleagues of mine at the Children's Health Council have authored test reviews and made other valuable contributions to the writing of this book. The list grows with each revision.

Joan Bisagno, M.S., Learning Disability Specialist
Polly Bredt, M.A., C.C.C., Speech and Language Pathologist
Barbara Fourt, OTR, Registered Occupational Therapist
Beth Harper, OTR, Registered Occupational Therapist
Marsha Silver, M.S., C.C.C., Speech and Language Pathologist
Karen Travis, M.S., C.C.C., Speech and Language Pathologist and Lawyer

The Children's Health Council is a private non-profit multidisciplinary clinic serving children of all ages who have mild to severe learning, language, motor, cognitive, and emotional disorders. All of the tests reviewed have been used in our clinic, and the strengths and limitations described are those we have experienced in our daily diagnostic work with children. We hope that our experience is helpful to you.

Carolyn Compton

Introduction

Educational assessment, in its broadest sense, is the gathering of information about a student's performance in school. When the student's school performance is deemed inadequate, educational diagnosis is used to investigate and define the student's particular pattern of academic strengths and skill deficiencies and to translate them into an individualized program. The diagnostician uses many tools—observation, interview, diagnostic teaching, and testing. Testing, then, is just one part of educational assessment.

This book reviews the instruments of educational testing, and their uses and misuses, within the total process of educational assessment for students in academic difficulty because of learning disabilities and/or related problems.

nia Achievement Tests (Tiegs and Clark, 1970), and the Sequential Test of Basic Skills (1958) all give teachers and parents important information about students' progress from year to year and about their academic relationship to other students at the same age and grade level.

But questions about an individual student's specific strengths and weaknesses are not easily answered by group achievement tests. Particularly for students with difficulties in academic areas, individual testing is essential to discover the pattern of strengths and weaknesses. This discovery can then lead to the development of an individual instructional program. Educational tests for students in academic difficulty have four main functions: screening, diagnosis, instructional planning, and measuring progress.

PURPOSE OF TESTING

The general purpose of educational testing is to answer educationally relevant questions about a student. Broadly, these questions are:

- What is the student's current functioning level in basic skills?
- What are the student's specific skill deficiencies, if any?
- What are the student's strengths?
- What and how shall the student be taught?
- How well is the student progressing?

The general school testing program attempts to answer these questions through group achievement tests given periodically throughout the grades. Such tests as the Iowa Test of Basic Skills (Lindquist and Hieronymus, 1956), the Califor-

Screening

The first phase of the diagnostic process is screening. A test or series of tests is given to a group of students who have something in common—age, grade level, or signs of a special problem, such as deficient fine motor coordination or poor reading performance. The results from screening tests provide a first look at a group of students to determine temporary groupings or to identify students in need of further testing. Kindergarten screening, for example, is popular in many districts as a means of determining which children may have difficulty in first grade. The goal of any screening program is to identify students in need of further individual diagnostic testing. The essence of screening is its quickness; therefore, test items must be carefully selected to measure critical skills.

Because most students who are screened do not receive further testing, we must take care to ensure that the screening procedures will properly identify those students in need of further evaluation. False positives—students identified as having disabilities when they do not—and false negatives—students with difficulties who slip through the screening process—are both serious problems. False positives can be corrected by referrals for individual testing, but false negatives do not get that opportunity.

Diagnostic Testing

In contrast to screening, diagnostic testing is usually a lengthy individual process. A battery of tests assesses the student's functioning not only in basic academic skills but also in processes believed to be essential for all learning—perception, memory, concept development, visual-motor skills, language development, and expressive skills. These tests assess the primary modalities used in the learning process—auditory, visual, and kinesthetic (or motor). Some attention is given to a possible cause for the academic problems, but much more attention is given to a description of their type and degree of severity.

The most common purpose of diagnostic testing is to determine a student's eligibility for special education services and programs. Pursuant to Public Law 94-142 (The Education for all Handicapped Children Act), every state has a set of rules and regulations that specify who is handicapped and what eligibility criteria a student must demonstrate to receive special education services.

In the case of students with specific learning disabilities, the eligibility criteria require that the student's test performance demonstrate a significant discrepancy between ability and achievement. While this discrepancy may be defined differently in different states, the process by which it is determined is diagnostic testing. What results from diagnostic testing is often, then, a placement decision. Students are admitted to or excluded from special programs, retained, placed in private schools, or referred for medical and psychological services on the basis of diagnostic testing. Thus, it must be carried out thoughtfully by experienced professionals who understand the importance of careful diagnostic decisions.

Instructional Planning

Following the diagnostic testing process and the placement decision, the instructional planning phase begins. While the information obtained from diagnostic tests is useful, rarely does it provide information specific enough for individual instructional planning. This planning is usually done by the special education teacher, who often needs to gather more specific information through informal inventories and curriculum-based assessment procedures.

Assessment, including educational testing, is an integral part of special education. It is the process that determines which students we work with, how we work with them, and how long they continue in our programs. Educational testing should never become too routine. Every student tested deserves to have an appropriate, well thought-out assessment planned and implemented. Critical decisions will be based on the result.

Measuring Progress

The final function of educational testing is to assess progress. Measuring pupil progress includes pre- and posttesting on formal and informal tests, daily charting of performance on specific tasks, and observing student performance in the classroom. Standardized tests, informal tests, and rating scales are usually used for this purpose.

ABUSES AND MISUSES OF TESTS

Many of the criticisms of educational tests are legitimate; in many instances tests have been abused and misused. One problem area in educational testing is the confusion of terms. As mentioned earlier, *assessment* is the total process of gathering information about a student's performance in school; diagnosis is one part of that process, and the diagnostician uses *testing* as one tool. Basing educational decisions on test results alone, without using the other tools of the diagnostician—observation, interview, and diagnostic teaching—is a misuse of tests. Viewing diagnosis as a once-only process rather than a continuous procedure is also a common error.

Anastasiow (1973, p.349) describes four other consistent abuses of tests:

• Generalizing the interpretation of test scores to groups not represented in the norming sample

• Overinterpreting scores—for example, focusing on a five-point gain in IQ score when five points is not statistically significant

• Teaching the answers to test questions in the belief that an improved test score alone will demonstrate pupil progress

• Violating students' confidentiality and privacy by revealing test scores to persons not directly involved with the educational program.

Wallace and Larsen (1978, p.22) add one other abuse to the list:

• Overgeneralizing the findings of a test, either by making decisions about an individual student based solely on performance on a group test or by labeling students on the basis of single test scores.

Hammill (1985, p.45) reminds us that tests don't diagnose. A student should not be considered learning disabled because he or she exhibits a discrepancy between ability and achievement; there may be other causes for that discrepancy. The role of the examiner is to consider all the factors, then make the diagnosis.

Salvia and Ysseldyke, in *Assessment in Special and Remedial Education* (1978), discuss the misuses of tests extensively. They divide testing errors into three types: the wrong test, the wrong interpretation, and "dumb" mistakes. A test may be wrong if it is technically inadequate, that is, invalid or unreliable. A test may also be wrong if it is used for the wrong purpose, such as using the Reading subtest of the Wide Range Achievement Test—Revised as if it were a measure of total reading. Finally, a test may be wrong when it is used with the wrong child—a child whose characteristics differ greatly from the norming sample.

The wrong interpretation of test scores, according to Salvia and Ysseldyke, is easily done. Two common errors are inferring causation from a student's test behavior and assigning a student to a group of students with similar test behavior on the basis of that test behavior alone. A good test can elicit performance that will define a student's skill deficiencies—but not the cause of them. And a student whose test performance is similar to that of retarded children is not necessarily retarded.

"Dumb" mistakes described by Salvia and Ysseldyke include such things as equating IQ scores on different tests and making clerical errors in scoring. Another "dumb" mistake is repeating the same test too frequently.

Testing is simply one diagnostic tool. When tests are part of a well-designed assessment procedure, planned and implemented by sensitive professionals, they provide important information about a student. But tests selected, administered, and interpreted incorrectly are worse than useless. They lead to incorrect and inappropriate placements and programs for children.

TYPES OF TESTS
There are many types of tests. To plan an appropriate testing program, one must understand the essential characteristics of each type.

Formal and Informal Tests
Formal tests are more appropriately called *standardized tests*. These may be group or individual tests. They have standardized procedures for administration, timing, and scoring. They are normed on a representative sample of students and may provide age and grade-level scores as well as standard scores, or percentiles, that allow the educator to compare a student with other students of the same age and grade. Once the standardized procedure has been altered, the norms are no longer valid, and legitimate comparisons cannot be made. Another term for formal or standardized tests is *norm-referenced tests*.

Informal testing does not produce normed scores. Informal tests are structured observations that appraise the student's performance without reference to other students. Informal tests are usually administered individually. Because there are no norms, the teacher can modify the test format, the timing, and the administration procedures to allow the student the best opportunity to demonstrate his or her skills. Test items can be selected to best reflect the curriculum being taught. Because the tests are not normed, interpretation of the results is very dependent on the skills of the examiner.

Individual and Group Tests
Some tests are designed to be administered individually, while others may be given to groups of students. Group tests save administration time and student time. They are appropriate instruments for assessing achievement in such skill areas as reading comprehension and math computation. They also measure student behaviors, such as persistence, pacing, and the ability to follow group instruction or to work independently. Often, learning-disabled and other special education students are exempted from group tests. As a result, their repertoires of group test-taking strategies are not well developed.

Individual tests generally allow the student more opportunities to demonstrate his or her skills. The examiner can establish rapport with the student and provide breaks to decrease anxiety or fatigue. The examiner also has more opportunity to clarify instructions and to encourage the student lacking in confidence. If presented skillfully, a test can hold the student's interest, and the examiner can elicit cooperation without deviating from standardized procedures. For these reasons, individual tests are recommended and usually required for the diagnosis of learning disabilities and other academic problems.

Diagnostic and Achievement Tests
Diagnostic and achievement tests can be either standardized or informal, group or individual. Diagnostic tests are designed to determine whether a student has a specific

learning disability and, if so, in what skill area or learning process it occurs. Some diagnostic tests, such as the Gates-McKillop-Horowitz Reading Diagnostic Tests, measure one specific academic skill area in depth. Others, such as the Goldman-Fristoe-Woodcock Auditory Skills Battery, attempt to assess several subskills of an important learning process. In diagnostic testing, observations of how the student does a task and the types of errors made are as important as the score. For this reason, individual diagnostic tests are usually more valuable than group tests in determining which students may have learning disabilities and in planning their instruction.

Achievement tests are designed to measure a student's present functioning level in basic academic skills. Items are selected to represent typical curriculum materials at specific grade levels. For example, a spelling test would include a graded list of words to be dictated by the examiner and written by the student. The score would reflect the student's present functioning level in spelling and suggest the instructional level. Evaluation of the student's error pattern on an achievement test is possible but not as easy as on a diagnostic test designed for that purpose. Achievement tests are often group tests, usually standardized and norm-referenced. They reflect curriculum content in a single area, such as mathematics, or in multiple areas, such as reading, mathematics, and spelling.

Aptitude Tests

Aptitude tests are often thought of as the opposite of achievement tests. Whereas achievement tests presumably measured learning, aptitude tests were thought to measure innate capacity or potential. Now the term *developed abilities* reflects the widely-accepted view that aptitude tests also reflect learning. Anastasiow makes the distinction that achievement tests measure school learning while aptitude tests measure broader, looser, less-controlled learning which occurs both in and out of school. While achievement tests are sometimes the best predictors of future performance (especially short term), achievement tests are generally used to assess current status and aptitude tests to predict future performance.

Criterion-Referenced Tests

Relative newcomers to the field of testing, criterion-referenced tests concentrate more on identifying the skills an individual student has mastered than on comparing that student to others of the same age or grade. The information obtained on these tests leads directly to instructional planning. Several terms are used to describe this testing process. *Curriculum-based assessment*, *object referenced assessment*, and *direct assessment* are all terms used in reference to the evaluation of pupil progress based on the curriculum.

In practice, eligibility and placement decisions are based on standardized, norm-referenced tests. While several authors describe the use of criterion-referenced testing for eligibility decision (Deno, 1985; Germann & Tindal, 1985; Marston & Magnusson, 1985), at present criterion-referenced testing is used primarily for instructional planning.

THE DIAGNOSTIC BATTERY

A major group of students for whom educational assessment is needed are those in academic difficulty because of suspected learning disabilities. The task of the diagnostician is to determine whether a student's academic problems are related to specific learning disabilities and, if so, what the nature and the degree of the disabilities are. From this information, a specific instructional program may be designed.

In designing a diagnostic testing battery for a student with suspected learning disabilities, the diagnostician must consider academic skill areas, learning processes and modalities, and the time and personnel available for testing.

Academic Skill Areas

If time and personnel are not an issue, what academic skill areas should be assessed in a complete educational evaluation? Table 1 serves as a guide to the major academic skill areas and their subgroups.

Each of these major areas could be further broken down into multiple subskills. Testing could go on forever, and sometimes, from the point of view of the parents, the student, and the teacher who referred the student, it seems as though it does. Fortunately, the constraints of time and personnel force some decisions about what areas should be assessed. Such decisions should be made by considering the following factors:

• *The concerns of the teacher or the parent in the referral or testing request.* If a student is referred because of difficulties in reading and spelling but exhibits superior math skills, the diagnostician may do a quick math screening but focus the evaluation on reading, writing, and spelling.

• *The age and grade of the student.* If the student is in first or second grade, the reading evaluation will focus on phonic skills, sight-word recognition, and oral reading rather than on advanced word analysis skills or silent reading comprehension.

• *Relevance of the area to classroom performance.* Oral spelling and oral math are often omitted because of their low frequency as classroom tasks. Similarly, written expression, an essential skill, should always be included.

Table 1. Academic Skill Areas

Reading

Decoding
  Phonic skills
  Sight-word recognition
  Oral paragraph reading
Comprehension
  Oral reading
  Silent reading
  Listening
  Comprehension in specific content areas

Writing

Penmanship
  Manuscript
  Cursive
Written Expression
  Fluency
  Syntax
  Mechanics
  Content

Spelling

Written
  Phonic words
  Irregular words
Recognition of Sight Words
Oral

Mathematics

Concepts
Computation
  Addition
  Subtraction
  Multiplication
  Division
Word Problems
  Oral
  Written

Oral Language

Receptive
  Vocabulary
  Listening comprehension
Expressive
  Articulation
  Morphology
  Syntax
  Semantics
  Pragmatics

Learning Processes and Modalities

The second factor to consider in designing the diagnostic testing battery is the basic psychological processes and the primary sensory modalities in which they occur. Table 2 provides an outline for assessing the basic psychological processes in the three modalities, or sensory channels, most commonly used in classroom learning.

The assessment of psychological processes and sensory modalities has been repeatedly criticized on several counts:

• Terms such as "memory," "attention," and "perception" are used differently in different test instruments (Ceci, Ringstorm, and Lea, 1981).

• The instruments used in process and modality testing have questionable validity and reliability (Arter and Jenkins, 1978).

• There is little evidence that the specific programming information yielded by these instruments is related to academic growth (Myers and Hammill, 1976; Arter and Jenkins, 1978).

Despite these criticisms, the assessment of psychological processes and sensory modalities continues to be a key component of the educational assessment of students with suspected learning disabilities. For students to qualify for special education programs, state law in California requires that the assessment results must, first, show a significant discrepancy between intellectual ability and achievement, and second, must demonstrate that the discrepancy is "directly related to a disorder in one or more of the basic psychological processes which include: attention, visual and auditory processing, sensory-motor skills, and cognitive abilities including expression, conceptualization, and association" (State of California, 1982).

Again, the learning processes selected for assessment should be based on the individual student's needs. If the teacher reports that the student has great difficulty following oral classroom instructions and giving oral reports, tests that assess auditory reception, auditory memory, and verbal expression will be selected. If the academic testing reveals confusion between words such as *boy* and *day* or *came* and *come*, tests in the area of visual perception would have high priority. Selecting tests to answer specific educational questions is more appropriate than administering a standard battery to all students; the latter frequently results in excessive testing (Wallace and Larsen, 1978, p. 71).

Process and modality tests are simply one part of the assessment process; they are neither perfect nor useless. They do often provide information about the tasks a student can do well—a part of the diagnostic process too often omitted.

Table 2. Process-Modality Chart

Modality	Process				
	Reception (initial receiving of information)	**Perception** (initial organizing of information)	**Association** (relating new information to other information)	**Memory** (short-term, sequential memory)	**Expression** (output)
Auditory (primary stimuli are auditory)					**Verbal expression**
Visual (primary stimuli are visual)					**Written expression**
Tactile/Kinesthetic (primary stimuli accompanied by motoric input)					**Motoric expression other than written or verbal**

Time and Personnel Available

The practicalities of time and personnel clearly affect the selection of tests in the diagnostic battery. Two hours of individual educational testing is generally considered a minimum amount of time for a basic educational evaluation; three to four hours would be more usual. Students with major learning disabilities, students who work slowly, or students who need frequent breaks and much encouragement often need several short testing sessions. Overtesting should be avoided: not only is it time-consuming, but it rarely leads to significantly more educationally relevant information.

Educational assessment is frequently done by a diagnostic team. The psychologist usually administers general intelligence tests and often tests of visual-motor development. The language therapist assesses receptive and expressive language skill, articulation, and auditory processing. The educational diagnostician tests academic performance and related learning processes. A perceptual-motor specialist examines gross and fine motor skills. When the educational diagnostician is a one-person team, the test battery must include a broader range of tests, particularly in the areas of concept development, language, and motor skills.

TEST SELECTION

Most educators have little trouble identifying the academic areas or learning processes to be tested. The chief problem is choosing the specific test to be used. Too often, tests are ordered rather than selected. Test selection should be based on the following criteria:

• Does the test answer the educational question being asked?

• Is the standardization sample appropriate for the student being tested?

• Is the test valid?

• Is the test reliable?

• Are the design and format appropriate for the student being tested?

• Is the content or skill area being measured appropriate for the age and grade of the student?

Educational Relevance

The most important question to ask in selecting a test is, What type of educational information do I need? Clearly, some tests should be given to every student, whereas other tests should be used only in highly specific situations. Screening tests should be quick and include items carefully selected to measure critical skills. Diagnostic tests must be thoughtful and yield information upon which placement decisions can be made and individualized program plans formulated. Tests used to measure pupil progress must be sensitive to the curriculum being taught. Random selection of tests, without careful consideration of the type of educational information the tests will yield, often results in overtesting or in trying to force a set of test scores to answer questions they were not intended to answer. The following examples illustrate this point.

Sycamore School District decided to give all students in their intermediate grades The Bender Visual Motor Gestalt Test. They designed group administration procedures and carried out the testing. Later, they realized the norms went only to the age of 9 years and were based on individual administration.

Maple School District decided to give a group standardized math test to all elementary-level students in the learning disability program in October and May to measure pupil progress in math. The test measured standard computation skills, but the curriculum being used was an experimental "new math" approach. Few students showed progress in math between October and May. Teachers had to spend spring parent conferences explaining that Johnny actually had made progress despite his test scores.

Standardization, Validity, and Reliability

Once the purposes of testing have been defined and specific educational questions have been posed, test selection should be based on the standardization sample, the validity, and the reliability of the tests available.

The composition of the standardization sample of a standardized test is an important factor. To standardize a test, the test author selects a population of students to whom he or she administers the new test. The performance of this group of students becomes the "norm." It is the author's responsibility to describe that population of students in depth—by age level, sex, racial background, socioeconomic level, intelligence level, and so forth. Examiners must learn to look for and pay attention to the composition of the norming sample to determine if that sample included students of the type being tested. Many standardization samples do not include minority groups or students with the same type of handicapping conditions as those to whom the test is typically given. Making judgments about a student's performance on a test with an inappropriate norming population is not a valid decision-making process and is one of the misuses of tests (Anastasiow, 1973).

Validity is another primary consideration in test selection. Does the test measure the skill area well? There are many types of validity.

• *Content validity* considers whether the skills being measured are critical to the academic task and whether the test reflects the curriculum.

• *Concurrent validity* asks if the test correlates well with other accepted criteria of performance in that subject or skill area.

• *Predictive validity* asks how well the scores correlate with some criterion for future success. Predictive validity is of particular importance for screening instruments.

• *Construct validity* questions the theory and assumptions under which the test was constructed.

• *Discriminate validity* considers whether each of the subtests does, in fact, measure a separate, distinct skill.

Again, consideration of test validity is of critical importance in all test selection. For some tests, studies of validity are readily available in the examiner's manual; for others, library research is necessary; for some, no evidence of validity is offered.

Reliability is the third important criterion for test selection. The consistency with which a test measures what it measures is a critical variable. Many factors influence a student's score on a test. Some of them come from within the student—attention, motivation, physical condition, anxiety, and so forth. The good diagnostician takes these factors into account when interpreting test scores. But other factors affecting reliability are part of the test itself—the length of the test, the clarity of instructions, the objectivity of the scoring, and others. The diagnostician must also learn to study the reliability data on a test and select the most reliable test that yields the needed educational information. Reliable answers to educational questions not asked are of little value, but unreliable answers to critical educational questions can cause placement and instructional errors.

Design and Format

The design and format of a test should also be considered in selection. Students with learning disabilities and other academic problems need tests that are simple in design, are clearly printed, and have easy-to-understand instructions. Whether a test is timed or untimed should also be considered. Sometimes it is important to know how rapidly a student can perform a given task. Reading, for example, is not a usable tool until it becomes fluent. Speed is also a critical variable in measuring writing ability. When speed is a factor, a timed test that will yield a score based on both accuracy and speed should be selected. Just as often, we need to know how much a student can do in a skill area when no time constraints are imposed. Untimed tests, or power tests, allow students to continue working until they reach a ceiling or complete the tests. When students are first learning a skill, untimed tests are usually more appropriate.

Careful consideration should be given to the type of response required by the tests; the format of a test should not penalize a particular type of student. Students with learning disabilities frequently have a short attention span, little motivation for school tasks, great anxiety about testing, and difficulty following directions. These characteristics frequently result in an impulsive style of test taking. Tests requiring multiple-choice or yes-or-no responses often lead to impulsive guessing with little monitoring of answers and are therefore often less appropriate with these students. Other tests place a high demand on auditory memory. Because auditory memory is frequently a weak area for students with learning disabilities, selection of a test that does not focus on this skill will yield more meaningful results.

Appropriateness of Content

Another factor in test selection is the appropriateness of the test content for the age and grade level of the student. Perceptual tests are much more appropriate at the primary grade levels, when perceptual skills are normally developing. Only the most impaired secondary students will demonstrate difficulties on perceptual tests. Bright students will have developed compensation techniques; their continued perceptual problems will be seen more clearly through error analysis of academic tasks. Oral reading tests are also more appropriate for primary and intermediate students. During those grades, oral reading is an important classroom skill. As students get older, oral reading tests give information about word recognition skills but may not yield accurate information about silent reading comprehension of content material—the more essential classroom task.

Inservice Training

Test selection should involve the full team of administrators, diagnosticians, and teachers. Available tests should be reviewed, and their standardization population, validity, and reliability should be studied. But careful test selection will be of little value unless it is followed by inservice training in administration and scoring procedures, test interpretation, and explanation of results to parents. Professionals involved in testing who do not take part in inservice training often use tests without critiquing their value. Inservice training sessions should serve as an ongoing evaluation of each test being given and its usefulness in providing answers to specific educational questions.

SPECIAL ISSUES IN TESTING

The Use of Grade-Level Scores

The type of test score most frequently reported by educational diagnosticians is the grade-level, or grade-equivalent, score. Even when percentiles and standard scores are provided in the test manual, many educational reports include only the grade scores. The reason for this is the easy communicability of the grade score; students, parents, and teachers all feel they understand its meaning. Despite repeated criticism of this procedure by experts in test construction, the practice has continued. The time has come to stop. Two sources support this point:

> Because the continued use of grade norms is professionally indefensible, the Board of Directors of the International Reading Association in 1980 has asked (1) that examiners abandon the practice of reporting and interpreting test performance in grade equivalents, and (2) that test authors and publishers eliminate such norms from tests (Brown, Hammill, and Wiederholt, 1978).

> Does anyone know how an assassination of the grade ratings could be accomplished? Perhaps a national hanging in effigy, a funeral, and a period of suitable mourning? Then a burial to put grade ratings to rest in honor beside their parent, the old Binet mental age constructs (Brill, 1979).

Brill's statement is taken from a speech given to school psychologists in San Diego in 1979 and later published as a technical report entitled *The Uses and Misuses of the WRAT*. He goes on to say that grade ratings give people—including professionals—false ideas of how learning takes place. Grade ratings should not be reported arithmetically as an indication of learning, because they represent the average scores of students in the sampling population at that grade level. Several other points about grade scores are important to keep in mind:

• They are not an equal-interval scale; the difference between grade levels 3.4 and 3.5 may be very different than the difference between grade levels 8.5 and 8.6 or even 3.5 and 3.6.

• They cannot be added and subtracted as raw scores, as standard scores can.

• They cannot be compared with the student's current grade placement.

This last point is very important. For example, if Richard's current grade placement is 6.3 (sixth grade, third month) and his WRAT reading grade is 5.1 (fifth grade, first month), we might say that he is one year and two months behind. This is an incorrect use of scores. If Richard's intelligence quotient is 110, his expected WRAT reading score is 7.1. This is the score to compare with 5.1. Better yet is a comparison of standard scores 110 and 94, the standard score that corresponds to the 5.1 grade equivalent.

The implications of Brown et al. and Brill's statements are very clear. Never report only grade scores when standard scores and percentiles are available; preferably, report the standard scores and percentiles and omit the grade scores. If a test yields only grade scores, don't use it; if you must, report the results only through discussion without scores.

While the above paragraphs deal with the grade level or grade equivalent score, it is important to note that the same criticism is equally true of the age-level or age equivalent score.

Evaluating Progress

Evaluating pupil progress is an essential part of every program for students with academic difficulties. Accountability demands that educators evaluate programs in terms of pupil progress, but measuring an individual student's growth is often not a simple process. The selection of tests that will not only provide valuable diagnostic information but also prove to be effective measures of pupil progress takes forethought and planning. The following factors may serve as general guidelines:

• Selecting tests that have alternate forms for retesting purposes is helpful only if the two forms have good statistical equivalency. In some tests, Form A or B frequently "seems" easier or usually results in higher or lower scores.

Such inconsistencies defeat the purpose of alternate forms. Research studies on "practice effect" are inconclusive with normal children, and even less is known about the practice effect of frequent test administrations with exceptional children, the most tested group.

• Selecting an individual test, such as the Woodcock Johnson Psycho-Educational Battery, or a coordinated series of tests, such as the Gates-MacGinitie Reading Tests, that covers a wide age range, allows for a measure of progress from year to year on the same instrument.

• Selecting tests with an appropriate level of difficulty for students is necessary in determining student progress. A test that is too hard or too easy gives little information on growth.

• Tests of progress should reflect the curriculum content. As the example of the Maple School District demonstrates, tests that do not measure the skills being taught show little pupil progress and require much explanation. Another example deals with oral reading tests. Tests of oral reading usually include a high percentage of sight words. If the student has been taught all year in a systematic phonics program, the retest score may not reflect his or her progress because exposure to sight words has been minimal. In this case, a measure of phonic skills that reflects the curriculum should be included in the retesting procedures. Testing oral reading with a timed test when speed reading has not been emphasized by the classroom teacher is another example of an impractical way to measure student progress.

• Reliability is a critical factor in selecting measures of pupil progress. In addition to the factors within the student and the test that affect reliability (discussed earlier), the teacher needs to be aware of several other reliability factors that affect measurement of progress. Difference scores are frequently used to document pupil progress; that is, a student is given a test in September and the same test (or its equivalent form) in May. The lower score is subtracted from the higher score, and the resulting difference score is used as an indication of growth or lack of progress. But several precautions are needed for this procedure. First, grade scores and percentile scores are not based on an equal-interval scale and should not be used for calculating differences. Raw scores or standard scores should be used. Second, difference scores are the most unreliable of test scores, because they combine the measurement errors of both test scores. Small gains or losses in achievement may not be reliable or statistically significant. Finally, difference scores that do reach statistical significance may not make any practical difference in instructional level and should not be overplayed.

• Tests with many subtests are particularly difficult to interpret in terms of student progress. Changes in the total test score often are used to document progress. However, total test scores are usually obtained by summing several subtest scores. Such a procedure often obscures progress in certain skills and lack of progress in others.

• Criterion-referenced tests provide important measures of pupil progress and should certainly be included together with well selected standardized tests.

Measuring Reading Comprehension

For many students with reading disabilities at the upper-elementary and secondary school levels, the reading problem is not decoding or word reading, but reading comprehension. Tests available in the area of reading comprehension, oral or silent, yield grade-level or percentile scores but offer little diagnostic information about the types of reading comprehension problems that the student demonstrates. Many skills make up reading comprehension—decoding, knowing word meanings, understanding content, organizing, recognizing tone and mood, inferring meaning, and many others. A task analysis of the reading comprehension process and developmental studies of progression of skills involved is needed. From this data, criterion-referenced tests can be designed. Meanwhile, diagnosticians need to remember that many factors of the test can affect reading comprehension scores:

• Level of material read (too easy or too difficult)
• Type of questions asked (specific facts or inferential questions)
• Type of response required (written, oral, multiple-choice, or essay)
• Length of time between reading and responding (immediate or delayed recall)
• Speed factor (timed or untimed)
• Instructions to the student

No global score can accurately reflect a student's reading comprehension. The conditions of the test must be considered.

Teachers who are designing individual programs to remediate reading comprehension should also consider the following factors in the student that may cause poor reading comprehension:

• *Poor decoding skills.* The most usual explanation for poor comprehension is that the student is reading material too difficult for his or her decoding skills.

• *Deficits in underlying language skills.* Weaknesses in vocabulary and sentence comprehension, due to inadequate language comprehension, are a frequent cause of low reading comprehension.

• *Experiential deficits.* Students may not have the experience necessary to understand the concepts being presented in the reading material.

• *Memory deficits.* Diagnosticians and teachers too often attempt to teach comprehension skills to students who already comprehend but who cannot recall the material.

• *Deficits in expressive skills.* Reading comprehension is often assessed by asking the student to express understanding of a passage verbally or in writing. The problem may not be in the comprehension but in the expressive part of this process.

 • *Specific comprehension deficits.* Many students need to be taught such specific skills as finding the main idea, recognizing mood and tone, and so forth.

When planning individualized reading programs, the teacher must study the diagnostic test information and the student's classroom performance to determine which of the above factors are contributing to the student's reading comprehension difficulties. The remediation programs should be very different for the student who has significant language disabilities and the student who needs to be taught specific comprehension skills.

In addition, it is risky to predict students' silent reading skills from their oral reading performance. The average reader usually has better comprehension in silent reading, but the student with learning disabilities frequently reads aloud with greater accuracy and comprehension. Oral reading focuses this student's attention, and hearing himself or herself read often improves comprehension. Measures of both kinds of reading should be included in a full diagnostic evaluation.

Determining Instructional Level

Test scores do not always make clear the level at which instruction should begin. Tests yield achievement scores which may or may not be helpful when deciding placement in a reading series. "Most series are not constructed according to readability formulas but rather according to a sequence of skills developed by the authors" (Lesiak and Johnson, 1983). Careful study of a student's test protocols yields important information about the type of reading series to select, but having the student read aloud a graded set of paragraphs from that series is the most useful process for determining instructional level.

In 1946, Betts (pp. 445–454) divided reading levels into categories dependent on the student's accuracy rate which are still our best guide for determining instructional level.

1. *Basal or independent level.* Student reads with 99 percent accuracy and 90 percent comprehension. Oral reading is fluent and well phrased. The student is free from tension and free to think about the content, because he or she is totally in control of the vocabulary, the sentence construction, and the content.

2. *Instructional level.* Student reads with 95 percent accuracy and 75 percent comprehension. He or she can use word analysis skills and makes good progress with teacher guidance.

3. *Frustration level.* Student reads with less than 90 percent accuracy and less than 50 percent comprehension. He or she becomes easily bogged down, tense, distractable, and sometimes resistive.

Betts's levels are very relevant for planning classroom instruction. Many, many students are being instructed in materials at their frustration level; that is, they are misreading more than one word in every 10. Halting and struggling over almost every word, they become very tense. This is not instruction; it is frustration.

Lesiak and Johnson (1983, pp. 12–17) describe two processes for placing a student in the appropriate reader. They are the informal reading inventory which uses Betts's levels, and a cloze test. In this procedure, graded passages are selected for oral reading and then every fifth word is deleted. The student supplies the word as he or she reads aloud. Independent Level requires at least 50% accuracy; Instructional Level is 30–50%, and Frustration Level below 30% accuracy. Several reading tests reviewed in Chapter One utilize a similar cloze procedure.

Students with good phonics instruction will often read with approximately the same accuracy rate in materials at a wide range of grade levels. In such cases, instructional level should be the highest level at which the student has 75 percent comprehension. Students with reading disabilities of the dyslexic type often make errors on little words (*the, he, they, from*). Their accuracy rate may also be the same across several grade levels, and they should be instructed at the highest level of good (75 percent) comprehension.

The Diagnostic Report

For many diagnosticians, the written report is the most difficult part of the educational assessment process. Describing a student's behavior during testing and analyzing the student's performance on several tests are very difficult tasks. The written diagnostic report ranges in length from a 12-page dissertation about the student's performance (which few people take the time or make the effort to read) to a 1-page listing of test scores. Between these extremes is a thoughtfully prepared 3- or 4-page report that helps the teacher, parent, or doctor understand more fully the student's classroom performance.

The following general outline has been useful in preparing written reports.

1. Identifying data
2. Reason for referral; purpose of testing
3. Behavioral observations during testing
4. Tests administered
5. Test results
6. Analysis of test results
7. Summary
8. Recommendations

Appendix C contains two examples of completed diagnostic reports using a similar format.

Identifying Data
The identifying data include such information as the student's name, birthdate, chronological age, grade, school, examiner's name, and date of testing.

Reason for Referral
This should be a brief statement of the present problem. It is helpful to know who referred the student, what behaviors were of concern, and the purpose of the testing.

Behavior During Testing
A most important section of the report is the description of the student's behavior during testing. Statements about the student's cooperation, attention, persistence, anxiety level, and response to the testing are important in assessing the reliability of the tests. Although the comments are subjective, based on the examiner's observation of the student, they do describe the student in the individual testing situation. The student may behave very differently from in the classroom—more attentive and cooperative or less so, more nervous and hyperactive or less so. The student's behavior may account for differences in performance and may provide clinical information critical to the assessment process.

Test Administered
These tests are often listed separately or combined with test results. Whenever possible, a brief description of the test itself should be included for readers who are unfamiliar with the test format. Some diagnosticians prefer to describe the tests on a separate page attached to the test report.

Test Results
All test scores are listed for each test or subtest adminstered.

Analysis of Test Results
The essence of the test report is in the analysis of the test results. The examiner discusses the student's performance on each test, summarizes the student's strengths and weaknesses in skills, and analyzes the various learning processes assessed. Examples are given to illustrate the kinds of errors the student has made. The examiner describes in detail the specific tasks the student has not mastered and summarizes the error pattern.

Summary Statement
The summary reviews the essential information about the student, reason for referral behavior, and test performance. The summary concludes with a specific statement of classification or diagnosis (Is the student mentally redarded? Does the student have a specific learning disability?). While the report may recommend that a student be considered for special education placement, only the Individual Education Planning team can determine eligibility.

Recommendations
These typically include a placement recommendation as well as teaching suggestions. In a well-written report, the recommendations flow logically from the description of the behavior and performance. The suggestions for teaching are based on task analysis and error analysis. They should incorporate analyses of the student's interests and strengths. They lead the teacher directly into curriculum planning. This section may also specify a date for reevaluation.

The written report described in this section is similar in format to those prepared by many psychologists and educational diagnosticians. In recent years, shorter standardized forms have been devised that allow test results to be written in quickly with little or no narrative concerning the student's behavior or performance. But a description of 16 separate tests with no analysis of their interrelationship is of little value. Such report forms, although expedient, often lead to stereotyped recommendations that do not follow logically from the student's behavior. The purpose of the written report is to communicate information about a student's performance that will enable teachers to plan and implement an appropriate instructional program and to communicate information to parents about their child's performance. As such, it is a critical document, one deserving of time and effort in preparation.

Communicating Test Results to Parents
In addition to providing information to the student's classroom teacher, the assessment process should help parents understand their child. Conveying the results of the diagnostic assessment to parents is usually the responsibility of the special education administrator, teacher, or psychologist. Conducting a parent conference that conveys clear and helpful information to parents is a very important skill.

Parents want to have the right to know whatever you know about their child's abilities and disabilities. They have the right to know your concerns and to express theirs. They need to have all of the information necessary to participate knowledgeably in any decision being made about their child's placement and program. This means that professionals involved in the assessment process have the responsibility to convey clear and accurate information. This does not mean giving the parents a list of numerical scores that have little meaning for them. Nor does it mean describing in detail a child's problems in terms like "perceptual disturbance" or "auditory closure." Nor does it mean talking with parents in such generalities ("Yes, Tom is a little behind in math") that they leave the office uncertain of the results of the assessment. The balance between being too technical and too general is very difficult, but essential, to achieve.

Some parents ask for specific numbers and terms. What is their child's IQ? What grade level is he or she reading at? Is the child dyslexic? Brain-damaged? Others ask few questions. But beneath the specific questions and the unasked questions, parents of all levels of sophistication are basically asking, Is something the matter with my child? What is it? Is the child going to be all right? What is the school going to do? How can we help?

The following guidelines can be used in preparing for a parent conference:

• Think about the most important information you want to share with the parents about their child. Be sure that the information is presented clearly and does not get lost in a morass of numbers and descriptions of behavior.

• Be certain you know what your recommendations will be. If the assessments have been done by a team, come to an agreement about recommendations before the parent conference. Parents want to hear the professional recommendations—not four conflicting views.

• Have all the information ready for the parent conference. Come prepared to answer such questions as, Who is the teacher of the special class? When can we observe? Do you know a good math tutor? How do we go about getting some counseling?

In a recent study titled "What Parents of the Learning Disabled Really Want from Professionals," Dembinski and Mauser (1977, p. 53) found that parents wanted professionals (teachers, psychologists, and physicians) to use terminology they could understand. They overwhelmingly disapproved of professional jargon. But the use of educational and psychological jargon is such a part of the professional role that teachers and psychologists must make a conscious effort not to overwhelm the parents with "jargonese." The following techniques have proven helpful:

• Review with the parents the reasons for referral and the school's concerns about the child. If the parents initiated the assessment, ask them to restate their concerns. Review the assessment process. Name the professionals who worked with the child and explain what they did. Be certain the parents know the names and understand the roles of all the people involved in the assessment process.

• Show the parents a few of the actual test items to demonstrate the task the student was asked to perform and the performance. Be certain to include examples of both the student's strengths and deficits. Rockowitz and Davidson (1979, p. 6) found it was better to present information about the child's strengths early in the conference. Too often, parents cannot hear the good news after a discussion of problems.

• Illustrate with examples how the student's skill deficiencies may be noted in the classroom, at home, and with friends.

• Encourage parent questions and comments by your manner. Try to draw both parents into the discussion. Be certain to schedule enough time for questions and discus-

sion.

• Don't avoid using terms such as *mental retardation, learning disability, dyslexia,* or *aphasia* if your evaluation clearly supports the diagnosis. Rockowitz and Davidson (1979, p. 6) echo the finding of several researchers that parents need a name for their child's problems.

• Give parents a written report. With some parents it is better to discuss the report point by point; with others it is better to just talk about the assessment results and have them read the report later. Explain clearly in the body of the report or on an attached sheet the meaning of terms such as *grade score, standard score, stanine,* and *percentile.*

• Before concluding, ask the parents to restate what they have learned from the conference. This gives the professional a chance to clarify any misconceptions.

• End the conference with a clear plan of what will happen next and whose responsibility it is to carry out each part of the process. Be aware of parents' feelings, and don't press them to make decisions until they have had a chance to think it over and talk to others.

THE TEST REVIEWS

The remaining chapters of this book present critical reviews of some of the most commonly used instruments in educational diagnosis. Each test is introduced with a data sheet that presents the essential data about the test. The purpose of the test, the major areas tested, and the age or grade range of the test are stated.

The data sheet also indicates whether the student's performance is timed, the amount of testing time required, and the amount of scoring/interpretation time necessary. If available, information on the norming sample is given. The data sheet also indicates whether a test has alternate forms for test-retest purposes.

Following the data sheet, the format of the test is described, and a critical review of the test's strengths and limiting factors is presented. Guidelines are given for the use of each test to minimize abuses and misuses of the test and to provide information for the diagnostician regarding administration and interpretation. But *85 Tests* is not intended to teach the reader how to administer any test. Even a person who is experienced in diagnostic testing needs to study the examiner's manuals and practice administering the test before using it with a student referred for testing.

Testing is one part of the educational assessment process—an important part—but not the only part. The educational diagnostician must work with parents, teachers, and others who know the students to gather information that will answer important educational questions accurately. This, after all, is the goal of educational assessment—a field of challenges and responsibilities.

GRANDADDIES
A Special Group of Tests

In the early 1960s, special education began to emerge as a clear specialty within the field of education. Innovative curriculum was devised specifically for exceptional students. Prospective teachers in the field were recruited to college and university programs where departments of special education were rapidly developing. Special education began its period of rapid expansion and advancement, culminating in P.L. 94-142 and categorical programs as we know them today. Similarly, the assessment of exceptional children began to be recognized as a specialty, and tests were developed specifically to diagnose the learning and language problems of exceptional children. Many of these tests focused upon language, perceptual-motor, and memory skills, attempting to analyze the sub-skills of these major areas of learning.

Several of these tests are still published today. Their technical characteristics are inadequate for making diagnostic, eligibility, placement, or instructional planning decisions; in some cases the skills they measure have not proved relevant to classroom performance. Despite their currently-recognized inadequacies, they have contributed greatly to the field of special education assessment. These authors provided us with a beginning, the first steps in a new field, and many of our most useful current diagnostic tools are based upon their work.

These five "grandaddies" are grouped together to highlight their contribution to the field.
- Illinois Test of Psycholinguistic Abilities
- Marianne Frostig Developmental Test of Visual Perception
- Myklebust Picture Story Language Test
- Purdue Perceptual Motor Survey
- Wepman Auditory Discrimination Test

Illinois Test of Psycholinguistic Abilities (ITPA)

S. A. Kirk, J. J. McCarthy, and W. D. Kirk
University of Illinois Press, 1961; revised 1968
54 East Gregory Dr., Champaign, IL 61820

Purpose	To assess how a child communicates with and receives communication from the environment and to provide a framework for planning remediation and developing instructional programs.
Major Areas Tested	Visual-motor and auditory-vocal skills
Age or Grade Range	2–10 years
Usually Given By	Psychologist Speech/language clinician
Type of Test	Standardized Individual
Scores Obtained	Age level Scaled
Student Performance Timed?	Yes (some subtests)
Testing Time	1 1/2 hours
Scoring/Interpretation Time	30–40 minutes
Normed On	962 average children from medium-sized towns and cities in the Midwest; 4 percent Black students
Alternate Forms Available?	No

FORMAT

The Illinois Test of Psycholinguistic Abilities (ITPA) materials consist of a manual, two books of test pictures, objects for description, visual-closure picture strips, and individual student record forms, all packaged in a carrying case.

The ITPA is based on Osgood's model of communication (Osgood, 1957), which postulates three dimensions to cognitive abilities: *channels* (auditory, visual, vocal, motor), *processes* (reception, association, expression), and *levels* (automatic, representational). The subtests of the ITPA represent these dimensions. There are ten basic subtests and two other supplementary tests.

The two levels postulated by Osgood are the representational and the automatic. At the *representational level* (or meaningful level), the processes of *reception, association,* and *expression* are assessed in the two major channels, auditory and visual. Functioning at the *automatic level* is assessed in the two major channels in terms of closure and sequential memory skills. The two supplementary tests provide additional information about automatic functioning in the auditory channel. The supplementary scores are not included when deriving the total or mean scores for the test.

Precise directions for administrating and scoring each subtest are contained in the manual. Raw scores are converted to age scores and scaled scores and are recorded on the summary sheet. Scaled scores are plotted on the profile sheet to provide a graphic representation of a student's performance.

An individual's test performance may be viewed in several ways. The total of the raw scores from the ten basic subtests is converted into a "psycholinguistic age," which provides an overall index of the student's level of psycholinguistic development. The raw scores are also translated individually into scaled scores. The mean scaled score for the normative population is 36, with a standard deviation of plus or minus 6. The student's own mean is derived by averaging the scaled scores of the ten basic subtests.

Discrepancies of plus or minus 10 from the student's own mean or the median scaled score are considered substantial. Using the student's mean or median scaled score as a reference point assists the examiner in viewing strengths and weaknesses.

| SUBTEST | REPRESENTATIONAL LEVEL | | | | | | AUTOMATIC LEVEL | | | | | |
| | AUDITORY-VOCAL | | | VISUAL-MOTOR | | | AUDITORY-VOCAL | | | VISUAL-MOTOR | | |
	Raw Score	Age Score	Scaled Score	Raw Score	Age Score	Scaled Score	Raw Score	Age Score	Scaled Score	Raw Score	Age Score	Scaled Score
AUDITORY RECEPTION												
VISUAL RECEPTION												
VISUAL MEMORY												
AUDITORY ASSOCIATION												
AUDITORY MEMORY												
VISUAL ASSOCIATION												
VISUAL CLOSURE												
VERBAL EXPRESSION												
GRAMMATIC CLOSURE												
MANUAL EXPRESSION												
(Supplementary tests) AUDITORY CLOSURE												
SOUND BLENDING												

SUMMARY SCORES:	Sum of Raw Scores	Composite PLA	Sum of SS	Mean SS	Median SS

ITPA Summary Sheet

In addition, patterns of performance may be found by analyzing the results further. Several ways of doing this are described by Kirk and Kirk in *Psycholinguistic Learning Disabilities* (1971). For example:

1. *Comparison of levels of organization.* The representational-level score is obtained by averaging age scores and scaled scores of tests at the representational level. The automatic-level score is obtained by averaging age scores and scaled scores of tests at the automatic level.

2. *Comparison of channels.* The auditory-vocal score is obtained by averaging age scores and scaled scores from auditory and verbal subtests. The visual-motor score is obtained by averaging age scores and scaled scores from visual and motor subtests.

3. *Comparison of psycholinguistic processes.* Scores for reception, association, and expression are obtained by averaging scaled scores for each process.

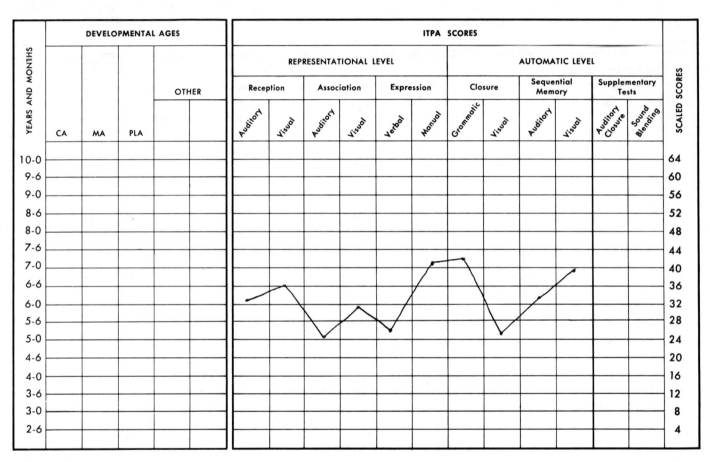

ITPA Profile Sheet

ITPA Subtests

Subtest	Description	Comments
Auditory Reception	Assesses the student's ability to derive meaning from verbally presented material. Questions of controlled length and structure are presented by the examiner. Vocabulary increases in difficulty. A simple yes or no response is required of the student. (*Do dogs eat? Do cosmetics celebrate?*)	The examiner is cautioned not to influence the student's response by inflection or facial expression. The simple response that is required makes it possible to test nonverbal children. However, some students may be tempted to give minimal involvement to the task and thereby respond in random fashion.
Visual Reception	Assesses the student's ability to match concepts presented visually. After brief exposure to a single stimulus picture, the student selects the correct match from four choices on the following page. Objects and situations conceptually similar to the stimulus are to be chosen.	Mild and moderate visual handicaps do not appear to affect performance on this subtest. It appears to measure central rather than peripheral processes (Bateman 1963).
Auditory Association	Assesses the student's ability to complete verbal analogies presented by the examiner. The vocabulary becomes more difficult as the task progresses. (*I sit on a chair; I sleep on a _____ . Years have seasons; dollars have _____ .*)	The student needs to grasp the analogy and to select the correct word that expresses it. Although included as a test of the process of association, the receptive and expressive processes are also involved. Careful analysis of a student's performance is needed to sort out the processes.
Visual Association	Assesses the student's ability to relate associated concepts, such as sock/shoe and hammer/nail. Stimulus and response pictures are presented on one page. At the lower level, the stimulus picture is surrounded by four choices. At the higher level, analogous relationships are employed. They follow the format "If this goes with this, then what goes with this?"	The process of selecting one of the pictures surrounding the stimulus picture is difficult for some children to understand. Some may imitate the examiner's model, pointing to all the pictures. At the higher level, it is possible for a student to choose the correct item without following the two-part analogy. Success at this level does not necessarily indicate an understanding of analogous relationships.
Verbal Expression	Assesses the student's ability to express concepts pertaining to familiar objects. The student is presented four objects individually—a ball, a block, an envelope, and a button—then asked to "Tell me all about this." The score is the number of discrete, relevant, and approximately factual concepts expressed. There is a one-minute time limit for each object.	This subtest, although labeled *Expression,* gives little information about the linguistic development of the student. Sentence use and grammar are not assessed. Rather, it is a test of cognitive awareness regarding objects and of the ability to express those concepts. A calm state, alertness to detail, and the ability to free associate and to respond within a time limit are basic to success on this subtest.
Manual Expression	Assesses the student's ability to demonstrate the use of objects through pantomime. A stimulus picture is presented, accompanied by the verbal request to "Show me what you do with a _____ ." The student's movements are recorded on a checklist of behaviors. Objects pictured include a guitar and binoculars.	Because this subtest assesses observation of and familiarity with objects in the environment, some students may be penalized by lack of exposure to such items as guitars and binoculars. Students respond best to this task when relaxed and uninhibited.

Subtest	Description	Comments
Manual Expression— *continued*		A study by McCarthy, reported in Kirk and Kirk (1971), found Down's Syndrome children to be superior in this area to other retarded children, and in relation to their other abilities. Many children with severe verbal language deficits do well on this measure of gestural language.
Grammatic Closure	Assesses the student's ability to complete verbal statements presented by the examiner. Each item consists of a complete statement followed by one to be completed with the correct word or grammatical inflection. Pictures serve as stimuli. (*Here is a boy. Here are two _____ . Each child has a ball. This is hers and this is _____ .*)	The ITPA was standardized on a basically Caucasian population. Standard American dialect was predominant. Therefore, responses of students from other populations may be informative, but they should not be scored. Students with speech defects were found to be deficient on this subtest in studies done by Ferrier (1966) and Foster (1963). This subtest does not provide complete analysis of grammatical form. Language sampling should be employed for more complete information.
Visual Closure	Assesses the student's ability to recognize a pictured object (or objects) when partially obscured in a scene. The task requires visual closure and figure-ground discrimination. A pointing response is used. There is a 30-second time limit.	Scanning ability and a reasonable searching procedure assist the student on this task. Also, an ability to function under time pressure is involved, although not explicitly stated.
Auditory Memory	Assesses the student's short-term memory for digits presented at the rate of two per second. Two trials are allowed. The digit series increase in length from two to eight numbers.	This subtest assesses immediate recall of unstructured, nonsyntactic material. Performance may be unrelated to short-term memory for other material, such as sentences. Because it requires verbal output, it may also be unrelated to tests of short-term retention of directions that are acted out rather than spoken. Performance on this subtest requires attention, a calm state, and retention of sequential material.
Visual Memory	Assesses the student's ability to reproduce sequences of nonmeaningful figures from memory. A pictured sequence is shown for five seconds; then the student places corresponding tiles in the same order. Two trials are allowed. Sequences increase in length from two to eight designs and include such patterns as lines and triangles.	This subtest requires a minimum of accumulated knowledge. Performance may be influenced by the ability to focus attention, function within a time limit, and retain sequential patterns. Patience and tolerance for a frustrating task are an aid. Some students are assisted by their verbal description of the designs. This helps the examiner understand a student's strategy but diminishes the test's value as a discrete measure of visual memory. This subtest only assesses memory of nonmeaningful pictorial material.

Subtest	Description	Comments
Auditory Closure (Supplementary)	Assesses the student's ability to supply mentally, then verbally, the sounds omitted in word(s) presented by the examiner. A progression from easier to more difficult vocabulary is used. Stimuli include ''airpla/'' (*airplane*) and ''auto/o/ile'' (*automobile*).	The student needs adequate hearing, good vocabulary, and attentive behavior to accomplish this task.
Sound Blending (Supplementary)	Assesses the student's ability to blend sounds spoken by the examiner at half-second intervals into words. At the lower end of the test, pictures are employed. The test progresses through synthesis of words with no picture clue (*f-i-s-h*) to nonsense words (*t-e-k-o*).	The upper limit for this subtest is below that for the test as a whole, specifically 8 years, 7 months.

Adequate hearing, auditory discrimination, and retention of sounds in sequence are required for adequate performance. Performance may also reflect training approaches. For instance, students in the primary grades who have been instructed in a phonic approach often do not reach a ceiling.

A recording is provided to ensure correct presentation. |

STRENGTHS OF THE ITPA

• The IPTA is widely used and highly respected. It has been carefully constructed, its organization derived from the Osgood and Sebeok (1965) model of communication. This model makes it possible to view an individual's strengths and weaknesses in terms of channels, levels of organization, and processes. The IPTA provides a basis for making observations about an individual's pattern of performance. Supplemented by other diagnostic measures, it assists in accurate diagnosis of learning and language problems.

• Directions for presenting and scoring the ITPA are well stated in the manual. The examiner will find the profile sheet useful in viewing an individual's strengths and weaknesses.

• The variety of tasks included in the test enables the examiner to alter task presentation to meet the needs of the student. Tasks requiring the greatest concentration can be presented when attention and interest are adequate. The visual tests provide a means for evaluating children with poor language skills and give them the opportunity to demonstrate normal functioning.

• The ITPA has been widely studied. Many publications are available to increase the examiner's understanding of the test. Courses are taught on its construction and administration, and a film is available to help prepare examiners.

LIMITING FACTORS OF THE ITPA

• The term *psycholinguistic abilities* used in the title of this test is misleading. The ITPA samples cognitive func-

tioning in verbal and nonverbal areas through different processes, but it does not analyze a student's psycholinguistic abilities.

• The ITPA purports to measure "discrete" functions. However, it is difficult to define and to develop tests that measure "discrete" functions. Subtests that are designed to assess nonlanguage functioning, such as Visual Memory, may still involve the use of vocabulary. Some students use labeling to retain the visual patterns.

• The ITPA was standardized on a limited sample of the population drawn from medium-sized towns and cities in the Midwest. Rural and metropolitan areas were not represented. Only 4 percent of the population was Black, and the number of Spanish-Americans is not even reported. Thus the usefulness of the ITPA for minority populations is extremely limited. The results must be interpreted with caution when used with minorities or students from lower socioeconomic classes. Reference to research on the use of the ITPA with these groups is included in Kirk and Kirk's book (1971).

• Caution is also advised in the interpretation of scores. Within the age range of 2 to 10 years, scores should be compared to the student's scaled score. To do this, all ten subtests must be given. Age scores should not be compared at these ages. Interpretation of scores is difficult at both the lower and upper ends of the age range. Many of the ITPA subtests do not provide a high enough ceiling. Above age 10, language-age scores, rather than scaled scores, should be used to describe performance.

• Accurate adminstration and meaningful interpretation of the ITPA require good preparation and experience. Its use

by untrained and inexperienced people is fraught with
danger, much as the use of IQ tests is. Its administration is
also more time-consuming than the manual would suggest.
Usually an hour and a half are required for its presentation,
and another hour for scoring and interpretation.

• The ITPA does not, and should not, stand alone as a
diagnostic tool. The examiner needs to know how to
interpret the results and to supplement the testing to obtain
needed information, whether academic, cognitive, or
linguistic.

• Studies on the validity of the ITPA are limited.
Factor-analytic studies of the ITPA have neither proven nor
disproven the construct validity of the test, according to the
authors (Kirk and Kirk, 1978, p. 64). A study by Elkins
(1972) analyzed construct validity and found that the
process and channel dimensions were verified but that the
representational and automatic levels were not clear.
Evidence of predictive validity is not presented. Though
Paraskevopoulos and Kirk (1969) state that scores deviating
from the child's mean make it more likely that the child will
have learning disabilities, no data is provided to support this
conclusion.

• Reliability data is summarized by Salvia and
Ysseldyke in their book on assessment (1978, p. 357).
Internal consistency is generally high in the ITPA, but
particular caution should be taken in interpreting the Visual
Closure and Auditory Closure subtests. Test-retest reliability
is significantly lower than internal-consistency reliability.
Salvia and Ysseldyke (1978) provide a summary of the
reliability data.

Marianne Frostig Developmental Test of Visual Perception (DTVP)

Marianne Frostig, in collaboration with Welty Lefever and John R.B. Whittlessey
Consulting Psychologists Press, Inc., 1961; Manual revised 1966
577 College Ave., Palo Alto, CA 94306

Purpose	To measure certain visual perceptual abilities and to detect difficulties in visual perception at an early age
Major Areas Tested	Visual perception
Age or Grade Range	3–8 years
Usually Given By	Special education teacher Occupational therapist Psychologist
Type of Test	Standardized Individual Group
Scores Obtained	Age level Scaled Perceptual quotient (PQ)
Student Performance Timed?	No
Testing Time	30–45 minutes (individual administration); 40–60 minutes (group administration)
Scoring/Interpretation Time	10–15 minutes
Normed On	2,116 white, middle-class students from southern California
Alternate Forms Available?	No

FORMAT

The Marianne Frostig Developmental Test of Visual Perception (DTVP) is a paper-and-pencil test. The test materials consist of an examiner's manual and monograph, expendable test booklets for the students, demonstration cards, and plastic scoring keys. The examiner must also supply four colored pencils or crayons (red, blue, green, and brown) and a pencil without an eraser for each student. For group administration, access to a blackboard is necessary for demonstration purposes.

During the testing session, the student completes tasks arranged in order of increasing difficulty in five areas of visual perception. The subtests and selected items from each are described below.

1. *Eye-Motor Coordination* (16 items). The student must draw continuous straight, curved, or angled lines between increasingly narrow boundaries or draw straight lines to a target.

2. *Figure-Ground* (8 items). The student must distinguish between intersecting shapes and find embedded figures. The

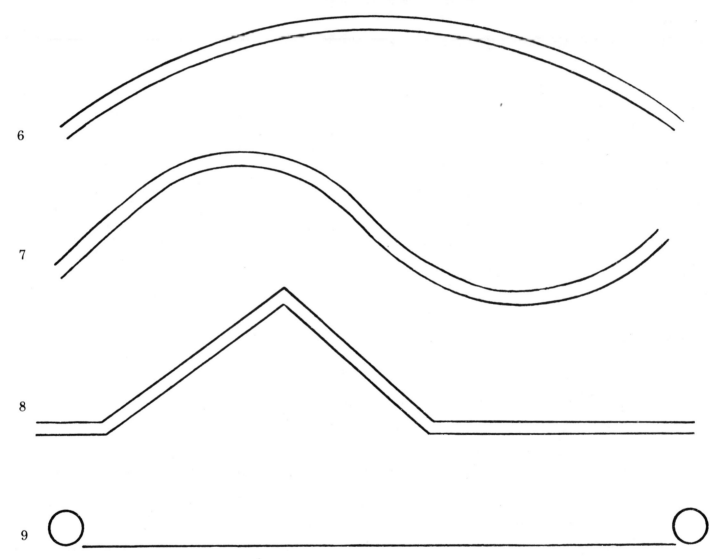

DTVP Eye-Motor Coordination

student must outline the hidden geometric forms with a colored pencil or crayon.

3. *Constancy of Shape* (17 items). The student must discriminate common geometric shapes (circles and squares), presented in different sizes, shadings, textures, and positions, from other similar shapes. The student must outline the recognized figures with a colored pencil or crayon.

4. *Position in Space* (8 items). The student must distinguish between figures in an identical position and those in a reversed or rotated position, marking the different figure.

5. *Spatial Relations* (8 items). The student must copy simple forms and patterns by joining dots.

The DTVP may be administered individually or in groups. The optimum number of students in a group depends on the age of the students. For example, a group of 8 to 10 is appropriate for kindergarten students, whereas 10 to 20 second graders may be tested simultaneously. Large groups require paraprofessionals who can circulate among the students to help monitor the test.

1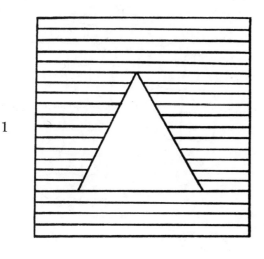

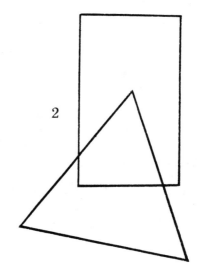 2

3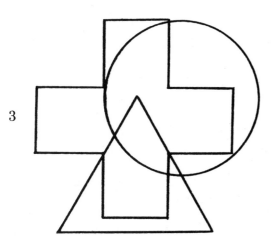

DTVP Figure Ground

4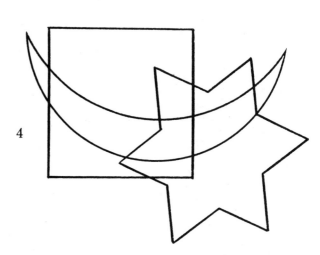

Instructions for the test are verbal, but there is an adaptation of the manual for hard-of-hearing, deaf, and non-English-speaking students. Additional examples and gestures are used.

Although the items are presented in one test booklet, parts of the test are omitted for nursery school and kindergarten students. The student may not erase, make corrections, or turn the test booklet. The test is not timed. Alternate, equivalent forms of the DTVP are not available.

Raw scores on each subtest are converted to age scores and scaled scores. The scaled scores on the five subtests are added to obtain a total test score; when divided by a student's age, the total score yields a perceptual quotient. Subtest scaled scores range from 0 to 20, with 10 as average and 8 or below indicating need for remediation. A perceptual quotient of 90 is suggested as the cutoff for children entering first grade; lower scores indicate the need for perceptual training.

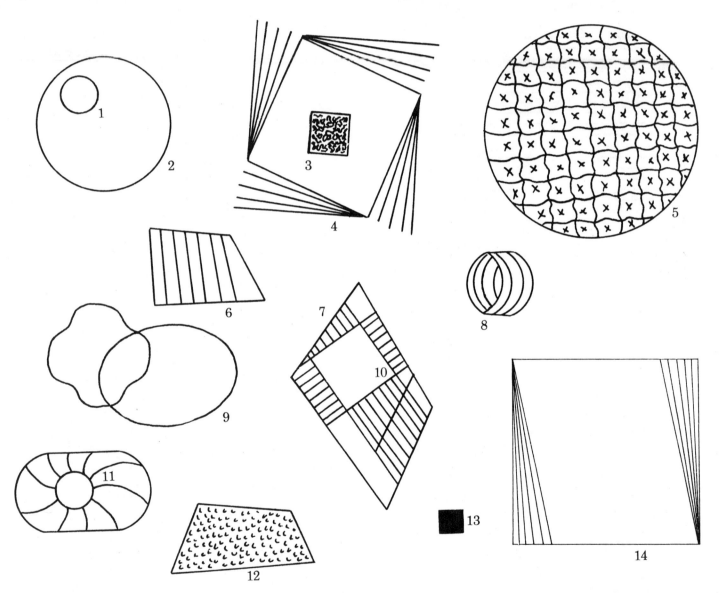

DTVP Constancy of Shape

STRENGTHS OF THE DTVP

• The DTVP is a well-known test, a forerunner in the field. It evaluates both visual perception and eye-hand coordination in young students. No expensive equipment is required. In addition to individual testing, the DTVP is useful as a screening instrument with groups of students. The test can also be used by the experienced clinician to gain diagnostic information on older students who have learning problems.

• The particular tasks on the DTVP are simple in design and arranged in order of increasing difficulty. The subtests can generally be performed quickly. For the most part, the directions for administering the test are clear. Examiner demonstration of each subtest, either on the blackboard or with demonstration materials, is especially helpful for the young student.

• The instructions for scoring the DTVP are fairly explicit. Examples are given that illustrate criteria for scoring each item. Scoring stencils provided for some items further increase objectivity. Time required for scoring is relatively short—approximately 10 minutes.

LIMITING FACTORS OF THE DTVP

• The DTVP purports to measure five distinct aspects of visual perception. Frostig's correlation studies indicate independence of the subtests. However, contradictory evidence has been found in several other investigations.

DTVP Position in Space

Such studies show that the DTVP subtests do not measure five different and relatively independent visual perceptual abilities. The degree to which the subtests measure one or more general visual perceptual factors also needs to be established (Hammill and Wiederholt, 1972).

• The process of transforming raw scores to scaled scores is very confusing. For example, in students over 8 years of age, someone who receives a perfect score on a subtest receives a scaled score of only 10, whereas younger students can make errors and get a higher score. Salvia and Ysseldyke (1978, p. 311) state, "The transformed scores for the DTVP are not only confusing; they are questionably derived and therefore absolutely must not be used in making diagnostic decisions."

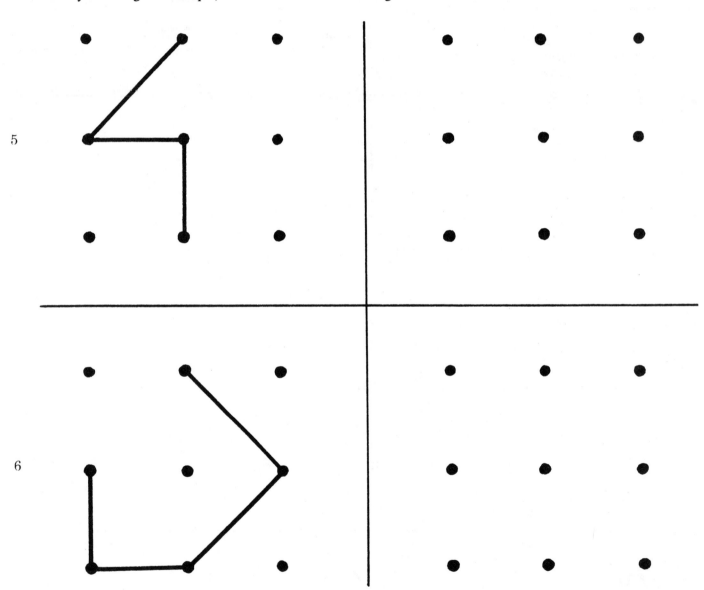

DTVP Spatial Relations

• The test items on the DTVP consist only of geometric forms and shapes; no letters or numbers are used. Although students may be able to distinguish a particular form from other figures presented in an identical, rotated, or reversed position, they still may not be able to differentiate letters having the same form but different positions (for example, *b* and *d*). The examiner should not conclude that a student's good performance on the DTVP automatically rules out difficulties in perceiving the symbols for language.

• Another difficulty with the DTVP is that visual perceptual skills are not measured apart from motor skills. The added motor component (tracing with a pencil), especially on the Figure-Ground subtest, contaminates the purity of the visual perceptual process. Visual perceptual abilities and motor skills should be measured as separate entities as well as integrative functions.

• Reliability results on the subtests range from .29 to .68, too low to be used in differential diagnosis. No reliability studies are given for students below age 5. Reliability on other tests is often low at this age level. This means that the results of a single administration to a preschooler should not be considered definitive of impairments in visual perception and eye-motor coordination.

• Validity studies reported in the manual were poorly designed and controlled (Salvia and Ysseldyke 1978, pp. 314-316).

Myklebust Picture Story Language Test (PSLT)

Helmer R. Myklebust
The Psychological Corporation, 1965; Record form revised 1985
555 Academic Court, San Antonio, TX 78204

Purpose	To assess various written language skills
Major Areas Tested	Written language
Age or Grade Range	7–17 years
Usually Given By	Special education teacher Speech/language clinician
Type of Test	Standardized Individual Group Norm-referenced
Scores Obtained	Age level Percentile Stanine
Student Performance Timed?	No
Testing Time	20–30 minutes
Scoring/Interpretation Time	20–30 minutes
Normed On	Metropolitan, rural, and suburban school populations in one midwestern state
Alternate Forms Available?	No

FORMAT

The Myklebust Picture Story Test (PSLT) is a test of written language most often administered individually, but it can be given to groups ranging in size from 8 to 10 students. More than 10 students may be tested simultaneously if additional test pictures are available. The test picture is a black-and-white photograph, 10 11/2 by 13 11/2 inches, that shows a young boy playing with dollhouse figures.

Other materials needed to administer the PSLT include the test manual and the printed record forms used for scoring. The manual is a clothbound book *(Development and Disorders of Written Language, Volume One)* containing administration and scoring procedures, as well as chapters discussing the author's ideas about the development of written language skills.

The examiners must supply the type of writing paper and pencils that the students are familiar with. Standard-size writing paper is suggested, because it affords the same potential story length for all students.

Administration of the PSLT requires simple oral directions. The examiner holds up the picture so that all can see, and says, "Look at this picture carefully." The examiner waits 20 seconds and says, "You are to write a story about it. You may look at it as much and as often as you care to. Be sure to write the best story you can. Begin writing whenever you are ready."

The picture is then placed in a central position, where it can be viewed by all students. It is permissible for a student to pick up the picture for close inspection. It should be replaced in a central position after the student finishes examining it.

Questions are answered neutrally. For example, a student might ask, "Should I write about how the boy is dressed?" A typical reply would be, "If you want to. Write the story the way you think is best." The examiner may encourage students to write something if they are having difficulty thinking of a story but must refrain from offering any suggestions that might influence the content of the story.

The PSLT is not timed; the students continue to write until they have completed their stories. Alternate, equivalent forms for test-retest purposes are not available.

STRENGTHS OF THE PSLT

• Tests measuring written expression are virtually nonexistent. The PSLT then, being the first of its kind, is a landmark test.

• The PSLT is easy to administer and requires no special training. The wide age range makes it a particularly good instrument for measuring the progress of a student's writing skills in relation to age. Separate norms are provided for boys and girls, reflecting sex differences in the development of written language at different age levels. Provision has been made for converting the raw scores into age and percentile equivalents and stanine ranks.

• Three attributes of language usage are evaluated by the PSLT. Scores are provided for the following scales: *Productivity* measures the length of the expression and includes counts of total words, total sentences, and words per sentence; *Syntax* measures the correctness of what is expressed and includes accuracy of word usage, of word endings, and of punctuation (errors of additions, omissions, substitutions, and word order are counted). *Abstract-Concrete* measures the meaning of the ideas being expressed on a continuum ranging from concrete to abstract. Norms for each of these measures were established developmentally for both boys and girls.

• The three aspects of language that are measured are useful because they make it possible to obtain a profile of a student's strengths and weaknesses in written language. For example, one student may write a story deficient in syntax but highly imaginative and abstract. Another student may write a syntactically correct story that is limited in ideation, tending toward the concrete. In planning a writing program, the teacher would study the student's performance on each of the three scales.

• Another diagnostic use of the PSLT is to compare the student's facility with the spoken and the written word. Initially the test may be administered by having the student tell a story about the picture. The next day the student is asked to write a story.

• Although the PSLT has not been standardized for spoken language, the findings from an oral test may be significant for remediation.

• The manual includes scored stories (illustrating normal and handicapped children), which are particulary helpful for the examiner who is learning how to score and interpret the PSLT. It will often be necessary to refer to these sample stories for comparison.

• The PSLT answered a critical need for a test of written language. In addition, volume 2 of *Development and Disorders of Written Language: Studies of Normal and Exceptional Children* (Myklebust, 1973) includes further analyses of the PSLT results for normal students and comparative findings for exceptional students—learning disabled, mentally retarded, socially and/or emotionally disturbed, speech handicapped, and reading disabled.

LIMITING FACTORS OF THE PSLT

• The norming procedures described in the test manual are inadequate. The sample came from only one midwestern state, and as yet there is no information available on geographic differences in written language development.

• The author claims that a wide range of socioeconomic levels and cultural backgrounds were included in the standardization sample. However, data regarding the racial breakdown or number of minority students included in the study are lacking. Caution should be the rule when using the PSLT norms with students from different cultural backgrounds.

• Another consideration concerning standardization is that only odd ages from 7 to 17 were sampled. The author interpolates scores for ages not tested. This is a questionable practice, especially because the standard deviations for the sampled ages are quite large.

• The author makes the statement that the PSLT appears to be a valid test but offers no evidence to support this assumption. No attempt was made to evaluate the face validity of the test. How motivating, for example, is the test picture in comparison with other pictures that might have been used?

• The author states that the test-retest reliability coefficients were statistically significant but does not report the data. The coefficients for the syntax scale seem to indicate that there is not sufficient interscorer reliability, especially with untrained examiners. This should be noted in the information on test administration.

Purdue Perceptual-Motor Survey (Survey)

Eugene G. Roach and Newell C. Kephart
The Psychological Corporation, 1966
555 Academic Court, San Antonio, TX 78204

Purpose	To assess perceptual-motor abilities, including both gross and fine motor skills
Major Areas Tested	Laterality, directionality, and perceptual-motor skills
Age or Grade Range	Preschool–grade 8
Usually Given By	Classroom teacher Physical education teacher Special education teacher Motor therapist Occupational therapist
Type of Test	Informal Individual Criterion-referenced
Scores Obtained	None (Profile only)
Student Performance Timed?	No
Testing Time	30–40 minutes
Scoring/Interpretation Time	10–15 minutes
Normed On	200 urban and rural elementary school students in Indiana, from grades 1–4 and from all socioeconomic levels; students with known achievement or motor problems excluded; 97 nonachievers of the same age and school used in a validation study
Alternate Forms Available?	No

FORMAT

The Purdue Perceptual-Motor Survey (Survey) is not a test but a series of tasks designed to provide the examiner with a structure for observing a student's motor skills. The materials consist of an examiner's manual and individual student record forms. Materials required are those usually found in a school setting—walking board, broom handle, small pillow, mat or rug, chalk and chalkboard, penlight. The manual includes information on the rationale and development of the test, directions for administering and scoring, and a set of cards for the form-copying task.

The Survey is composed of 11 subtests organized into 5 major skills areas. It provides 22 item scores.

In order to secure the student's best performance, each subtest has four possible levels of administration:

1. *Unstructured Instruction.* The student is given general verbal directions for the task, and the examiner then observes how the student performs. For example, on the Walking Board subtest, the student would be told simply, "Walk to the other end."

2. *Verbal Directions.* If the student cannot perform the task at the unstructured instruction level, the examiner gives more explicit verbal directions, such as, "Step up on the board here and walk forward slowly to the other end."

3. *Demonstration.* At this level, the examiner helps the student by saying, "Do it like this" and then demonstrating the task for the student to imitate.

Survey Subtests

Skill Area	Subtest
Balance and Posture	1. *Walking Board.* Student is asked to walk on a walking board four inches wide and six inches off the ground to obtain a measure of dynamic balance. Three scores are obtained: forward, backward, and sidewise.
	2. *Jumping.* Student is asked to jump and hop on each foot and both feet in a series of eight tasks designed to measure laterality and rhythm.
Body Image	3. *Identification of Body Parts.* Student is asked to point to nine common body parts.
	4. *Imitation of Movements.* Student is asked to imitate a series of 17 arm positions to measure the ability to translate visual information into a motor act.
	5. *Obstacle Course.* Student is asked to step over, step around, and duck under a broom handle to assess spatial orientation.
	6. *Kraus-Weber Test of Physical Fitness.* Student is asked to raise upper body and legs from a prone position to test physical strength and muscular fitness.
	7. *Angels in the Snow.* Student is asked to perform a series of tasks requiring moving specific limbs individually and in pairs.
Perceptual-Motor Match	8. *Chalkboard.* Student is asked to perform a series of four chalkboard tasks assessing visual-motor coordination, with particular emphasis on directionality and mid-line problems.
	9. *Rhythmic Writing.* Student is asked to reproduce a series of eight continuous writing motifs. Rhythm, accuracy, and orientation on the chalkboard are observed and scored.
Ocular Control	10. *Ocular Pursuits.* Student is asked to perform a series of four visual-tracking exercises.
Form Perception	11. *Developmental Drawings.* Student is asked to copy seven geometric forms to assess visual-motor coordination.

4. *Guided Movements.* If the student cannot initiate the task, the examiner physically guides his or her movements.

The level of structure that the student requires for each task is noted, together with other observations of performance, on the individual record forms. Each item is rated on a four-point scale following the guidelines in the examiner's manual. All scores are recorded on the record forms. Because the survey is not intended as a test but as a structured observation, the rating scores are not translated into age scores or percentiles but are simply used as a guide to adequate or inadequate performance.

STRENGTHS OF THE SURVEY

• The Purdue Perceptual-Motor Survey provides a structure for assessing a variety of gross and fine motor tasks in elementary school students. The manual is clearly written, and directions for administration and scoring are easy to follow. Little equipment is necessary, so the Survey is an inexpensive way to assess motor skills. The Survey is intended to be used as a structured observation. The increasing assistance provided for the student in the four levels of task administration is very helpful in determining the type of instruction each student will need, and the profile of strengths and weaknesses helps the teacher plan appropriate perceptual-motor activities.

• The Survey was developed from the theoretical framework described by Kephart (1960) in *The Slow Learner in the Classroom.* This book is very helpful to the teacher who is planning a perceptual-motor program. Also helpful are the checklists of motor performance provided by Chaney and Kephart (1968) in *Motoric Aids to Perceptual Training.*

LIMITING FACTORS OF THE SURVEY

• The Survey should be used as it was intended—as an informal assessment procedure. Normative data was gathered on a limited sample of students. Although the test-retest reliability was high in one study reported in the manual, the four-point rating scale for each item clearly leads to subjective scoring decisions. The five skill areas are general categories rather than discrete motor functions. There is much overlapping, and a differential diagnosis of motor disabilities should not be attempted from this informal scale.

• Validity studies, which were carried out with a very small sample, demonstrated that students who are low achievers academically performed more poorly on the Survey than high-achieving students. Even in the authors' studies, performance of the motor tasks did not improve with age or socioeconomic class. There is not sufficient evidence to document the authors' claim that performance of these tasks is "necessary for acquiring academic skills by usual instructional methods" (Examiner's Manual, p. iii).

• Although the Survey is an informal test, it requires a skilled examiner. Many of the tests are difficult to administer, and the observations of student performance take the eye of a person trained and experienced in motor skills.

• The manual does not provide any guidelines for interpreting the profiles or subtest patterns. Such information would be very helpful to the teacher who is inexperienced in the area of motor development.

Wepman Auditory Discrimination Test

Joseph M. Wepman
Western Psychological Services, 1958, revised 1973, 1987
12031 Wilshire Blvd., Los Angeles, CA 90025

Purpose	To evaluate the student's ability to recognize fine differences that exist between phonemes in English speech
Major Areas Tested	Auditory discrimination
Age or Grade Range	5–8 years
Usually Given By	Special education teacher Speech/language clinician
Type of Test	Standardized Individual
Scores Obtained	Rating scale
Student Performance Timed?	No
Testing Time	10–15 minutes
Scoring/Interpretation Time	5–10 minutes
Normed On	1,800 children aged 4–8; sample stratified by age, ethnic background, geographic region, and socioeconomic background
Alternate Forms Available?	Yes

FORMAT

The materials for the Wepman Auditory Discrimination Test include a brief manual and forms for recording individual responses. The manual contains some information on test development, directions for administration, and guidance in the interpretation of test results.

The test consists of 40 pairs of monosyllabic meaningful words. The words were selected from the *Lorge-Thorndike Teacher's Word Book* of 30,000 Words (1944). Of the 40 word pairs, 30 differ by only one sound: *muss-mush*. The 10 word pairs that do not differ are included as false choices and aid in the judgment of test validity.

The words in each pair are of equal length. Comparisons are made between 13 initial consonants, 13 final consonants, and 4 medial vowels. Consonants chosen for contrast are within the same phonetic category—for example, the stops /p/, /t/, and /k/. Vowel comparisons are based on such criteria as the part of the tongue that is raised; the height of the tongue; and the position of the lips.

The word pairs are read by the examiner. The student indicates whether the words pronounced were the same or different. No pictures are used, and the examiner pronounces the words with lips covered. Thus, visual skills are not involved. A rating scale is used to interpret a student's performance. The scale provides descriptions of ability ranging from "very good development" to "below the level of the threshold of adequacy" for the ages 5 to 8 years.

STRENGTHS OF THE WEPMAN AUDITORY DISCRIMINATION TEST

• This test is a brief, inexpensive, and relatively simple tool for assessing auditory discrimination ability. The test is carefully constructed. Word length and complexity of test items are controlled.

• Test-retest reliability is high. The existence of equivalent forms provides the examiner with a good reevaluation procedure.

LIMITING FACTORS OF THE WEPMAN AUDITORY DISCRIMINATION TEST

• Some young handicapped children may have difficulty understanding the concept of *same/different*. A low score may represent difficulty in grasping that concept or in sustaining attention for the task, rather than auditory discrimination difficulty. This problem was found in clinical practice and was verified by Blank (1968) in her research.

• This test provides a measure of auditory discrimination of isolated word pairs. Additional testing or observation is necessary to assess discrimination skills of other types and in other situations, such as conversational speech and discrimination of sound against a background of noise.

• Although many phonemic contrasts are presented, others are missing. For instance, the sounds /ng/, /l/, r/, /j/, and /ch/ are not included in the discrimination tasks. In addition, the contrast of voiced/voiceless consonants (for example, *bad-bat*) is not included. Also, only a limited number of vowel discriminations are assessed.

CHAPTER ONE
Academic Tests

The assessment of skills in basic academic areas is one of the primary purposes of educational testing. This chapter contains 25 tests that assess student functioning in the basic academic skill areas of reading, writing, spelling, and mathematics.

The first section includes 10 multiple subject tests presented in alphabetical order. In the last edition of this book, *A Guide to 75 Tests for Special Education*, there were only four tests in this category. The large increase documents examiners' interest in comprehensive test batteries. The Basic Achievement Skills Individual Screener is a relative newcomer to the field. The BASIS provides measures of reading comprehension, math calculation and word problems, spelling, and written language. The four Brigance Diagnostic Inventories are popular and comprehensive criterion-referenced batteries. The Diagnostic Achievement Battery (DAB) includes not only reading, writing, and math, but the oral language skills of listening and speaking. The Kaufman Test of Educational Abilities (KTEA) provides both brief and more comprehensive screening of reading, spelling, and math across the grades. A new test, the Norris Education Achievement Test (NEAT) provides reading in context a writing sample as well as decoding, spelling, and math. The well-known Peabody Individual Achievement Test (PIAT–R) uses a multiple-choice format to assess the basic skills plus general information. And finally, the best known and widely used brief test of academic skills continues its same format in its revised form, the Wide Range Achievement Test (WRAT-R).

The second section of the chapter contains ten tests specific to reading. In alphabetical order, the first test is the Decoding Skills Test (DST), a new well-constructed criterion-referenced test, followed by the Durrell Analysis, an old favorite battery of multiple reading skills. The Gates-MacGinitie Reading Tests (GMRT) include silent reading assessment at all grade levels and, with the Gates-McKillop-Horowitz Reading Diagnostic (RDT), is similar to the Durrell in format. Four tests of oral paragraph reading are included: The Gilmore Oral Reading Test and the Gray Oral Reading Test are very similar in form, while the Spache Diagnostic Reading Scales (DRS-81) includes silent reading and word analysis skills as well. The Slosson Oral Reading Test (SORT) is the shortest test of word reading available. The Test of Reading Comprehension (TORC) provides interesting subtests to assess the comprehension area of reading. The new revised form of the Woodcock Reading Mastery Test (WRMT-R) is the most comprehensive test of the group. For an overview of the reading tests, see Appendix D.

In the spelling and writing section of this chapter, there are only three tests reviewed. This is a decrease since *75 Tests*, perhaps because many of the multiple subject tests now include spelling and written language subtests. The three tests reviewed in this section are very different. The Boder Test of Reading-Spelling Patterns is a criterion referenced test for identifying dyslexic students. The Test of Written Language (TOWL) assesses written language through an original paragraph writing task. The Test of Written Spelling (TWS-2) is just what its name describes.

Math also is assessed in many of the multiple subject batteries. For that reason, only two separate math tests are reviewed in this section. The Enright™ Diagnostic Inventory of Basic Arithmetic skills is a very comprehensive assessment of computation. And the popular Key Math

Diagnostic Arithmetic Test covers a wide range of age levels and skills.

Some tests are difficult to categorize. The Slingerland Screening Tests for Identifying Children with Specific Language Disability and the Malcomesius Specific Language Disability Test are clearly tools for assessing academic skills. They include sections related to writing, spelling, and phonics. However, the primary contribution of these tests to educational assessment is in the area of perception and memory, so they are reviewed in Chapter Two.

Basic Achievement Skills Individual Screener (BASIS)

The Psychological Corporation, 1983
555 Academic Court, San Antonio, TX 78204

Purpose	To provide both norm-referenced and criterion-referenced information in basic academic skills
Major Areas Tested	Mathematics, reading, spelling, and writing
Age or Grade Range	Grades 1–12
Usually Given By	Psychologist Educational diagnostician Counselor Administrator Special education teacher Any trained person
Type of Test	Individual Criterion-referenced Norm-referenced Standardized
Scores Obtained	Grade level Percentile Age level Stanine
Student Performance Timed?	No
Testing Time	45–60 minutes
Scoring/Interpretation Time	15–30 minutes
Normed On	3,296 students in grades 1–12; sample balanced for race and socioeconomic background; 4% mainstreamed disabled students; additional 232 18–23-year-old adults included
Alternate Forms Available?	No

FORMAT

The Basic Achievement Skills Individual Screener (BASIS) is an individual test of reading, math, spelling, and writing achievement. It covers grades 1 through 12 and provides both norm-referenced and criterion-referenced information.

The materials consist of a manual containing directions for administration and scoring as well as technical information; the BASIS content booklet, which includes the reding passages and readiness activities; and BASIS record forms. The student writes directly on these consumable forms for the Mathematics, Spelling, and Writing subtests. The forms also include a summary of the student's performance in both norm-referenced and criterion-referenced scores.

Four subject areas are assessed by the BASIS:

1. *Mathematics.* This subject includes five items at the readiness level: addition; subtraction; multiplication; division of whole numbers, fractions, and decimals; and word problems using basic computation skills.

2. *Reading.* This subtest includes a few items at the readiness and beginning reading levels (letter naming, word matching, word reading, and sentence reading). It primarily assesses reading comprehension through a cloze procedure. The student reads orally a passage with six words missing and fills in appropriate words based on meaning.

3. *Spelling.* In this subtest, the student writes single words dictated by the examiner.

4. *Writing.* This subtest consists of a 10-minute writing sample on a standardized topic ("Your Favorite Place"). The examiner reads the sample for an overall or holistic impression of its content, organization, vocabulary, sentence structure, and mechanics. The impression is then matched against an average sample for the student's grade, and the student's sample is rated average, above average, or below average as compared to the sample.

A student may be given all four subtest areas or single areas selected by the examiner. When the complete test is given, the Mathematics subtest is given first.

The grade-referenced cluster is the basic unit of administration of the BASIS. The content of each subtest area is divided into eight clusters of items, a cluster for each grade level, 1 through 8. All of the items in each cluster for each subject area must be administered at one time. If the student passes the criterion or minimum number of items for each cluster, he or she moves on to the next level. If the student does not pass the criterion, the examiner drops two grade-level clusters to obtain a basal. The basal/ceiling process, then, is done through levels rather than through single items. The basal is the lowest level at which the student passes criterion; the ceiling is the lowest level at which the student

---

7 (a) $\begin{array}{r} 4283 \\ \times\ 315 \\ \hline \end{array}$ (b) $\dfrac{2}{3} = \dfrac{6}{\square}$ (c) $67\overline{)7303}$

(d) $\begin{array}{r} 7.03 \\ \times\ 4.6 \\ \hline \end{array}$ (e) $5.94 + 3.4 =$ (f) $.14\overline{)7.42}$

DICTATED:

(g) In the gym, we set up 10 rows of chairs with 12 chairs in each row. 125 more people can sit on the bleachers. How many people can sit in the gym in all?

DICTATED:

(h) Jan has $3\frac{4}{5}$ yards of canvas cloth. She needs $1\frac{2}{5}$ yards to make a floor for her tent. How many extra yards of cloth will Jan have?

BASIS Mathematics Cluster

does not pass the criterion.

A grade-referenced cluster in Mathematics consists of six computation items and two word problems.

Criterion is usually five out of eight correct. A grade-referenced cluster in Reading is one paragraph with six omitted words; criterion is usually four out of six. The Spelling grade-referenced cluster is six dictated words with the usual criterion being four correct.

Following the test completion, raw score points for items correct, plus those below the basal level, are totaled in each subject area and converted to a variety of scores: grade equivalents, stanines, and percentile ranks based on grade and age. In addition, a grade-referenced placement is determined. The grade-referenced placement score describes the student's instructional level in each subject area. In Reading, it represents the last level at which a student reached criterion, a level of 50–67 percent accuracy on the cloze procedure. In Mathematics and Spelling, it represents the first level at which the student did not achieve criterion, a level of about 60–70 percent accuracy. In addition to these norm-referenced and criterion-referenced scores, other diagnostic information is elicited by error analysis of math, reading, and spelling performance.

STRENGTHS OF THE BASIS

• The BASIS is obviously designed to provide the quick screening information usually obtained through the Wide Range Achievement Test. Many of the limitations of the WRAT have been eliminated by including reading comprehension, word problems, and written language. The advantages of a single instrument measuring basic skills quickly over a wide age range have been maintained. The BASIS is a good initial screening tool. It is especially useful as a quick survey of a new student's skills.

• The student testing materials are well designed, with large print and in a format familiar to students. The manual is clearly and concisely written.

• The combining of norm referenced scores with criterion referenced information allows for a variety of interpretations of student performance. Actually the interpretation needed is minimal as the BASIS content is directly classroom related.

• The Reading subtest provides an excellent measure of reading comprehension. The cloze procedure requires the student to understand not only individual sentences but also complete paragraphs. Although oral reading accuracy is not scored, the examiner gains very useful information about a student's decoding skills.

• Including two word problems in every level of the Mathematics subtest is a helpful factor.

• Good reliability and validity data are provided in the manual. The BASIS is very reliable for such a short test, and content validity is strong for the narrow range of skills assessed. Careful attention was given to the standardization sample.

• The manual and the record forms provide good information about procedures for error analysis in each subtest.

The Writing subtest is a unique feature of the BASIS. There are very few, if any, adequate measures of written language skills which actually assess a student's writing (as opposed to grammar or punctuation). It is easy for students to write to the topic "A Favorite Place," and in 10 minutes the examiner can gain important information about the student's skills. The grade level samples provide a useful reference point. The subject area of written language does not allow as precise a measurement as the other basic skills, and the holistic approach of evaluating writing is a useful one.

LIMITING FACTORS OF THE BASIS

• Although the BASIS includes a few items at the readiness level, as in other wide range achievement tests, it is not a good instrument for measuring the skills of first grade students.

• Although the BASIS provides norms for students through high school and beyond, the content of the materials used only reaches eighth grade level. The test is best used in grades 2–8.

• The words for the Spelling subtest were selected from grade-level spelling series, and they reflect all of the inconsistencies of those series. While they may yield an adequate grade referenced score, they give little information about a student's skills and do not reflect the skills of students taught in a systematic phonics approach.

• Although the BASIS manual is clearly written, the organization of the manual with the record forms is confusing. In Reading, the passing criteria are printed on the record forms, in Math and Spelling they are not. The possible correct answers for Reading are in an appendix. The examiner must be very familiar with the materials to administer the test smoothly.

• Although the authors have clearly explained the limitations of grade equivalent scores, their inclusion is questionable. It is too easy for the inexperienced examiner to confuse the grade equivalent score and misuse it as a grade placement recommendation.

Brigance® Diagnostic Inventories
(Brigance Inventories)

Albert H. Brigance
Curriculum Associates, Inc., 1976–1983
5 Esquire Rd., North Billerica, MA 01862

Purpose	To assess preacademic, academic, and vocational skills and to provide a systematic performance record to help teachers define instructional objectives and plan individualized educational programs
Major Areas Tested	Reading, writing, spelling, mathematics, language, and motor skills
Age or Grade Range	Preschool–grade 12
Usually Given By	Classroom teacher Administrator Special education teacher Paraprofessional Psychologist Teaching aide
Type of Test	Informal Individual (some group subtests) Criterion-referenced
Scores Obtained	Grade level (some subtests) Age level (some subtests)
Student Performance Timed?	No
Testing Time	15–90 minutes (depending on purpose of testing)
Scoring/Interpretation Time	15–30 minutes
Normed On	Not normed, but field-tested in 30 states and 2 provinces of Canada
Alternate Forms Available?	No, except for some subtests in the Diagnostic Comprehensive Inventory of Basic Skills

FORMAT

There are four Brigance® Diagnostic Inventories (Brigance® Inventories) designed to assess basic competencies at different grade levels. Together, the four instruments evaluate more than 500 skill sequences from preschool through grade 12. The materials for each Brigance® Inventory consist of an examiner's notebook and individual record books. The notebook is designed to lie flat on the table between the examiner and the student. It includes directions for administering each subtest, test items, scoring criteria, and instructional objectives in behavioral terms. When the assessment is oral, the student works directly from the student page; when a test requires writing or when group testing is done, the student page is reproduced in multiple copies.

The individual student record books provide a means of recording ongoing progress. The student's responses are recorded by the examiner in the record book in a different color each time the test is administered. A grade-level profile is charted after each administration to provide a graphic summary of student achievement. Observation of student behavior can also be noted.

The Brigance® Inventories are informal. Administration directions are given, but the examiner is encouraged to adjust the procedures to meet the needs of the student. The only question being asked in each subtest is: "Has the student mastered this skill, or is more instruction needed?" Developmental ages or grade-level scores are provided for a few key subtests in each inventory, but, basically, the tests are not norm-referenced. Their purpose is to assess basic skills, define instructional objectives, assist teachers in program planning, and provide a continuous measure of progress.

INITIAL CLUSTERS VISUALLY

SKILL: Can articulate correct sound when cluster is presented visually.

> **DIRECTIONS:** Point to the first letters (sh).
>
> **Say:** *Look at these letters. Tell me the sound they have when they are together at the beginning of a word.*
>
> If the student does not understand, explain the first blend.
>
> **Say:** *These letters have the sound of sh as in shock or shape.*
>
> See *NOTE #2* and the next page for alternate method of administration.

NOTES:

1. You may wish to check the student's understanding of the voiced and unvoiced "th."

   Say: *Can you tell me the other sound "th" makes?*, after the student has given one sound.

2. An alternate method of assessing this skill is to present the initial clusters in combination with a vowel. The results of the alternate method may have more validity if the student has been taught by a method which always presents the clusters in combination with a vowel such as Duggins or *Words in Color*. See next page for alternate administration.

DISCONTINUE: After three consecutive errors.

TIME: 10 seconds per response.

ACCURACY: Give credit for each correct response.

OBJECTIVE: When presented with a list of 33 blends and digraphs (clusters) listed in an order commonly taught, the student will indicate the sound_____(quantity) of the consonants have or make in the initial position.

Brigance Inventories Examiner's Page for Initial Clusters Visually

STRENGTHS OF THE BRIGANCE® INVENTORIES

• Each inventory is a comprehensive battery of assessments, including many skills for a wide age range of students. By careful selection of subtests appropriate for each student's age and skill level and for the purpose of the testing, assessment can be completed quickly.

• The Brigance® Inventories are intended to lead directly to instructional objectives and program planning; if used correctly, they do.

• The inventories can be administered by teaching aides or para-professionals under supervision.

• The inventories provide a well-organized recordkeeping system.

• The inventories include some unique subtests. Skills such as alphabetizing, dictionary and reference book use, interpretation of graphs and maps, and knowledge of geometry are not assessed in other instruments.

• The Spanish Edition of the Diagnostic Inventory of Basic Skills is very helpful in assessing the instructional needs of Spanish-speaking students.

LIMITING FACTORS OF THE BRIGANCE® INVENTORIES

• The informal format somewhat encourages teachers or teaching aides to administer the Brigance® Inventories without preparation. This often results in too lengthy, inappropriate, or haphazard assessment. Careful selection of tests, preparation of materials, and study of data-recording procedures are essential if the instruments are to be available.

• The Brigance® Inventories are good informal tests of skill mastery. Their usefulness as more stringent diagnostic tools is not justified given their lack of technical information.

sh ⟶	wh	th (v)	th (u)	st
sw	gr	sp	fl	gl
sl	pl	cl	bl	tr
cr	sc	dr	ch	fr
pr	br	sm	sk	wr
qu	spr	thr	scr	shr
str	spl	squ		

Brigance Inventories Initial Clusters Visually

- The Brigance® manuals contain only brief descriptions of the field testing. More complete information about the school districts included would be helpful.

- No reliability data is presented for any of the Brigance® inventories. Reliability is difficult to obtain when the subtests are not administered in a standardized manner. However, at a minimum, data should be presented for those subtests with alternate forms to establish their equivalency.

- Suggestions for discontinuing testing on subtests should generally be ignored. The Brigance® is a criterion-referenced test, and its purpose is to assess exactly what skills a student has mastered. Students tend to know scattered items (some abbreviations, some contractions), so all items need to be assessed. Also, in the Brigance®, item order was determined by examining typical basal series; therefore the order of difficulty will depend upon the instructional program, and it is inappropriate to use ceiling procedures.

- Teachers need to be aware that the Brigance® Inventories assess many specific academic skills; however, they do not tell the user how well or how poorly a student is doing in any subject areas. They should be used in conjunction with good norm referenced tests both at the time of initial assessment and in measuring progress.

- The Brigance® Inventories should not be used for grade placement decisions. The lack of reliability and validity data do not permit the instrument to be used for this purpose.

Scope of the Brigance® Inventories

Inventory	Grade Range	Skills Assessed	Comments
Diagnostic Inventory of Early Development (Yellow Notebook)–1978	Preschool–2	Preambulatory motor Gross and fine motor Self-help Prespeech Speech and language General knowledge Readiness Writing Math	Assesses infant and preschool development in many areas from birth through six years. The social-emotional domain is not assessed. Developmental ages based upon extensive review of the developmental literature are given for most of the 98 skill sequences. These ages are guides for when a skill is usually learned and should not be used for placement decisions.

Diagnostic Inventory of Basic Skills (Blue Notebook)–1976	K–6	Readiness
		Reading
		   Word recognition
		   Fluency
		   Analysis
		Vocabulary
		Handwriting
		Grammar
		Spelling
		Math
		   Computation
		   Measurement
		   Geometry
			Comprises the original Brigance® Inventory with 141 subtests covering a variety of academic tasks in key subject areas. This inventory is available in Spanish. A small pamphlet lists which subtests are appropriate to administer for a particular grade. The grade level scores provided for some subtests are not based on a standardization sample.

Diagnostic Inventory of Essential Skills (Red Notebook)–1981	4–12	Reading
		   Word recognition
		   Oral Reading
		   Comprehension
		   Analysis
		   Reference
		Writing
		Spelling
		Math
		   Computation
		   Fractions
		   Decimals
		   Percents
		   Measurement
			While advertisements list this inventory as appropriate for grades 4–12, it was clearly designed for secondary students in special education. Measures minimal competencies in academic and vocational skills. Includes rating scales for health practices and attitudes, self-concept, job interview skills, auto safety, speaking and listening skills. A guide lists tests appropriate for each grade level. Grade placement scores on some tests are not norm-referenced and their use is questionable. The Reading Comprehension subtest was revised in 1982; it can be purchased from the publisher to replace pages in the 1981 edition. The revised form is one of the best measures of passage comprehension for secondary students available.

Diagnostic Comprehensive Inventory of Basic Skills (Green Notebook)–1983	K–9	All Skills in Diagnostic Inventory of Basic Skills Speech Listening Percents Metrics Reading Comprehension	Designed for use in elementary and middle schools. Expands Diagnostic Inventory of Basic Skills to grade 9. Adds new subtests, particularly in the areas of speech, listening, and reading comprehension. More than half of the skills can be assessed in groups. A guide lists tests appropriate for each grade level. Has two forms for many subtests to provide for pre- and post-testing; however, no data is provided on the equivalency of these forms and the scores are not norm-referenced. They should not be used as a measure of progress.

Diagnostic Achievement Battery (DAB)

Phyllis L. Newcomer and Dolores Curtis
Pro-Ed, 1984
5341 Industrial Oaks Blvd., Austin, TX 78735

Purpose	To identify students who are significantly below their peers in language and academic skills; to determine their strengths and weaknesses; to document progress; and to serve as a research instrument.
Major Areas Tested	Listening, speaking, reading, writing, and mathematics
Age or Grade Range	6–14 years
Usually Given By	Educational Diagnostician Special educational teacher
Type of Test	Individual Norm-referenced Standardized
Scores Obtained	Percentile Standard Score
Student Performance Timed?	Yes, on some subtests
Testing Time	1–2 hours
Scoring/Interpretation Time	20–30 minutes
Normed On	1,534 students from 13 states; sample was balanced for sex, place of residence, race, geographic region, and occupation of the parents and compared with the Statistical Abstracts of the United States, 1980
Alternate Forms Available?	No

FORMAT

The Diagnostic Achievement Battery (DAB) is a relatively new individual test of academic achievement. The DAB was developed to fill the need for a single assessment device to measure spoken language, written language, and applied mathematics. The materials for the DAB consist of the manual, student worksheets for the written subtests and math calculation, and a three-page examiner's form which contains the test items for the oral tests and a record of scores. The manual provides an extensive discussion of the test model, instructions for administration, scoring, and interpretation, norms tables, and data on test standardization and technical properties.

In the DAB, three major constructs are measured: spoken language, written language, and mathematics. The two language constructs are assessed in both the receptive and expressive mode: listening and speaking, reading and writing. In math, only Applied Mathematics is assessed. The 12 subtests which the DAB authors developed to measure the three constructs reflect the achievement skills delineated by P.L. 94-142. The examiner may choose to give the whole test or individual subtests.

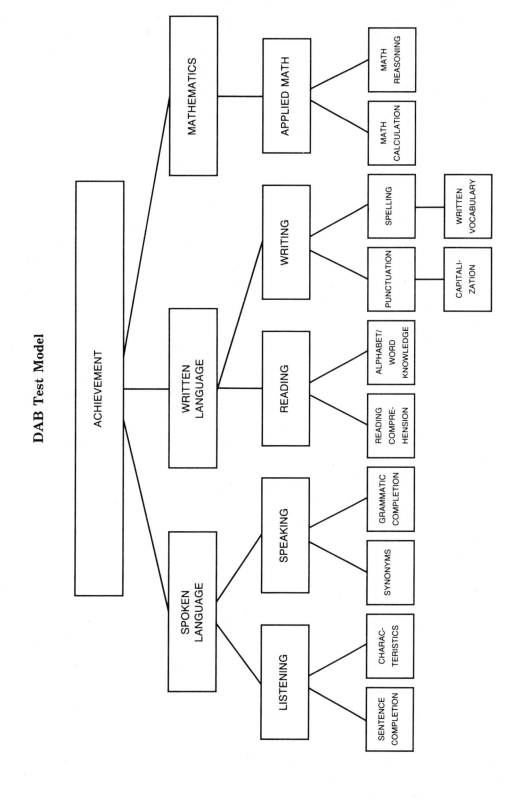

DAB Test Model

Listening

1. *Story Comprehension* (35 items). The examiner reads aloud brief stories of increasing length, and the student answers questions about them.

2. *Characteristics* (35 items). The examiner reads aloud a brief statement, and the student decides whether it is true or false.

Speaking

3. *Synonyms* (25 items). The examiner says a word and the student supplies a word with the same meaning.

4. *Grammatic Completion* (27 items). The examiner reads unfinished sentences and the student supplies the missing morphological form.

Reading

5. *Alphabet-Word Knowledge* (65 items). The first 25 items include matching letters and words, recognizing and naming letters, and recognizing beginning and ending consonants. These items are only administered to students who cannot read at least three of the five words in the 40-word list which comprises this subtest.

6. *Reading Comprehension* (35 items). The student silently reads short stories of increasing length and answers questions about them by the examiner.

Writing

7 and 8. *Capitalization and Punctuation.* The student is given a paragraph without capitals or punctuation and is asked to insert correct capitals and punctuation marks. Separate scores are calculated for each subtest. A 15-minute time limit is imposed.

9. *Spelling* (20 items). The student writes words dictated by the examiner.

10. *Written Vocabulary.* The student is shown three pictures that represent a modified version of The Tortoise and the Hare. He or she is encouraged to write a story based on the pictures that has a beginning, a middle, and an end. The maturity of the vocabulary is measured by counting the number of words with seven or more letters. A 15-minute time limit is imposed.

Applied Mathematics

11. *Mathematics Reasoning* (30 items). The student is asked a question involving a math concept or operation and asked to answer it without using pencil or paper. Pictures are used for the younger students. "Art drove 55 m.p.h. for 10 hours. How far did he drive?" "Which pie is divided into fourths?"

12. *Mathematics Calculation.* The student is given a page of math calculations arranged in order of increasing diffi-

culty. A 15-minute time limit is imposed.

Starting levels according to age are indicated on the examiner's form for each subtest. Ceiling levels, which differ for each subtest, are also clearly indicated. In this way students are tested only over an appropriate range for their age. Each subtest begins with one sample item to illustrate the task. The raw score for each subtest is converted into a percentile rank and a standard score with a mean of 10 and a standard deviation of 3. Subtest scores can then be combined into 9 composite scores called quotients. Quotients are standard scores with a mean of 100 and standard deviation of 15.

STRENGTHS OF THE DAB

• The DAB is a well-designed and well-normed technically strong test. Test-retest reliability is good, and validity data reported in the manual is strong.

• The DAB manual is comprehensive and clearly written. The administration and scoring procedures are well described. The discussion of the DAB Test Model is interesting to read. The manual also includes a well-written discussion of the problems with group tests.

• The DAB measures a wide variety of skills which are directly related to classroom performance. Interpretation of test results to teachers, parents, and older students is not difficult due to the familiarity of subtest tasks. The comprehensiveness of the test adds to its usefulness for special educators in the public schools.

LIMITING FACTORS OF THE DAB

• The authors note two areas of inconsistency in the technical data on the DAB. The internal consistency of the test was lower for 13-year-olds than for any other age group. This suggests some type of a sampling error in that age range. Also, the Synonyms Subtest is not as reliable as the other subtests and examiners are advised to interpret it cautiously for individual students and to put more confidence in the Speaking Composite score.

• The DAB is a long test. For students at the upper end of the age norms, it may require two hours to administer. While the tasks are varied on each subtest, they all have a "school-like" quality that could be overwhelming to the student who is not doing well in school. Administering the test in two sessions or selecting only critical subtests or composites is recommended.

• Many of the subtest tasks such as those in Spelling, Math Calculation, Capitalization, and Punctuation are familiar to the students; others such as those in Characteristics require a new type of thinking. For these subtests, additional examples or training items would be very useful.

• No guidelines are given as to the appropriate age range for using the Capitalization and Punctuation subtests. The reading level of the paragraph makes it too difficult for most students below fourth grade.

• Similarly, the Written Vocabulary subtest, which gives the student credit for using words of seven letters or more in length, is inappropriate for students below age eight. A seven-year-old would receive a scaled score of 10 with no words of that length. Guidelines for appropriate subtests for younger students would add to DAB's usefulness.

• For older students, perfect scores on several subtests yield scaled scores of 15 or less. For example, a 12 1/2-year-old with a perfect score on Alphabet-Word Knowledge would only receive a scaled score of 13. By studying the norm tables for the age of the student to be tested, the examiner can select subtests appropriate for older students. There are other tests in several of the areas which are more appropriate for older students because of their range of difficulty.

• Two starting levels are provided for most subtests; one for students aged 6–8 and one for students 9 and over. For students in the older range who don't obtain a basal score, the examiner must go back to the first item on the subtest. A progression downward from the starting level until a basal is reached would reduce testing time, an important consideration on this lengthy test.

• On several subtests additional information is needed to interpret a student's performance. For example, on Synonyms a student may not know the meaning of the stimulus word or may have word finding problems which make it difficult for him to supply a synonym.

• On Math Reasoning, some of the questions are quite long; poor auditory memory or auditory comprehension may cause errors rather than lack of math skills. Examiners should consider these types of possibilities when they interpret an individual student's performance.

Kaufman Test of Educational Achievement (KTEA)

Alan S. and Nadeen L. Kaufman
American Guidance Service, 1985
Publishers Building, Circle Pines, MN 55014

Purpose	To measure school achievement in grades 1–12
Major Areas Tested	Reading, spelling, mathematics
Age or Grade Range	Grades 1–12
Usually Given By	Educational diagnosticians Special educational teachers Psychologists
Type of Test	Individual Standardized Norm-referenced
Scores Obtained	Age level Stanine Grade Level Standard Percentile
Student Performance Timed?	No
Testing Time	20–30 minutes (Brief Form); 60–75 minutes (Comprehensive Form)
Scoring/Interpretation Time	10–15 minutes
Normed On	Stratified random sample of 589 students in 25 cities in 15 states; sample balanced for sex, geographic region, socioeconomic status, and educational level of the parents
Alternate Forms Available?	The 2 forms, Brief and Comprehensive, may be used as alternate forms

FORMAT

The Kaufman Test of Educational Achievement (KTEA) is an individually-administered test of academic skills in reading, spelling, and math for the first through twelfth grades. Two forms are provided, Brief and Comprehensive. The Brief Form globally samples reading, spelling, and mathematics; the Comprehensive Form separates reading into decoding and comprehension and math into applications and computation. The materials for each form consist of a manual, an easel book for presentation of test items, individual forms for recording responses and profiling scores, and a parental reporting form. The subtests for the Brief Form are:

Mathematics (52 items). Assesses basic math computation skills as well as applications and reasoning. Computations are done with pencil and paper while concept and applications are read by the examiner and often have accompanying pictures.

Reading (52 items). Assesses reading of single words and reading comprehension. The comprehension items often require a gestural response.

Spelling (40 items). Assesses spelling through writing a dictated word list of increasing difficulty.

In the Comprehensive Form, mathematics is separated into a Mathematics Applications and a Mathematics Computation subtest with 60 items each. Reading is broken into Decoding (60 items) and Comprehension (50 items). The Spelling test format remains the same.

The authors recommend that the Brief Form be used unless there is a particular reason for needing the more specific information on the Comprehensive Form. On the response forms, starting points according to grade are indicated for each subtest. Items are grouped into units, and testing is discontinued whenever a student makes errors on all the items in a unit.

Raw scores for each subtest are converted into age scores, grade scores, stanines, percentiles and standard scores (mean: 100; standard deviation: 15). On the back of the response form, standard scores can be graphed to give a profile of a student's performance. Procedures are given in the manual for determining if subtest differences are significant.

STRENGTHS OF THE KTEA

• The KTEA is a well standardized reliable quick test of academic achievement. The Brief Form compares favorably with the WRAT-R, the BASIS, and the NEAT, in terms of time, content, and technical properties.

• The comprehensive form also provides criterion-referenced assessment data to analyze student errors.

• Strong internal consistency and test-retest reliability results are presented in the manual; extensive validity studies are also reported. Spring and fall norms are provided for both forms of the KTEA.

LIMITING FACTORS OF THE KTEA

• The Reading Comprehension items require silent reading and a gestural response. Many students are resistant to this task, perhaps feeling shy or foolish. When a student doesn't respond, the examiner needs to explore further to find out if he cannot read the item or doesn't want to respond.

• Although paraprofessionals may administer the KTEA, the manual suggests that trained examiners do the interpretation.

• The Report to Parents was intended to explain the results of the KTEA in non-technical terms. It is quite wordy and raises more questions than it clarifies.

Norris Educational Achievement Test (NEAT)

Janet Switzer
Western Psychological Services, 1988
12031 Wilshire Blvd., Los Angeles, CA 90025

Purpose	To provide a rapid screening measure of basic academic skills as well as a reliable measure of pupil progress
Major Areas Tested	Reading, writing, spelling, arithmetic
Age or Grade Range	Preschool–12th grade
Usually Given By	Classroom teacher Special education teacher Psychologist Administrator
Type of Test	Individual Normed Group (some subtests)
Scores Obtained	Standard Percentile Age Stanine Grade
Student Performance Timed?	Yes (some subtests)
Testing Time	30 minutes
Scoring/Interpretation Time	15 minutes
Normed On	3,000 students from 50 school districts in 19 states; sample balanced for community size, parent education level, ethnic background, age, grade, and sex
Alternate Forms Available?	Yes

FORMAT

The Norris Educational Achievement Test (NEAT) is an individual test of reading, spelling, math, and writing achievement. Norms are provided for grades 1 through 12, including 11th and 12th graders "planning to go to college."

The materials consist of an examiner's manual which includes directions for administration, scoring, and interpretation, and a Master Booklet in which either the student writes his or her own answers or the examiner records student responses. Equivalent Forms A and B are provided for test-retest purposes.

The NEAT is composed of the six subtests described below:

1. *Readiness*. Given to students in second grade or younger, Readiness is composed of three tasks assessing skills prerequisite for writing, arithmetic, and reading. Fine Motor Coordination is assessed through a form copying task; both speed and accuracy are scored. Math Concepts evaluates basic concepts such as size, shape, counting, number writing, and adding groups. Letters includes matching, naming, and giving letter sounds. Separate scores are given for each subtest, as is a total Readiness score.

2. *Word Recognition*. The student reads aloud single words increasing in difficulty from primer through college level. In addition to tabulating correct responses, the examiner also notes the "slowing point," the item on which the student's reading speed slowed down.

3. *Spelling*. A written spelling test in the usual classroom format; the examiner pronounces a word, uses it in a sentence, and pronounces it again. Words range from primer through high school level.

4. *Arithmetic*. A standard test of math computation including basic operations with whole numbers and fractions. A 10-minute time limit is imposed; if the student is still working at the end of the 10 minutes, he is given a different colored pencil and allowed to continue. Scores for both speed and "power" are obtained.

5. *Oral Contextual Reading and Recall*. The student reads aloud paragraphs of graded difficulty. The paragraphs are composed of words from the Word Recognition subtest. This allows a comparison of the student's word reading in isolation and in context. Each student begins this test with a paragraph that includes words at the level at which he or she has read with 90% accuracy on Word Recognition. Each paragraph is prefaced by an Orientation Cue from the examiner. For example, "This is a story about people wanting improvement in one of their town's roads. They tell the newspapers."

Following the oral reading, the student is asked four recall questions to assess reading comprehension. A basal-ceiling procedure combining reading errors and recall questions is used to determine whether the student continues with more difficult paragraphs or drops back to lower levels.

Only "significant context reading errors" are scored; these include words which are significantly changed or where the meaning is altered. Minor errors (boys/boy, says/said) or repetitions are not scored as errors. Recall questions are to be answered with words in the paragraph, not words in the Orientation Cue. Scores for speed, accuracy and recall are calculated.

6. *Composition*. The student writes an original composition on the topic "On My Next Vacation" (Form A) or "On My Next Weekend" (Form B). A five-minute time limit is given, and compositions are scored on a number of empirical bases including word count, word analysis, and punctuation, which can be objectively and quickly scored. Qualitative criteria will also be included. Students below second grade or students who are unable to write may dictate the composition.

STRENGTHS OF THE NEAT

• The NEAT is a new test. When this review was written, only prepublication information was available. The NEAT is clearly designed to provide the quick screening information usually obtained through the WRAT, and, less frequently, the BASIS. The assessment of basic skills in reading, writing, spelling, and math in one instrument over a wide age range is an obvious strength of all three tests. The NEAT offers several features not available in the other tests:
—Equivalent forms A and B for test-retest purposes
—Measures of both reading recognition and reading comprehension
—A comparison of a student's word recognition skills with contextual reading skills using the same vocabulary
—Measures of math speed and power
—More complete skills assessment at Readiness level
—A standardized measure of written language

• The test format and tasks presented are very familiar to students as they were selected to represent usual classroom tasks. This feature of the NEAT increases the use of administration and makes interpretation of a student's scores directly applicable to classroom performance.

• The NEAT was authored by a clinician. As a result, the test procedures and the manual instructions provide many opportunities for gathering sensitive diagnostic information. One example is the "slowing point." On the Reading Recognition test the examiner notes the point at which the student "slows down", shifting from sight reading to word analysis. Another example is the way in which the spelling tests on Form A and Form B are structured. Item 33, Form A is city; Item 33, Form B is cent. By analyzing a student's reponses to Form A and later, in posttesting, to Form B, specific skills learned (such as the soft sound of c) can be documented. This procedure is followed in Arithmetic as well.

• The directions for administration are clear and sensitive to student needs. The examiner is given good instructions for scoring procedures while administering the test. For example, Word Recognition is to be scored while the student is completing Arithmetic. This allows the examiner to ascertain the correct level for beginning Oral Contextual Reading.

LIMITING FACTORS OF THE NEAT

• The NEAT is a new test. Norm tables reflecting a nationwide standardization sample are in preparation. Reliability and validity data are currently being gathered. The value of the NEAT as a screening instrument as well as a measure of student progress cannot yet be evaluated.

• The Oral Contextual Reading and Recall Test is a unique measure of reading skills. The directions for administering and interpreting this subtest are complex, in part due to their unfamiliarity. Extensive examples of "significant" and "minor" errors are needed to help the examiner unfamiliar with this concept. In addition, examples are needed for scoring the recall questions. It is difficult to understand the difference between "words in the paragraph" and "words in the Orientation Cue."

Peabody Individual Achievement Test–Revised (PIAT–R)

Lloyd M. Dunn and Frederick C. Markwardt, Jr.
American Guidance Service, Inc., 1989
P.O. Box 99, Circle Pines, MN 55014–1796

Purpose	To provide a wide-range screening measure of reading, spelling, mathematics, written language, and general information
Major Areas Tested	Mathematics, reading, spelling, and general information
Age or Grade Range	Grades K–12
Usually Given By	Classroom teacher Paraprofessional Special education teacher Any trained person Psychologist
Type of Test	Standardized Individual Norm-referenced
Scores Obtained	Age equivalent Grade equivalent Standard Percentile
Student Performance Timed?	No
Testing Time	30–40 minutes
Scoring/Interpretation Time	25–30 minutes
Normed On	National standardized sample of 1,738 K–12 students based on U.S. Census projections for a representative school sample for the year 1990. Sample was stratified by sex, geographic region, socio-economic status, and race or ethnic group
Alternate Forms Available?	No

FORMAT

The Peabody Individual Achievement Test (PIAT-R) is the 1989 edition of the PIAT, which was originally published in 1970. The major features of the original PIAT have been retained. However, item content and art work have been updated and many new items have been included.

The PIAT-R materials consist of four easel kits of test items, each containing the directions for subtest administration; individual test records to record student responses; and one manual which includes procedures for general administration, scoring and interpretation, the norms tables and technical information. Separate Response Booklets are needed for the Written Expression subtest. Optional materials include a cassette for the Pronunciation Guide and a carrying bag.

The PIAT-R consists of 5 subtests given in the order listed below. The test combines short answer and multiple-choice questions; no writing is required. Suggested starting points are given for each subtest, and a basal and ceiling procedure is used to reduce testing to a critical range for each student. The five subtests are:

1. *General Information.* This subtest contains 100 questions that are read to the students and answered orally. The content includes science, social studies, fine arts, and sports.

2. *Reading Recognition.* This subtest includes 100 items. It begins with letter matching and naming. The remaining items are single words that the student reads aloud. The words were selected from a basal reading series using both sight word and phonic approaches.

3. *Reading Comprehension.* This subtest includes 82 multiple-choice items. For each item, the student is presented with a page that contains one sentence to be read silently. The next page contains 4 illustrations, and the student selects the picture which best illustrates the sentence.

4. *Mathematics.* This subtest includes 100 multiple-choice items ranging from matching numbers to high school geometry and trigonometry. The questions are read to the student, who then selects the correct answer from 4 visually-presented choices. All computation must be done mentally.

5. *Spelling.* This subtest includes 100 items which assess the student's ability to recognize the correct spelling of a word. The examiner pronounces the word, and the student selects the correct spelling from 4 visually-presented choices. No written spelling is required.

While the PIAT-R was standardized on the above 5 subtests given in the prescribed order, selected subtests can be given for individual students. Age level, grade level, percentile ranks, and standard scores are provided for each subtest and for the PIAT-R total. In addition, a Total Reading Score can be obtained by combining the results for the Reading Recognition and Reading Comprehension subtests.

The test records include two profiles for graphic presentation of an individual student's test results. The Developmental Score Profile may be used to plot grade or age equivalents, while the Standard Score Profile is used for plotting standard scores.

In addition to the five main subtests, the PIAT-R includes an optional subtest to assess written expression at two levels: Level I, for kindergarten and first grade, tests prewriting skills such as writing one's name, copying letters and words, and writing letters and words from dictation. Level II, for grades 2–12, asks the student to write a story about a stimulus picture. Level II is scored on a three point scale using 24 criteria that range from legibility to story completeness and use of metaphors. Grade-based stanines are used to report scores for both Levels I and II. In addition, a 15-point developmental scaled score is available for Level II. Because the psychometric characteristics of the Written Expression subtest score is not incorporated into the PIAT-R total score.

STRENGTHS OF THE PIAT-R

Note: The PIAT-R was not available for use with students at the time of this test review. The following strengths and limitations are based upon the author's knowledge of characteristics of the earlier edition which have not changed.

• The PIAT and PIAT-R provide a quick rough estimate of achievement levels. The multiple-choice items allow the test-taker to move quickly, and the variety of items holds student interest. These factors make the PIAT and PIAT-R especially useful for screening underachieving secondary students.

• Used in conjunction with other diagnostic tests, the subtests of the PIAT-R can provide useful information. The Mathematics subtest includes items that assess a student's problem-solving skills more effectively than a straight computation test would. The picture format of the Reading Comprehension subtest is a unique way to measure the important skill of sentence comprehension. For students who have not previously had an intelligence test, the General Information subtest can provide a quick estimate of overall functioning.

Perhaps most useful is a comparison of a student's Spelling score in the PIAT-R (which requires only recognition of the correct spelling) with written spelling performance on a test such as the Wide Range Achievement Test-R (p. 61). For example, suppose two sixth-grade students obtained the grade scores shown here:

	WRAT-R Spelling Grade Level	PIAT-R Spelling Grade Level
Student A	4th B	5.8
Student B	4th B	4.7

Both students are performing significantly below grade level on written spelling. Student A, however, has the ability to recognize correct spelling, as her PIAT-R score indicates, thus demonstrating some visual memory skills. The remedial program for Student A would attempt to capitalize on that visual memory, and the expectations for performance in such skills as proofreading and dictionary work would be higher than would be for Student B.

• The new Written Expression subtest is a valuable addition to the PIAT-R. Standardized tests of written language which actually require the student to write a paragraph, with the exception of the TOWL (p. 98), have been notably lacking in the field. The validity of this PIAT-R subtest cannot be determined until it is used in the field, but the efforts of the authors to include it should be applauded.

LIMITING FACTORS OF THE PIAT-R

• The PIAT-R was not intended to be a comprehensive diagnostic instrument in any of the subtest areas. For students with academic problems, it should serve only as a guide for further, in-depth, testing.

• When interpreting a student's performance on the PIAT-R, it is necessary to keep in mind the exact task presented on each subtest. The broad general subtest names (Mathematics, Reading Recognition, Reading Comprehension, Spelling, and General Information) do not describe the tasks. For example, the examiner must be careful not to make general statements about a student's spelling based on the PIAT–R alone, because the task of recognizing correct spelling is quite different from written spelling (the more usual classroom task). Also, such a statement as, "Student C is two years below grade level in math" may be very inaccurate if based on the PIAT–R alone; the student's computation skills may be excellent.

• The multiple-choice format used on the Mathematics, Reading Comprehension, and Spelling subtests is appropriate for a screening tool but may yield very inaccurate results for individual students. For example, the impulsive student often selects an answer without thinking, whereas the student with sophisticated test-taking skills may puzzle out an answer by the process of elimination without really knowing the information.

• As with any test made up of subtests, there is a tendency to focus attention on a comparison of subtest scores; that is, to discuss Student A's performance in spelling compared to her performance in math. The PIAT–R manual discusses the problems in this type of analysis and presents guidelines for interpreting differences between raw scores on subtests. The examiner should study these guidelines carefully to avoid overinterpretation of subtest differences.

• Data on the reliability and validity of the PIAT-R were not available at the time this review was written.

Wide Range Achievement Test–Revised (WRAT-R)

Sarah Jastak and Gary S. Wilkinson
Jastak Associates, Inc., 1984
1526 Gilpin Ave., Wilmington, DE 19806

Purpose	To assess skills in reading, spelling, and arithmetic
Major Areas Tested	Reading, spelling, and arithmetic
Age or Grade Range	5 years–adult
Usually Given By	Classroom teacher Special education teacher Psychologist
Type of Test	Standardized Individual Norm-referenced
Scores Obtained	Standard Percentile
Student Performance Timed?	Yes
Testing Time	20–30 minutes
Scoring/Interpretation Time	15 minutes
Normed On	5,600 children and adults from all socioeconomic groups and all ranges of intellectual ability in seven states
Alternate Forms Available?	No

FORMAT

The Wide Range Achievement Test—Revised (WRAT-R) is the sixth revision of the WRAT, originally published in 1937. The materials for the WRAT-R consist of the administration manual and individual test blanks for each level of the test. The administration manual includes descriptions of the subtests, directions for administering and scoring, norms tables, reliability and validity data, and interpretation guide lines.

The test is divided into two levels. Level 1 is for students between the ages of 5 years, 0 months and 11 years, 11 months. Level 2 is for persons 2 years of age and older. Norms are provided through 74 years of age.

Each level of the WRAT-R contains three subtests:

1. *Reading*. Recognizing and naming letters and pronouncing single words.

2. *Spelling*. Copying marks, writing the name, and writing single words from dictation.

3. *Arithmetic*. Counting, reading numerals, solving oral problems, and performing basic written computation skills.

"The WRAT-R was intentionally designed to eliminate, as totally as possible, the effects of comprehension." (Administration Manual, p. 1) It is designed to measure the process of decoding in reading, encoding in spelling, and basic arithmetic computation.

The three subtests can be given independently. When all three are given, no particular order is required. The WRAT-R usually is given individually, but group procedures for the Spelling and Arithmetic subtests are described in the manual.

In Level 1, each of the subtests begins with some pre-academic tasks. In the Reading section, the prereading skills assessed include naming letters in the student's name, matching 10 letters by form, and naming 13 letters of the alphabet. The prespelling test consists of copying 18 geometric marks and writing names. The prearithmetic test includes counting, reading 5 digits, showing 3 and 8 fingers, identifying which number is more, and doing 3 oral addition and subtraction problems. Students between the ages of 5 and 7 are routinely given the pretests. Older students are given the pretests only when they cannot achieve a basal level on the Reading, Spelling, or Arithmetic subtest. Level 2 students who cannot achieve a basal level are also given the pretests.

The items in each subtest are arranged in order of difficulty. The student continues working until a ceiling level is reached in Reading (10 consecutive errors) and Spelling (10 consecutive errors) or until the time limit expires in Arithmetic (10 minutes).

A raw score for each subtest represents the number of correct responses prior to reaching the ceiling. Full credit is given for the preacademic tasks if they are not administered. Raw scores are converted into standard scores and percen-tiles for age as well as grade equivalents. The grade equivalents are represented by scores such as 2M, 4B, or 10E (mid-second, beginning 4th, end of 10th respectively). Norms tables are provided for six-month age groups from 5–13 years and for one or more year age groups from age 14 and older.

STRENGTHS OF THE WRAT-R

• The WRAT-R is undoubtedly the best known and most widely used quick measure of individual achievement in basic academic skills. Students of all ages and skill levels can be tested to get an estimate of academic performance that can serve as a first step in diagnostic evaluation.

• Although equivalent forms of the WRAT-R are not available, the wide age range covered by the test makes it a valuable tool for assessing the progress of an individual student over several years. The WRAT-R is inexpensive in terms of materials and time. It is relatively quick to administer and score.

• The elimination of the numerical grade score is to be applauded. Grade scores are often misused, and the reporting of standard scores and percentiles is much more appropriate.

• The new test blanks for level 1 and level 2 are much easier to read and less intimidating to students. For testing visually handicapped students, large print editions of the test blanks are available.

• The 1978 norms for the WRAT greatly overestimated the abilities of primary grade students. The new norms for the WRAT-R seem to be more accurate at the younger age levels.

LIMITING FACTORS OF THE WRAT-R

• *In Uses and Misuses of the WRAT,* a technical report published by Jastak Associates, Inc., the limitations of the WRAT are described very well. They apply equally to the WRAT-R. This report, together with WRAT-R, Monograph 1 (Wilkinson, 1987), is issued by the publisher to avoid misuse of the test and should be "must" reading for every examiner.

• Because the WRAT-R is so easy to give and to score, it is frequently overused and misused. It must be viewed as an initial estimate of a student's basic academic skills and not as a complete diagnostic instrument. Too often students are admitted to or excluded from special programs on the basis of their WRAT-R scores alone. An investigation of the content of WRAT-R subtests indicates that such a use of the test is not warranted.

The Reading subtest assesses word recognition only. The student simply reads aloud a list of single words. There is no measure of sentence reading, paragraph reading, or comprehension. Some students can decode single words, but cannot decode sentences and paragraphs, the more essential reading tasks. And, of course, good decoders with poor comprehension are not identified on the WRAT-R.

Similarly, the Arithmetic subtest raises many content questions. Because it is a straight computation test, student performance depends on the curriculum that has been taught. Students who have not been taught skills in fractions cannot obtain a fourth-grade score. Students instructed totally in the "new math" may get unrealistically low scores. Also, there is only one example of many types of problems. In addition, the 10-minute time limit on the arithmetic test affects the scores of older students, who may work slowly. If possible, they should be given an opportunity to complete as many problems as they can; then two scores should be reported, one within the 10-minute limit, and one after the time limit was extended.

• The manual states that the WRAT-R is a valuable tool for instructional planning when the examiner analyzes the types of errors a student makes on the three subtests. No guidelines for this type of informal assessment are given.

The table that follows illustrates error analysis on the spelling subtest. Information of this type should be included in the manual if the WRAT-R is to be used for instructional planning.

• The manual discusses the use of the WRAT-R with learning disabled students; however, no learning disabled students are included in the standardization sample.

• The technical characteristics of the WRAT-R are described briefly in the manual and also in WRAT-R, Monograph 1 (Wilkinson, 1987). Reliability and validity studies are sketchy for such a widely-used test. It is the misuse of the WRAT-R which is its greatest limitation. According to Witt, the WRAT-R is not precise enough to be an instrument for diagnosis or placement. "Instead its use is roughly equivalent to doing inner ear surgery with a chain saw." (Witt, 1986, p. 89) "Clearly the time saved in using the WRAT-R is not worth the potential cost in diagnostic errors which are likely (in fact probable) when using this thread bare test." (Witt, 1986, p. 89)

Analysis of Spelling Errors

Word	Spelling	Error Type	Teaching Strategy
cat	*ɔat*	Letter reversal (kinesthetic)	Dictation, visual-motor training
boy	*doy*	*b/d* confusion (visual-kinesthetic)	Visual discrimination, visual-motor training
will	*well*	Vowel discrimination (auditory)	Auditory discrimination, word patterns (*ill*)
make	*mack*	Vowel error and visual recall	Silent-*e* rule, dictation
say	*sae*	Poor visual recall	Word patterns (*ay*), word tracing
grown *explain*	*grone* *explane*	Poor visual recall	Word tracing
enter *advice*	*inter* *edvice*	Vowel discrimination (auditory)	Auditory discrimination, dictation
surprise	*suprise*	Incorrect pronunciation (auditory)	Auditory-kinesthetic feedback, visual cuing, color coding
cut *cook*	*kut* *kook*	Poor visual recall	Word tracing
light *dress* *watch*	*lite* *dres* *woch*	Poor visual recall	Word tracing, color coding

Decoding Skills Test (DST)

Ellis Richardson and Barbara DiBenedetto
York Press, 1985
2712 Mt. Carmel Road, Parkton, MD 21120

Purpose	To identify reading disabled students and provide a diagnostic profile of their decoding skill development
Major Areas Tested	The decoding process of reading
Age or Grade Range	First to fifth grade reading level
Usually Given By	Reading specialist Classroom teacher Special education teacher
Type of Test	Diagnostic Criterion referenced
Scores Obtained	No scores are obtained
Student Performance Timed?	No
Testing Time	20–30 minutes
Scoring/Interpretation Time	15–20 minutes
Normed On	Not normed
Alternate Forms Available?	No

FORMAT

The Decoding Skills Test (DST) is an individually-administered criterion referenced instrument which provides a variety of types of diagnostic information about a student's decoding skills. The materials consist of the Manual of Instructions, The Presentation Book, from which the student reads, the Basal/Ceiling and Passage Scoring Key Card, Individual Scoring Booklets, and the Phonic Profile Worksheet. A stop watch is also necessary for administering the test. The Manual of Instructions includes discussion of the test design, uses of the DST, directions for administration, scoring and interpretation, as well as reliability and validity data.

The DST has three subtests:

1. *Basal Vocabulary* is composed of 11 word lists representing reading levels from preprimer through a 5.2 reader. Words were selected from high-occurrence words in 10 common basal reading series; both phonic-linguistic and conventional basal vocabulary series were used. The Basal-Finder procedure has the student read the first three words of each 10-word list until an error is made. Then the examiner begins with the Main List, starting one level lower than the list on which the error occurred and continues with successively lower paragraphs until the student reads 8 of 10 words correctly. The student continues reading the higher lists until he misses more than 5 words in a list or completes List 11.

2. *Phonic Patterns* is composed of four sections which each contain six 5-word lists. The six word lists assess the following phonic patterns; cvc, ccvc, cvce, ccvce, cvvc, ccvvc. The 4 sections are monosyllabic real words, polysyllabic real words, monosyllabic nonsense words, and polysyllabic nonsense words. Students begin with the first word in each section and continue until they make 10 consecutive errors or complete the section. The same procedure is followed for each of the 4 sections. The presentation of both real and nonsense words enables the examiner to discover not only the student's specific phonic knowledge, but also how well the student transfers phonic skills to new words.

3. *Contextual Decoding* consists of eleven passages which correspond with the 11 reading levels in Subtest 1. The 10 Subtest 1 words are embedded in the passage, as are 6 words from Subtest 2. Students begin with the passage at the same level as their basal list in Subtest 1. The basal level is the highest passage in which the student reads at least 8 of the target words from Subtest 1 correctly. A ceiling is reached when the student misses more than five target words in one passage. Thus, in the DST, target words are measured twice, once in isolation and once in context. This allows a direct comparison of the student's contextual decoding with his decoding of single words. Subtest 3 is timed to allow a measure of reading rate, and five sample recall questions test comprehension.

Following the completion of the three subtests, the examiner scores the student's performance to obtain several types of diagnostic information. This information is outlined in the table that follows.

Following the scoring of each subtest, the examiner transfers the scores to the face page of the Scoring Booklet. If the student's raw score on the 120-item Phonic Pattern Subtest is at least 10, the examiner can obtain more diagnostic information by completing the Phonic Pattern Profile. A separate worksheet is provided for this purpose. By following directions presented in the manual carefully, the examiner can gain good information about a student's consonant patterns, vowel patterns, syllabic patterns, and phonic transfer. The information is then transferred to the face sheet of the Scoring Booklet in profile form.

STRENGTHS OF THE DST

• The DST is a unique test in concept and in structure. The careful construction of the word lists, phonic tests, and passages provide the examiner with a wealth of valuable information about a student's decoding skills. The comparison of decoding in isolation and decoding in context as well as the measures of phonic transfer are two examples. The information is so designed to lead directly to instructional planning.

• The manual is complete and clearly written. Examples are given to illustrate scoring procedures. The chapter on interpretation is very helpful.

• Although the manual states that the DST is useful from first to fifth grade, it can be used very effectively with older students who continue to have decoding problems.

• The Contextual Decoding Subtest has two ceiling procedures. The standard procedure has the student read until more than 50% of the target words are read incorrectly. For those students who are clearly struggling with contextual decoding, the option is given to stop when the student reads less than 80% of the target words correctly. This is a sensitive consideration for the student for whom this process is very painful.

• The careful test construction procedures of the DST ensure its content validity. Test-retest reliability is good, and studies of good and poor readers support the criterion validity of the test.

• Despite the lack of alternate forms, the careful construction of the DST allows it to be used as a sensitive measure of progress.

LIMITING FACTORS OF THE DST

• As is noted in the manual, the DST takes time to learn to administer and score. The information obtained is different from that on most reading tests, and the scoring procedures, particularly for the phonic profile, are laborious until the examiner has given several tests.

• The cursory measure of comprehension could be discarded. Its inclusion tempts the examiner to use it in determining instructional level. The DST is strictly a decoding test and should be used that way.

• In the Interpretation Section, the author provides guidelines for Reading Rate and Error Rate. For example, a reading rate of 50–60 words per minute at instructional level is described as average. No data are cited to support these guidelines.

Diagnostic Information Obtained From DST Subtests

Subtest	Diagnostic Information
Basal Vocabulary	1. Instructional Level. The grade equivalent of the student's basal level word list, the list on which 8 out of 10 words were read correctly. 2. Frustration Level. The grade equivalent of the student's ceiling level word list, the list on which less than 5 out of the 10 words were read correctly.
Phonic Patterns	1. Phonic Transfer Index (PTI). A measure of the ability to transfer phonic skills to new words; obtained by dividing the number of real-word/nonsense word pairs read correctly by the total number of real words read correctly. Separate phonic transfer indices are calculated for monosyllabic and polysyllabic words.
Contextual Decoding	1. Instructional Level. The grade equivalent of the basal passage. 2. Frustration Level. The grade equivalent of the ceiling passage. 3. Reading rate. 4. Error rate. 5. Percentage of phonic words corect in context. 6. Percentage of comprehension questions correct.

Diagnostic Reading Scales—Revised (DRS-81)

George D. Spache
CTB/McGraw-Hill Division, 1963; revised editions 1972, 1981
Del Monte Research Park, Monterey, CA 93940

Purpose	To evaluate oral and silent reading abilities and auditory comprehension
Major Areas Tested	Oral and silent reading and listening comprehension
Age or Grade Range	Grades 1–7
Usually Given By	Special education teacher Diagnostician trained in reading assessment
Type of Test	Standardized Individual Criterion-referenced (supplementary phonics tests)
Scores Obtained	Grade level (supplementary phonics tests) Instructional level Independent level Potential level
Student Performance Timed?	Optional
Testing Time	45–60 minutes
Scoring/Interpretation Time	15 minutes
Normed On	534 students in grades 1–8; sample balanced for race, sex, and geographic area; poor readers and high ability students excluded from sample
Alternate Forms Available?	Yes

FORMAT

The Diagnostic Reading Scales—Revised (DRS-81) is the third revision of the Spache Diagnostic Reading Scales first published in 1963 and revised in 1972. The materials consist of an examiner's manual, an individual expendable record book for use by the examiner, and a reusable spiral-bound book for use by the students.

An examiner's cassette provides a model for administration of the DRS-81, and a technical manual provides more extensive statistical data. A stopwatch is also needed.

The battery includes 3 graded word recognition lists, 2 reading selections at each of 11 levels (ranging from grades 1.6 to 7.5 in difficulty), and 12 supplementary word analysis and phonics tests:

Initial Consonants
Final Consonants
Consonant Digraphs
Consonant Blends
Initial Consonant Substitution
Auditory Recognition of Initial Consonant Sounds
Auditory Discrimination
Short and Long Vowel Sounds
Vowels with *r*
Vowel Diphthongs and Digraphs
Common Syllables
Blending

1. *Word Recognition Lists.* These graded word lists yield a tentative level of performance and are used to determine the level of the initial passage the student should be able to read orally in the next part of the test.

2. *Oral Reading.* The student reads each paragraph aloud and answers orally questions asked by the examiner. Most of the seven or eight questions for each paragraph require factual recall, but a few interpretive questions are included. Oral reading errors, including reversals, omissions, substitutions, mispronunciations, repetitions, and hesitations are recorded by the examiner. Oral Reading stops when the student makes more accuracy errors than the maximum allowed for the paragraph or does not answer the minimum number of comprehension questions required.

3. *Silent Reading.* The student reads silently the paragraph just higher in difficulty than the last one read orally. Comprehension is assessed again by oral answers to questions asked by the examiner. Silent Reading stops when the student does not answer the minimum number of questions required on a given paragraph.

4. *Auditory Comprehension.* The examiner reads to the student the paragraph just higher than the last one read silently. Comprehension is assessed in the same manner.

5. *Supplementary Phonics Tests.* Any or all of the phonics tests (see the list above) may be administered to the student to obtain a detailed analysis of the student's word attack skills and phonics knowledge. Grade equivalent scores are

provided for the phonics tests, although the author cautions using these as "norms"; the tests are essentially criterion referenced.

Two forms of the reading passages (R and S) are provided for test-retest purposes.

The scores obtained on the DRS are Instructional Level (Oral Reading), Independent Level (Silent Reading), and Potential Level (Auditory Comprehension).

Instructional Level is defined as "the level at which the student reads orally and comprehends as well as 68 percent of the standardization population at that level." The author feels that this level is likely to be found acceptable by the average classroom teacher for group reading practice.

Independent Level is the highest level the student can read silently with no less than 60 percent comprehension. It represents the upper limit for materials the student is expected to read independently.

Potential Level is the highest level to which the student can listen with at least 60 percent comprehension. It represents the level to which a student's reading level can theoretically be raised as a result of an appropriate remedial program.

STRENGTHS OF THE DRS-81

• The DRS-81 assesses word recognition and oral and silent reading in one battery. It is fairly easy to administer and takes relatively little time. Although the scores are not useful, the tests provide good information about a student's reading skills. For example, an analysis of specific errors gives clues to how the student attempts to read. Error analysis is crucial for determining the instructional needs of a student. To facilitate analysis of types of errors, the student record book contains a Work Analysis Checklist and a Checklist of Reading Difficulties.

• The Supplementary Phonics Tests are helpful in revealing the nature of word analysis skills. They include tasks involving initial and final consonants, blends, vowels, and word endings. In most cases the words used are nonsense words and for most subtests the item is correct when the element being tested is correct. For example *mat* for *man* is correct for initial consonants. These criterion-referenced tests can identify specific skills that need to be mastered.

• In addition to the standard test procedures, the manual contains useful suggestions for further informal analysis of reading difficulties. For example, the examiner may wish to present to the student words in isolation that were misread in context. Then the examiner can compare a student's success with words in context to success with them in isolation.

• Students failing in reading often feel threatened by a reading test. In the DRS-81, the passages that the student reads are not marked by grade level, an important and sensitive consideration.

• The author is sensitive to the problems of assessing

oral reading in students with nonstandard English. The manual contains an excellent section on typical pronunciations of certain words by students who speak Black dialect or are of Hispanic background. The pronunciation tendencies of Puerto Rican immigrants are carefully outlined, and an outline of procedures for testing any student with a dialect is included.

• The author's broad knowledge of reading is shared with the examiner through the excellent manual, which should be read by every examiner.

LIMITING FACTORS OF THE DRS-81

• The DRS-81 must be administered by a person with considerable clinical experience in reading diagnosis because analysis of reading performance is often a subjective evaluation. Accurate recording of oral reading errors depends heavily on the judgment of the examiner.

• The terms *Instructional, Independent* and *Potential Reading Levels* have been used consistently with informal reading inventories. They have certain meanings within that context. In the DRS-81, the terms have a different meaning. Examiners need to be aware of these differences as they interpret scores to teachers who are more familiar with the informal reading inventories. The independent level in DRS-81 suggests that a student can read independently at a level above his instructional level. This assumption is not documented and does not fit with the common view that the independent level is below the instructional level. Rather than using silent reading as a measure of the independent level as described in the manual, the examiner would do better to assess silent reading at the same levels as oral reading using the alternate form, R or S.

• The comprehension questions at all levels are short-answer questions, the majority of which are straight recall of facts. For the student with a short-term memory problem, the comprehension score can be quite misleading. An alternative way of assessing comprehension that does not depend so heavily on immediate memory would add to the test's usefulness.

Adding other fundamental types of comprehension questions would be helpful at the upper grade levels.

For example, the test does not cover such skills as the ability to grasp the main idea, the ability to weave together the ideas in a selection, or the ability to draw inferences from a short passage.

The short-answer comprehension questions pose some real concerns. Questions designed on the yes-or-no model are handicapped by a 50 percent probability of getting any question correct simply by guessing. This kind of question is all too prevalent at the upper-grade levels. For example, seventh-grade-level questions include, "Can we skim all kinds of reading?" and, "Is marble always white?"

Answers to many other questions seem quite obvious, so that any student with sufficient experience and knowledge can derive the correct answers regardless of how well he or she has read the passage. Typical questions are, "What color was his wagon?" (second grade); "How do birds help us?" (fifth grade); "What kind of flowers do poppies have?" (fifth grade). The superficial understanding required by such comprehension questions is a serious drawback.

• The measurement of reading rate as fast, average, or slow similarly presents special concern. A student may have many reading rates, depending on such factors as the difficulty of the material, the content of the passage, and the purpose for which it is being read. In view of these factors, the silent reading rate on the DRS-81 does not appear to be too meaningful.

• The examiner should keep in mind that performance on the Supplementary Phonics Tests can be directly related to the type of reading instruction a student receives. For instance, a student in a phonics-oriented program may perform much better on these tests than a student who is being taught by sight-word methods. As the manual states, the phonics tests do not possess any degree of reliability to justify grade norms. Omitting them entirely would be a better practice.

• The standardization sample for the DRS-81 is very small; the 534 students were reduced to 290 for data analysis. Validity and reliability data were adequate, but the small size of the sample limits the generalizability of the test. The DRS-81 is best used as an informal diagnostic test rather than as a norm referenced instrument.

Gilmore Oral Reading Test (GORT)

John V. Gilmore and Eunice C. Gilmore
The Psychological Corporation, 1968
555 Academic Court, San Antonio, TX 78204

Purpose	To assess oral reading accuracy and comprehension skills
Major Areas Tested	Oral reading
Age or Grade Range	Grades 1–8
Usually Given By	Classroom teacher Special education teacher
Type of Test	Standardized Individual Norm-referenced
Scores Obtained	Grade level Percentile range Stanine Rating scale
Student Performance Timed?	Optional
Testing Time	15–25 minutes
Scoring/Interpretation Time	15 minutes
Normed On	Over 4,000 students from a wide range of socioeconomic levels in six school districts throughout the United States
Alternate Forms Available?	Yes

FORMAT

The materials for the Gilmore Oral Reading Test consist of a manual of directions, the booklet from which the student reads paragraphs, and the individual record blanks for recording the student's reading errors and answers to comprehension questions.

Two equivalent forms are available—Forms C and D (A and B are out of print). Each form consists of 10 paragraphs carefully constructed from graded vocabulary in basal readers. The paragraphs are graduated in length and difficulty from the primer through the eighth-grade level. The paragraphs increase in difficulty due to more multisyllable words, more complex sentence structure, and content which interests increasingly older students. The 10 paragraphs form a continuous story that is introduced with an illustration. Forms C and D are both printed in the same booklet, but separate record blanks are provided for each.

The examiner introduces the test through the illustration and selects a paragraph about two years below the student's expected reading level. The student reads the paragraph aloud, and the examiner times the reading with a stopwatch and marks any errors. The examiner reads the five comprehension questions following each paragraph, and the student answers orally. The testing stops when the student makes 10 or more accuracy errors in one paragraph.

Separate grade-equivalent, percentile, and stanine scores are obtained for accuracy, comprehension, and rate of reading. Performance ratings are also provided. Here is an example of what a sixth grader's scores might look like.

A Sixth Grader's Scores on the Gilmore Oral Reading Test

Score	Accuracy	Comprehension	Rate
Stanine	3	8	
Percentile band	11–22	89–95	
Grade equivalent	4.2	5.3	
Performance rating	Below average	Above average	Fast

STRENGTHS OF THE GILMORE ORAL READING TEST

• This is one of several good standardized oral reading tests. It provides a means of assessing a student's oral reading accuracy, comprehension, and rate. A system for analyzing the student's oral reading errors is built into the test format.

• Careful analysis of the error pattern of an individual student can lead directly to planning a corrective program. For example, a student who waits for prompting from the examiner needs to be taught how to use word analysis skills and needs to be encouraged to sound out new words; the student who makes frequent "substitutions" may need to learn to monitor oral reading with comprehension clues.

• The wide grade range of the Gilmore Oral Reading Test, together with its equivalent Forms C and D, make it a good instrument for measuring pupil progress through test-retest procedures.

• An added advantage of the test is that the timing is optional and separate from the scoring for accuracy and comprehension. The examiner may decide whether using the stopwatch will cause anxiety in a student that would significantly affect performance. Eliminating the timing simplifies test administration and does not affect the accuracy and comprehension scores.

• A special edition of the GORT is available for the visually handicapped and may be obtained from the American Printing House for the Blind in Louisville, Kentucky.

LIMITING FACTORS OF THE GILMORE ORAL READING TEST

Users of this test should be aware of several factors that significantly affect interpretation of test results.

• The accuracy score is the only reliable and valid score on the test. The system for obtaining a comprehension score often results in a spuriously high score. This is because of a procedure that gives "bonus" points for paragraphs above the ceiling level. The authors make the assumption that, if a student could read the next paragraph after reaching the ceiling (that is, after making 10 errors), he or she would be able to answer almost the same number of questions as on the ceiling paragraph. The result of this assumption is the scoring system shown here. Students frequently receive comprehension scores well above their accuracy scores, not because they answered the questions correctly, but simply because of the bonus system.

• Because the comprehension questions on the Gilmore Oral Reading Test require only recall of specific facts from the paragraph and no interpretation or abstract reasoning, comprehension scores rarely reflect the student's functioning level in classroom materials. It is safe to say that, if the student's comprehension score is higher than the accuracy score, it means little in terms of actual skills. However, if the student's comprehension score is lower than the accuracy score, beware! Given the types of questions and the bonus

Scoring System for the Comprehension Section of the Gilmore Oral Reading Test

Paragraph Number	Comprehension (number correct)	
1	5 ⎫	
2	5 ⎬ Credited	
3	4 ⎭	
4 Basal	3 ⎫	
5	4 ⎪	
6	3 ⎬ Actually read	
7 Ceiling	4 ⎭	
8	3 ⎫	
9	2 ⎬ "Bonus points"	
10	1 ⎭	

scoring system, a low comprehension score may reflect serious comprehension or memory problems that require further assessment.

• The vocabulary of the test is drawn from basal readers, which usually have a sight-word emphasis. Particularly at the lower levels, students who are being instructed in a phonic or linguistic approach are often unable to demonstrate their reading gains. For example, a student may have made great progress during the year in learning letter names, sounds, and phonically regular three- and four-letter words. These gains will not be seen on pre- and posttesting, because linguistically regular words are not featured. Parents and teachers need to understand that the Gilmore Oral Reading Test will not reflect growth until the child also masters a basic sight-word vocabulary.

• The content of the upper-grade paragraphs of this test deals with the vocational aspirations of male and female students. Professionals today may find the orientation offensive (Dick prepares to be a doctor or scientist, but Mary considers secretarial work or nursing).

• Examiners inexperienced in oral reading assessment need to practice several times to establish their skills in using notations for indicating oral reading errors.

• As is typical of most oral reading tests, all accuracy errors are weighted the same; that is, a repeated word counts the same as a mispronounced word. Recent research suggests that errors which do not affect comprehension should be penalized less.

Error Types on the Gilmore Oral Reading Test

Error Type	Definition	Example
Substitution	Real word is replaced by another	*Step* for *stop*; *father* for *farther*
Mispronunciation	Word produced is not a real word	*Frist* for *first*; *at'end* for *attend*
Lack of response	Student does not attempt word within five seconds	
Disregard of punctuation	Student does not pause for periods or commas	
Insertion	An extra word or words are added	*the* *The boy and girl came home.*
Hesitation	Student pauses at least two seconds before attempting word	
Repetition	A word, phrase, or sentence is repeated	
Omission	One or more words are omitted	*This is the best place to (have a) picnic.*

Durrell Analysis of Reading Difficulty
(Durrell Analysis)

Donald D. Durrell and Jane H. Catterson
The Psychological Corporation, 1937; revised 1955, 1980
555 Academic Court, San Antonio, TX 78204

Purpose	To assess strengths and weaknesses in various reading skills and subskills
Major Areas Tested	Oral and silent reading, listening comprehension, word analysis skills, spelling, and handwriting
Age or Grade Range	Grades 1–6
Usually Given By	Special education teacher
Type of Test	Standardized Individual Norm-referenced
Scores Obtained	Grade level
Student Performance Timed?	Yes (some subtests)
Testing Time	30–90 minutes (depending on number of subtests given)
Scoring/Interpretation Time	15–30 minutes
Normed On	200 students at each grade level, 1–6, from five states representing each region of the U.S.; included only children in the average range of the Metropolitan Achievement Test; consideration given to language backgrounds, socioeconomic status, ethnicity, and curriculum
Alternate Forms Available?	No

FORMAT

The materials for the Durrell Analysis of Reading Difficulty (Durrell Analysis) consist of the examiner's manual of directions, individual record booklets for recording each student's responses, a tachistoscope with word lists to accompany specific subtests, and a book containing the paragraphs for the Oral Reading, Silent Reading, and Listening Comprehension subtests. The manual includes directions for administering and scoring tests and for interpreting test results. It also includes brief information on test construction and standardization.

The Durrell Analysis contains 19 subtests designed to assess a student's performance on various types of reading tasks. The examiner selects only those subtests appropriate for each student's reading level. Subtests may be given in any order.

Following the administration of each subtest, the examiner scores the test and calculates the grade-level score according to procedures in the manual. The results of the major subtests are plotted by grade-level scores on the

Durrell Analysis Subtests

Subtest	Reading Grade Level	Task	Timed?	Normed?	Additional Information Gained?
Oral Reading	1–6	Reading aloud a series of paragraphs graded for difficulty; answering comprehension questions	Yes	Yes	Error patterns in oral reading
Silent Reading	1–6	Reading silently a series of graded paragraphs; aided and unaided recall	Yes	Yes	Eye movements per line, imagery, sequential recall
Listening Comprehension	1–6	Listening to graded paragraphs; answering comprehension questions	No	No	Comparison to silent reading
Word Recognition	1–6	Reading word lists of graded difficulty, presented by tachistoscope; time for analysis given on words not recognized	Yes	Yes	Comparison of sight-word vocabulary and word analysis skills
Listening Vocabulary	1–6	Listening to a series of words and indicating the category to which they belong by pointing to a picture (Child hears the words *glow* and *elated* and points to a picture of the sun and a smiling face, respectively.)	No	Yes	Comparison of reading vocabulary and listening vocabulary
Sounds in Isolation	1–6	Giving sounds of letters, digraphs, blends, phonograms, prefixes, suffixes	No	Yes	
Spelling Test	2–6	Writing dictated spelling words correctly from a graded list	No	Yes	Comparison of phonic and sight spelling
Phonic Spelling	4–6	Writing dictated words exactly as they sound	No	Yes	Patterns of spelling errors
Visual Memory of Words (Primary)	3 and below	Recalling words presented visually and locating them in a list of similar words	Yes	Yes	

Subtest	Reading Grade Level	Task	Timed?	Normed?	Additional Information Gained?
Visual Memory of Words (Intermediate)	3–6	Recalling words presented visually and writing them	Yes	Yes	
Identifying Sounds in Words	3 and below	Listening to a word pronounced by the examiner and finding one that begins with the same sound from three printed choices	No	Yes	Ability to perceive beginning blends and ending sounds
Prereading Phonics Abilities Inventories					
Syntax Matching	Nonreaders–1	Recognizing that a sentence is composed of single words (Child looks at the phrase *come here*. Examiner says, ''Come here,'' and asks, ''Which word is *here*?'')	No	Yes	
Identifying Letter Names in Spoken Words	Nonreaders–1	Listening to a word and giving the initial letter by name	No	Yes	
Identifying Phonemes (Letter Sounds) in Spoken Words	Nonreaders–1	Listening to a word and giving the initial sound	No	Yes	
Naming Lower-case Letters	Nonreaders–1	Naming lowercase letters in printed words	No	Yes	
Writing Letters from Dictation	Nonreaders–1	Writing letters from dictation with picture cues provided (''Write a *t* in the box next to the picture of a tree.'')	No	Yes	
Writing from Copy	Nonreaders–1	Copying four words (given only to children who are unable to write from dictation)	No	No	
Naming Uppercase Letters	Nonreaders–1	Naming uppercase letters in isolation	No	No	
Identifying Letters Named	Nonreaders–1	Pointing to letters, either lower-case or uppercase, named by the examiner (given to children who are unable to name letters)	No	No	

profile chart on the front of the individual record booklet. The profile provides a graphic representation of the student's strengths and weaknesses in reading. A checklist of instructional needs is also included in the individual record booklets, as are specific checklists of difficulties on individual subtests. These checklists, together with the profile chart, form the basis for an individualized remedial program.

STRENGTHS OF THE DURRELL ANALYSIS

• The Durrell Analysis was developed to help reading teachers understand the reading process and plan individual reading programs. To reach this goal, a wide variety of subtests are included. When used wisely, they yield a wealth of information about a student. The Durrell Analysis is one of the few tests that allow assessment of oral and silent reading, listening comprehension, word analysis skills, and spelling all in the same battery. The variety of subtests allows for testing of nonreaders as well as readers with high intermediate-grade skills.

• While maintaining the same general format, the revised Durrell Analysis includes several important changes in the third edition. The content of the reading and listening paragraphs has been updated for sex and ethnic balance. New normative data using a wider geographic sample is included. New measures of listening vocabulary allow direct comparison between reading and listening skills. New measures have been added to the prereading skills section.

• The manual is well organized and clearly written. The checklists for recording reading difficulties are helpful in bridging the gap between test scores and daily performance.

• The Durrell Analysis includes several unique subtests. Listening Vocabulary provides a measure of a student's understanding of single spoken words by assessing the student's ability to place them in categories. Phonic Spelling is a good measure of auditory analysis for intermediate students. Syntax Matching is a creative measure of the basic concept that sentences are made up of single separate words.

LIMITING FACTORS OF THE DURRELL ANALYSIS

• Although the third edition of the Durrell Analysis has been renormed, only grade scores are provided. No standard scores are included, and the grade scores themselves are of little value.

• On the Oral Reading and Silent Reading subtests, the grade scores are based on speed and vague scoring of comprehension questions. There is no rationale provided for basing instructional level on speed, and there are serious ambiguities in the directions for scoring comprehension. For example, the manual states, "Generally speaking, the scoring of the comprehension questions should be generous.... If the child...answered that the little brown dog played with 'three or four other dogs,' one might assume that knowing that

there was more than one other dog was worth half-credit." (The story says "two dogs.") Such vague scoring criteria invalidate the use of the grade scores, which were questionable to begin with.

• The technical characteristics of the Durrell Analysis are very weak. The standardization sample is poorly described, no test-retest reliability studies are presented, and validity is not well substantiated. The Durrell Analysis is best thought of as an informal inventory.

• In considering the Durrell Analysis as an informal inventory, it is important to note which reading skills are poorly assessed or omitted. First, reading comprehension on both the Oral Reading and Silent Reading subtests is limited to recall of specific facts. No interpretation or generalization is required. Second, tachistoscopic presentation, such as that used on the Word Recognition subtest, is often confusing for poor readers and gives inaccurate information regarding their word recognition skills. Word lists or flashcard procedures are often more accurate. Third, no subtests assessing discrimination or recognition of vowel sounds (long or short) are included. Fourth, no pure auditory tests of discrimination or blending are included.

• The authors of the Durrell Analysis discuss the comparison of the student's raw score on Listening Vocabulary and Word Recognition. While the equivalency of lists of words is well done, the tasks are too dissimilar to compare. Word Recognition is decoding only, while Listening Vocabulary requires both comprehension of the single words and categorization skills.

Gates-MacGinitie Reading Tests (Third Edition)

Walter H. MacGinitie and Ruth K. MacGinitie
The Riverside Publishing Company, 1989
8420 Bryn Mawr Avenue, Chicago, IL 60631-3476

Purpose	To measure silent reading skills from pre-reading through high school
Major Areas Tested	Silent reading vocabulary and comprehension
Age or Grade Range	Grades 1–12
Usually Given By	Classroom teacher Special education teacher
Type of Test	Standardized Group Norm-referenced
Scores Obtained	Stanine Grade equivalent Normal curve equivalent Extended scale score Percentile rank
Student Performance Timed?	Yes
Testing Time	50–60 minutes
Scoring/Interpretation Time	15 minutes
Normed On	Nation-wide sample of 42,000 K–12 students based on the 1980 U.S. Census stratified according to geographic region, district enrollment size, and socio-economic levels
Alternate Forms Available?	Yes

FORMAT

The Third Edition of the Gates-MacGinitie Reading Tests is the latest edition in a long tradition of reading tests begun in 1926 by Arthur I. Gates. The Gates Silent Reading Test and the Gates Primary Reading Tests were the original tests. In 1965, Gates and Walter MacGinitie authored the first edition of the Gates-MacGinitie Reading Tests, following in 1978 with the second edition and in 1989, with the third edition. The basic purpose of the test series is to provide teachers and school administrators with a means of evaluating the reading levels of students throughout their school careers. The format is a group-administered test of multiple-choice questions assessing vocabulary and paragraph comprehension. In the third edition, nine levels of tests are available from the pre-reading level (late kindergarten) through twelfth grade. Alternate forms (K and L) are available from Levels 3 through 10/12 for test-retest purposes. The chart below describes the subtests available at each level.

Level	Subtest

PRE	PreReading Evaluation
	  Literacy Concepts
	  Reading Instruction Relational Concepts
	  Oral Language Concepts (Linguistic Awareness)
	  Letters and Letter-Sound Correspondence

R	Beginning Reading Skills
	  Use of Letter-Sound Correspondence:
	    Initial consonants and consonant clusters
	    Final consonants and consonant clusters
	    Vowels
	  Use of Sentence Context

1, 2	Vocabulary. A test of word recognition or de-coding; student matches words with pictures. Comprehension. Student chooses picture which illustrates a passage.
3, 4, 5/6 7/9, 10,12	Vocabulary. A test of word knowledge; student choses word or phrase which means most nearly the same as the test word. Comprehension. Student selects best answer to questions about prose passage or verse.

The test materials include test booklets for each student at each level. Hand scorable editions are available at each level; at the lower levels (K–3) machine scorable booklets are available, while at the higher levels (4–10/12) students may mark their answers in test booklets or on machine- or hand-scorable answer sheets. Self-scorable answer sheets are also available at the higher levels. Teacher's manuals for Directions for Administration and manuals for Scoring and Interpretation are provided for each level. The latter include directions for scoring and using the norms tables, meaning and interpretation of test scores, and comprehensive remediation strategies. Out-of-level norms are available for all forms of the test. Scoring keys and Class Summary Records are provided at each level. A Decoding Skills Analysis Form is provided for levels 1 and 2; this form allows the teacher to analyze an individual student's errors in phonic skills.

STRENGTHS OF THE GATES-MACGINITIE READING TESTS

• The Gates-MacGinitie Reading tests are well known and well normed. Because they are group tests, they are efficient and appropriate for screening purposes to determine which students are in need of diagnostic testing.

• The wide age range and alternate forms make the Gates-MacGinitie Tests excellent for test-retest purposes, that is, to determine the progress that an individual student has made in a remedial program. Many school districts use them routinely in fall and spring with both regular and special education students.

• At levels 1 through 10/12, the Vocabulary and Comprehension subtests are scored separately; a student may be given one or both parts.

• The teacher's manuals are well organized, well written, and easy to use.

• The third edition provides four different levels of tests for the end-of-kindergarten through first grade students. These tests—levels PRE, R, 1, and 2—assess skills in the child who is about to be taught to read through the first grader who is considerably above average.

• The Gates-MacGinitie Reading Tests are designed for group administration and contain many features to facilitate this process. Administration procedures are clearly presented, and there are ample practice items to acquaint students with the test format. Identical sample pages make possible testing students at several levels in the same classroom. For example, the sample items are the same for levels 4 through 10/12. A wide range of norms are available at each level; for example, for level 5/6, norms are provided for grades 4 through 9.

• In the standardization process, equating testing was done with 25,000 students so that norms for the second edition and third edition could be linked to measure progress on students given the old edition.

• Improvements have been made in the content of the comprehension test items at all levels. In addition to questions requiring specific facts, the questions require higher reading skills, such as interpretation and generalization.

• Rather than an as single words, vocabulary items are presented in short sentences or phrases which suggest their parts of speech. The authors have been careful not to give a context which suggests the meaning of the word, as a Vocabulary test would then become a Comprehension test.

• Great efforts were made during test construction to assure that the tests would be valid measures of knowledge and skills acquired in standard school reading programs.

LIMITING FACTORS OF THE GATES-MACGINITIE READING TESTS

• The Gates-MacGinitie Reading Tests measure silent reading skills, a critical area of reading competence. In any silent reading test, analysis of errors is difficult. For example, in Level 4, Form K, Vocabulary item 37, the test word is *soothe* and the choices are *bathe, hold, calm, straighten,* or *call* as possible synonyms for *soothe.* If the student marks *straighten,* the examiner does not know which of the following occurred: (1) The student read the word *calm* as *clam;* (2) the student did not know the meaning of *soothe* and confused it with *smooth;* or (3) the student did not know the meaning of *calm.* Because analysis of errors on silent reading tests is difficult, the low scoring student should be administered an individual oral reading test such as the Gray Oral Reading Test (p. 84) or the Gilmore Oral Reading Test (p. 70).

• Factors of inattention and impersistence may affect a student's performance on any group test. As special education students frequently display these problems, scores must be used with caution.

• Information on test reliability was not available for review at the time of this writing.

• The lack of a Decoding Skills Analysis form above level 2 implies that students in third grade and higher have mastered basic phonic skills. For many special education students this is not true, and a phonic analysis process would be helpful. Such students should be given an individual phonics test such as those included in the Gates-McKillop-Horowitz Reading Diagnostic Tests (p. 81) or the Woodcock Reading Mastery Tests (p. 92).

Gates-McKillop-Horowitz Reading Diagnostic Tests (Gates-McKillop-Horowitz)

Arthur Gates, Anne McKillop, and Elizabeth Horowitz
Teachers College Press, second edition 1981
Teachers College, Columbia University, 1234 Amsterdam Ave., New York, NY 10027

Purpose	To assess strengths and weaknesses in reading and related areas
Major Areas Tested	Oral reading, word analysis, and related skills
Age or Grade Range	Grades 1–6
Usually Given By	Classroom teacher Special education teacher Diagnostician trained in reading disorders
Type of Test	Standardized Individual
Scores Obtained	Grade level Age level (some subtests) Rating scale
Student Performance Timed?	No
Testing Time	40–60 minutes (depending on number of subtests given)
Scoring/Interpretation Time	15 minutes
Normed On	600 children in grades 1–6 from public and private schools, urban and rural areas, and minority groups (Black and Spanish)
Alternate Forms Available?	No

FORMAT

The Gates-McKillop-Horowitz Reading Diagnostic Tests (Gates-McKillop-Horowitz) are a revised edition of the 1962 Gates-McKillop Tests. They are a battery of subtests designed to be used with individual students in elementary school and include tasks from the readiness level through such advanced skills as syllabication. Subtests are selected based on the student's reading level and particular reading difficulties. No specific order of administration is required.

The materials consist of a reusable booklet that contains the materials to be read by the student; a booklet in which the student and the examiner record responses; and a manual that includes the rationale for the tests, directions for administering and scoring, grade-level scores, and interpretive ratings.

The 15 subtests included in the Gates-McKillop-Horowitz are shown in the table that follows. Grade scores that may be converted into a rating of high, medium, low, or very low are given for the four general ability tests that assess oral reading, word recognition, and spelling. These grade scores allow comparison of each student with others at the same grade level. On the diagnostic tests of specific skills, such as recognition of vowel sounds, the student's raw score or number correct is compared with the norming sample and is rated average, above average, or below average.

STRENGTHS OF THE GATES-McKILLOP-HOROWITZ

• The most obvious advantage of the Gates-McKillop-Horowitz battery is that many critical skills are included. Through thoughtful selection of subtests, the skilled examiner can develop a testing battery appropriate for a beginning reader or a struggling intermediate student. Careful selection of subtests allows every student some successful reading experiences during testing, while the examiner obtains maximum diagnostic information. The variety in the format and the informal tone of the procedures hold the interest of most students.

• Comparison of students' performances on various subtest pairs also yields invaluable diagnostic information. A few examples:

1. Words: Flash Presentation and Words: Untimed allow the examiner to compare sight-word vocabulary and word analysis skills on words of equivalent difficulty.

2. Auditory Blending and Recognizing and Blending Common Word Parts offer an auditory-visual comparison, blending with auditory stimuli only, and blending skills with printed words.

This type of diagnostic information can be obtained when the Gates-McKillop-Horowitz is used by a skilled examiner. Other features, such as the checklist of difficulties for the Oral Reading subtest and the discussion of interpretation of test results in the manual, are excellent.

LIMITING FACTORS OF THE GATES-McKILLOP-HOROWITZ

• The test was normed on 600 children. Only limited information regarding the composition of the norming sample is given, and no studies of reliability or validity are reported. The lack of these critical pieces of information strongly suggests that the Gates-McKillop-Horowitz should be used as an informal battery to obtain information about a student's skills in a variety of reading tasks. The information is excellent, but the grade scores are of little value.

• The Oral Reading passages are stilted in style and content. No measure of comprehension is included. The examiner should substitute another oral reading test (Gilmore Oral Reading Test, Gray Oral Reading Tests, Spache Diagnostic Reading Scales) or devise comprehension questions for the Gates-McKillop-Horowitz in order to get some measure of oral reading comprehension.

• The first edition of these tests included three subtests that were of great diagnostic value: Recognizing the Visual Form of Sounds in Nonsense Words, in Initial Letters, and in Final Letters. The new edition has added nothing in technical soundness and is less valuable as an informal diagnostic instrument.

Gates–McKillop-Horowitz Subtests

Subtest	Task
Oral Reading	Student reads orally seven paragraphs ranging in difficulty from grades 1 to 6. Errors recorded by the examiner and classified by type. No comprehension questions included.
Reading Sentences	Student reads four sentences with phonetically regular words.
Words: Flash Presentation	Tachistoscope presents a graded list of words at half-second intervals. Tests sight recognition of single words.
Words: Untimed	Presentation of same word list as above, but student is given opportunity to use word analysis skills.
Knowledge of Word Parts: Word Attack	
Syllabication	Student is asked to read a list of nonsense words (*rivlov*, *kangadee*). The skill being measured is syllable blending.
Recognizing and Blending Common Word Parts	Student reads a list of nonsense words made up of common word parts (*stade*, *shemp*, *whast*). If student is unable to read the whole word, the examiner may show how to break it into an initial blend and a common ending and then blend it back together (*wh-ast—whast*).
Reading Words	Student reads 15 one-syllable nonsense words.
Letter Sounds	Student is shown printed letter and is asked to give its sound.
Naming Capital Letters	Student is shown printed uppercase letter and is asked to name it.
Naming Lowercase Letters	Student is shown printed lowercase letter and is asked to name it.
Recognizing the Visual Form (Word Equivalents) of Sounds	
Vowels	Student is shown five vowels and is asked to indicate which one is in a nonsense word pronounced by examiner (*vum*, *keb*, *hote*, *sate*).
Auditory Tests	
Auditory Blending	Student listens to word pronounced by examiner, with parts separated by quarter-second intervals; student pronounces whole word (*d-ar-k—dark*).
Auditory Discrimination	Examiner pronounces pairs of words, and student identifies them as same or different (*dim—din*, *weather—wetter*).
Written Expression	
Spelling	Words from Words: Flash Presentation and Words: Untimed are presented to the student for oral spelling.
Informal Writing	Student is encouraged to write an original paragraph on a topic of his or her choice.

Gray Oral Reading Tests—Revised (GORT-R)

J. Lee Wiederholt and Brian R. Bryant
Pro-Ed, 1986
5341 Industrial Oaks Blvd., Austin, TX 78735

Purpose	To measure growth in oral reading and to aid in the diagnosis of oral reading problems
Major Areas Tested	Oral reading
Age or Grade Range	6 1/2–18 years
Usually Given By	Special education teacher Psychologist Diagnostician trained in reading disorders
Type of Test	Standardized Individual Norm-referenced
Scores Obtained	Standard Percentile
Student Performance Timed?	Yes
Testing Time	15–30 minutes
Scoring/Interpretation Time	15 minutes
Normed On	1,400 students in 15 states; sample balanced for sex, race, ethnicity, and age; both urban and rural communities included in sample
Alternate Forms Available?	Yes

FORMAT

The Gray Oral Reading Test (GORT-R) is a revised edition of the widely used oral reading test originally authored by Dr. William S. Gray in 1915 and subsequently revised several times. The materials consist of two equivalent forms, A and B. Both A and B are included in a single spiral-bound Student Book of reading passages. There are 13 independent paragraphs of gradually increasing difficulty for each form. Each paragraph is followed by five multiple-choice questions designed to measure various types of reading comprehension. Individual Profile Examiner Record forms include reprints of each passage as well as places to record types of errors, the amount of time used to read each paragraph, and the student's scores. The GORT-R Manual includes administration and scoring procedures, interpretation guidelines, norm tables, and information on test development. A stopwatch is also needed to administer the test.

Guidelines are given to help the examiner decide with which paragraph to begin the testing. Each paragraph is preceded by a "prompt" which the examiner reads to the student.

This story is about a very courageous woman. Read the story to find out what she did.

The prompt is intended to give the reader a purpose for reading. The student reads the paragraph aloud while the examiner records errors and time. Then the examiner reads along with the student five comprehension questions, each with four possible responses, and the student selects the correct response.

Basal and ceiling levels are based upon comprehension performance rather than accuracy. The basal paragraph is the highest paragraph on which the student answers *all* of the comprehension questions correctly. The ceiling is reached when the student answers less than 3 of the 5 questions about a paragraph correctly.

For each paragraph read, the student obtains a Passage Score (combination of speed and accuracy), and a Comprehension Score (number of correct responses). The Passage Scores are summed, as are the Comprehension Scores, and converted to percentiles and standard scores. The standard scores are then combined into an Oral Reading Quotient, which can also be expressed as a percentile.

In addition to providing an accuracy score, examiners are encouraged to analyze five types of oral reading errors:

1. *Meaning similarity*. Replacing a printed word with another word similar in meaning (*moment* is read *minute*).

2. *Function similarity*. Replacing a printed word with another word of similar syntactic function (*flown* is read *fleed*).

3. *Graphic-phonemic similarity*. Replacing words with words similar in appearance (*felt* is read *fell*).

4. *Multiple errors*. More than one type of error in a misread word (*struck* is read *hit*).

5. *Self-correction*. Allows analysis of student strategies.

STRENGTHS OF THE GORT-R

• The GORT-R is one of several good reading tests that all follow the same general format. Its wide range and equivalent forms allow for both an initial measurement of oral reading proficiency and a measure of progress.

• The unique feature of the GORT-R is that speed of reading is an integral part of the accuracy score. In other oral reading tests, timing is optional, but here the rate of reading is considered of equal importance to the number of errors. Particulary with older students, the Passage Score, which combines speed and accuracy, is more predictive of classroom performance.

• The analysis of the types of reading errors which an individual student is making (provided in the manual) leads more directly to strategies for remediation.

• The comprehension questions on the GORT-R differ in several ways from those found on other oral reading tests. The multiple choice format not only allows for more standardized scoring than open-ended questions, but also aids the student with recall problems. The examiner reads the questions and answers aloud with the student, ensuring that the student reads each possible response, reducing impulsive responses. The questions have been designed to measure not only literal comprehension and recall of facts, but also inferential, critical, and affective reading skills. The following questions illustrate this strong feature of the GORT-R.

What probably explains how the children got into this situation?

How do you think she feels during the ordeal?

What is the best name for the story?

How do you think the story ends?

• The "prompt" preceeding each paragraph is a very useful feature. It serves to focus the student's attention and to provide a framework and reason for reading.

• The Examiner's Manual is clear and well organized and includes a great deal of information about analyzing a student's performance.

• The GORT-R is well-normed and standardized. Extensive reliability and validity data are published in the manual. They support the technical merits of this test.

LIMITING FACTORS OF THE GORT-R

• For students with reading disabilities, the timing aspect of the GORT-R causes increased pressure. Because these are the students for whom the most accurate diagnostic data is needed, another test may need to be used with students whose performance is significantly affected by the stopwatch.

- It is questionable whether speed of reading is an important criterion for beginning readers. The beginning reader who reads slowly and cautiously but without errors is penalized by the GORT-R scoring system. And for students with reading difficulties related to impulsiveness, reading speed may not be a desirable characteristic.

- Basing the basal and ceiling on the comprehension skills of the student is a questionable procedure. Many students with strong decoding skills do not get an opportunity to display them; they read only one or two paragraphs before they reach a ceiling due to comprehension problems. Conversely, students with poor decoding skills struggle painfully through many paragraphs due to their ability to "comprehend" the general context. The GORT-R is a very discouraging test for the bright student with serious decoding problems.

- The upper paragraphs of the GORT-R are very difficult to read. The sentences are very complex and the subject matter and vocabulary unfamiliar for most secondary students. These factors combined with the timed aspect of the test also make it very discouraging for the student with significant reading or language difficulties.

- In the manual, the authors state that research findings indicate that accuracy errors such as omissions, additions, reversals, and dialectical errors are less important than other error types, yet in the scoring system they count equally. For example, an omission is counted as an error just as a substitution is. If certain errors are not as important, perhaps they should not affect a student's score in the same way.

Slosson Oral Reading Test (SORT)

Richard L. Slosson
Slosson Educational Publications, Inc., 1963
P. O. Box 280, East Aurora, NY 14052

Purpose	To provide a quick measure of reading ability
Major Areas Tested	Word reading
Age or Grade Range	First grade through high school
Usually Given By	Classroom teacher Special education teacher School psychologist Counselor
Type of Test	Standardized Individual Norm-referenced
Scores Obtained	Grade level
Student Performance Timed?	No
Testing Time	3–5 minutes
Scoring/Interpretation Time	2–3 minutes
Normed On	108 students enrolled in grades 1–12; (National norming in progress)
Alternate Forms Available?	No

FORMAT

The Slosson Oral Reading Test (SORT) is an individual test of word reading for students in grades 1–12.

The materials consist of a single page. The front side of the page describes the purpose of the test, the validity and reliability data, the directions for administration and scoring, and the norms table. The 10 word lists are printed on the reverse side. The student reads the words from one sheet while the examiner records responses and the student's score on an identical sheet.

The 10 word lists of the SORT each contain 20 words. They cover 10 reading levels (primer, grades 1–8, and high school). Words were selected from standard school readers.

The examiner selects the word list which he thinks the student will be able to read without error. If the student makes an error, the examiner drops back each preceeding list until the student reads all 20 words correctly. Then the examiner takes the student through each higher list until the student is unable to read any of the words correctly. The examiner is given sugestions on ways to move the student along the list at a rate of about 5 seconds per word. The examiner marks correct words with a *t*, errors with a /. Errors include mispronunciations, omissions, and hesitations of more than 5 seconds.

The number of correct responses is totaled at the end of each list. A total score is obtained equalling the total number of correct responses on all lists read plus any words below the starting level. Using the norms table printed on the test form, the total raw score is converted to a grade level score.

STRENGTHS OF THE SORT

• The SORT is the epitome of the quick and easy test. It takes less than 10 minutes to administer and score.

• Despite its quickness, the SORT has adequate reliability and validity data to support its usefulness as a screening of word reading.

• A large print edition (SORT Form A) for use with Adult Literacy Programs and Visually and Verbally Handicapped students is available from the publisher. A word list flip card edition which prints the word lists on separate cards is also available.

LIMITING FACTORS OF THE SORT

• The SORT was standardized on a population of 108 students from grades 1–12. No other information is given about the sample regarding age, place of residence, ethnic background, reading abilities or disabilities. Therefore, SORT grade equivalent scores have little meaning. Research studies have consistently found that the SORT over-estimates reading levels.

• Obviously, the SORT only measures one dimension of reading, word identification. Given this, its low correlation

with WRAT must be due to the selection of words on one or both lists.

• The authors suggest that due to its high test-retest reliability, the SORT may be used for measuring pupil progress. However, measuring pupil progress on a test which only yields grade level scores is a poor practice. (See Introduction.)

Test of Reading Comprehension (TORC)

Virginia L. Brown, Donald D. Hammill, and J. Lee Wiederholt
Pro-Ed, 1978; revised 1986
5341 Industrial Oaks Blvd., Austin, TX 78735

Purpose	To provide a normed measure of silent reading comprehension
Major Areas Tested	Reading comprehension
Age or Grade Range	7–18 years
Usually Given By	Classroom teacher Special education teacher
Type of Test	Standardized Individual Group Norm-referenced
Scores Obtained	Scaled (each subtest) Standard (total test)
Student Performance Timed?	No
Testing Time	30–120 minutes
Scoring/Interpretation Time	40–90 minutes
Normed On	2,492 students in 13 states balanced for sex, age, and city and rural populations
Alternate Forms Available?	No

FORMAT

The Test of Reading Comprehension (TORC) is an instrument for measuring silent reading comprehension in students from grades 1 through 8. The 1978 edition was revised in 1986. The test may be individually or group administered. The materials consist of an examiner's manual, student booklets, answer sheets, individual student profile sheets, and separate response forms for the Reading the Directions of Schoolwork subtest.

Four subtests form the General Reading Comprehension Core:

1. *General Vocabulary* (25 items). The student reads three stimulus words that are related in some way (*teeth, nose, arm*) and selects two words from a group of four (*hair, air, legs, too*) that are related to the stimulus words. Both answers must be correct.

2. *Syntactic Similarities* (20 items). The student reads five sentences and selects the two that are most nearly alike in meaning. For example:

It was her wagon.
It was not her wagon.
It was his wagon.
The wagon was not hers.
It was not his wagon.

Both responses (in this example, the second and fourth sentences) must be correct.

3. *Paragraph Reading* (6 paragraphs). The student reads a paragraph and five questions. A multiple-choice format is used for all five questions. The student is required to select the "best" title, recall story details, draw an inference, and draw a negative inference (*Which sentence could* not *go in the story?*).

8. *Sentence Sequencing* (10 items). Each item includes five randomly ordered sentences that, when ordered properly, will create a meaningful paragraph. The student orders the sentences. Scoring is based on relational order rather than specific sequence.

Note: Sentence Sequencing was an optional test in the 1978 edition. It is now an integral part of the Reading Comprehension Core. To allow TORC users to be able to use their old forms, it has not been renumbered.

Diagnostic Supplements, which are four additional subtests, are used to gain a more comprehensive evaluation of strengths and weaknesses in a student's reading comprehension:

4. *Mathematics Vocabulary* (25 items). The student reads three stimulus items (*more than, longer, bigger*) and selects two words from a group of four (*blue, larger, food, greater*) that are related to the stimulus words. Both answers must be correct.

5. *Social Studies Vocabulary* (25 items). The student reads three stimulus items (*Congress, govern, court*) and selects two words from a group of four (*law, anarchy,*

combustion, legislature) that are related to the stimulus words. Both answers must be correct.

6. *Science Vocabulary* (25 items). The student reads three stimulus items (*tendon, ligament, muscle*) and selects two words from a group of four (*bone, medulla, carbonate, cartilage*) that are related to the stimulus words. Both answers must be correct.

7. *Reading the Directions of Schoolwork* (25 items). The student reads a common teaching instruction and carries it out. (*Number these words in alphabetical order.*) This subtest is designed to be used with younger or remedial readers (below fourth-grade level).

On all subtests, the student begins with item 1 and proceeds until a ceiling is reached. Ceiling criteria are clear in the examiner's manual. For each subtest, a raw score (number correct) is computed and converted into a scaled score and percentile using tables based on age. Scaled scores have a mean of 10 and a standard deviation of 3. The four core tests are combined into a reading comprehension quotient (RCQ) with a mean of 100 and a standard deviation of 15, allowing easy comparison of a student's TORC scores with other measures of intellectual and language functioning.

STRENGTHS OF THE TORC

• The TORC is subtitled *A Method for Assessing the Understanding of Written Language*. It is based upon the latest research on reading comprehension and psycholinguistics. Subtests are designed to assess the reader's ability to "construct meaning" from the printed word. Examiners are urged to read the manual carefully to understand the rationale for the test and avoid misinterpretation.

• Several of the subtests are unique in content and format and offer new understandings of the reading comprehension process.

• The examiner's manual is clear and complete. Directions for administration and scoring are easy to follow.

• Administrative options, such as answer sheets or booklets, one sitting or several, are included, making administration easier.

• Attention has been paid to reliability, validity, and construction of norms, all of which are clearly reported in the manual. Test-retest reliability is strong.

• No grade-equivalent scores are provided. Since the statistical problems of grade scores are overwhelming, it is to the authors' credit that they do not provide them.

• The procedures for small and large group testing are well described in the manual, including specific discussion of students who should always be tested individually.

• The TORC Summary Sheet has some interesting aspects. There is a place to indicate to whom test results have been released and/or interpreted. Quick check lists allow the examiner to indicate any special characteristics of the examiner, the environment, or the student at the time of testing. Finally, there is a brief space for summarizing intepretations and recommendations. The Summary Sheet fits with the TORC philosophy of an interactional theory and provides a model for a brief test report.

LIMITING FACTORS OF THE TORC

• The standardization sample of the 1986 TORC was changed from the 1978 standardization sample in two ways: 1) the 6 year old subjects were dropped because research indicated the TORC was not suitable for this age; 2) the sample was augmented with students from four major census areas. The 1986 sample is compared with the 1985 Statistical Abstract of the United States and is balanced for sex, geographical area of residence, rural/metropolitan residence, and age. However, there is still no description of the population regarding race, linguistic background, or reading ability. Until this is done, scores of learning disabled or minority students must be interpreted with caution.

• Several of the TORC subtests measure abilities rarely taught in classrooms. In particular, Syntactic Similarities measures the ability to recognize that two sentences mean the same thing, a very unfamiliar task. Many students need more teaching of this type of task than that provided in two examples. Because of this, scores on the subtest and, therefore, the RCQ, are suspect.

• The content area vocabulary tests are recommended to be used for students in the intermediate and upper grades to screen their readiness for reading in content areas. The vocabulary is so specific to topics previously taught that it has little value as either a screening test or a measure of progress.

• The theoretical constructs underlying the TORC are new and complex. Interpretation of scores is difficult. The TORC is best used in conjunction with other measures of reading skills.

• A major concern about the TORC is that it has attempted to cover too wide an age range with too few items (Hood, 1985). It is certainly true that the TORC is a very short test of silent reading comprehension compared with such tests as the Gates-MacGinitie.

• Whether the variety of tasks used on the TORC will compensate for the few items of each type, only time and research will tell. Validity studies using the TORC have shown low but significant correlations with other group reading comprehension tests such as the California Achievement Test and the SRA Achievement Series. The correlations are expected to be low due to the different construct of reading comprehension embodied in the TORC.

• There is no indication on the 1986 manual that the TORC has been revised. As the changes in scoring procedures and norms are significant, the 1986 manual should be labeled Revised Edition *on the cover,* or the test should be renamed TORC-2. Many clinicians are undoubtedly unaware that they are using the older edition. Changes are outlined below.

CHANGES IN THE 1986 TORC

1. More description of the rationale for subtests.

2. Inclusion of Sequencing Sentences as one of the required tests composing the Reading Comprehension Quotient rather than an alternate or substitute subtest.

3. Augumented standardization sample with 6-year-old students dropped and population increased at upper age levels.

4. Increased age range for use of test from 6 1/2–14 1/2 years to 7–18 years.

Woodcock Reading Mastery Tests—Revised
(WRMT-R)

Richard W. Woodcock
DLM Teaching Resources, 1987
One DLM Park, P. O. Box 4000, Allen, TX 75002

Purpose	To provide a comprehensive measure of reading ability across a wide age range
Major Areas Tested	Reading
Age or Grade Range	Grades K–college senior Adults to age 75+
Usually Given By	Special education teacher Classroom teacher Psychologist Trained paraprofessional (administration and scoring only)
Type of Test	Standardized Individual Norm-referenced
Scores Obtained	Age level Relative performance index Grade level NCE (normal curve equivalent) Percentile Standard
Student Performance Timed?	No
Testing Time	30–60 minutes
Scoring/Interpretation Time	30–45 minutes
Normed On	6,089 Subjects in 60 diverse U.S. communities; 4,201 K–12 students; 1,023 college students; 865 adults. Population balanced for geographic region, community size, sex, race, Hispanic origin, and socioeconomic status
Alternate Forms Available?	Yes

FORMAT

The Woodcock Reading Mastery Tests—Revised (WRMT-R) are a revised edition of the original Woodcock Reading Mastery Test published in 1973. It is an individually-administered comprehensive battery of subtests which assess various aspects of reading across a wide age range. The materials include a manual, an easel kit for presenting the test materials, and individual test records for recording student responses and scores. The WRMT-R has two forms, G and H. Separate easel kits and test records are needed for each form. Form G includes the complete test battery, four subtests of reading achievement, two readiness subtests, and a two-part supplementary check list. Form H includes only the four reading achievement subtests. A separate record form, G&H, may be used if both forms of the test are administered.

The subtests in Form G, the complete battery, are:

Readiness Cluster

1. *Visual-Auditory Learning.* This subtest is taken from the Woodcock-Johnson Psychoeducational Battery. The student learns a battery of unfamiliar visual symbols representing familiar words. The student then "reads" test stories composed of these 28 symbols. Visual-Auditory Learning is a 134-item paired associate learning task.

2. *Letter Identification.* The 51 items of this subtest assess the student's ability to identify by name or sound the letters of the alphabet. Upper and lower case and manuscript and cursive forms are presented.

Basic Skills Cluster

3. *Word Identification.* The student reads aloud words ranging in difficulty from the preprimer through the college level. One hundred six items are presented (*you, watch, already, urgent, cologne, carnivorous*).

4. *Word Attack.* This 45-item subtest assesses the student's ability to pronounce nonsense words (*raff, chad, yeng, cigbet, bafmotben*) using phonic and structural analysis skills.

Reading Comprehension Cluster

5. *Word Comprehension.* The Word Comprehension test is comprised of three subtests, each measuring a different level of cognitive processing:

5A. *Antonyms.* This 34-item subtest requires the student to read a word and respond orally with a word opposite in meaning (*enemy–friend, profit–loss*).

5B. *Synonyms.* The student is required to read the word and state a word similar in meaning. Thirty-three items are presented (*zero–none, nothing, zip; tint–color, shade, dye*).

5C. *Analogies.* This subtest contains 79 items that test knowledge of word meaning using an analogy format. The student reads a pair of words and ascertains their relationship. Then he reads a third word and applies the same relationship to supply a word to complete the analogy.

foot–toes; hand–_____
duet–quartet; two–_____
famine–hunger; epidemic–_____

The three Word Comprehension subtests are organized in such a way that it is also possible to assess a student's skills in four vocabulary areas:

General Reading Vocabulary. 30 words. (*whisper, frolic*).
Science-Mathematics Vocabulary. 40 words. (*doe, meter*).
Social Studies Vocabulary. 38 words. (*migrate, wigwam*).
Humanities Vocabulary. 38 words. (*soprano, plot*).

6. *Passage Comprehension.* This subtest includes 68 items designed to assess reading comprehension. It uses a modified cloze procedure. The student reads a two or three sentence paragraph silently; when he comes to a blank he supplies an appropriate word based upon the meaning of the paragraph. For example:

Each day Midas counted his gold. Each day, after he had _____ it, he wished for more.

A person can buy stocks on margin. That is, he pays only part of the price in cash, which is the margin. To pay the _____ he borrows from his broker, paying interest on the loan.

The WRMT-R is constructed so that students are tested only on those items within their operating range. The operating range is assumed to extend from a basal level marked by six consecutive correct reponses to a ceiling level of six consecutive incorrect responses. On two subtests, Visual-Auditory Learning and Word Attack, all students begin at the first item. For the other four subtests, a starting point table based on estimated reading grade level is provided.

The WRMT-R provides a variety of test information; error analysis, age and grade equivalent scores, a relative mastery index, instructional range, percentile ranks, and standard scores are provided separately for each subtest. Five cluster scores are also provided; Readiness, Basic Skills, and Reading Comprehension (Word Identification, Word Attack, Word Comprehension, Passage Comprehension), Total Reading-Full Scale and Total Reading-Short Scale (Word Identification, Passage Comprehension). The use of cluster scores results in higher validity.

The WRMT-R test record form provides two primary and three supplementary diagnostic profiles that offer a graphic display of a student's performance. The supplementary profiles allow the incorporation of test results from the Woodcock-Johnson Psychoeducational Battery and the Goldman-Fristoe-Woodcock Auditory Skills Test Battery.

STRENGTHS OF THE WRMT-R

• The WRMT-R maintains the basic features of the original test while incorporating several changes and additions. These changes increase the diagnostic value of the test. The major changes are:

1. The Letter Identification Test is not included in the Total Reading Score.

2. The Word Comprehension Test has been expanded to include antonyms and synonyms as well as analogies. In addition, a student's reading vocabulary in four content areas can be assessed.

3. Several tests include one or more training items to ensure that the student understands what is expected of him.

4. The norms have been extended to include college, university, and non-school-attending adults.

• The Supplementary Letter Checklist can be used in an informal manner to gain more information about a student's knowledge of letter names and sounds. This is especially useful with young children or students with very low reading levels.

• A Word-Attack Error Inventory is provided to aid the examiner in error analysis of the Word Attack Test. This inventory provides useful information for instructional program planning for a student with poor word attack skills. However, the directions for completing this inventory are poor and require a very knowledgeable examiner for useful interpretation.

• The Word Comprehension Test is designed to assess three levels of cognitive processing. Antonyms require the simplest cognitive skills as many of the responses will be at the word association level (*day-night*). Synonyms is a more difficult task as the student must supply a word that is similar in meaning as most of the words do not have another word which is exactly the same in meaning. Analogies requires the highest level of cognitive processing because it requires the understanding of relationships.

• The Total Reading-Short Scale cluster provides a quick estimate of global reading ability through the administration of just two subtests, Word Identification and Passage Comprehension. The correlation between this cluster and Total Reading-Full Scale is very high.

• A micro computer scoring program, ASSIST™ (Automized System for Scoring and Interpreting Standardized Tests) is available. For examiners using the test extensively, ASSIST™ will save time and diminish clerical scoring errors. ASSIST™ is compatible with Apple II and with IBM PCs.

• A Report to Parents is also available from the publisher. This report conveys test results and a brief interpretation of the student's performance in a form that is more understandable to parents.

• Equivalent Forms G and H allow for retesting or may be combined to increase precision and validity. Raw scores can be plotted on the diagnostic profiles. This allows the examiner to obtain information quickly; more complete analysis can be formulated later. The raw score profile can be used to give immediate feedback to the student during the actual testing process. This is especially desirable with older students.

LIMITING FACTORS OF THE WRMT-R

• The split-half reliability data for the WRMT-R included in the manual is quite strong for the grade levels reported. However, many grade levels are not reported, and no test-retest reliability data is presented.

• Limited data on validity is presented. The inclusion of data using the 1973 Woodcock Reading Mastery Test "because the psychometric characteristics of the WRMT and the WRMT-R are so similar that many generalizations are valid" is a very questionable procedure.

• No information is given as to the inclusion or exclusion of special education students in the norming population.

• The WRMT-R manual includes a lengthy discussion of how to calculate the Aptitude-Achievement Discrepancy. This calculation presumably allows the examiner to compare the student's actual achievement on the WRMT-R with aptitude measures such as the Reading Aptitude Cluster of the Woodcock-Johnson Psychoeducational Battery or the Wechsler Intelligence Scale for Children-Revised. However, the calculation is based upon *estimated* correlations between these tests and reading abilities. In addition, the final number, the percent of the population with the same size discrepancy, has little meaning in terms of diagnosis, placement, or program planning.

The Boder Test of Reading-Spelling Patterns

Elena Boder and Sylvia Jarrico
The Psychological Corporation, 1982
555 Academic Court, San Antonio, TX 78204

Purpose	To differentiate specific reading disability, or developmental dyslexia, from non-specific reading disability; to classify dyslexic readers into one of three subtypes; to provide guidelines for remediation
Major Areas Tested	Reading Spelling
Age or Grade Range	First grade through adult
Usually Given By	Teacher Speech/language clinician Reading specialist Psychologist Physician
Type of Test	Informal Individual Diagnostic
Scores Obtained	Grade level Age level
Student Performance Timed?	No
Testing Time	30 minutes
Scoring/Interpretation Time	30–45 minutes
Normed On	Not normed
Alternate Forms Available?	No

FORMAT

The Boder Test of Reading-Spelling Patterns is a unique test in concept and design. The purpose of the test is to determine whether or not an individual student is dyslexic, and if so, within which of three subtypes that student may be classified. This determination is based on a student's reading and spelling error patterns. The test materials consist of a manual, student forms for the reading and spelling tests, examiner's recording forms, and a diagnostic summary form.

The student is administered an oral reading test consisting of graded word lists. Beginning at the indicated level, the student reads a 20-word list; the odd-numbered words are phonetically regular; the even-numbered words are non-phonetic. The initial reading is a flash presentation. One second is allowed per word. If the student does not read the word on sight, he or she is given 10 seconds to decode the word before going on to the next word. The examiner records the student's responses, checking "flash", "untimed", or "not read" appropriately.

Thirteen graded word lists are provided, pre-primer through adult. If a reading problem is suspected, the examiner begins with the pre-primer list; otherwise, the test begins two grades below the student's actual grade level, but no higher than the 5th grade list. A ceiling is reached when the student reads six or fewer words in a list correctly on sight presentation. The examiner then determines the student's reading level, which is defined as "the highest grade level at which the student reads at least 50% of the word list on sight presentation." A Reading Age is calculated by adding 5 to the Reading Grade Level. A Reading Quotient is determined by the usual formula:

$$\text{Reading Quotient} = \frac{\text{Reading Age} \times 100}{\text{Chronological Age}}$$

For each word list read, the examiner tabulates the number of words read flash and untimed and the number of words not read. Subtotals are calculated for phonetic and non-phonetic words.

Next the examiner prepares an individual spelling test by selecting 10 *known* words from the student's sight or *flash* list and 10 *unknown* words from the student's *not read* list. Five phonetic and 5 non-phonetic words comprise each list.

When the examiner administers the spelling test, the *known* words are dictated in the usual way—pronounced, used in a sentence, and pronounced again. For the *unknown* words, the student is told to "try to write the words the way they sound." The examiner pronounces the word and asks the student to repeat it aloud and then write it. *Known* words are scored for correctness only; *unknown* words are scored for their phonetic equivalence to the dictated words. For example, *flite* for *flight*, *kedl* for *kettle*, and *onrubol* for *honorable* are scored as GFE's (good phonetic equivalents).

Based upon his or her reading-spelling pattern, the student is classified as one of five reader subtypes; normal, nonspecific reading disability, dysphonetic, dyseidetic, or mixed dysphonetic-dyseidetic. The author defines the dysphonetic subtype category as one in which the student exhibits weakness in the auditory analytic function and the dyseidetic subtype category as one in which the student exhibits weakness in the visual gestalt function.

STRENGTHS OF THE BODER TEST

• The Boder, used in conjunction with other reading tests, is a very useful tool when the question being asked by the parent is, "Is my child dyslexic?" The author has defined the term and delineated several basic subtypes in a clear manner, which is helpful in understanding the disorder.

• The discussion of the subtypes in the Interpretation chapter of the manual is excellent. It not only clarifies the types of dyslexic readers, but distinguishes the dyslexic reader from the normal reader and the student with a non-specific reading disorder.

• The word lists of the Boder are carefully constructed. Not only do they include half phonetic, half non-phonetic words, they include only words which are introduced at the same grade level in both reading and spelling.

• In states in which the eligibility criteria for admission to special education require documentation of a processing disorder, the Boder is a useful test. Defects in the auditory analytical function and the visual gestalt function are clearly documented.

• Alphabet tasks are included for the student who is a non-reader or who has a sight vocabulary below the pre-primer level. Reciting the alphabet, naming the letters, giving letter sounds, and writing the alphabet test require auditory and visual memory and give important diagnostic information on the non-reading student. Other informal diagnostic tasks are described in the manual, such as syllabicating tasks and drawing a clock face from memory. These tasks provide clinical information that is helpful not only in formulating the diagnosis but also in planning remediation.

• Studies of interrater reliability, test-retest reliability, and internal consistency are reported in the manual. In addition, extensive research validating the construct validity of the Boder subtypes is reported. An extensive reference list is also provided.

• The guide to remedial intervention presented in the manual provides helpful information for classroom teachers and tutors working with students with specific reading disability.

LIMITING FACTORS OF THE BODER TEST

• The Boder test is more difficult to administer than it appears. Procedures for testing the limits of a student's sight vocabulary are difficult to understand through the complex instructions presented in the manual. Also, constructing the individual spelling test is initially very difficult and requires much practice before it can be done quickly. Examiners unfamiliar with the test should not only study the manual thoroughly but also administer the test in two sessions with the first several students tested. By giving the reading test one day and the spelling another, the examiner can prepare the spelling test between sessions.

• The Boder subtypes are not as easy to identify as the manual proclaims. There are many students who do not quite fit the criteria for dysphonetic or dyseidetic. In particular, it takes time and experience to interpret the performance of remediated students, who may not exhibit clear patterns. This pattern is occurring with increasing frequency as remedial programs become more widespread. The authors recognize these problems, and a future edition of the manual will address these issues more thoroughly and empirically (Boder and Jarrico, personal communication, July, 1988).

• The high school word list is designated grades 10–12. However, no directions are given as to what grade to use to determine Reading Grade, Reading Age, and Reading Quotient. The same problem occurs with the Adult list.

• The rules for determining if a student's misspelling is a GFE (good phonetic equivalent) are ambiguous. For example, any vowel may be substituted in an unstressed syllable, making *rimembr* a GFE, but not *remimbr*. An *e* may be added to any word except when it converts the spelling or misspelling into another word; so *lisne* for *listen* is a GFE, but not *hale* for *hall*. These rules are difficult to apply. Since the Boder subtypes are all based upon the percentage of GFEs, the rules need to be much more logical and unambiguous.

• More attention should be given to the analysis of reading errors. The authors stress the analysis of spelling errors, and examples are given of typical reading error patterns for each subtype. But systematic evaluation of the reading pattern is also crucial if remedial reading programs based on test performance are to be designed.

• A single test should not be used to make any diagnosis, especially not one as complex as dyslexia. The Boder should be used as part of a battery given to students with known or suspected reading disabilities, not as an isolated diagnostic tool.

Test of Written Language (TOWL)

Donald D. Hammill and Stephen C. Larsen
Pro-Ed, 1978; 1983
5341 Industrial Oaks Blvd., Austin, TX 78735

Purpose	To identify students with written language disabilities, to identify strengths and weaknesses in writing, and to document progress in writing
Major Areas Tested	Written language
Age or Grade Range	Grades 2–12
Usually Given By	Classroom teacher Special education teacher Educational diagnostician Psychologist
Type of Test	Individual Group Standardized Norm-referenced
Scores Obtained	Percentile Standard
Student Performance Timed?	No
Testing Time	40–60 minutes
Scoring/Interpretation Time	15–20 minutes
Normed On	3,418 students balanced for sex, place of residence, and grade level in 14 states
Alternate Forms Available?	No

FORMAT

The Test of Written Language (TOWL) is one of the few standardized assessments of students' written language skills. The materials consist of a manual containing administration and scoring directions, as well as theoretical and statistical background, individual student answer booklets, and a summary and profile sheet for recording each student's scores.

On the student answer form is printed a three-part picture depicting life on another planet. In scene one, the environment of the planet is deteriorating; scene two shows the movement by spaceships to a new planet; in scene three, humans and space creatures join together in a cooperative life. Using this stimulus, the student is asked to write a story using all three pictures. This sample of spontaneous writing and other measures compose the six subtests of the TOWL:

1. *Vocabulary*. Students receive one point for every correctly spelled word that contains seven or more letters.

2. *Thematic Maturity*. Students receive one point for each of 20 criteria included in their stories. Among the criteria are writing in paragraphs, giving personal names to the characters, having a definite ending, and expressing a philosophical or moral theme.

3. *Handwriting*. If the student wrote in cursive, the handwriting is matched against five samples in the manual demonstrating degrees of legibility. A score of 0 to 10 is obtained. Students who wrote in manuscript do not receive a handwriting score.

4. *Spelling*. The student is given a separate 25-word spelling test. The test is a shortened form of the Larsen-Hammill Test of Written Spelling using words from both the Predictable Words list and the Unpredictable Words list. One point is given for each word spelled correctly.

5. *Word Usage*. The student is given 25 sentences with words missing to complete. The word usage test assesses the student's knowledge of correct grammar (regular and irregular plurals, past tenses, comparatives, and pronouns). (For example: *He built the house all by* _____ . *One sheep is in the barn; two other* _____ *are in the field.*)

6. *Style*. The student rewrites 25 sentences with correct punctuation and capitalization. (*she is mrs smith.*) The sentence must be totally correct to receive one point.

Raw scores for each section are converted into percentiles and standard scores. The standard scores for the six subtests are totaled and transformed into a total test score, the written language quotient (WLQ). The WLQ has a mean of 100 and a standard deviation of 15. If a student did not obtain a score on a specific section (such as handwriting), a score for that section is prorated by averaging the student's other standard scores.

No grade scores are provided in the 1983 edition, in line with the author's position that grade scores are too often misinterpreted and are less statistically reliable than standard scores.

STRENGTHS OF THE TOWL

• The need for a standardized test to measure written language is apparent to every diagnostician in the field. The other highly used instrument, the Myklebust Picture Story Language Test, has serious drawbacks. The use of the standardized picture stimulus to gather a spontaneous

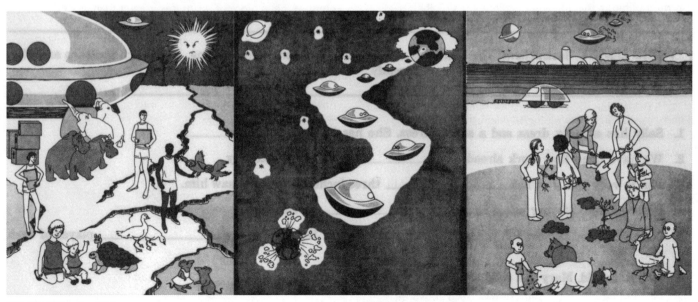

TOWL Stimulus Picture

writing sample together with standardized measures of spelling, grammar, and mechanics is a creative approach to this difficult assessment problem.

- The TOWL picture is interesting to students of all ages and generally produces a good writing sample.

- The group format allows for efficient testing of a whole class followed by individual analysis of strengths and weaknesses.

- Administration and scoring procedures for the TOWL are very clear. The addition of sample stories for scoring practice is a helpful feature.

- The TOWL manual is clear and well written. The section on informal assessment of written language is very helpful to the teacher.

LIMITING FACTORS OF THE TOWL

- While the TOWL picture produces a reasonably good spontaneous writing sample, the assessments of that sample seem contrived and of little value in evaluating a student's program needs. For example, while rating vocabulary on the length of the words used may be theoretically sound, it is not as meaningful as a system that indicates the types of words (parts of speech, common or unusual words) a student is currently using and not using. It also eliminates credit for the short but unusual word.

- Also, the Thematic Maturity criteria seem very arbitrary. A student who writes dialogue or a story personalizing the characters in the picture will receive a very high score that may have little to say about the writer's overall thematic maturity.

- There are many standardized spelling tests. Therefore, it is disappointing that the authors did not assess the student's spelling *in the context of the story*. Difficulties with standardizing that procedure are obvious, but an attempt would be applauded. A way of assessing Word Usage and Style in the context of the story also would have made the TOWL a much more valuable assessment tool.

- Even though the TOWL reports many validity studies comparing the TOWL with the Myklebust Picture Story Language Test, the Test of Reading Comprehension, the Test of Adolescent Language, and the Test of Language Development, impressions of clinicians are that the validity is questionable. For students in suburban communities, the subtest scores and WLQ seem to overestimate a student's abilities. Many students reported by their teachers to be doing very poorly in written language in school obtain average or higher scores on the TOWL. Such results may be due to the inherent problems of assessing such a global skill as written language with one writing sample, or they may be due to the limitations in the subtests described above. In either case, examiners should be extremely cautious about reporting individual students' scores without information

about their writing skills in other situations.

- Although the TOWL was designed to measure progress in a writing program, the lack of an alternate picture or other subtests makes it inappropriate to use as a pre-and posttest. A student could make great gains in written language that would not be reflected in retesting on the TOWL.

- Although the WLQ is a reliable score, in reality it has little meaning as it combines many very diverse skills. Use of a single score to denote a student's functioning in an area such as written language is over-simplified.

- The standardization sample does not describe the inclusion of handicapped students; the ethnic and language backgrounds of the sample are also not described.

- Test-retest reliability studies reported in the manual suggest that the WLQ and 4 subtests have adequate stability; Thematic Maturity and Vocabulary are questionable.

- The authors caution that TOWL results should not be interpreted as meaning that a child has a particular disability, i.e., dysgraphia, learning disability, language impairment. Poor scores on the TOWL can reflect many other factors, not the least of which is poor instruction in written language. If a diagnosis is needed, TOWL results should be used only in conjunction with other comprehensive assessments.

- No holistic system of evaluating the student's writing is provided. The authors concentrated on developing the objective measures of vocabulary and thematic maturity. Given the weaknesses of these measures, a means of holistic assessment would be very helpful. This is usually done by providing samples of written paragraphs and instructions to read a paragraph for total impression rather than specific aspects of the composition. "Holistic scoring is based on the premise that a piece of writing is greater than any of its parts." (Mullis, 1984, p. 16.)

- The summary of the six subtests into a total test score, the Written Language Quotient, seems useless given the great difference between the subtests. Clearly, scores on tests such as spelling and thematic maturity reflect very different skills. Combining them into one score seems to be a questionable procedure.

Larsen-Hammill Test of Written Spelling (TWS–2)

Stephen Larsen and Donald Hammill
Pro-Ed, 1976; revised 1986
5341 Industrial Oaks Blvd., Austin, TX 78735

Purpose	To provide a standardized, reliable, and valid measure of written spelling
Major Areas Tested	Written spelling
Age or Grade Range	Grades 1–12
Usually Given By	Classroom teacher Special education teacher
Type of Test	Standardized Individual Group Norm-referenced
Scores Obtained	Percentile Standard
Student Performance Timed?	No
Testing Time	15–25 minutes
Scoring/Interpretation Time	10 minutes
Normed On	3,805 children in 18 states; sample was balanced for race, sex, ethnicity, residence, and geographic area
Alternate Forms Available?	No

FORMAT

The Larsen-Hammill Test of Written Spelling (TWS-2) is a revised edition of the original test published in 1976. The TWS-2 uses essentially the same format as the TWS, a dictated written spelling test. The age range has been expanded to include grades 1–12. The materials consist of an examiner's manual and individual Summary/Response forms. The manual includes the test rationale, administration and scoring directions, interpretation suggestions, norms tables, and data on the technical aspects of the test. The Summary/Response forms provide a place for the students to write the dictated words as well as a place to record TWS-2 and other test scores.

The TWS-2 includes two subtests or lists of spelling words. The first list includes 50 Predictable Words—words that follow basic spelling rules. The second list contains 50 Unpredictable Words—words that essentially have to be memorized. For example:

Predictable Words:	Unpredictable Words:
let	*eight*
stop	*fountain*
spend	*collar*
strange	*requisite*
tardy	*sure*
district	*awful*
tranquil	*campaign*

The examiner pronounces each word, uses it in a sentence, and pronounces it again. The student writes each word.

The same word lists are used with students at all grade levels. Entry levels for different grades are outlined in the manual. The testing is discontinued when the student misspells five consecutive words on each of the two lists. If the student has not spelled five consecutive words correctly on each list, the examiner returns to the entry level and tests downward until a basal is reached. Modifications of this procedure for group testing are given in the manual.

In addition to raw scores, the TWS-2 gives a percentile and standard score based on 6-month age intervals for each word list. Raw scores for the two lists are summed and percentiles and standard scores provided for the total test.

STRENGTHS OF THE TWS-2

• The TWS-2 is a well-constructed, well-normed, easy-to-administer test. The revised edition includes several changes which make the test more usable. These include an extended age range and greater reliability at the younger age levels. The addition of entry levels for different grades is a helpful addition. In keeping with the Pro-Ed philosophy, age and grade level scores have been replaced with standard scores and percentiles.

• Dividing the words into two types allows the classroom teacher to plan an appropriate individualized spelling program. For example, two beginning fourth-grade students might receive the scores on the table shown here. As the table shows, Student A has significantly more difficulty with unpredictable words than with predictable words and needs a spelling program that focuses on techniques for memorizing sight words. Student B is having more difficulty with rule-based words and needs a systematic approach to this type of spelling.

While both students exhibit "average" spelling skill, their instructional needs are quite different. Examples of four types of spelling patterns are presented in the manual: low scores on both lists; very low scores on both lists; stronger spelling scores for predictable words; and stronger spelling scores for nonpredictable words. Brief guidelines for interpretation and planning for these patterns are included.

• The reliability and validity data presented in the manual supports the technical soundness of the TWS-2.

Two Fourth Graders' Scores on the TWS-2

	Student A		Student B	
	%tile	SS	%tile	SS
Predictable Words	73	109	19	87
Unpredictable Words	26	90	68	107
Total Test	55	102	48	99

LIMITING FACTORS OF THE TWS-2

• The Summary/Reponse forms require the students to write in all of the dictated words on one page in small spaces. This is an overwhelming format for the poor speller. Using regular notebook paper is recommended.

• The description of the standardization samples gives little information on the school status of the students. It is not clear if handicapped students were included in the sample. Further validity studies regarding the identification power of the TWS-2 with learning disabled students are needed.

Enright® Diagnostic Inventory of Basic Arithmetic Skills (Enright®)

Brian E. Enright
Curriculum Associates, Inc., 1983
5 Esquire Rd., North Billerica, MA 01862

Purpose	To assess knowledge of basic facts and computation skills in mathematics
Major Areas Tested	Math computation
Age or Grade Range	Grades 1–6 (and remedial classes in secondary school)
Usually Given By	Classroom teacher Special education teacher Educational diagnostician
Type of Test	Criterion-referenced Individual Group Standardized
Scores Obtained	None
Student Performance Timed?	No
Testing Time	Varies with skills of the student
Scoring/Interpretation Time	15–30 minutes
Normed On	Students primarily in Louisiana and in five other states
Alternate Forms Available?	Yes (some parts)

FORMAT

The Enright® Diagnostic Inventory of Basic Arithmetic Skills (Enright®) is a comprehensive instrument for assessing a student's math computation skills. The materials consist of an examiner's notebook and individual arithmetic record books. The loose-leaf examiner's notebook is designed to lie flat on the table between the examiner and the student for individual testing.

The Enright® provides three levels of information:

1. The grade level at which basic math computation skills are commonly taught.

2. Assessments of 144 basic computational skills

3. An analysis of error patterns

Each of the basic skills assessed has been referenced to five basal mathematics series selected for their nationwide use. Through tables in the examiner's notebook, it is possible to determine the grade level at which a particular skill, such as adding two-digit numbers and regrouping ones, is typically taught. This information is useful in determining sequential curriculum.

The 144 basic computational skills are assessed in a very systematic manner. First, the student is administered the Wide Range Placement Test. This 26-problem screening test establishes a starting point for assessing a student's competency in addition, subtraction, multiplication, and division of whole numbers, fractions, and decimals. For students whose area of difficulty is known, this step may be omitted.

Once it is determined which operations the student needs help with, the Skill Placement Test for that operation is given. Shown here is the Skill Placement Test for Addition of Whole Numbers. The purpose of this test is to determine the student's competency within the sequence of skills required in adding whole numbers. One problem for each critical step in the sequence is provided. The examiner's page corresponding to this Skill Test provides the grade level at which the skills are usually taught, a description of each type of problem, and an instructional objective for the skill sequence.

The student's first error on the Skill Placement Test determines which Skill Test will then be given. For example, if a student's first error is adding and regrouping two three-digit numbers from left to right, the student is given the Skill Test for that step in the operation, shown here with the corresponding examiner's page.

NAME: Rick Lowe

(Give Skill Test A-12.)

1.
$$\begin{array}{r} 4 \\ +5 \\ \hline 9 \end{array}$$

2.
$$\begin{array}{r} 6 \\ +7 \\ \hline 13 \end{array}$$

3.
$$\begin{array}{r} 3 \\ 1 \\ +5 \\ \hline 9 \end{array}$$

4.
$$\begin{array}{r} 74 \\ +\ 5 \\ \hline 79 \end{array}$$

5.
$$\begin{array}{r} \overset{1}{5}7 \\ +\ 5 \\ \hline 62 \end{array}$$

6.
$$\begin{array}{r} 65 \\ +22 \\ \hline 87 \end{array}$$

7.
$$\begin{array}{r} \overset{1}{3}7 \\ +59 \\ \hline 96 \end{array}$$

8.
$$\begin{array}{r} \overset{1}{6}8 \\ +74 \\ \hline 142 \end{array}$$

9.
$$\begin{array}{r} \overset{1}{2}8 \\ 45 \\ +14 \\ \hline 87 \end{array}$$

10.
$$\begin{array}{r} \overset{1}{3}5 \\ 56 \\ +64 \\ \hline 155 \end{array}$$

11.
$$\begin{array}{r} \overset{1}{6}37 \\ +256 \\ \hline 893 \end{array}$$

12.
$$\begin{array}{r} \overset{2}{5}89 \\ +345 \\ \hline 8116 \end{array}$$

Enright Skill Placement Test, Addition of Whole Numbers

This part of the process is a unique feature of the Enright®. The student computes five problems. On the examiner's page, each test item is printed with the correct response. The most common incorrect responses are also provided. By matching the student's response with one of the incorrect responses, the examiner can determine which type of error a student has made. The Enright® identifies 198 distinct error types. These have been grouped into seven error clusters. The error pattern information clarifies for teachers the approach a student is taking to arrive at an answer. This information leads directly to an individualized remedial program. Students with errors in the same error clusters may be grouped for instruction. Following remediation, the second five items on the Skill Test are administered as a posttest. A criterion of 80 percent accuracy is recommended. When all of the skills in an operation that the student had made errors on have been retaught, the alternate form of the Skill Placement Test may be given as a posttest.

A Basic Fact Test is provided for addition, subtraction, multiplication, and division. Two forms are available for each operation. Each form consists of 50 basic facts. One form of the Basic Fact Test is usually given after the Skill Placement Test. Students who do not know the basic facts may still understand the computational process and should be allowed to use manipulatives or facts tables for the Skill Placement Tests. Calculators are not permitted because they give a complete answer and do not allow error analysis. The alternate form of the Basic Facts Test may be used as a posttest.

The student's performance is recorded in the arithmetic record book. The booklet has 13 sections to correspond with the 13 operations assessed in the Enright®. The record tracks a student's progress in the acquisition of computation skills by dates and also provides information about error types. A color-coding system allows one record book for each student to be used throughout the elementary grades.

Skill Placement Test — A. Addition of Whole Numbers   Form A

DIRECTIONS: Give each student a copy of **S-8** and a pencil. Tell the students to start with the first test item and to compute the test items *in order*. Tell the students to stop when they have computed as many of the test items as they can.

SKILL: Adds whole numbers.

GRADE LEVELS TAUGHT: 1.0 to 3.0

ARITHMETIC RECORD BOOK: Page 2

MATERIALS: Copy of S-8 and a pencil.

ASSESSMENT METHODS: Individual or group written response.

DISCONTINUE: When student has completed as many of the test items as he or she can.

NEXT:
1. Give **Basic Facts Test: Addition**, pages 38–39. (See **NOTE** 2.)
2. The letter and number above each test item in the **Answers** represent the matching skill test. Give the skill test that corresponds to the letter and number of the first test item computed incorrectly.

NOTES:
1. You may wish to use Form A of the **Skill Placement Test** as a pretest and Form B as a post test.
2. Before skill testing, the examiner should determine if the student has difficulty with basic addition facts. Such a weakness can interfere with the gathering of accurate information about student ability to compute.

Answers for Form A

A-1 $^{1.0}$ $\begin{array}{r} 4 \\ +5 \\ \hline 9 \end{array}$	A-2 $^{1.6}$ $\begin{array}{r} 6 \\ +7 \\ \hline 13 \end{array}$	A-3 $^{1.6}$ $\begin{array}{r} 1 \\ 6 \\ +1 \\ \hline 8 \end{array}$	A-4 $^{1.6}$ $\begin{array}{r} 74 \\ +\ 5 \\ \hline 79 \end{array}$
A-5 $^{2.3}$ $\begin{array}{r} 57 \\ +\ 5 \\ \hline 62 \end{array}$	A-6 $^{2.2}$ $\begin{array}{r} 65 \\ +22 \\ \hline 87 \end{array}$	A-7 $^{2.3}$ $\begin{array}{r} 37 \\ +59 \\ \hline 96 \end{array}$	A-8 $^{2.9}$ $\begin{array}{r} 68 \\ +74 \\ \hline 142 \end{array}$
A-9 $^{3.0}$ $\begin{array}{r} 28 \\ 45 \\ +14 \\ \hline 87 \end{array}$	A-10 $^{3.0}$ $\begin{array}{r} 35 \\ 56 \\ +64 \\ \hline 155 \end{array}$	A-11 $^{2.7}$ $\begin{array}{r} 637 \\ +256 \\ \hline 893 \end{array}$	A-12 $^{2.9}$ $\begin{array}{r} 589 \\ +345 \\ \hline 934 \end{array}$

OBJECTIVE: By _____(date)_____, when given twelve test items for adding whole numbers, _(student's name)_ will compute with 100% accuracy: (list as appropriate)

A-1	Two Numbers with Sum Less Than 10	A-8	Two 2-Digit Numbers, Regrouping Ones and Tens
A-2	Two 1-Digit Numbers with Sum Greater Than 10	A-9	Three 2-Digit Numbers, Regrouping Ones
A-3	Three Numbers with Sum Less Than 10	A-10	Three 2-Digit Numbers, Regrouping Ones and Tens
A-4	2-Digit Number to a 1-Digit Number, with No Regrouping	A-11	Two 3-Digit Numbers, Regrouping Ones
A-5	2-Digit Number to a 1-Digit Number, Regrouping Ones	A-12	Two 3-Digit Numbers, Regrouping Ones and Tens
A-6	Two 2-Digit Numbers, with No Regrouping		
A-7	Two 2-Digit Numbers, Regrouping Ones		

Enright Examiner's Page for Addition of Whole Numbers

(Directional 105.)

NAME: Rick Lowe

a.	b.	c.	d.	e.
2 24**6** +386 X 5114	3 66**8** +279 X 8120	2 43**9** +194 X 5115	2 13**9** +595 X 6116	4 38**4** +468 X 7116

368	557	295	746	453
+486	+277	+439	+189	+269

Enright Skill Test A-12

ADDITION: TWO 3-DIGIT NUMBERS, REGROUPING ONES AND TENS

SKILL: Add two 3-digit numbers, regrouping ones and tens.

GRADE LEVEL TAUGHT: 2.9

STUDENT RECORD BOOK: Page 2

ASSESSMENT METHODS: Individual or group written response.

ACCURACY: At least 4/5 (80%) on the test items. When the review items are used for post testing, 4/5 (80%) is also required.

NOTES:
1. **Uses Fingers** Check to see if student adds by using his or her fingers.
2. **Addition Facts** Refer to page 2 of the *Student Record Book* if the student's error does not fit an error pattern. These kinds of random errors indicate a need for basic fact instruction and practice.

REVIEW ITEMS:

a. 368 +486 **854**	**b.** 557 +277 **834**	**c.** 295 +439 **734**
d. 746 +189 **935**	**e.** 453 +269 **722**	

(A-12)
OBJECTIVE: By _____(date)_____ , when given five test items for adding two 3-digit numbers, regrouping ones and tens, __(student's name)__ will compute the numbers with at least 4/5 (80%) accuracy.

	a.	b.	c.	d.	e.
	246 +386 **632**	668 +279 **947**	439 +194 **633**	139 +595 **734**	384 +468 **852**

ERROR ANALYSIS

a.	b.	c.	d.	e.		
51212	81317	51213	61214	71412	**Regrouping 1:** Writes entire sum of each column without regrouping. *	6|8 +7|4 1 3|1 2
522	837	523	624	742	**Regrouping 4:** Writes ones in ones place, but does not regroup tens.	① 57 + 5 5 2
722	1037	723	824	942	**Regrouping 5:** Regroups tens from ones column into hundreds column. †	1 637 +256 9 8 3
5114	8120	5115	6116	7116	**Directional 105:** Adds left to right, writes tens, regroups ones, and writes sum of ones column.	A 3|B 6|8 +7|4 1|1 5

Examiner's Notes:

* If the student is adding from left to right, he or she will have the same answer shown here. Check to see if the student is adding from left to right instead of from right to left.

† These answers show that the student correctly regroups tens from tens column into hundreds column.

Enright Examiner's Page for Skill Test A-12

A class record sheet and individual progress record forms that may be used for discussions with parents are also available.

STRENGTHS OF THE ENRIGHT®

• This instrument promises to be very useful for diagnosticians and classroom teachers. There are few good math tests, and the Enright® provides not only a sequential assessment of computational skills but also an analysis of errors, which leads directly to objectives and curriculum planning.

• Although the test is designed for elementary grade students, it obviously can be used effectively with students with poor computation skills in junior or senior high school.

• The record book for tracking the progress of an individual student over the years is very helpful.

LIMITING FACTORS OF THE ENRIGHT®

• Although the Enright® can be used with first and second graders, it is of limited value until the process of regrouping in addition and subtraction has been introduced.

• The grade-level information provided on each Skill Test should be used only to identify the grade level at which the skill is commonly taught. It is not appropriate to attach grade-level scores to a student's performance.

• The Enright® is a test of computation skills only. Math concepts and applications are not assessed. A complete math curriculum would need to include many other skill areas.

• The Enright® is long and cumbersome to give. The results may not be worth the effort as there are other, informal, ways to assess a student's computational difficulties.

Enright Error Clusters

Error Cluster	Definition	Example
Regrouping	Little understanding of place value	$\begin{array}{r} 68 \\ +74 \\ \hline 1312 \end{array}$
Process Substitution	Process changed in mid problem	$\begin{array}{r} \overset{2\!\!\!/}{\cancel{3}}27 \\ -164 \\ \hline 363 \end{array}$
Omission	Step in process or part of answer left out	$\begin{array}{r} 51 \\ 6\overline{)346} \\ \underline{30} \\ 6 \\ \underline{6} \\ 0 \end{array}$
Directional	Steps performed in wrong direction or order	$\begin{array}{r} 3 \\ 68 \\ +74 \\ \hline 115 \end{array}$
Placement	Correct computation, but numbers written in wrong place	$\begin{array}{r} 6 \\ +7 \\ \hline 31 \end{array}$
Attention to Sign	Wrong operation performed	$\begin{array}{r} 4 \\ +5 \\ \hline 20 \end{array}$
Guessing	Lack of basic understanding; random answers	$\begin{array}{r} 3 \\ 1 \\ +5 \\ \hline 315 \end{array}$

Key Math—Revised (Key Math–R)
A Diagnostic Inventory of Essential Mathematics
Austin J. Connolly
American Guidance Service, Inc., 1988
Publishers' Building, Circle Pines, MN 55014-1796

Purpose	To provide a comprehensive assessment of the understanding and applications of mathematics concepts and skills
Major Areas Tested	Mathematics
Age or Grade Range	Preschool–Grade 9
Usually Given By	Classroom teacher Special education teacher Psychologist Paraprofessional
Type of Test	Standardized Individual Criterion-referenced
Scores Obtained	Grade equivalent Standard Score Age equivalent Stanine Percentile Normal Curve Equivalent
Student Performance Timed?	No
Testing Time	60–75 minutes
Scoring/Interpretation Time	30–45 minutes
Normed On	Nationwide sample of 1,798 students in grades K–9. Sample was standardized for geographic region, grade, sex, socioeconomic status, and race or ethnic group according to U.S. Census Reports of 1983 and 1986.
Alternate Forms Available?	Yes

FORMAT

The Key Math—Revised materials include a test manual, two easel kits for presentation of the test items, and individual test records for recording student responses. Colorful stimulus materials and directions for administering each item are sequentially displayed simultaneously to the examiner and the student in the easel kits. Most subtests require verbal responses to questions asked by the examiner in conjunction with the pictorial materials. The computation subtests assess written math skills. The Key Math—Revised is an individually administered test consisting of 13 subtests grouped into three mto three major areas. The following is a listing of the three areas and their subtests.

The *Basic Concepts Area* assesses the foundation knowledge upon which elementary mathematics is based.

Subtests   Numeration
                      Rational Numbers
                      Geometry

The *Operations Area* assesses basic computation skills.

Subtests   Addition
                      Subtraction
                      Multiplication
                      Division
                      Mental Computation

The *Applications Area* assesses the use of knowledge and computational skills.

Subtests   Measurement
                      Time and Money
                      Estimation
                      Interpreting Data
                      Problem Solving

For all of the subtests of the Key Math—Revised, students complete only those items appropriate to their range of ability. This range extends from a basal level established by three consecutive correct responses to a ceiling level marked by three consecutive errors.

A wide variety of scores are available from the test. For each subtest, raw scores are converted to percentile ranks and standard scores with a mean of 10 and a standard deviation of 3. The subtest scores within an area are combined to yield a grade or age equivalent, a percentile rank, and a standard score (mean of 100, standard deviation of 15) for each of the three areas. These scores are then combined to yield standard scores, percentiles, age and grade equivalents, stanines, and NCEs for the total test. This information can be graphically presented on the Score Profile. Standard errors of the mean are given so that confidence bands at different levels can be displayed. Information is given to allow the examiner to decide whether differences between area scores are statistically different.

STRENGTHS OF THE KEY MATH—R

• The Key Math–R has many excellent features. It is a criterion-referenced instrument based on the developmental sequence of skill acquisition and logical thinking. Extensive clinical training and experience in test administration are not required to administer the Key Math–R, making it a helpful screening and diagnostic tool.

• The Key Math–R is a highly motivating test for students because of the broad range and diversity of item content and the use of colorful and stimulating materials. The new version includes contemporary pictures and questions that hold the interest of a wide range of students—including those having difficulty with math!

• Because of its diagnostic structure and almost total lack of reading and writing requirements, the test is particularly useful for students with a wide range of intellectual abilities and for those who are learning disabled.

• The revised edition of the Key Math includes 13 instead of 14 subtests. A subtest on Rational Numbers was added to expand items from whole numbers and fractions to decimals and percents. Subtests on Estimation, Data Interpretation, and Problem Solving were added. Problem solving incorporates the old Word Problems subtest with additional problems requiring the identification of extraneous and missing information.

• The Key Math–R provides a more detailed analysis of a student's math skills than any test available. By comparing test scores among the three areas, it is possible to identify students who have excellent computation skills but do not understand concepts and, conversely, those who seem to have poor math skills when only their computation skills are weak. In addition to analysis by area, it is possible to determine each student's knowledge within the particular domain of each subtest. For example, in the Interpreting Data subtest, items are divided into Charts and Tables, Graphs, and Probability and Statistics. The test record allows you not only to do item analysis but also to identify strengths and weaknesses in that area based on the performance of the norming population with the same score in that subtest. This procedure, entitled Summary of Domain Performance, leads directly to instructional planning.

• The Key Math–R is well standardized, using a nationwide sample of students stratified according to U.S. Census figures of 1983 and 1986.

• Extensive reliability data is provided in the manual. Studies of split-half, alternate form, and item response reliability are reported, documenting reliability coefficients in the .70s and .80s for the subtests and in the .80s and low .90s for the areas and total test scores. In addition, the standard error of the mean is reported for each score to allow more reliable interpretation of an individual student's profile.

- The Key Math–R was carefully constructed to represent mathematical content in grades K–9 as well as a developmentally sequenced progression of math knowledge and skills. Research studies documenting its validity are found in the manual.
- A Report to Parents form is available describing the test, the student's performance, and ways in which the results may be used to benefit the student.
- A computerized scoring procedure, Key Math–R ASSIST (Automated System for Scoring and Interpreting Standardized Tests) is available from the publishers. ASSIST provides a printout summarizing and interpreting data with suggestions for future instruction.

LIMITING FACTORS OF THE KEYMATH–R

- The Key Math–R is very long to administer, score, and interpret. The materials are motivating, and many students are able to demonstrate great persistence using the colorful picture-materials. Despite the basal-ceiling procedure, the test requires at least two testing sessions. For these reasons, it will probably be used only with students for whom the primary concern is math.
- Some of the subtest changes in Key Math–R eliminated unique tests from the original Key Math. Numerical Reasoning was eliminated; Time and Money were combined into one subtest; and Missing Elements was included in Problem Solving. Due to their importance as skills of daily living, more assessment of the time and money concept is needed than that provided in one subtest. Also, Missing Elements was a unique test of language understanding in math which yielded valuable information about a student; this information is not available in Key Math–R.

A

INDIVIDUAL TEST RECORD

KeyMath
R E V I S E D

a diagnostic
inventory of
essential
mathematics

AUSTIN J.
CONNOLLY

Student's Name _____ Sex: M/F

School _____ Grade _____

Mathematics Teacher _____

Examiner _____ Date _____

	YEAR	MONTH	DAY
Test date			
Birth date			
Chronological age			

DATA FROM OTHER TESTS

Test	Date	Results

SCORE SUMMARY

Derived-score tables are in Appendix E of the *Manual*. For standard scores and scaled scores, indicate your selection of grade or age and fall or spring norms by circling the number of the appropriate table:

Standard Scores and Scaled Scores	Grade	Age
Fall norms (August–January)	Table 1	Table 2
Spring norms (February–July)	Table 3	Table 4

See Table 9 for percentile ranks, stanines, and normal curve equivalents. Obtain grade equivalents and age equivalents from Tables 10 and 11, respectively.

BASIC CONCEPTS AREA

Numeration
Rational Numbers
Geometry

Raw Score / Standard Score / %ile Rank

Grade/Age Equivalent

1.

OPERATIONS

Subtest: Addition, Subtraction, Multiplication, Division, Mental Computation

Raw Score / Scaled Score / %ile Rank

Copy

OPERATIONS AREA
Raw Score / Standard Score / %ile Rank
Grade/Age Equivalent

2.

APPLICATIONS

Subtest: Measurement, Time and Money, Estimation, Interpreting Data, Problem Solving

Raw Score / Scaled Score / %ile Rank

APPLICATIONS AREA
Raw Score / Standard Score / %ile Rank
Grade/Age Equivalent

3.

TOTAL TEST

1. + 2. + 3. = Total Test Raw Score

Standard Score / %ile Rank / NCE (optional) / Stanine (optional) / Grade Equivalent / Age Equivalent

KeyMath Diagnostic Profile

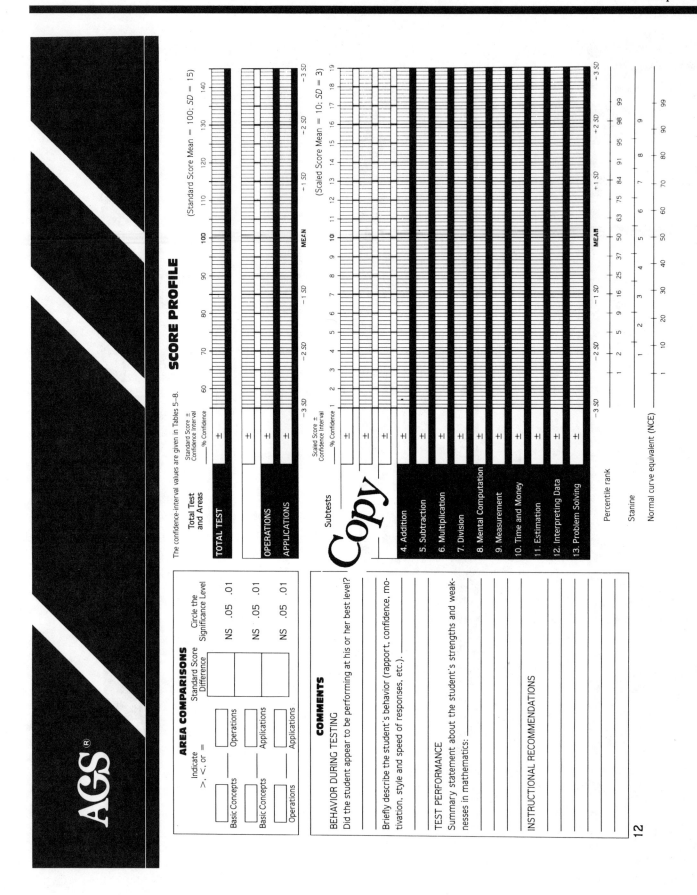

SCORE PROFILE

The confidence-interval values are given in Tables 5–8.

AREA COMPARISONS

Indicate >, <, or =   Standard Score Difference   Circle the Significance Level

Basic Concepts ———— Operations   NS .05 .01
Basic Concepts ———— Applications   NS .05 .01
Operations ———— Applications   NS .05 .01

COMMENTS

BEHAVIOR DURING TESTING
Did the student appear to be performing at his or her best level?

Briefly describe the student's behavior (rapport, confidence, motivation, style and speed of responses, etc.).

TEST PERFORMANCE
Summary statement about the student's strengths and weaknesses in mathematics:

INSTRUCTIONAL RECOMMENDATIONS

12

CHAPTER TWO

Perception, Memory, and Visual Motor Skills

Despite controversy over their concurrent and predictive validity, tests of perception and memory are routinely used in assessing students' academic skills. In some states, the eligibility criteria for entrance into special education programs for students with specific learning disability require the documentation of a processing disorder.

Although their relationship to academic skills may require further definition, perception and memory are clearly processes required for learning. As mentioned in the introduction, if these process tests are used in conjunction with tests that assess basic academic skills, they can provide information that is useful in understanding a student's learning disorder.

This chapter reviews six tests of perception and memory. In alphabetical order, the first two tests assess auditory skills. The Goldman-Fristoe-Woodcock Auditory Skills Battery (GFW Battery) is a comprehensive group of tests to assess auditory processes. The Lindamood Auditory Conceptualization Test (LACT) assesses auditory discrimination and sound sequencing as related to reading and spelling.

Next comes a unique series of tests designed to identify students with dyslexia. The Malcomesius Specific Language Disability Test, the Slingerland Pre-Reading Screening Procedures, and the Slingerland Screening Tests for Identifying Children with Specific Language Disability all include informal measures of auditory and visual memory as well as kinesthetic memory skills. The last test in the section, Visual-Aural Digit Span (VADS) compares a student's visual and auditory memory for digits.

In addition to Chapter Five, Gross and Fine Motor Skills, the reader who is interested in perception and memory is also referred to Chapter 6, General Intelligence Tests and

Developmental Scales, as many of these tests contain subtests in these areas.

This chapter concludes with five tests which assess visual perception and fine motor coordination. The first two are well known design copying tasks—the Bender Visual Motor Gestalt Test (BVMGT) and the Beery-Buktenica Test of Visual-Motor Integration (VMI). The Motor-Free Visual Perception Test (MVPT) assesses various areas of visual perception without the motor component. The Test of Visual Motor Skills (TVMS) and the Test of Visual Perceptual Skills (Non Motor) (TVPS-Non Motor) are two tests by the same author, the first a design copying task and the second a test of visual perception.

Readers who are specifically interested in the area of fine motor assessment are referred to the tests in Chapter Five, Gross and Fine Motor Skills.

Goldman-Fristoe-Woodcock Auditory Skills Test Battery (G-F-W Battery)

Ronald Goldman, Macalyne Fristoe, and Richard W. Woodcock
American Guidance Serivice, Inc., 1974, 1975, 1976
Publishers Bldg., Circle Pines, MN 50014

Purpose	To identify persons who are deficient in auditory skills and to describe their auditory deficiencies
Major Areas Tested	Auditory attention, discrimination, memory and sound-symbol relationships
Age or Grade Range	3 years to adult
Usually Given By	Speech language clinician Audiologist Educational diagnostician Psychologist
Type of Test	Standardized Norm-referenced Individual
Scores Obtained	Standard Percentile Stanine Age equivalent
Student Performance Timed?	Taped administration requires a set pace for student response
Testing Time	3 hours for complete battery
Scoring/Interpretation Time	20–30 minutes
Normed On	5,773 subjects, aged 3–80 years, from California, Florida, Maine, and Minnesota. The majority were in the 9–18-year age range and from Minnesota. The sample was 7.2% black and 4.2% other non-white races. The Reading of Symbols Subtest was standardized on a different nationwide sample of 4,790 subjects as part of the Woodcock Reading Mastery Test
Alternate Forms Available?	No

FORMAT

The Goldman-Fristoe-Woodcock Auditory Skills Test Battery (G-F-W-Battery) is a series of individual tests which assess a broad range of auditory skills representing increasing cognitive complexity.

The materials for the complete battery consist of five easel-kits, each with their own manual and testing materials, individual response forms, battery profile forms, and a technical manual for the entire battery. A high quality tape recorder is required as the test is administered on tape; earphones are recommended, but not required.

The battery is composed of 12 tests in four categories. The battery can be given in its entirety or the examiner may select one or several tests to administer. Training procedures are provided before each test to ensure that the student understands the task and knows the names of the pictures used in the test items. No basal/ceiling procedures are used so all students are administered complete subtests. However, there are provisions for a shortened form for Part 4 described in the manual.

Raw scores for each of the tests are converted to percentiles, standard scores, stanines, and age equivalents. The results of each test can be plotted on the battery profile form to give a graphic summary of a student's performance in auditory skills.

STRENGTHS OF THE G-F-W BATTERY

• The G-F-W Battery assesses a wide range of auditory skills. The tests are well constructed and the taped administration ensures standardized procedures. Scoring procedures are easy and quick to complete.

• Every subtest begins with training procedures to teach students the vocabulary necessary for the visual stimuli. Although these procedures add to the length of the test, they allow a clearer assessment of auditory skills.

• The technical manual documents and discusses the relationship between auditory perception skills and articulation, reading, and spelling.

• The two diagnostic inventories, the Sound Confusion Inventory and the Reading Error Inventory provide good criterion-referenced information on individual students.

LIMITING FACTORS OF THE G-F-W BATTERY

• The technical characteristics of the G-F-W Battery are weak. While extensive research studies are presented in the Technical Manual, several important issues are not considered. For example, test-retest reliability studies were not done by the author, and a subsequent study by Bann and Gengal (1984) suggests that reliability is questionable. The poor reliability limits the usefulness of the battery in individual program planning.

• In addition, no studies of concurrent validity were reported. A study of construct validity which was reported failed to support the G-F-W Battery as a measure to identify mild speech and learning disabilities in the younger students.

• The G-F-W Battery is long to administer in its entirety. Several sessions are needed with younger students not only because of the length of the test, but because of the fatigue which occurs in long tests of auditory processing.

Organization of the G-F-W Battery

Easel	Category	Tests	
1	Auditory Selective Attention (ASA)	Auditory Selective Attention	ASA is an assessment of a student's ability to attend under increasingly difficult listening conditions. The student looks at four pictures and selects the one named by the examiner. The background conditions are quiet, fan-like noise, cafeteria noise, and voice.
2	Diagnostic Auditory Discrimination (DAD)	DAD, Part I	DAD is a diagnostic assessment of speech-sound discrimination. If problems are found, DAD provides a description of sound confusions. The student looks at two pictures and points to one named by the examiner. The pairs of words differ in only one phoneme (yawn/lawn). If the student scores below the 25th percentile on Part I, Parts II and III are given in the same manner.
3	Diagnostic Auditory Discrimination (DAD)	DAD, Parts II and III	
4	Auditory Memory	Recognition Memory Memory for Content Memory for Sequence	Three measures of short-term auditory memory: *Recognition Memory:* student listens to a list of words read by examiner and answers yes if he has heard the word in the list before. *Memory for Content:* student looks at array of 2–12 pictures and points to two not named by the examiner. *Memory for Sequence:* examiner reads sequences of 2–8 words; student arranges pictures in the same order as named by the examiner.
5	Sound Symbol	Sound Mimicry	Student repeats single nonsense words spoken by the examiner.
		Sound Recognition	Student points to picture of word spoken by examiner one sound at a time.
		Sound Analysis	Student repeats part of a word as directed by examiner.
		Sound Blending	Student repeats word pronounced by examiner one sound at a time.
		Sound-Symbol Association	Student "memorizes" syllable names for nonsense forms.
		Reading Symbols	Student reads list of nonsense words.
		Spelling of Sounds	Student spells list of nonsense words.

Lindamood Auditory Conceptualization Test, Revised Edition (LACT)

Charles Lindamood and Patricia Lindamood
DLM Teaching Resources, 1970; revised 1979
One DLM Park, Allen, TX 75002

Purpose	To measure auditory discrimination and the ability to identify the number and order of sounds in a sequence
Major Areas Tested	Auditory perception
Age or Grade Range	Preschool–adult
Usually Given By	Special education teacher Speech/language clinician Remedial reading teacher Paraprofessional
Type of Test	Standardized Individual
Scores Obtained	Grade level
Student Performance Timed?	No
Testing Time	10–15 minutes
Scoring/Interpretation Time	10–15 minutes
Normed On	660 students in grades K–12 from a range of socioeconomic and ethnic backgrounds in a California school district; subsequently, 52 K–12 students from another California school district were added
Alternate Forms Available?	Yes

FORMAT

The materials for administering the Lindamood Auditory Conceptualization Test (LACT) include a manual, two examiner's cue sheets (one in Spanish), individual record sheets, and a set of 18 half-inch colored cubes (three each of red, yellow, blue, green, white, and black). The manual contains directions for administration and scoring, information on test construction, and suggestions for interpreting results. A tape is provided for the examiner to use as a guide for the pronunciation of individual sounds and syllable patterns.

The LACT test consists of four parts:

1. *The Precheck*. This part contains five items designed to determine whether the student can demonstrate knowledge of the following concepts: same/different, numbers to 4, left-to-right order, and first/last.

2. *Category I, Part A*. The student must identify the number of isolated sounds heard from a list of 10 items, and decide whether they are the same or different.

3. *Category I, Part B*. The student is given six items and asked to identify not only the number of isolated sounds heard and their sameness or difference, but also their order.

4. *Category II*. From a list of 12 items, the student must determine the number of sounds in a syllable and changes in the sound pattern when sounds are added, omitted, substituted, shifted, or repeated.

The Precheck is given to determine that the student understands the basic concepts necessary to obtain a valid test score. If knowledge of the Precheck concepts is not demonstrated, the test is discontinued. Categories I and II are each preceded by demonstration procedures.

In the LACT, the student manipulates colored blocks to indicate understanding of sound patterns. Each block represents a sound. There is no constant relationship between a specific color and a specific sound, so the student may select any colors. Different sounds within a pattern are represented by different colors.

As the examiner pronounces each sound pattern, the student may use visual cues (the examiner's lip movements) to aid discrimination; the examiner notes this diagnostic information. Patterns may not be repeated unless an environmental noise interferes with the student's hearing. Testing is discontinued after five consecutive errors in Category I. In Category II, the student is given an opportunity to do another similar pattern after an error. Testing is discontinued after five errors in Category II.

Points are given for each correct block pattern, and on that basis a raw score is obtained. The raw score is converted to a weighted score (one point for each correct response in Category I, Part A; three in Category I, Part B; and six in Category II). A single weighted score is obtained for the total tests; no subtest scores are provided. The examiner then compares the weighted score with a table that provides recommended minimum scores for each grade level. These minimum scores should be considered predictive of success in reading or spelling at or above that grade level.

Two equivalent forms, A and B, are available for reevaluation purposes.

STRENGTHS OF THE LACT

• The LACT provides a means of evaluating auditory perception skills related to reading and spelling without using written symbols. The student need not have knowledge of sound-symbol associations to demonstrate auditory perception skills. This makes the LACT a valuable tool for assessing auditory perception in beginning or remedial readers.

LAC Test Format

Category	Examiner Pronounces	Student's Block Pattern
Category I, Part A	Three same sounds (/b/, /b/, /b/)	Three same colors
	Two different sounds (/t/, /m/)	Two different colors
Category I, Part B	Two same sounds followed by one different sound (/s/, /s/, /p/)	Two same colors followed by one different color
Category II	Two different sounds in a syllable (/al/)	Two different colors
	New sound added at beginning of a syllable (/pal/)	New color added at beginning
	Change in last sound of a syllable (/pab/)	Change in last color

Many tests are available for assessing auditory discrimination of whole words. (See the Wepman Auditory Discrimination Test and the Goldman-Fristoe-Woodcock Test of Auditory Discrimination.) Other tests assess sound blending or auditory synthesis. (See the Illinois Test of Psycholinguistic Abilities.) The LACT, however, assesses analysis of the number and order of sounds as well as discrimination. These skills are crucial in reading and spelling.

• The Precheck section of the LACT is excellent. It allows the examiner to assess quickly the student's knowledge of the basic concepts necessary to take the test. Once it is determined that the student understands these basic concepts, errors on the test can more accurately be related to skill deficiencies in auditory perception.

• The manual provides an excellent presentation of how auditory perception, reading, and spelling relate to each other. Teachers and clinicians will find the discussion of follow-up remediation techniques and the authors' interpretation of test performances helpful.

• The LACT can be used with a wide age range of students. The alternate test forms make it a usable tool for evaluating progress in a remediation program.

• A study of test-retest reliability using alternate forms of the LACT demonstrated good reliability. The data was not presented by age level, which would have been more helpful.

• The Spanish Cue Sheet is sensitive to the language customs of Spanish-speaking children and adults. Both formal and informal verb types are presented.

LIMITING FACTORS OF THE LACT

• The LACT is not an easy test to administer, and extensive practice is recommended before using it with students suspected of auditory disorders. Although the administration manual is clearly written, the process of using colored blocks to illustrate sound patterns is a difficult one. Category II, in particular, requires extensive verbal explanation, and many students become confused if the examiner is not quite skilled in test administration. The order of items in Category II is particularly difficult to administer.

• Students with intellectual deficits or delays in concept development have difficulty learning the relationship between the colors and the sounds. They may continue to believe that there is a direct relationship between color and sound, such as red always equals /p/. This confusion is seen in such statements as, "There aren't enough colors." Such students may actually be able to spell the syllables in Category II (illustrating good auditory analysis) without being able to do the block patterns.

• The LACT authors have chosen to allow students to use visual cues (lip movements) to aid their auditory discrimination. It is true that visual cues are usually avail-

able in natural conversations. However, it is important for the examiner to note carefully whether or not the student uses visual cues. If the student does not, teaching him or her to do so is a good first step in remediation. If they are used extensively, it is important for the teacher to realize that, in activities where the student does not have direct contact with the speaker, auditory perception may be quite poor.

• The score obtained on the LACT is difficult to interpret. For example, suppose a third-grade student obtains a total test score of 60. According to the minimum scores table in the manual, a score of 61 is the minimum score predicting high probability of successful reading and spelling performance in high-first-grade material. Does this mean that the third-grade student's auditory perception skills are at a first-grade level? Or that the student should be instructed in first-grade material? The interpretation becomes even more confusing with an older student. A score of 93 is the minimal score for predicting reading and spelling success for the second half of fifth grade, but 99 is the minimum recommended score for 7th grade through adult. The lack of clarity in test score interpretation suggests that the LACT is better used as an informal test—a task-analysis approach to auditory perception, rather than a standardized test yielding grade-level scores.

• Throughout the manual, reading and spelling are treated as identical tasks requiring the same auditory perception skills. Validity studies should be done to separate these two processes. Although the authors feel that the reading method the student has been taught does not affect performance on the LACT, this seems questionable. Students with phonics training have clearly had more practice with auditory analysis than have sight-word readers.

• All of the validity studies of the LACT are based on comparisons with the WRAT, 1978 edition, not the revised edition (WRAT-R), which has substantially different norms.

• The standardization sample of the LACT is not well described and was drawn from a very limited geographic region. Examiners must be cautious about the generalizability of test results.

• The LACT can be given to Spanish-speaking students by using the examiner's cue sheet in Spanish. The minimal grade scores recommended are the same for both English and Spanish students. It is not clear whether the Spanish form of the LACT has been tested for reliability or validity.

Malcomesius Specific Language Disability Test (MSLDT)

Neva Malcomesius
Educators Publishing Service, Inc., 1968
75 Moulton St., Cambridge, MA 02238-9101

Purpose	To identify students with a specific language disability
Major Areas Tested	Auditory, visual, and kinesthetic skills related to reading, writing, and spelling
Age or Grade Range	Grades 6–8
Usually Given By	Classroom teacher Special education teacher
Type of Test	Informal Group
Scores Obtained	None (guidelines for evaluating test performance)
Student Performance Timed?	Yes
Testing Time	1 1/2 hours
Scoring/Interpretation Time	20–30 minutes
Normed On	Not normed
Alternate Forms Available?	No

FORMAT

The materials for the Malcomesius Specific Language Disability Test (MSLDT) consist of a teacher's manual, test booklets for the students, and a set of cards and charts used in administering the test. As in the Slingerland Tests, the MSLDT is not a test of oral language but rather a test of visual, auditory, and kinesthetic skills related to reading, spelling, and writing.

Because the Malcomesius Test was designed as an upward extension of the Slingerland Tests (junior high school level), the 10 subtests are almost identical to those in the Slingerland Tests, Forms A to D. The tests are also designed for group administration. The table below compares the Malcomesius subtests to those of the Slingerland. It is interesting that, in the Spelling—Auditory to Motor subtest, the focus is on sound-symbol association rather than correct spelling. Thus the following words would be considered correct: *dubious-doobious; exceed-excead.*

The MSLDT does not include any of the individual auditory tests that are found in the lower levels of the Slingerland Tests.

STRENGTHS OF THE MALCOMESIUS TEST

• As in the Slingerland Tests, the Malcomesius Test battery includes a series of school-related tests to aid the classroom teacher in identifying students with specific language disability. There are few tests designed for adolescents, and the Malcomesius Test provides a means of assessing the auditory, visual, and kinesthetic skills of this age group on tasks related to classroom performance.

LIMITING FACTORS OF THE MALCOMESIUS TEST

• The MSLDT is subject to the same limiting factor as the Slingerland Tests; the most serious of these is a lack of norms.

• No reliability or validity data are reported.

• The author seems to assume that the only difference between beginning readers and more mature readers is the length of the words they can process and the speed with which they can process them. This is shown by the fact that the items for sixth, seventh, and eighth graders are all the same; only time limits differentiate them. It may well be that

Comparison of the Malcomesius and Slingerland Subtests

Malcomesius Subtest	Description	Corresponding Slingerland Subtest
1. Paragraph Copying	Requires copying paragraphs from a wall chart	1
2. Near-Point Copying	Requires copying a list of words	2
3. Visual Discrimination	Requires matching visually similar words (*innuendo, inunendo, innuendo, inuennbo, innuenbo*)	4
4. Visual Perception and Recall	Requires identifying correct words and number sequences presented visually (*barbraian, barbarian, bardarian, darbraian*)	3
5. Visual Kinesthetic Recall	Requires writing phrases after a visual presentation (*Keep quite quiet.*)	5
6. Auditory Discrimination	Requires discrimination of words that sound very much alike (*trick, trek*)	None
7. Auditory Kinesthetic Memory	Requires writing phrases from dictation (*parents of the girl*)	6
8. Auditory-Visual Integration	Requires listening to a word or sequence of numbers and selecting it from four similar choices presented visually (*9,586; 6,589; 9,856; 9,589*)	8
9. Comprehension	Requires listening to a paragraph and writing it	None
10. Spelling—Auditory to Motor	Requires writing a list of 20 dictated words with focus on sound-symbol association, *not* correct spelling (*dubious-doobious, exceed-excead*)	None

an entirely different set of tasks should be used to identify these older disabled readers, rather than those used with the elementary students assessed by the Slingerland Tests.

• Subtests 9 and 10 are particularly poorly labeled. Subtest 9 is much more a measure of written language skills and sequential memory than it is of comprehension, and subtest 10 cannot be called spelling when the scoring directions specifically say, "Do not count spelling."

• The teacher's manual includes a page of "General Directions for Evaluating the Tests." This page contains a number of statements about specific language disability that are presented as fact when they really represent the author's opinion. The person using the Malcomesius Test needs to be alert to these statements and to avoid conclusions about a student's learning disability based on performance on this test alone.

Slingerland Pre-Reading Screening Procedures

Beth H. Slingerland
Educators Publishing Service, Inc., 1968; revised 1976, 1977
75 Moulton St., Cambridge, MA 02238-9101

Purpose	To identify bright children with difficulties in the auditory, visual, and kinesthetic modalities that may indicate specific language disability
Major Areas Tested	Auditory, visual, and kinesthetic skills related to beginning reading
Age or Grade Range	Grades K–1
Usually Given By	Classroom teacher Special education teacher Psychologist Adminstrator
Type of Test	Informal Group
Scores Obtained	Rating scale (guidelines for evaluating test performance)
Student Performance Timed?	Yes
Testing Time	20–25 minutes each for three test sessions
Scoring/Interpretation Time	15–20 minutes
Normed On	Not normed
Alternate Forms Available?	No

FORMAT

The materials for the Slingerland Pre-Reading Screening Procedures consist of student booklets, cards and charts for three subtests, and a teacher's manual. Practice pages and markers are also provided. The tests are designed to be used with groups of kindergarten children who have not yet been introduced to formal reading. The recommended group size is 15 children. At least one monitor is needed to help the children locate the right page and to prohibit them from copying each other's work. The students use pencils without erasers and are taught to bracket their errors so that self-corrections can be noted.

The Slingerland Pre-Reading Screening Procedures contain 12 subtests to be given to the group and a set of individual auditory tests. The 12 subtests are:

1. *Visual Perception* requires matching single-letter and two-letter combinations.

2. *Visual Perception* requires visual matching of three-letter combinations.

3. *Visual Perception and Memory* requires visual memory of geometric and letter forms.

4. *Near-Point Copying* requires copying geometric and letter forms. Space is provided on both sides of the geometric and letter forms for left-handed and right-handed students.

5. *Auditory-Visual Perception* requires listening to a spoken direction and marking the appropriate picture. In Figure 67 the examiner says, "Mark the picture of the bird flying to its nest."

6. *Letter Recognition* requires marking the visual symbol of the letter name pronounced by the examiner. In Figure 68 the examiner says, "Mark the *f*."

7. *Visual-Kinesthetic Memory* requires visual perception and memory of geometric forms. The student draws the forms from memory after being shown a model.

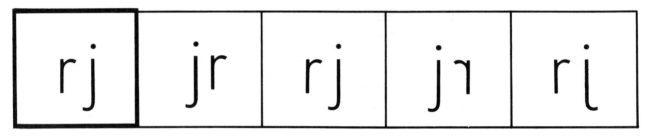

Slingerland Pre-Reading Screening Procedures, Procedure 1, Visual Perception

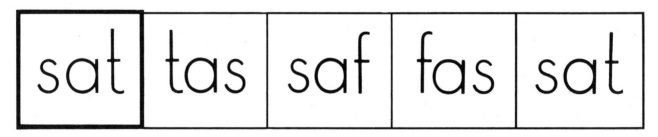

Slingerland Pre-Reading Screening Procedures, Procedure 2, Visual Perception

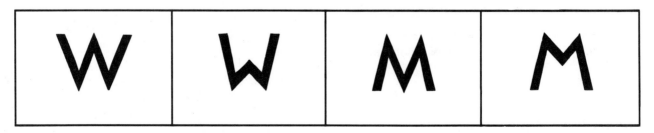

Slingerland Pre-Reading Screening Procedures, Procedure 3, Visual Perception and Memory

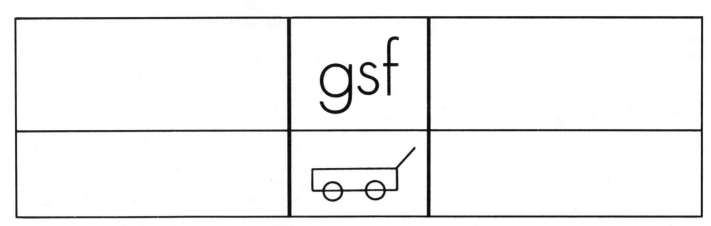

Slingerland Pre-Reading Screening Procedures, Procedure 4, Near-Point Copying

Slingerland Pre-Reading Screening Procedures, Procedure 5, Auditory-Visual Perception

**Slingerland Pre-Reading Screening
Procedures, Procedure 6, Letter Recognition**

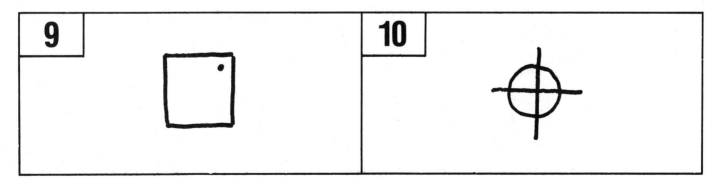

Slingerland Pre-Reading Screening Procedures, Procedure 7, Visual-Kinesthetic Memory

8. *Auditory Perception with Comprehension* requires listening to a story and indicating comprehension by marking a picture. For instance, for the illustrations shown here, the examiner would tell the following story: *Jane said to her little sister, "I wish you would go to the big table and get the little box for me. Something for you is in the little box." Mark the picture that shows where Jane wanted her sister to go.*

9. *Far-Point Copying* requires copying geometric and letter forms from a wall chart.

10. *Auditory Discrimination* requires listening to sets of three words and indicating if the words are the same or different. In Figure 72 the examiner says, "Slap, slap, slab." The student marks XX in the space between the two balloons, because the three words do not sound the same. When the words all sound the same, the student marks / / in the space.

11. *Auditory-Visual-Kinesthetic Integration* requires listening to the name of a letter, selecting it from three printed letters, and copying it. In Figure 73 the examiner says, "Copy the letter *B* in the last box in the row."

12. *Auditory-Visual Association* requires identifying pictures that begin with a specific sound pronounced by the examiner. For instance: "You see a book, a pencil, and a

table. Mark the picture of the one that begins with the sound *t*."

The individual auditory tests include the following:

1. *Echolalia* requires repeating a word several times.

2. *Reproducing a Story* requires listening to and retelling a story.

The Slingerland Pre-Reading Screening Procedures are not normed for age or grade-level scores. However, a five-point rating scale (high, high-medium, medium, low-medium, and low) for evaluating student performance is given, as well as specific guidelines for scoring the tests. Alternate forms for test-retest purposes are not available.

STRENGTHS OF THE SLINGERLAND PRE-READING SCREENING PROCEDURES

• The Slingerland Pre-Reading Screening Procedures are a well-planned battery of readiness tests. They have been carefully designed to include tasks that assess a student's skills in all modalities: auditory, visual, and kinesthetic, alone and in combination. The teacher's manual is well organized, and the directions are very clear. The idea of using practice pages to train the students in the proper procedures is excellent. One part of the practice pages is a "This Is Me" picture, which yields a great deal of informa-

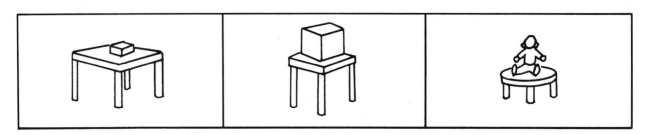

Slingerland Pre-Reading Screening Procedures, Procedure 8, Auditory Perception with Comprehension

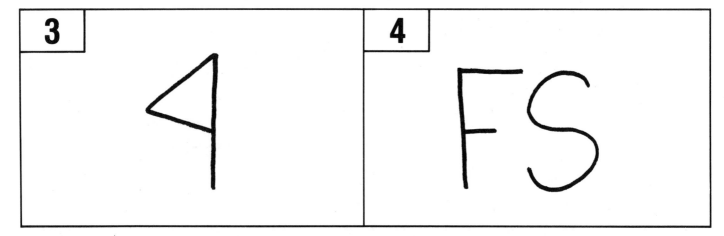

Slingerland Pre-Reading Screening Procedures, Procedure 9, Far-Point Copying

tion about the student's readiness skills. Although the subtests are timed, this is primarily to keep the group testing moving along and does not put serious constraints on the students. The teacher's manual gives excellent discussions of the subtests and the skills being measured by each. The Slingerland Pre-Reading Screening Procedures are an excellent contribution to the field when used as a group screening measure (1) to give the first-grade teacher extensive information on the modality strengths and weaknesses of a class of beginning readers and (2) to identify children who may need further individual testing.

LIMITING FACTORS OF THE SLINGERLAND PRE-READING SCREENING PROCEDURES

• The Slingerland Pre-Reading Screening Procedures must be considered informal tests at this time. No age or grade norms are provided. The five-point rating scale is

based on the test results of several hundred children just entering first grade in school districts throughout the United States, but no further information about the sample is given.

• The Slingerland Pre-Reading Screening Procedures were designed to identify children who would enter first grade using the Slingerland adaptation of Orton-Gillingham (Gillingham and Stillman, 1960) techniques as a curriculum. The teacher's manual interprets test performance from the Orton-Gillingham point of view. This is not a serious problem in using the tests, but the teacher should be aware that a statement such as "The brighter the child, the more opportunities there have been for language learning" is an opinion, not a statement of fact.

• The author suggests that the Slingerland Pre-Reading Screening Procedures be used with the Pintner-Cunningham Primary Test of general intelligence (1966). This suggestion points out the need to be cautious about diagnosing any

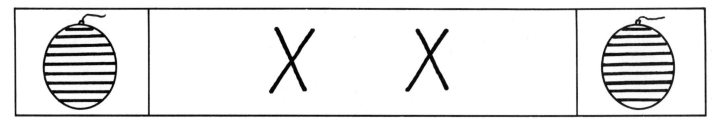

Slingerland Pre-Reading Screening Procedures, Procedure 10, Auditory Discrimination

Slingerland Pre-Reading Screening Procedures, Procedure 11, Auditory-Visual-Kinesthetic Integration

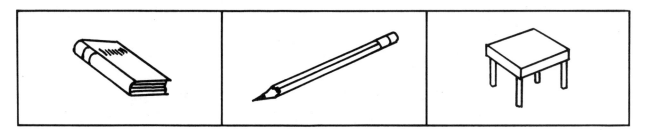

Slingerland Pre-Reading Screening Procedures, Procedure 12, Auditory-Visual Association

child's learning disabilities on the basis of one test.

• Recent factor analytic studies of the Slingerland Pre-Reading Screening Procedures identified four factors— visual motor processing (subtests 4,7,9), prereading (subtests 1 and 2), and language processing (subtests 5 and 8). The prereading factor was the best predictor of school success in first and second grades, with visual processing the next strongest. The fact that these findings were true of both reading and math suggests that the Slingerland Pre-Reading Screening Procedures assess a general readiness factor rather than skills specific to reading.

• The same studies suggest that the procedures over-identify at-risk kindergarten children, especially those from lower socioeconomic backgrounds.

Slingerland Screening Tests for Identifying Children with Specific Language Disability (SST)

Beth Slingerland
Educators Publishing Serivce, Inc., Forms A, B, C, 1962; revised 1970; Form D, 1974
75 Moulton St., Cambridge, MA 02238-9101

Purpose	To identify students with a specific language disability or inadequate perceptual-motor skills, and children who compensate for inadequate perceptual-motor skills
Major Areas Tested	Visual, auditory, and kinesthetic skills related to reading and spelling
Age or Grade Range	6–12 years
Usually Given By	Classroom teacher Special education teacher Psychologist Administrator
Type of Test	Informal Group
Scores Obtained	None (guidelines for evaluating test performance)
Student Performance Timed?	Yes
Testing Time	1–1 1/2 hours
Scoring/Interpretation Time	30–40 minutes
Normed On	Not normed
Alternate Forms Available?	No

FORMAT

The Slingerland Screening Tests for Identifying Children with Specific Language Disability (SST) is a series of pencil-and-paper tests published in five forms for various grade levels.

Form	Grade Level
Pre-Reading	End of kindergarten to beginning of first grade
A	End of first grade to beginnign of second grade
B	End of second grade to beginning of third grade
C	End of third grade to beginning of fourth grade
D	Fifth and sixth grades

Despite the name, the SST is not language tests. They do not assess the typical language skills such as syntax, vocabulary, and language comprehension. Rather, they test auditory, visual, and kinesthetic abilities related to reading, writing, and spelling. Specific language disability (SLD) is another term for developmental dyslexia.

The materials for each form include the students' booklets, in which they write their answers, and a set of cards and charts for the examiner. Although the Slingerland Tests are not normed and therefore provide no age- or grade-level scores, standardized administration procedures are described in the examiner's manuals. One manual is provided for the Pre-Reading Test; a second includes the instructions for Forms A, B, and C; and a third is available for Form D. Directions for scoring and guidelines for evaluating test performance are also included in the manuals.

The Slingerland Tests (and the teaching method) are based on Orton-Gillingham techniques for teaching reading and spelling through a multisensory approach. The linkages among auditory, visual, and kinesthetic modalities are the essence of the model. The tests are designed to assess these linkages.

Forms A, B, C, and D of the Slingerland Tests include the same eight group subtests. Form D includes an additional group subtest. Forms A, B, C, and D also include a series of audityry subtests to be given individually at the conclusion of the group subtest. The eight basic subtests and the individual auditory tests are described in the table shown here. Although the number and difficulty of the items within each subtest vary in each form, the skill being measured remains the same. This format allows assessment of student progress on the same series of tasks in grades 1–6.

Because of the different format, the Slingerland Pre-Reading Screening Procedures are reviewed separately.

Slingerland Subtests

Subtest	Description	Modality	Relationship to Classroom Skills
1. Far-Point Copying	Student copies paragraph from a chart on the wall	Visual, kinesthetic	Assesses visual-motor skills related to handwriting
2. Near-Point Copying	Student copies single words printed at top of page on lines at bottom	Visual, kinesthetic	Assesses visual-motor skills related to handwriting
3. Visual Perception Memory	Student is shown a word card for 10 seconds and then asked to find the word in a group of four visually similar words (*mnoey, mouey, woney, money*)	Visual	Assesses visual memory skills related to reading and spelling
4. Visual Discrimination	Student is asked to match words containing many easily confused letters (*lady, daly, laby, baby, lady*)	Visual	Assesses basic visual discrimination without memory component or written response
5. Visual Kinesthetic Memory	Student is shown word or design card for 10 seconds and then asked to write or draw the word or design	Visual, kinesthetic	Assesses the combination of visual memory and written response, which is necessary for written spelling
6. Auditory Kinesthetic Memory	Examiner dictates sequences of letters, numbers, and words, and then the student writes what the examiner dictated	Auditory, visual, kinesthetic	Combines auditory perception and memory with written response, skills necessary for dictation lessons
7. Initial and Final Sounds (Level D includes vowel sounds)	Examiner pronounces a word, and the student writes the initial or final sound (*shimmer—sh; clasp—p*)	Auditory, visual, kinesthetic	Assesses auditory discrimination and sequencing related to basic phonics with a written response
8. Auditory-Visual Integration	Examiner pronounces a word, and the student selects it from a group of four visually similar words (*baddy, babby, dabby, daddy*)	Auditory, visual	Assesses visual discrimination related to word recognition
9. Following Directions (Form D only)	Examiner gives a series of directions requiring a written response (*Write the alphabet. Do not use capital letters. Put a comma after each letter.*)	Auditory, kinesthetic	Assesses auditory memory and attention with a written response
Individual Auditory Tests (Forms A, B, C, and D)			
Echolalia	Examiner pronounces a word or phrase and the student repeats it four or five times aloud (*animal-animal-animal-animal*)	Auditory, kinesthetic	Assesses auditory-kinesthetic confusion related to pronunciation
Word Finding	Examiner reads a sentence with a missing word, and the student fills in the missing word (*A long yellow fruit is called a _____ .*)	Auditory	Assesses comprehension and the ability to produce a specific word on demand; word-finding problems often identify children with specific language disability
Story Telling	Examiner reads a story aloud, and the student retells it	Auditory	Assesses auditory memory and verbal expression of content material

STRENGTHS OF THE SLINGERLAND TESTS

• Beth Slingerland, the author of the tests, is an experienced teacher of students with specific language disabilities. She developed the tests for use in publis schools, and they reflect her knowledge of teaching. The subtests measure skills that are directly related to classroom performance.

• Students with specific language disabilities have deficits in auditory, visual, and kinesthetic skills and the intergration of these three systems, or modalities. Through careful analysis of a student's errors on the Slingerland Tests, a teacher can determine which modalities are the weakest and plan a remedial program accordingly. In contrast to the Illinois Test of Psycholinguistic Abilities, the Slingerland subtests measure the modalities with regular academic tasks, which makes them much more usable for the classroom teacher.

• The Slingerland Tests were designed as screening instruments. They can be administered by classroom teachers to total classroom groups. They are an economical way to identify students with difficulties in visual, auditory, or kinesthetic skills.

• As in all test batteries, some subtests are better than others. The three subtests measuring visual processing are particularly useful in determining the level of a visual perception problem. For example, the following performance on these three tests is very typical of students who have difficulty reading:

Visual Perception Memory (test 3): 80 percent correct
Visual Discrimination (test 4): 100 percent correct
Visual Kinesthetic Memory (test 5): 50 percent correct

These scores are interpreted to mean that, as the visual process becomes more complex, and when memory and a written response are required, the student's performance is poorer. In contrast is this typical performance of another student with reading difficulty:

Visual Perception Memory (test 3): 50 percent correct
Visual Discrimination (test 4): 70 percent correct
Visual Kinesthetic Memory (test 5): 95 percent correct

In this case, the kinesthetic (written) responses seem to increase the efficiency of the visual process.

LIMITING FACTORS OF THE SLINGERLAND TESTS

• At the present time, the Slingerland Tests must be viewed as informal tests. Although very specific directions for administration are given and complex scoring procedures are presented, no norms are provided. Thus, judgments about an individual student's performance are very subjective, depending on the sophistication of the examiner. The author stresses the need to develop local norms, which is probably true but not very realistic.

• One advantage of the Slingerland Tests is the fact that they use skills related to classroom tasks. But precisely because they measure classroom tasks, the tests are long and difficult for many students to take. Several subtests require extensive writing, and many students become discouraged. Because the items were selected to produce the visual and auditory sequencing and discrimination errors characteristic of studetns with specific language disability, many students become frustrated and require a great deal of emotional support to complete the test.

• There seems to be no rationale for the number or order of items within a subtest. There is no systematic increase in the difficulty of items, other than increasing vocabulary difficulty from Form A through Form D.

• Administration procedures are complex and difficult. Scoring procedures are long and also difficult, especially in view of the fact that the tests are not normed. The tests require considerable study before they can be used successfully.

• The terminology of the Slingerland Tests is very confusing. The term *specific language disability* requires explanation because it is often confused with oral language problems of other types. The titles of the subtests have no meaning to teachers or parents who have not seen the subtest items. School districts jthat choose to use this test need to devise a system of scoring, reporting scores, and describing results that are easily understood.

• Of great concern is the fact that the Slingerland Tests are frequently used as the only instrument to diagnose a student as having specific language disability. Such a practice is highly questionable for any single test and particularly for a nonstandardized, nonnormed instrument.

• A technical manual is now available that includes reliability and validity data on the SST (Forms A, B, C, D). Statistics on test-retest and interrater reliability indicate that reliability is better for Form C that for Forms A or B. The reliability data for individual subtests is below acceptable limits, while total test scores were acceptable. This would indicate that when reliable data for identification purposes is needed, the test should be given in its entirety.

• The studies of concurrent validity, reported in the technical manual, have different results depending upon ages of the students and form of the SST. When compared with Comprehensive Tests of Basic Skills (CTBS), Forms B and D appear to have grteater validity than A and C.

• Although the SST is intended to identify students with specific language disability or developmental dyslexia, there is no evidence that they are more precise in the identification of this type of learning problem than they are in identifying students with other types of specific learning disabilities.

The Visual Aural Digit Span Test (VADS)

Elizabeth M. Koppitz
Grune & Stratton, Inc., 1977
Orlando, FL 32887

Purpose	To provide a clinical tool to help diagnose specific learning problems in school children; and as a quick screening test for school beginners to identify learning problems
Major Areas Tested	Intersensory integration, sequences, and short term memory
Age or Grade Range	5 1/2–12 years
Usually Given By	Special education teacher School psychologist Educational diagnostician
Type of Test	Individual Standardized Norm-referenced
Scores Obtained	Age equivalent Percentile Grade equivalent
Student Performance Timed?	Yes
Testing Time	15–20 minutes
Scoring/Interpretation Time	15–20 minutes
Normed On	810 normal public school students; K–6th grades. Sample included a cross section of socioeconomic levels in urban and rural areas. All geographical sections of the country were included, but the majority were from New York State. The sample was balanced for age, sex, and ethnicity; no physically or mentally handicapped children were included
Alternate Forms Available?	No

FORMAT

The Visual Aural Digit Span Test (VADS) is a brief individual test which assesses sequencing and memory in a variety of modalities.

The materials needed to administer a VADS test include a set of 26 VADS stimulus cards, a VADS test scoring sheet, a pencil, and a watch. The rationale, administration and scoring procedures, norms tables, discussion of score patterns, and technical data on the test are contained in a book, *The Visual Aural Digit Span Test* (Koppitz, 1977).

The VADS consists of four subtests, each of which presents sequences of numbers for the student to recall. The mode of presentation and response varies with each subtest. The four subtests are:

I. *Aural-Oral (A-O)*. The student listens to sequences of digits pronounced by the examiner and repeats them back in correct order. This is the familiar digit span test found in several other test batteries. It requires the processing of auditory sequential material. It is a test of rote auditory memory.

II. *Visual-Oral (V-O)*. The student reads the sequences of digits and repeats them orally in the correct order. The subtest requires visual-oral integration and recall. This process is similar to that expected in reading.

III. *Aural-Written (A-W)*. In this subtest, the student listens to the digit series and responds in writing. The subtest measures auditory-visual integration with a written response. This is similar to the process required for spelling or dictation.

IV. *Visual-Written (V-W)*. This subtest requires the student to read the series of digits and write them from memory. It assesses intrasensory integration, visual input, and writing output. Similar skills are required when a student is asked to write material from memory.

The four subtests are given individually in one sitting in the order listed above. Entry points and ceiling procedures are described in Koppitz's book. In subtests I and III the examiner pronounces the digits at the rate of one per second. In subtests II and IV the student reads the digit sequences aloud and may study them for 10 seconds before the card is taken away. For subtests III and IV the student's responses are written on a single unlined piece of paper.

Each subtest is scored in the same way. The raw score is the number of digits in the longest series the student recalled correctly. Therefore the highest score obtainable on each subtest is 7.

Eleven scores are obtained from the VADS test—four for the subtests plus these seven combination scores:

Aural Input: (A-O) + (A-W)
Visual Input: (V-O) + (V-W)
Oral Expression: (A-O) + (V-O)
Written Expression: (A-W) + (V-W)
Intrasensory Integration: (A-O) + (V-W)

Intersensory Integration: (V-O) + (A-W)
Total VADS: (A-O) + (V-O) + (A-W) + (V-W)

Means and standard deviations for subtest scores are given for each age group. Six-month intervals are reported below seven years and yearly intervals thereafter. Percentile scores are presented for individual subtests and composites by age.

STRENGTHS OF THE VADS

• The VADS test is quick to administer and score. There are few materials, and the test is inexpensive. The rationale for the test is based on the experienced author's observation that students who do poorly in overcoming their learning problems have serious deficits in intersensory integration, sequencing, and recall. Digits were selected rather than letters to eliminate the anxiety produced by letter forms in poor readers. The rationale of the test is clearly explained in Koppitz's book.

• The administration procedures are clearly written and easy to follow. The author has provided good procedures for ensuring that the students can read and write the numbers on the subtest where those skills are required.

• Extensive information is provided to aid the examiner in making clinical observations of each student's performance. Observing student strategies and error patterns adds to the clinical diagnostic value of the test. Analysis of the ways the student writes his numerals on the unlined page can also be helpful. The techniques are similar to those recommended for users of the Bender Developmental Visual Gestalt Test by the same author.

LIMITING FACTORS OF THE VADS

• The VADS measures a very narrow range of behavior, short term recall of digits. Examiners should be cautious about generalizing the information into broad areas of memory. Certainly the small size and unscientific composition of the sample makes it clear that the VADS should be used as a screening device, rather than as a diagnostic tool.

• The selection of digits rather than alphabet letters for the test may have been a wise decision. However, one must be cautious about generalizing from recall of digits to recall of letters. The integration and recall processes may be quite different.

• The Koppitz book is interesting reading, providing extensive information on the test and its interpretation. However, a separate examiners manual with administration and scoring procedures and norms would facilitate administration greatly.

• The technical inadequacies of the VADS severely limit its usefulness. The one reported reliability study was poorly designed. While several studies of validity are reported, they are methodologically weak (Webster and Whitley, 1986).

There is no data presented which supports the VADS predictive validity or its concurrent validity with actual school performance. Examiners must consider the VADS a rough screening test. It does not have the technical merit to make differential diagnosis or to identify potential learning disabilities.

134   Chapter Two

The Bender Visual Motor Gestalt Test (BVMGT)

Lauretta Bender
The American Orthopsychiatric Association, Inc., 1946; Koppitz Developmental Scoring System, 1963, revised 1975; Pascal and Suttell Scoring System, 1951
49 Sheridan Ave., Albany, NY 12210

Purpose	To assess level of maturity in visual-motor perception and to detect emotional disturbances
Major Areas Tested	Visual-motor integration and emotional adjustment
Age or Grade Range	5–11 years (Koppitz Developmental Scoring System) 15–50 years (Pascal and Suttell Scoring System)
Usually Given By	Psychologist Special education teacher
Type of Test	Standardized Individual Group
Scores Obtained	Age level Percentile
Student Performance Timed?	No
Testing Time	10 minutes (individual administration) 15–25 minutes (group administration)
Scoring/Interpretation Time	10–20 minutes
Normed On	1,100 students from the Midwest and East, including public school children in rural, small town, suburban, and urban areas; 1974 sample included Blacks, Orientals, Mexican-Americans, and Puerto Ricans (norms refer to Koppitz standardization)
Alternate Forms Available?	No

FORMAT

The Bender Visual Motor Gestalt Test (Bender) is a series of nine abstract designs to be copied in pencil by the student. The figures illustrate certain principles of Gestalt psychology. The designs, printed on four-inch by six-inch cards, are presented one at a time. The student copies each design, with the sample before him or her. When the student finishes drawing a figure, the card is removed and the next card is placed at the top of the paper. A modification of the test requires the student to recall the designs from memory after initial performance.

The Bender is usually administered individually but can be given to a group of students. As a group test, different techniques have been devised for administration: projecting the designs onto a screen or wall, using enlarged stimulus cards, using individual decks of cards for each student, or using special copying booklets.

The standard individual administration of the Bender permits the student to erase and rework the reproductions. More than one sheet of paper may be used, and although there is no time limit on this test, data presented by Koppitz (1963) shows the average time required to complete the test along with the critical time limits. Timing the test, then, can be useful. Manipulation of the stimulus cards is allowed, but they must be replaced in the original position before the student begins copying. If the student rotates the paper while copying a design, it should be returned to its original position before the next figure is presented.

There is no basal or ceiling level on the Bender. The student copies all nine designs, which are presented in a specified order. Alternate, equivalent forms for test-retest purposes are not available.

The original Bender did not include any formal scoring system. However, as the test became more popular in clinics and schools, several scoring systems were developed. One of the most frequently used was devised by Elizabeth Koppitz, a clinical psychologist who used the test extensively with children with learning and emotional disorders. Koppitz's book, *The Bender-Gestalt Test for Young Children* (1963), describes a scoring system, age norms for children between the ages of 5 and 11 years, and reliability and validity data. Volume 2 of the same book (Koppitz, 1975) presents a revised scoring system, a norming population expanded to include minority groups, and a compilation of the research available on the test. These two books are essential for scoring and interpreting test performance.

In the Koppitz scoring system (described in detail in her books), errors are counted for distorting the shape of the design, perseverating, falsely integrating two forms, and rotating forms. The student's total error score is converted to a developmental-age score. Volume 2 provides tables for converting the total number of errors to both age-equivalent and percentile scores. Koppitz reports that these types of errors are most indicative of minimal brain dysfunction.

STRENGTHS OF THE BENDER

• The Bender is a quick, reliable, easy-to-administer test that is generally nonthreatening and appealing to students. It is popular with psychologists and is a widely used clinical instrument. The test is inexpensive and requires few materials.

• The Bender provides developmental data about a student's maturity in visual-motor integration. Of equal value is the important clinical information that can be obtained by observing a student's behavior while taking the test. For example, the experienced examiner notes such behaviors as excessive erasing and reworking of the designs, rotation of the drawing paper, time needed to complete the test, the spatial organization of the designs on the paper, and the student's attitude during testing. Two students may achieve the same score on the Bender, even producing similar-looking finished protocols, but the clinical observations of the two students may be very different. The behaviors observed during testing provide valuable diagnostic insight.

• Research has also supported the use of the Bender to detect emotional problems. Koppitz (1975) has developed two new emotional indicators (Box around Design and Spontaneous Elaboration, or Addition to Design) to add to her previous list of 10 (Confused Order, Wavy Line, Dashes Substituted for Circles, Increasing Size, Large Size, Small Size, Fine Line, Careless Overwork or Heavily Reinforced Lines, Second Attempt, and Expansion). She reports that the presence of three or more emotional indicators on a student's final product suggests the need for further psychological evaluation.

• The group adaption of the Bender is particularly economical in terms of time. Combined with other brief tests, it is moderately effective as a screening instrument, to identify high-risk students in need of further evaluation. Used in a pretest-posttest manner, the Bender can also be used as a means of evaluating the effectiveness of perceptual-motor training programs.

• The development of various scoring systems to meaningfully quantify a student's performance on the Bender has increased the test's utility. In addition to the Koppitz system for children, the Pascal and Suttel Scoring System has proven useful for adult protocols.

LIMITING FACTORS OF THE BENDER

• The Bender can be interpreted both intuitively and objectively. In either case, the examiner must be highly trained and experienced to effectively analyze the test protocols and to observe and evaluate the student's behavior while taking the test. For example, the designs may result from difficulties in immaturity in visual perception, motor coordination, or the integration of perceptual and motor skills. Less experienced examiners should definitely be cautioned against interpreting the Bender through subjective, intuitive procedures; use of an objective scoring system is more appropriate. Considerable experience is also necessary to achieve a high degree of score reliability with the Bender.

• In spite of recent improvements in the Koppitz Developmental Scoring System, the procedures still contain a high degree of subjectivity. The examiner must compare the student's reproductions with the model according to specific criteria. Scoring a Bender protocol can take considerable time because of the careful inspection required.

• Koppitz reports that the Bender can be used as a measure for detecting neurological impairment (minimal brain dysfunction). The Bender may be helpful in this regard when used in conjunction with other tests and with intellectual evaluation, medical evaluation, and social history. Such a diagnosis should *never* be made on the basis of Bender performance alone.

• Projective interpretations of the Bender should be employed with caution. The emotional indicators can discriminate between well-adjusted and emotionally disturbed groups of students but cannot be used for a definitive diagnosis of an individual child. The 12 indicators can differentiate neurotic, psychotic, and brain-damaged students only when accompanied by other tests and background data.

• The Bender is limited by age because of its developmental ceiling. The test distinguishes between students with outstanding or average visual-motor perception and those with immature perception only for students between the ages of 5 and 8. Most normal 10-year-old students can copy the Bender designs without any difficulty. Scores are meaningful for older students only if their perceptual-motor development is below the 9-year-old level.

• As a group test, the Bender has certain drawbacks. The examiner cannot observe and supervise each student individually; therefore some of the clinical value of the test is lost through group administration. For very immature and hyperactive students who cannot work independently, individual administration is more appropriate.

• A last consideration is the use of the Bender in research studies. The reported findings on using the test as a means of predicting academic achievement have often been contradictory. Further investigation might clarify these discrepant findings. More research is also needed to determine what the recall method of the Bender measures and what diagnostic implications this procedural variation holds. Another area that needs to be more fully explored and substantiated concerns the recent finding that the rate of development in visual-motor perceptual skills differs among students of various ethnic groups.

• Given the conflicting results of research using the Bender, it is best to think of this test as a measure of visual-motor integration through design copying, rather than as a test of intelligence, emotional disturbance, or minimal brain damage.

The Developmental Test of Visual Motor Integration (VMI–3R)

Keith E. Beery
Modern Curriculum Press, 1982, 1989
13900 Prospect Rd., Cleveland, OH 44136

Purpose	To help prevent learning and behavior problems through early screening identification
Major Areas Tested	Visual-motor integration
Age or Grade Range	Preschool through adult; norms provided ages 4–17.11
Usually Given By	Classroom teacher Special education teacher Occupational therapist Psychologist
Type of Test	Standardized Individual Group
Scores Obtained	Age level T Score Percentile Normal curve equivalent Standard
Student Performance Timed?	No
Testing Time	10–15 minutes
Scoring/Interpretation Time	10 minutes
Normed On	5,824 students between the ages of 2 years, 6 months and 19 years, balanced for ethnicity, income level, place of residence, and sex based on 1980 U.S. census figures
Alternate Forms Available?	No

FORMAT

The Developmental Test of Visual-Motor Integration (VMI–3R) was first published in 1967 and renormed in 1982. In the 1989 version, the test remains the same while scoring procedures and norms have been upgraded.

The materials for the VMI-3R consist of the manual and individual test booklets. The VMI is a pencil-and-paper test. It may be presented to groups of students, but is more often used individually. The test booklet presents 24 geometric forms for the student to copy. The forms are printed in heavy black outlines and arranged three to a page, with a space below each one for the student to copy that form. The format is clear and uncluttered, and the forms are arranged from the simplest to the most complex. The student copies the forms and may not erase or rotate the book. The test is not timed, and the student continues working until three consecutive errors are made. Although the same booklet is used for students of a wide age range, the student only copies forms within his or her ability. The raw score consists of the total number of forms copied correctly before reaching the ceiling; this score is converted to an age score, standard score, and percentile using the tables in the manual.

The VMI is published in two forms. The Long Form contains all 24 geometric forms and covers the age range of 2 to 15 years. The Short Form is somewhat less expensive, contains only the first 15 geometric forms, and is recommended for students between 2 and 8 years of age. Alternate, equivalent forms for test-retest purposes are not available.

STRENGTHS OF THE VMI

• The VMI–3R is a well-constructed test. The 24 geometric forms were chosen over letter forms because they were equally familiar to children of varying backgrounds. The forms are developmentally sequenced, with careful thought to increasing task complexity. The wide age range makes the VMI–3R a good instrument for screening purposes as well as for measurement of student progress.

• The VMI–3R is an enjoyable test for most students. The directions are clear and easy to understand. The beginning forms allow even young or seriously impaired students to experience success, whereas the more complex forms present a challenge for the adolescent student. The

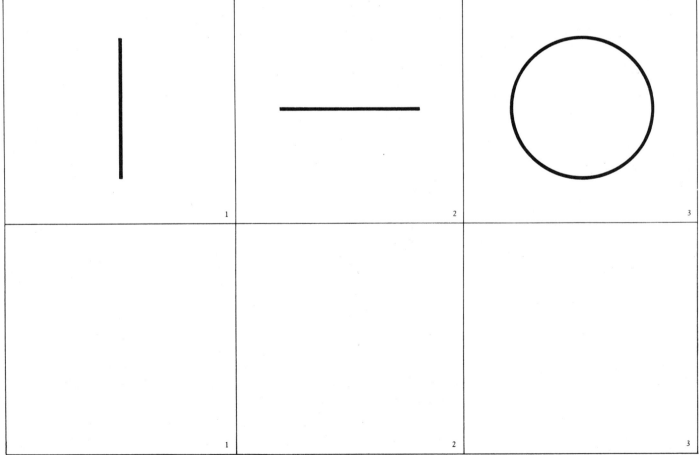

VMI, Items 1, 2, 3

test requires no verbal responses and therefore can be used with children with hearing impairments or language disabilities. It is a good test to use as a warm-up in an early part of a diagnostic battery.

• As were the older editions, the VMI–3R is a quick test to administer and score and yet yields good information about a major area of learning.

• The VMI–3R has clear directions for administration and is a good instrument for the classroom teacher to use with small groups of students. The provision of age norms for each item provides the teacher with a basis for understanding which types of geometric forms can be expected to be mastered next. This is, if a student can complete the right oblique line (/) and the left oblique line (\) successfully, we can expect that next the student will probably learn to reproduce the oblique cross (x). Extensive developmental data, including age scores for imitating forms at the younger ages, is provided in the manual.

• The VMI–3R manual is particularly helpful in describing the process of visual-motor integration and in outlining a sequence of visual-motor training activities.

• In the 1989 edition of the VMI, several important changes have been made in administration and scoring procedures which have greatly added to the value of the test.

• Instructions are given to the students in the group administration to, "Do your best on both the easy and the hard ones." Previously, students' rapid, careless approach to the easier items often resulted in lower scores. (This instruction should be given to individual students as well, although it has been omitted from the Individual Administration instructions.)

• Excellent guidelines are given to help the examiner tease out the differences between the visual perception and motor coordination aspects of a student's performance. The examiner is also encouraged to teach the young, inexperienced child how to make a few forms and then retest in two weeks. Children without deficits in this area will usually learn and retain the process.

• The scoring range of the VMI–3R has been expanded from 24 to 50 points by weighting each form according to age norms. In this manner, the more difficult forms are given four points while the simplest forms are worth one point. This expansion closes the gaps between the age groups and allows a higher

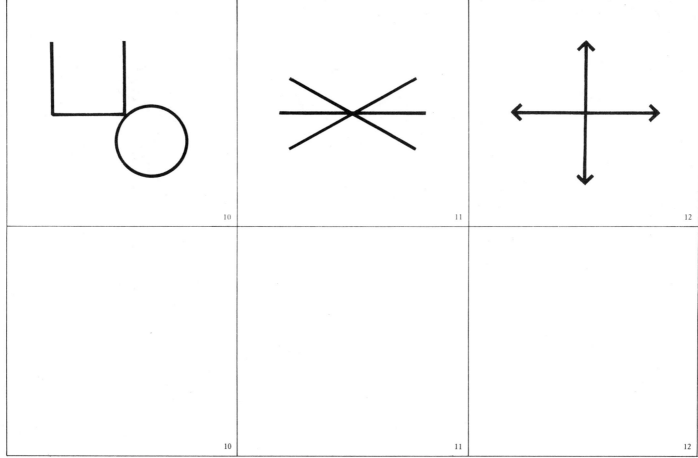

VMI, Items 10, 11, 12

DEVELOPMENTAL TEST OF VISUAL-MOTOR INTEGRATION
Copyright © 1967 by Keith E. Beery and Norman A. Buktenica

range of scores for older students.

• More specific criteria are described for scoring each form. This is important because the VMI–3R is still scored on a credit/no credit basis for each form. The two-page summary scoring provided near the end of the manual is helpful for the experienced VMI–3R examiner.

• The VMI–3R now uses standard scores with a mean of 100 and standard deviation of 15 to allow more direct comparison with other standardized tests.

LIMITING FACTORS OF THE VMI

• Although the VMI–3R has age norms for students up to 17.11 years old, it seems most useful with preschool and primary-age students. It can be used as either an individual or group test with one set of age norms. If used as a group test, monitors should be provided to keep students from rotating the book or skipping forms. The expanded forms have made the test more valid at the upper age levels. However, the norming sample has a small number of students at ages 15 and older, and scores should be used with caution. The size and composition of the standardization sample indicates that the norms are most adequate for

the 5- to 13-year old gage range.

• The VMI–3R does not measure spatial organizational skills. Each form is copied in the space provided. A student may have much more difficulty on a test like the Bender Visual Motor Gestalt Test, where nine forms are copied on a blank piece of paper. A very low score on the VMI–3R often reflects an impulsive, careless approach to the test, and this must be sorted out from true deficits in visual-motor integration.

• Despite the increased specificity for scoring forms provided, clearly the author relies upon the examiner's experience to score the test correctly. In one place he states that an inexperienced examiner will recognize when an older child has hastily copied the simplest forms which are clearly within his ability and "take such behaviors into account in scoring." (VMI–3R Manual, p. 24.) Such nebulous statements are in fact true for the experienced scorer, but research described in the manual clearly documents the need for training in scoring procedures for the not-so-experienced examiner.

• The reliability and validity studies presented in the manual provide no data but summary statements only.

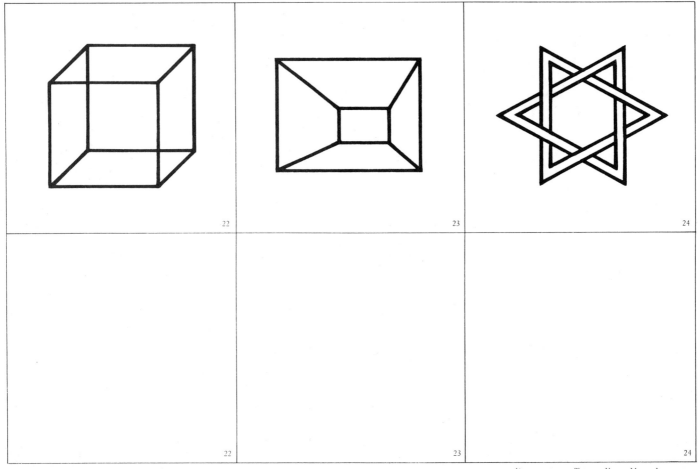

VMI, Items 22, 23, 24

Motor-Free Visual Perception Test (MVPT)

Ronald P. Colarusso and Donald D. Hammill
Academic Therapy Publications, 1972
20 Commercial Blvd., Novato, CA 94947

Purpose	To measure overall visual perceptual processing ability
Major Areas Tested	Visual perception
Age or Grade Range	4–9 years
Usually Given By	Classroom teacher Special education teacher Occupational therapist
Type of Test	Standardized Individual
Scores Obtained	Age level Perceptual quotient (PQ)
Student Performance Timed?	No
Testing Time	10–15 minutes
Scoring/Interpretation Time	15–20 minutes
Normed On	881 urban, suburban, and rural children from all races and economic levels in 22 states
Alternate Forms Available?	No

FORMAT

The materials required for administering the Motor-Free Visual Perception Test (MVPT) are the test manual, the book of test plates, and an individual scoring sheet. The test consists of 36 items arranged into five sections, each section with its own demonstration item and instructions.

Section 1. From an array of four drawings, the student selects a drawing of a geometric form that matches a stimulus drawing. The first three items in this section require matching by spatial orientation; the remaining five items require recognizing the correct form in a rival background. (See Item 6, from Section 1, shown here.)

Section 2. The student selects the geometric form that is the same shape as the model but is rotated, darker, or a different size. On some items in this section, the correct figure must also be distinguished from a rival background. (Section 2, Item 12.)

Section 3. The student is first shown a stimulus drawing and is then asked to choose it from memory from an array of four similar drawings. (Section 3, Item 15.)

Section 4. The student selects, from an array of incomplete drawings, the drawing that would, if completed, match the model. (Section 4, Item 29.)

Section 5. The student selects from four drawings the one that is different. The difference involves a change in spatial orientation of the drawing or a part of the drawing. (Section 5, Item 34.)

The examiner tallies the number of correct responses in all five sections to determine the raw score. This score can then be converted to an age equivalent, a perceptual quotient, and with some computation, a standard score. Each of these scores represents the student's performance on the total test; separate scores are not given for each section.

STRENGTHS OF THE MVPT

• The motor-free aspect of this test makes it a useful diagnostic tool, because it helps to detect which component of visual-motor integration activities may be causing an individual student's difficulty. When used as part of a test battery that includes tests of visual-motor integration and various aspects of coordination, it can make an important contribution to delineating the specific problem area and setting up an appropriate intervention program.

A   B   C   D

MVPT, Section 1, Item 6

• The MVPT is easy to administer, and although it must be given individually, it is not excessively time consuming. The scoring procedure is simple and objective. Administering the test requires no disposable materials, except for the one-page scoring sheet, making it a relatively inexpensive test to give.

• The method of reporting scores is quite useful; the availability of age scores, perceptual quotients, and standard scores makes it easy to compare a student's performance on this test to performance on other tests. In addition, the availability of scores in several forms serves as a system of checks and balances against the pitfalls of the individual scoring systems.

• The authors' use of the standard error of measurement in reporting age-equivalent scores is useful because it requires the examiner to view the student's score as a range within which the "true" score is likely to fall. The examiner is also cautioned to take into account the standard error of measurement when intepreting perceptual quotients, although this is not "built into" the reporting of these scores (unlike the age-equivalent scores).

• The test directions are, for the most part, clear and simple. However, language-impaired students sometimes have difficulty understanding what is expected on the visual closure items, and the standard procedure outlined in the manual does not permit much additional explanation.

• The MVPT's reliability is acceptable for students aged 5 years to 8 years, 11 months but is borderline for 4-year-olds. Construct validity is acceptable for students aged 5 years to 7 years, 11 months.

LIMITING FACTORS OF THE MVPT

• The authors caution that guessing, random answering, and perseveration are factors that must be considered in interpreting scores on this and most other tests. A raw score of less than 10 indicates less than chance performance and cannot be interpreted with confidence.

• No information is given about the selection of the normative sample nor about the proportions of subgroups included in the sample.

• The sample populations for students aged 4 years through 4 years, 11 months and for students aged 8 years, 6 months through 8 years, 11 months were too small to allow confident test interpretation for students in these age groups.

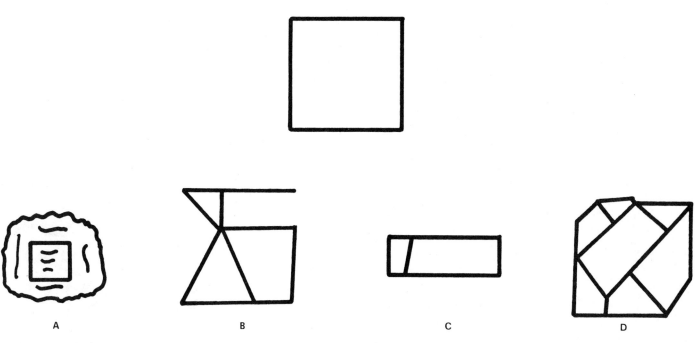

A   B   C   D

MVPT, Section 2, Item 12

- The high success rate on each item for 7-year-olds makes the MVPT nondiscriminatory at the upper age limits.

- The content validity of the test is open to question. The authors state that the test assesses five areas of visual perception: spatial relationships, visual discrimination, figure-ground perception, visual closure, and visual memory. For each of the five types, other researchers are cited who have measured similar aspects of visual perception. However, the authors do not establish adequately that these five areas are mutually exclusive or that they represent all aspects of visual perception.

- Some of the definitions of perceptual categories are vague and confusing. This is complicated by the division of the test into five unlabeled sections that do not seem to correspond in all cases with the perceptual categories the authors have defined. Section 1, for example, includes five figure-ground items, as well as three items that the authors would, it seems, include in their definition of spatial relations.

- The number of items in each perceptual category ranges from 5 to 11. Because the test provides only a total score, the larger percentage of items on visual closure, for example, means that a student with this difficulty may achieve an unrealistically low score.

- No information is provided about the test's construct validity for 4-year-olds and 8-year olds.

- In studying the MVPT's criterion-related validity, the authors did not correlate MVPT scores exclusively with other motor-free tests, thus introducing too many variables for accurate interpretation. This problem was further complicated by using a homogeneous sample for the interest correlations.

A   B   C   D

MVPT, Section 3, Item 15

A   B   C   D

MVPT, Section 4, Item 29

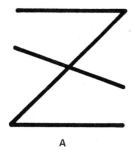 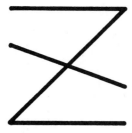 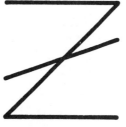 

A   B   C   D

MVPT, Section 5, Item 34

Test of Visual-Motor Skills (TVMS)

Morrison F. Gardiner
Children's Hospital of San Francisco, 1986
Publications Dept., Box 3805, San Francisco, CA 94119

Purpose	To determine a child's visual-motor functioning; to provide practical information on how a child perceives non-language forms and translates with his or her hand what is visually perceived
Major Areas Tested	Visual perception and eye-motor coordination
Age or Grade Range	2–13 years
Usually Given By	Teacher Language therapist Counselor Occupational therapist Diagnostician Psychologist
Type of Test	Individual or group Standardized Norm-referenced
Scores Obtained	Age level Standard Percentile Stanine
Student Performance Timed?	No
Testing Time	5–10 minutes
Scoring/Interpretation Time	5–10 minutes
Normed On	1,009 children between the ages of 2 and 13 in the San Francisco Bay Area
Alternate Forms Available?	No

FORMAT

The Test of Visual Motor Skills (TVMS) consists of a series of 26 geometric forms for a student to copy. Each form is printed on a separate page in the test booklet. No basal or ceiling procedures are used. Each student, regardless of age, is encouraged to attempt each drawing. If it is clear that the student is experiencing difficulty, the examiner may stop when the child fails four consecutive designs. No erasing is permitted. Both individual and group administration are possible.

The materials for the TVMS consist of a manual containing directions for administration and scoring, technical information, and norms tables, and individual test booklets in which the students copy the designs. Each design is given a score of 0, 1, or 2. A zero indicates the student was unable to copy the form with any degree of accuracy; a score of 1 indicates some minor errors; a score of 2 indicates that the child copied the design with precision. A total test score is obtained and is converted into a motor age, standard score, percentile, and stanine. Guidelines are given to assist the examiner in analyzing the student's performance for various types of motor problems, such as directionality, confusion, or perseveration.

STRENGTHS OF THE TVMS

• The TVMS is an easily administered, quick test of design copying, one of the basic visual-motor tasks.

• The two-point scoring system gives students some credit for designs which are almost correct. This is an advantage for children who work quickly and make careless mistakes on designs which they obviously could copy correctly. The scoring system is also more sensitive to small gains in measuring progress than a pass/fail system.

LIMITING FACTORS OF THE TVMS

• The TVMS measures the same skill as the Test of Visual Motor Integration. The author has made changes in format designed to enhance the test; that is, each design is printed on a separate page, and a two-point scoring system is used. Other than the scoring system, the changes are inconsequential.

• The standardization sample is small and not well described by the author. Other than the fact that the children were all in school, the author gives no demographic data except age.

• Little reliability or validity data is provided. What is included is poorly described.

• The author states that the TVMS can be administered to a group. However, no guidelines are given for age, size of the group, or how to manage the mechanics of page turning and individual encouragement recommended in the manual.

The usefulness of group testing is questionable; if a young child needs an assessment of visual-motor functioning, he or she needs more attention to performance than can be given in a group.

Test of Visual-Perceptual Skills (Non-Motor) (TVPS)

Morrison F. Gardiner
Special Child Publications, 1982
Box 33548, Seattle, WA 98133

Purpose	To determine a child's strengths and weaknesses in non-motor visual perception
Major Areas Tested	Visual perception, divided by the author into the following areas: visual discrimination, visual memory, visual-spatial relations, visual form constancy, visual sequential memory, visual figure-ground, and visual closure
Age or Grade Range	4–12.11 years
Usually Given By	Regular or special education teacher Psychologist Occupational therapist Optomestrist Any professional familiar with psychological or educational tests
Type of Test	Individual Standardized
Scores Obtained	Standard (scaled and perceptual quotient) Percentile Age level
Student Performance Timed?	No
Testing Time	10–30 minutes
Scoring/Interpretation Time	10 minutes
Normed On	962 private and parochial school children in the San Francisco Bay Area; 86% white, 14% nonwhite
Alternate Forms Available?	No

FORMAT

Materials for the Test of Visual-Perceptual Skills (Non-Motor) (TVPS) consist of a test manual, a book of 144 test plates, and individual record forms. For each of the seven subtests, the examiner presents a trial item to determine that the student understands the task, and then presents each test item in sequence until a ceiling level is reached for that subtest. No basals are established. Each subtest has 16 items. The individual subtests are described below.

Visual Discrimination. The student selects, from an array of five forms, the form which matches a model. Selection requires distinctions ranging from gross rotations to subtle directional differences, and from global distortions of shape to subtle differences in the spacing of lines within the forms.

Visual Memory. The student is shown a single form, and is then asked to identify it from memory from an array of similar forms.

Visual-Spatial Relations. From an array of five forms, the student identifies the form that is different from the others. Most differences are rotations or reversals of the entire form; some involve reversals of part of the form.

Visual Form Constancy. The student selects the form which matches the model from an array of five similar forms. Selection involves recognizing the required shape despite changes in size, spatial orientation, shading, and/or rival background.

Visual Sequential Memory. The student is shown a sequence of forms and is then asked to identify it from memory from an array of four similar sequences. The items progress from a sequence of two forms to a sequence of nine forms.

Visual Figure-Ground. The student selects the form that matches the model from an array of four similar forms, each embedded in a rival background.

Visual Closure. From an array of four incomplete forms, the student selects the one that would match the model if it were complete.

Following administration of all seven subtests, the examiner tallies raw scores to obtain the various derived scores, both for the test as a whole and for the individual subtests.

STRENGTHS OF THE TVPS

• The TVPS is an extremely easy test to administer and score. Instructions in the manual are clear and simple. The manual provides a clear description of the seven areas of visual perception in question, as well as a general definition of visual perception.

• No verbal responses are required from the student, and receptive language requirements are minimal, making the test useful for students with limited language abilities. Standardized procedure permits additional instruction on the trial items when needed, so that difficulty understanding the test is rarely a problem.

• Speed is not a factor in the scoring, so that a student with generally slow response time is not penalized. The test provides the opportunity for the examiner to make informal observations about the student's apparent processing or response speed, but only accuracy counts in the scoring.

• The process of test construction is clearly described in the manual. Potential items were field tested and selected on the basis of correlation with total test scores, subtest scores, and age. Adequate correlations are reported between item order and item difficulty, suggesting that the items are arranged in order of difficulty, and lending confidence to the use of the ceiling procedures.

• The low correlations reported among the individual subtest scores suggest that they do assess different skills, although whether they assess the specific skills they were designed to assess has not been adequately established.

LIMITING FACTORS OF THE TVPS

• Some students find the test tedious. Although the author notes administration times ranging from 7 minutes for younger students to 15 minutes for older students, clinical experience suggests that some methodical students take much longer to respond. Unless an early ceiling is reached, the test involves studying 112 items; the mere size of the book of test plates is discouraging to some students.

• The quality of the drawings is variable, and at times may interfere with test performance. Subtle differences between items meant to be identical (sometimes differences in proportion, sometimes in thickness of lines) may seem more significant to the student than the intentional differences between test items.

• Although the author describes the purpose of the test in terms of determining strengths and weaknesses in different areas of visual perception, no explanation is provided for why this specific information might be useful, or how the different factors may relate to academics or other functional skills.

• Content validity is not adequately addressed. The author notes that he has determined the "important factors of visual perception" through a literature review, but the literature review is not presented. He has then attempted to represent these seven factors in the seven subtests of the TVPS but presents no documentation that the subtests successfully tap these specific factors. Finally, the author comments that the seven factors, represented by the seven subtests of the TVPS, "provide a comprehensive sampling of an individual's visual-perceptual skills." Again, no supporting data is provided. Questions remain regarding whether the broad area of visual perception can be divided into seven mutually exclusive but collectively comprehensive factors, and whether the seven subtests of the TVPS measure these specific factors.

• The author's discussion of criterion-related validity is weakened by lack of a clear criterion for comparison, given the lack of similar tests of non-motor visual perceptual skills. The discussion of diagnostic and predictive validity is also weak, as the author does not adequately address the issue of what the test should predict or diagnose.

• No information is presented in the manual regarding test/retest reliability or interrater reliability; only internal consistency was measured.

• Norming procedures were questionable. The normative sample was restricted to students in the San Francisco Bay Area and was not adequately described. Although the scaled scores are based on age groups divided into one-year intervals in the normative sample, interpolations were used to provide scores at four or six month intervals at some age levels. This is a questionable procedure.

• As the author notes, the test does not discriminate well at the upper ages. Performance tends to rise quickly in the early years and then level off, with very little increase in performance among the older ages (10 to 12 year olds). It is unknown whether this occurs because these skills have reached their peak development by this age or because the test does not have sufficiently difficult items to discriminate well among 10- to 12-year olds. The author's suggestion that the norms for 12-year olds be used for individuals aged 13 to adult is questionable.

• Poorly established reliability and validity as well as limitations in norming procedures are a serious weakness in this test. The TVPS may be useful to augment the experienced examiner's clinical judgment in assessing the student's strengths and weaknesses in visual perceptual skills, but specific scores should be used only with extreme caution.

CHAPTER THREE
Speech and Language Tests

The primary, first-learned language system is oral. Long before children come to school, they develop skills of listening and speaking that enable them to communicate with others. The secondary language system, written language, is learned in school. Difficulties in the acquisition of reading and writing often have their basis in the student's oral language skills. This chapter deals primarily with the assessment of oral language, with its reception and expression. The tests reviewed here are usually given by speech and language therapists or clinicians. However, several of the newer tests include measures of written language, of reading and writing. These tests are more likely to be given by educational diagnosticians.

A complete speech and language evaluation includes assessment in the five major components of language:

1. *Phonology*. This is the sound system that constitutes spoken language. Phonemes such as /k/ and /f/ have no meaning in isolation, but their combination in specific sequences creates words.

2. *Morphology*. Morphemes are the smallest meaningful units of language. They are usually words like *picnic*, *work*, or *slow*, but they may also be grammatical markers signifying specific concepts, such as plurality (*picnics*), tense (*worked*), or shifts from adjective to adverb (*slowly*).

3. *Syntax*. This is the grammatical aspect of spoken language, the system for ordering words into meaningful sequences. Grammatical structure plays an important role in the comprehension and production of spoken language.

4. *Semantics*. This includes the meaning of words, sentences, and paragraphs. Vocabulary is a basic part of semantics.

5. *Pragmatics*. This includes the rules governing the use of language in context. Such features as conversational turn-taking and topic maintenance affect ability to communicate effectively.

A speech and language clinician assesses both the receptive and expressive processes of each of these five components. For example, in the area of syntax:

Receptive: Can the student comprehend past tense?
Expressive: Can the student express ideas in past tense?
In the area of semantics:

Receptive: What is the level of the student's listening vocabulary?
Expressive: What is the level of the student's spoken vocabulary?

The first section includes four tests of articulation and two methods for analyzing oral language samples. These types of tests and procedures require the training and expertise of a speech and language pathologist. The first procedure is the Developmental Sentence Scoring (DSS), a well-known method for analyzing a language sample. Four tests of articulation competence are included: The Fisher-Logemen Test of Articulation Competence, The Assessment of Phonological Processes, the Goldman-Fristoe Test of Articulation, and the Templin-Darley Tests of Articulation. The section ends with a review of the Tyack-Gottsleben Language Sampling, Analysis, and Training Handbook, another procedure for analyzing oral language samples.

The second section includes 16 tests of language development:

Auditory-Visual Single Word Picture Vocabulary Test. A measure of receptive vocabulary.

Boehm Test of Basic Concepts—Revised. A preschool kindergarten receptive measure.

Clinical Evaluation of Language Fundamentals—Revised. A battery of receptive and expressive language tests.

Expressive One-Word Picture Vocabulary Test. A picture naming test for elementary school students.

Expressive One-Word Picture Vocabulary Test (Upper Extension). A picture naming test for adolescent students.

Peabody Picture Vocabulary Test—Revised. A measure of receptive vocabulary.

Preschool Language Scale. Receptive and expressive skills.

Receptive One-Word Picture Vocabulary Test. A measure of receptive vocabulary.

Sequenced Inventory of Communication Development—Revised. Receptive and expressive verbal skills.

Test of Auditory Comprehension of Language—Revised. A Battery of receptive language tasks.

Test of Adolescent Language—2. Includes both oral and written skills.

Test of Language Development—2—Primary. Primary battery of oral language tests.

Test of Language Development—2—Intermediate. Intermediate batteries of oral language tests.

Test of Word Finding. New measure of word retrieval.

Token Test for Children. Measures ability to follow oral directions.

The Word Test. Evaluates the semantic aspects of expressive language.

Many of the tests in this chapter were designed to be used with preschool children, attesting to the importance of the speech and language area in the assessment of very young children.

Many of the tests reviewed in this chapter lack validity for students from bilingual backgrounds. Those who are interested in the assessment of Spanish-speaking children are referred to the bilingual (Spanish-English) language tests in Chapter Four.

Developmental Sentence Scoring (DSS)

Laura Lee and R. A. Koenigsknecht
Northwestern University Press, 1974, 1988
625 Colfax, Evanston, IL 60201

Purpose	To provide a systematic procedure for analyzing a student's grammatical structure and for estimating the extent to which the student has learned generalized grammatical rules enough to use them in conversation
Major Areas Tested	Grammatical structure of spoken language
Age or Grade Range	2–7 years
Usually Given By	Speech/language clinician
Type of Test	Individual
Scores Obtained	Percentile
Student Performance Timed?	No
Testing Time	30–60 minutes
Scoring/Interpretation Time	2 hours
Normed On	200 white monolingual children between ages 2 and 7 years, from middle-income homes where standard American English was spoken
Alternate Forms Available?	No

FORMAT

Developmental Sentence Scoring (DSS) involves obtaining a conversational language sample by using stimulus materials that the student is interested in, such as toys or pictures provided by the clinician. A corpus of 50 different, consecutive, intelligible, nonecholalic, complete (subject and verb) sentences is used for analysis. The authors state that this procedure, therefore, is appropriate only for students who use complete sentence structures at least 50 percent of the time. Fragmentary utterances are discarded from the sample. Detailed information about elicitation of the sample and the acceptability of various utterances in the language corpus is provided by the authors in the book containing the test (Lee and Koenigsknecht 1974).

The utterances are evaluated in terms of eight grammatical features that psycholinguistic research has found to be early components of language. Research has also provided information about their developmental progression. These features are based on transformational generative grammar (Chomsky 1957, 1965) and case grammar (Brown 1973; Fillmore 1968).

The grammatical criteria includes the following:
1. Indefinite pronouns and/or noun modifiers
2. Personal pronouns
3. Main verbs
4. Secondary verbs
5. Negatives
6. Conjunctions
7. Interrogative reversals
8. *Wh*- question words

Each grammatical form present in a sample utterance is independently assigned and scored from 1 to 8 points according to a weighted scoring system. The weighted scores indicate a developmental sequence of grammatical growth within each category. Furthermore, an additional sentence point may be added if the entire utterance is correct in all aspects—syntactically as well as semantically. This sentence point is designed, in part, to account for other grammatical features not individually scored, such as plurals, possessive makers, word order, and prepositions.

Comprehensive scoring guidelines are provided by the authors in both tabular and narrative form. Emerging structures may be indicated by inserting attempt marks (–) under the appropriate categories. A model chart format for listing and scoring the transcribed sentences appears in the authors' book (Lee and Koenigsknecht 1974), but practical tables must be made by the clinician. The DSS scoring procedure is illustrated in Table 20.

Scores for the 50-sentences utterance sample are totaled; then the mean score per sentence is computed. This is the Developmental Sentence Score (DSS), which is compared with the normative data available for the student's chronological age. Percentile values have been computed for the

ninetieth, seventy-fifth, fiftieth, twenty-fifth, and tenth percentile ranks at six-month intervals for ages 2 to 7. An estimate of the student's expressive language level can be obtained by finding the age range where the DSS is approximately equivalent to the fiftieth-percentile score.

The authors suggest, in addition, that students scoring close to the tenth percentile for their age receive further speech and language evaluation and be considered potential candidates for therapy. When DSS is used to measure progress, the authors state that students might be dismissed from therapy when their scores approximate the lower limits of the normal range for their age group. However, other important factors, such as conceptual development and auditory skills, must be taken into consideration.

STRENGTHS OF DSS

• DSS is an inexpensive language assessment procedure, with an authors' book that provides all the information necessary for administration and interpretation. Transcription forms are not provided, but they can easily be designed by the clinician.

• Because DSS is a detailed, painstaking procedure, a thorough reading of the author's book is necessary. Comprehensive information about various utterance types in the language corpus is included. Numerous examples illustrate the method of developmental scoring. The convenient chart provided by the authors usually contains enough specific scoring information to meet the requirements of typical language samples. Background psycholinguistic research and essential language-sampling techniques are also concisely presented.

• It is felt that 50 spontaneous and complete sentences is a reasonable number to use in assessing language-impaired children. There is no sufficient evidence that supports the collection of larger samples for analysis purposes. In fact, established criteria do not yet exist for determining adequate sample size for linguistic analysis.

• A significant amount of diagnostic information can be obtained by examining the scatter of scores on DSS charts, because consistent error categories and stereotyped structures are indicated in repetitive scoring patterns. The chart makes it especially easy to see what structures are missing and what forms the child is consistently substituting for others.

• Many psycholinguistic researchers and therapists of language-disordered students have espoused language-sampling measures such as DSS over traditional tests of morphological and syntactic competency. They feel that conversational speech places a "grammatical load" on the student because it requires the student to combine several transformations into single sentences. As a student gains linguistic competence with age, one can expect progressive growth in the grammatical load of his or her utterances. This increasing load results from mastery of new, higher-level morphological forms and syntactic stuctures as well as growth in the number of forms and structures that the student can incorporate into a single utterance. DSS assesses the impact of both these developmental aspects. In addition, rule consistency and frequency of usage can also be assessed more accurately in conversational speech than under rigid testing conditions.

• The validity of a test of conversational language behavior is difficult to assess directly because adequate and appropriate external criteria are lacking. Therefore, determining the internal consistency of DSS and the consistency of repeated applications with different clinicians and different stimulus materials becomes more significant.

Validity of the DSS construct was established when the test was normed on 200 children from middle-income homes. Validity was indicated by the significant differences between age groups in the overall scoring procedure, as well as by all the component grammatical categories. Further validity was obtained through verification of the grammatical hierarchies in a reciprocal averaging procedure that resulted in a minor revision of the original weighted scoring system of DSS, presented in 1971.

High reliability coefficients obtained by DSS lend major support to the scoring procedure. The overall internal consistency was .71 (estimated by coefficient Alpha), and the reliability coefficient for the overall DSS was .73.

LIMITING FACTORS OF DSS

• DSS is a highly time-consuming procedure as compared with other conventional language-assessment techniques. Inherent in it are great opportunities for errors in transcribing and scoring the language samples. To minimize such errors, it is recommended that clinicians transcribe and score their own samples, using the authors' book to clarify the scoring procedure when necessary.

DSS Scoring Procedure*

Sentence	Indefinite Pronoun/ Noun Modifier	Personal Pronoun	Primary Verb	Secondary Verb	Negative	Conjunction	Inter-rogative Reversal	Wh-Question Word	Sentence Point	Total
I want to eat.		1 I	1 want	2 to eat					1	5
What you doing?		1 you	– are (omitted)					2 what	0	3
The dog won't go in the house.			4 won't go		5 won't				1	10
She's trying to take it off.	1 it	2 she	1 is trying	5 to take					1	10
He drinked all the milk.	3 all	2 he	– drinked/ drank						0	5
Look at me!		1 me	1 look						1	3
He said, ''Where's my house?''		2, 1 he, my	2, 1 said, is				1 where is my house?	2 where	1	10

*Numbers in columns indicate points assigned to each element.

• Caution should be exercised in comparing a student's DSS with the percentile scores presented by authors. The sample used to obtain normative data for each six-month age period was small (20 individuals). Furthermore, criteria used to determine the "normalcy" of these subjects' language appears to have been inadequate. The only objective, standardized measure of adequate language skill was a score within one standard deviation of the mean for age on the Peabody Picture Vocabulary Test–Revised. Other criteria included normal developmental histories without reports of overt hearing problems, severe misarticulations, or discernible behavioral problems. More intensive evaluation of language skills with other standardized measures should have been undertaken.

• The usefulness of DSS is limited by the fact that the end product is a score rather than a descriptive, composite picture of the student's linguistic performance. Errors merely reduce a student's overall score without specifying the incorrect generalizations he or she may be using. A score may be spuriously high simply because the student uses many words.

• The authors have stated that an essential purpose of DSS is the planning of remediation goals. However, the absence of a descriptive summary sheet that examines performance on individual grammatical criteria tends to defeat this purpose. In addition to the lengthy assessment process, the clinician must also summarize the student's linguistic performance by reviewing individual sentence errors. Moreover, appropriate goals for language therapy cannot be developed solely from examination of DSS error patterns but require more detailed knowledge found through other language measures.

• The DSS procedure is appropriate only for students who can produce 50 complete sentences within a reasonable time. Clinicians should be aware that Lee and Koenigsknecht (1974) have developed an alternate method of language-sampling analysis for students exhibiting lower-level language development.

• The DSS was designed solely to assess the linguistic performance of students who have learned standard American English. Further research is needed to systematize analysis of other dialects of English as well as other languages. Allen Toronto (1972) has developed a scoring system similar to DSS for the Spanish language (see Screening Test of Spanish Grammar). It is not a translation of DSS but a developmental scale of Spanish grammatical forms, and it can help clinicians differentiate between bilingual interference with language development and a disability in the student's native language.

• DSS uses a limited number of discrete grammatical criteria. Although there is little doubt that these are essential components of language development, such basic grammatical criteria as plurals, possessive markers, adverbs, and prepositions have been omitted.

• The authors claim that DSS is a useful tool for evaluating progress during therapy, but it should be limited to the assessment of longitudinal changes and not applied to short-term changes. Research has shown that a significant practice effect can be produced when the DSS is repeated over a short time (four applications over two weeks). Furthermore, when DSS is used as an objective measure of grammatical growth during an interim and posttherapy assessment procedure, it is essential that the same stimulus materials be used to minimize test variables as much as possible.

The Fisher-Logemann Test of Articulation Competence (Fisher-Logemann)

Hilda B. Fisher and Jerilyn A. Logemann
Riverside Publishing Company, 1971
8420 West Bryn Mawr Rd., Chicago, IL 60631

Purpose	To examine a student's phonological system in an orderly framework and to facilitate the recording and analysis of phonetic notations of articulation and the comprehensive and accurate analysis and categorization of articulation errors
Major Areas Tested	Articulation
Age or Grade Range	3 years–adult (Picture Test) 9 years–adult (Sentence Articulation Test)
Usually Given By	Speech/language clinician
Type of Test	Individual Criterion-referenced
Scores Obtained	None
Student Performance Timed?	No
Testing Time	10 minutes (screening test); 25 minutes (complete test)
Scoring/Interpretation Time	15–20 minutes
Normed On	Not reported
Alternate Forms Available?	Yes

FORMAT

The Fisher-Logemann Test of Articulation Competence (Fisher-Logemenn) is made up of two parts, the Picture Test and the Sentences Articulation Test. The materials consist of 109 picture stimuli on 35 hardboard cards in an 8 1/2- by-11-inch folio, two sets of 8 1/2- by- 11 inch record forms, and a test manual. The manual contains detailed instructions for administering each part of the test, as well as directions for recording responses and distinctive-feature analysis of the misarticulations.

The Picture Test uses spontaneous identification of colorful picture stimuli to assess the production of 25 single-consonant phonemes, 23 consonant blends, 12 single vowels, and 4 diphthongs. Single-consonant productions are evaluated in each of the syllabic positions in which they occur in the English language. This test uses only words that have the test consonant phoneme next to a vowel. Therefore, consonants may occur in "prevocalic" (*dog*), "intervocalic" (le*tt*er), and "postvocalic" (do*g*) positions. Test words were chosen on the basis of familiarity and frequency of occurrence in the vocabulary of young children.

The picture folio can be converted easily into a convenient easel for presentation of the picture stimuli. The stimulus word, test phoneme, and item number corresponding to the record form are printed on the back of each card, which faces the examiner. A suggested "prompting phrase" is printed under the test word for use if a verbal prompt is necessary to elicit the response.

The two sets of record forms provide an abundance of useful information for the examiner. Transcriptions for the Picture Test are made on both sides of a single sheet. Productions of consonant phonemes are recorded on the front of the sheet, and articulation of consonant blends and vowel phonemes are transcribed on the back. The front of the sheet is organized into a chart that highlights the nature of the articulation deficit by distinctive-feature analysis. The distinctive-feature analysis includes place of articulation, voicing, and manner of formation. Some unique features of this recording sheet include:

- A description of each single-consonant phoneme in terms of its distinctive features. For example, the *t* sound is listed as a voiceless, tip-alveolar phoneme produced as a stop consonant.
- Space for recording the specific types of misarticulation patterns, which are discussed and listed in the Phonetic Notation section of the test manual.
- International Phonetic Alphabet (IPA) symbols for each sound.
- Common spelling of each phoneme.
- The developmental age for each sound. This is the age at which 90 percent of the children are expected to have achieved mastery of the sound in all syllabic positions (Hejna, 1959). As an example, the chart indicates that 90

percent of all 7-year-olds should be able to articulate correctly the /s/ phoneme.

On the reverse of this recording form, productions of consonant blends using the phonemes /s/, /r/, and /l/ are transcribed. Spaces are provided for noting the phonemic contexts discovered to be least and most conducive to adequate productions of each. Vowel productions are also recorded on this side of the sheet and are organized in terms of place of articulation (front, central, back) and degree of constriction (high, mid, low).

The Fisher-Logemann also contains a rapid screening form of the Picture Test. This short form comprises 11 selected cards with marginal tabs for easy location. Productions of phonemes thought to be most commonly misarticulated are assessed.

The Sentence Articulation Test consists of a single card on which there are 15 sentences to be read by the student. The test evaluates production of every single-consonant sound in all three syllabic positions as well as all vowel phonemes in English. The sentences require third-grade or higher reading level. Each cognate pair of consonants (phonemes with the same place of articulation and manner of formation) is assessed in the same sentence, but consonant sounds with no cognates are grouped by similarity in the manner of production—for example, the nasal phonemes /m/ and /n/. The test phonemes are indicated by IPA symbols before each sentence, and the letters corresponding to the sounds are underlined within the utterances. (*G*eorge is at the *ch*ur*ch* wat*ch*ing a ma*g*ic show.) Spaces for recording misarticulations are provided above each test sound.

A summary of the student's sentence misarticulations may be recorded on the back of the record form. Each manner of formation and place of articulation is listed, followed by the sentence number in which the phonemes of that specific type are assessed.

STRENGTHS OF THE FISHER-LOGEMANN

- The Fisher-Logemann is available in a convenient test folio that converts easily into an easel for displaying the stimulus pictures. Its compact size makes it portable and easy to store.
- The test manual is well organized and concisely written. Detailed information on test development and administration and on recording and analyzing responses is supplemented by sample test protocols and a listing of common dialectal variations.
- This instrument is a comprehensive diagnostic tool. Articulation is assessed in both single-word productions and connected speech. Vowel sounds as well as single consonants and blends are included. Many conventional articulation tests do not contain stimulus items that specifically evaluate vowel production. Consequently, the articulation of

these sounds must be assessed independently by the examiner.

• The further value of the Fisher-Logemann as a diagnostic tool lies in its adaptability to either comprehensive assessment of articulation or quick screening. It is therefore appropriate for use in public school systems where rapid measures of articulation must be made or as part of lengthier diagnostic evaluations that require in-depth testing. Because a single record form is used for both the screening and complete versions of the word test, it is possible to switch easily to the in-depth form if multiple articulation problems are revealed by the screening.

• The stimulus pictures are interesting and colorful and therefore elicit the stimulus words easily in most testing situations. Alternate pictures have been provided for students who might be affected by geographical differences in pronunciation and by dialect factors. Care was also taken to choose items for the Picture Test with which students are known to have maximum familiarity: 90 percent of the selected words are included in the Kindergarten Union Word List, a study of preschool vocabulary, and 74 percent are found in the Horn Word List of the most frequently used vocabulary items of children through age 6. The same criterion of familiarity was used in choosing the reading vocabulary for the Sentence Articulation Test.

• An excellent feature of the Fisher-Logemann is its information about the phonological variations that should be expected for several dialect groups. Common variations among standard and class dialects in different regions of the United States are presented in footnotes on both record forms. Dialect notes in the test manual list phonemic substitutions for several native dialects (general American, Eastern, New York City and environs, Southern, and Black) and describe foreign dialect influences from Spanish, Italian, French, German, and Russian and the Scandinavian, Oriental, and Eastern European languages. Such vital information broadens the use of this tool and aids the clinician in making an appropriate diagnosis of either an articulation deficit or a dialect variation.

• Perhaps the most innovative facet of the Fisher-Logemann is the organization of its record forms. They are easy to use, yet they allow the examiner to note an abundance of useful information. Particularly useful are the guidelines for distinctive-feature analysis, which describe phonemes according to the factors that govern their discrete production. The result, therefore, is not only knowledge of the phonemes a student has misarticulated, but also the specific rules of sound production that have been violated. For example, if a student consistently substitutes /p/ for /f/ and /b/ for /v/, examination of the record form immediately reveals difficulties with manner of formation and place of articulation—although the concept of voicing is intact. Furthermore, the examiner can determine that bilabial stop pho-

nemes are being subsituted for labiodental fricatives. Immediate access to such information aids greatly in planning appropriate therapy.

• Many conventional articulation tests assess the production of phonemes in initial, medial, and final positions within a word. But this type of analysis does not allow for assimilation effects. Stimulus words are not selected with careful attention to the influence of surrounding phonemes on pronunciation of the test phonemes; they may be preceded or followed by either consonant or vowel sounds. But the Fisher-Logemann uses prevocalic, intervocalic, and postvocalic positioning to account for these assimilation factors. The coarticulation effects of dissimilarly produced consonant sounds are eliminated. This method of organization enables the clinician to evaluate sound production within a systematized phonology rather than as isolated occurrences.

• The judgment of whether stimulus items provide a representative sample of a student's phoneme production is essential in determining the content validity of an articulation test. The Fisher-Logemann demonstrates content validity by assessing all the consonant and vowel sounds in the English language. Furthermore, stimulus words were chosen on the basis of their frequency in the vocabulary of young children.

LIMITING FACTORS OF THE FISHER-LOGEMANN

• Inherent in the organization of a formal articulation test like the Fisher-Logemann is a limitation imposed by the environment in which articulation skill is assessed. Conversational usage of speech sounds is not evaluated. Experienced clinicians are aware that students can often produce a sound correctly in single words while making errors in less restrained conversation. The Sentence Articulation Test does provide some assessment of articulation in connected speech, but this cannot be considered a measure of spontaneous production. Furthermore, because the Sentence Articulation Test can only be used with students at a third-grade reading level, evaluation of connected speech cannot be completed with younger students, beginning readers, or students with reading disability; yet these are the groups of students who are most likely to display articulation errors.

• The developers of the Fisher-Logemann do not provide any information in the manual about the reliability of their assessment instrument. It appears that studies to determine test-retest reliability as well as inter- and intra-rater reliability have not been performed.

The Assessment of Phonological Proceses— Revised (APP-R)

Barbara W. Hodson
The Interstate Printers and Publishers, 1980, 1986
Jackson at Van Buren, Danville, IL 61832

Purpose	To provide a phonological assessment instrument for highly unintelligible children
Major Areas Tested	Phonology
Age or Grade Range	No age range given. Estimated range 2 years and older
Usually Given By	Speech/language pathologist
Type of Test	Individual Criterion-referenced
Scores Obtained	Percentage of occurence Phonological deviancy score Severity interval
Student Performance Timed?	No
Testing Time	15–20 minutes
Scoring/Interpretation Time	1–2 hours
Normed On	Not normed
Alternate Forms Available?	No

FORMAT

The Assessment of Phonological Processes—Revised (APP-R) is a revision of the original APP published in 1980.

The APP-R was designed for highly unintelligible children. Results indicated not only the presence of a disorder, but also the degree of severity, and a direction for planning remediation.

The APP-R kit includes two sets of pictures, five packets of phonological forms, and a manual. The manual has general administration procedures for both the screening and full assessment modes, transcription as well as scoring, accountability and dismissal considerations, and a design for phonological remediation. All scorable categories are described with examples, including segment omissions, class deficiencies, and phonological processes. A case study, complete with pre- and post- transcription, phonological analysis, and course of remediation is provided. The test is administered using objects (boat, jump rope, etc.). These are not in the kit. Examiners are encouraged to gather these objects, supplementing with pictures when necessary.

The first step in administering the APP-R is to divide the objects into five separate groups to match the five columns on the Recording Sheet. The objects are emptied one group at a time in front of the child, who is instructed to choose a toy (or picture) and say its name. If the child does not name an object, the examiner is to say the name and ask the child to name it, preferably after some intervening time. Specific methods for eliciting responses are provided.

The author recommends that the child's responses be audiotaped for later verification. A continuous speech sample is also to be elicited to document later intelligibility gains in spontaneous conversation.

Three forms are necessary when administering the APP-R.

The child's productions are written on the recording sheet. Specific procedures, including the use of a check mark for correct production, a slash mark through omitted sounds, etc., are outlined as is the use of diacritic symbols useful in transcribing deviations. After the transcriptions of the child's utterances are verified, they are transferred to the analysis sheet. Check marks are placed in columns which correspond to the phonological processes evidenced. The first four columns are for segment omissions. Columns 5–10 are class deficiency columns. The fourteen following columns are provided for "miscellaneous error patterns," which are common phonological processes.

The summary sheet is where check marks from the analysis form are totaled and transferred to the designated lines for the 10 basic omission and class deficiency processes. A percentage of occurrence score, a phonological deviancy score, phonological processes average, and severity interval can be calculated. Two screening protocols, the Preschool and Multisyllabic, contain 12 stimulus words

each. Questions are provided at the bottom of each form as guidelines to determine whether further assessment is indicated.

The authors state that the time required for completion of the screening and full assessment modes varies with the experience of the examiner and the severity of the phonological disorder. Nevertheless, estimates were four to five minutes for the preschool screening, fifteen minutes for the multisyllablic screening, and less than an hour for the full 50-item assessment.

STRENGTHS OF THE APP-R

• The choice of object stimuli makes data collection a much more natural and easy process when testing preschool, developmentally delayed, or difficult to test children.

• The time required to administer the 50-item assessment usually does not exceed the 20 minutes stated by the author. In this amount of time, the entire administration can usually be achieved in one session.

• Although most of the objects needed for the test are relatively easy to find, the addition of pictures for difficult to find objects is extremely helpful.

• Both the Preschool and Multisyllabic screening forms are very practical and useful methods for fast data collection. This is one of the few multisyllabic screening tests available for school age children. The words chosen for the Preschool form are likely to be familiar to speakers of American English. The criterion for referral for full assessment at the bottom of each screening form makes this a quick decision-making process.

• This analysis provides the clinician with excellent information to plan phonological remediation for her client. Both the manual and author's book, *Targeting Intelligible Speech*, describe in detail how to select target patterns and plan remediation cycles. (Hodson & Paden, 1983).

• Percentage of occurrence scores are useful for posttreatment accountability measures.

• This is an extremely useful measure for its intended population, the highly unintelligible child. It is based on "state of the art" research in the field of child phonology.

• This manual is a good resource for the description of 29 phonological processes.

• Both Spanish and computerized versions of the APP-R are available.

LIMITING FACTORS OF THE APP-R

• This test is not easy to use. Clinicians must have some prior knowledge of phonological processes in order to use this analysis with some degree of comfort.

• The time required to analyze the 50-item test often exceeds one hour. Although this assessment is highly useful for planning remediation, it may be too complicated and time consuming for many clinicians to use simply as a diagnostic tool.

•   There is no normative data in the test manual. The author does give basic guidelines for normal 2, 3, and 4 year olds. No detail, apart from its evolution from a retrospective study of several hundred client's records, about how severity ratings of age compensatory points were devised is included.

•   Re-entering the child's productions from the recording sheet to the analysis sheet is a time consuming and cumbersome process.

•   Many of the words chosen for the Spanish APP–R are not easily represented in object form. There are no picture stimuli for this version. A good number of these words were not easily recognizable to Spanish speaking preschool children of Mexican descent.

The Goldman-Fristoe Test of Articulation (GFTA)

Ronald Goldman and Macalyne Fristoe
American Guidance Service, Inc., 1969; revised 1972, 1986
Publishers' Bldg., Cirlce Pines, MN 50014

Purpose	To provide systematic assessment of articulation of the consonant sounds in English
Major Areas Tested	Articulation
Age or Grade Range	2–16 years
Usually Given By	Speech/language clinician Audiologist
Type of Test	Individual Criterion-referenced
Scores Obtained	Percentile
Student Performance Timed?	No
Testing Time	20 minutes
Scoring/Interpretation Time	15–20 minutes
Normed On	38,884 students in grades 1–12 throughout the United States plus an additional 852 children aged 2–5
Alternate Forms Available?	No

FORMAT

The materials for the Goldman Fristoe Test of Articulation (GFTA) include the response form, a manual, and an easel device for displaying stimulus pictures. The 8 1/2 by 11 sprial-bound easel contains 35 large and colorful pictures. Each response form provides room for recording and comparing an individual's speech responses from the three GFTA subtests:

1. *Sounds-in-Words*. Productions of single-consonant sounds and of 11 common consonant blends are elicited by identification of pictures illustrating common objects and activities. The examiner asks, "What is it?" to elicit the test phoneme and then may pose additional relevant questions to produce the desired response. Consonant phonemes are classified as occurring in initial, medial, and final positions of the stimulus words. Medial position, according to the authors, does not necessarily refer to the middle consonant in a word, but rather to some internal position within a polysyllable. Not all of the consonant phonemes are evaluated in each of three positions; a few are omitted because of the rarity of their occurrence in the English phonological system.

The stimulus words are printed on the back of the picture, facing the examiner, with the letters representing the test phonemes set off in bold type and with extra spacing around them. The numbers corresponding to the record sheet are indicated above the test phonemes.

2. *Sounds-in-Sentences*. The examiner reads two short stories aloud to the student while showing a corresponding set of pictures. In presenting each story, the examiner emphasizes the "key words" that appear in bold type on the examiner's side of the easel kit. These words contain the phonemes being evaluated in the subtest, those sounds considered by the authors most likely to be misarticulated by children. The student is then asked to retell the story in his or her own words, using the illustrations as memory aids. These pictures help provide some control over the content of the speech sample. The examiner is encouraged to prompt the student to produce any key words not elicited by the pictures.

3. *Stimulation*. This subtest evaluates the student's ability to produce previously incorrect phonemes correctly, in the context of syllables, words, and sentences, with stimulation by the examiner. The student is instructed to watch the examiner closely and to try to repeat the sound heard. Only phonemes that were misarticulated in the Sounds-in-Words subtest are evaluated and only in the word position (initial, medial, final) where the errors originally occurred. Stimulation pictures in this subtest list specific syllables, words, and sentences for testing stimulability of each phoneme. If the student is unable to imitate a sound accurately in any of the three contexts, "multiple stimulation" is used, whereby the examiner repeats the phoneme three times before the student

is asked to reproduce it again. Whenever a student is unable to articulate a phoneme correctly with multiple stimulation, testing for that sound should be discontinued. The Stimulation subtest provides valuable information concerning the sounds that may most readily be remediated by speech therapy.

The test phonemes on the response form are coded by color to designate the word positions being evaluated and also by number to designate the location of the sound on the response matrix. Blue always indicates the initial position within a word, yellow the medial position, and green the final position. Responses from the Sounds-in-Words and Stimulability subtests are recorded on one side of the form. To the left of these columns is a list of the key words as they are written on the easel. During the Sounds-in-Sentences subtest, the examiner is to place a check mark above each correctly articulated sound, or to mark the subject's subsitution or omission above the misarticulated sounds. These notations must later be transferred to the Sounds-in-Sentences matrix on the other side of the response form. Side-by-side comparison of responses on all three subtests is possible by folding over the Sounds-in-Sentences response matrix. The authors state that this test was designed to accomodate two levels of evaluation depending upon the qualifications of the tester. The first is to judge for the presence of error only for the purpose of referring a child for therapy. The second level is to judge for the type of error for therapeutic planning and determination of severity of the disorder. Standard notations to be used for each of these levels of assessment are reviewed in the manual. These range from an X-mark to signify an error to the sound substitution produced accompanied by diacritic markings. A mild distortion is marked "2," while a severe distortion is given a "3."

STRENGTHS OF THE GFTA

• The GFTA uses large and colorful pictures that are highly interesting to most students, making it relatively easy to elicit the stimulus words under usual circumstances.

• The directions for test administration are clear and concise, making this an easy test to use. The manual also contains good information on test rationale and construction.

• The pictures and word selection make this test quite useful for the preschool child. In the 1986 version, norms have been extended to include the 2 year old.

• The unique value of the GFTA is the variety of contexts in which phonemic production is evaluated. Not only is articulation performance in single-word production evaluated, but so is articulation in a controlled connected speech sample.

• Although the GFTA is designed for analysis of consonant production, articulation of vowels may also be judged. All the vowel sounds of English are present in the Sounds-in-Words subtest, and an alert examiner may obtain information on the student's production of these phonemes.

• The GFTA does provide normative data based on results of the National Speech and Hearing survey (Hull et al., 1971, 1972), of 38,884 children aged 6.0 to 16+. Additional percentile rank norms for children aged 2.0 to 5.11 for the Sounds-in-Words subtest are also available. These are based on the 1983 sample of 852 children used to standarize the Khan-Lewis Phonological Analysis, a procedure designed for use with the Goldman-Fristoe. (Khan-Lewis, 1986)

• Test-retest reliability was determined by retesting 37 articulatory defective children between the ages of 4 and 8. The median agreement for the Sounds-in-Words subtest was 95%, and the median agreement for the Sounds-in-Sentences subtest was 94%.

LIMITING FACTORS OF THE GFTA

• A major weakness of the GFTA is the complicated format for recording responses. Although the form is color-coded to indicate sounds occurring in initial, medial, and final positions within the words, it is often difficult to locate these phonemes rapidly on the response matrix. Even highly trained diagnosticians may have difficulty evaluating several phoneme productions within a single word and then recording these judgments in various places on the response matrix while maintaining the attention of the student. If an examiner attempts to record all the responses while administering the test, a more definitive judgment than "acceptable" or "unacceptable" production is difficult to make. In order to use this tool to make an accurate assessment of articulation, it is frequently necessary to tape record the session and to transcribe errors at a later time. This obviously extends the time needed to complete the evaluation.

• The GFTA is not available in a screening form and therefore may be too lengthy for use in public school screenings. Administration of the entire test is approximately 20 minutes, and the examiner may have difficulty maintaining the attention of young students or students who exhibit multiple articulation errors.

• Although the test manual does provide detailed information about interpreting students' responses, no consideration for dialect variations has been included. Frequently the speech and language clinician may be asked to evaluate the articulation of a non-native English speaker or an individual from a different section of the United States. Some basic information on expected articulation variations for major dialect groups—such as Americans residing in the southern, northeastern, or midwestern United States or Mexican-American students—would certainly enhance the value of this tool.

• In the organization of this test, attention was not given to using the rules that govern production of specific speech sounds. The test provides information on which phonemes are misarticulated by the student, but it does not give information about what kind of errors occurred in terms of manner of formation or place of articulation. The examiner is not instructed to give a complete phonetic transcription of the full word even though a space is now provided for this on the response sheet for use with the Khan-Lewis Phonological Analysis. Distinctive feature theory and phonological processing have not been incorporated into the test. This limits the examiner's ability to diagnose discreetly and plan remediation.

• Information gleaned from the stimulability subtest would again be greatly enhanced if the examiner were to transcribe the entire word. In this way, movement toward adult production could be visible.

• The reliability of this articulation test may be judged by the consistency with which the same response is recorded for each phoneme in initial, medial, and final positions within the stimulus words. Test-retest reliability was obtained for the Sounds-in-Words and Sounds-in-Sentences subtests only. Measures of interrater and intrarater reliability were obtained only for the Sounds-in-Words subtest. The lack of research to determine interreliability and intrareliability for the Sounds-in-Sentences and Stimulation subtests is clearly a weakness of this tool.

• The content validity of a measure of articulation skill must involve stimulus items that provide a representative sample of a student's phoneme production. The developers of this test do not provide substantial information concerning the choice of the stimulus words, nor do they discuss the influence on articulation of such variables as word frequency and the grammatical function of a specific sound. Some measure of content validity, however, is assured by the fact that all but one of the consonants contained in the English language are assessed in the Sounds-in-Words subtest.

The Templin-Darley Tests of Articulation
(Templin-Darley)

Mildred C. Templin and Frederic L. Darley
The University of Iowa, 1960; revised 1969
The University of Iowa, Iowa City, IA 52242

Purpose	To assess general accuracy of articulation (Screening Test); to assess production of a wide range of speech sounds in a variety of word positions and phonetic contexts (Diagnostic Test); to evaluate consistency of production of various types of speech elements (Iowa Pressure Articulation Test)
Major Areas Tested	Articulation
Age or Grade Range	3 years–adult
Usually Given By	Speech/language clinician
Type of Test	Individual
Scores Obtained	Age level
Student Performance Timed?	No
Testing Time	15 minutes (Screening Test); 25–30 minutes (Diagnostic and Iowa Pressure Articulation Test)
Scoring/Interpretation Time	10 minutes (Screening Test); 15–20 minutes (Diagnostic and Iowa Pressure Articulation Test)
Normed On	480 white, monolingual public school children aged 3–8 years in Minneapolis and St. Paull, Minnesota; children of normal intelligence with no gross evidence of hearing loss
Alternate Forms Available?	No

FORMAT

The Templin-Darley Tests of Articulation (Templin-Darley) make up a compact diagnostic instrument comprising three separate tests; (1) the Screening Test, (2) the Diagnostic Test, and (3) the Iowa Pressure Articulation Test. A manual contains detailed information on test administration, the stimulus words and pictures, the normative data, and a general discussion of diagnostic procedures and research in the field of articulation. Record forms must be ordered from the publisher separately.

The total test contains 141 sound elements, many of which occur in more than one test. These stimulus elements can be organized into several different diagnostic units by using the record form overlays provided. Any combination of these diagnostic units may be administered, depending on specific diagnostic needs.

1. *Screening Test.* This test consists of the first 50 pictures in the manual, which are used to elicit the sounds found to be good predictors of articulation problems in preschool and kindergarten students. Cut-off scores have been provided for ages 3 to 8, at six-month intervals, based on the number of sounds correctly articulated. The authors state that these scores should be used to separate a student with adequate articulation from those requiring more in-depth articulation testing.

2. *Diagnostic Test.* This 42-item grouping of single consonants contains 22 stimulus sounds assessed in the initial position of words and 20 consonant phonemes in the final position. Use of the appropriate record form overlay identifies the items to be evaluated in this section. The mean number of consonant sounds correctly produced by children aged 3 to 8 years is provided at one-year intervals for comparison purposes.

3. *Iowa Pressure Articulation Test.* This test contains 43 items selected to assess the adequacy of a student's intraoral pressure for phoneme productions. This subtest, then, can be used to evaluate velopharyngeal closure and nasality. The stimulus consonants consist of fricative, plosive, and affricate sounds that have been found to require greater intraoral breath pressure than other phoneme types.

4. *Additional consonant cluster groupings.* These may be used to determine the phonetic contexts in which the student produces specific consonants adequately.

5. *Groupings of vowels and diphthongs.* This test assesses production of 11 vowel sounds, 5 diphthongs, and 1 consonant-vowel combination. Mean scores at one-year intervals for students 3 to 8 years old are provided for vowel and diphthong groups.

For young students, the examiner displays each picture and elicits the stimulus word by asking, "What is this?" or by using the questions and statements printed on the back of each card (such as, "What's pouring out of the chiminey?"). The phonetic symbols are also printed on the back of the

cards, with the item numbers corresponding to the record form. The examiner is encouraged to have the student imitate the stimulus word if the student does not produce it spontaneously with only the picture as motivation.

There are 141 stimulus sentences (in addition to the 141 sound elements) for assessing the articulation of older students who are able to read and for whom the use of picture stimuli seems inappropriate. The phonemes tested in the sentence format correspond to those evaluated by the picture stimuli. Two test words containing the stimulus sound are included in each sentence.

The Templin-Darley record form lists each test phoneme, provides space for recording articulation performance, gives an outline for analyzing the test results, and allows for further comments. Sections are included for listing phonemes that are consistently misarticulated throughout the testing and for recording error sounds noted in the student's conversational speech. The authors suggest using standard phonetic notations to indicate correct sound productions (✓), substitutions (enter phoneme uttered), omissions (–), distortions (X), nasal emissions (ne), and no response (nr).

After the student's responses have been recorded, the examiner should test the stimulability of the misarticulated sounds. The student should be asked to imitate each error phoneme in isolation, in a syllable, in a word, and in a sound cluster within a word. Space is provided on the record form for recording the student's imitative performance.

STRENGTHS OF THE TEMPLIN-DARLEY

• The Templin-Darley is perhaps the most comprehensive and versatile set of articulation tests available, and it can be used for testing the articulation of both adults and children. It is applicable for screening large groups in a public school setting, for obtaining a detailed analysis of articulation skill in order to determine the need for therapy, and for describing a pattern of misarticulations to aid in planning remediation goals. It is a practical investment for those on a limited budget, because it is a single instrument that can serve several diagnostic purposes.

• In addition to detailed information on administration and interpretation of the test, the manual includes a lengthy discussion about articulation testing and research. It is an excellent resource tool for speech pathology students and for clinicians who do not have extensive diagnostic experience.

• A unique feature of the Templin-Darley is the Iowa Pressure Articulation Test, which provides for quick screening of a student's velopharyngeal competency. However, normative data was obtained for presumably normal students and consequently does not relate specifically to those with cleft palates or velopharyngeal incompetency.

• The ability of a student to imitate a particular phoneme is an important consideration in the choice of a sound for remediation. This factor is often omitted in the format of articulation tests. The Templin-Darley, however, includes evaluations of the stimulability of error sounds in several phonemic contexts (in isolation, in a syllable, in a word, and in a sound cluster).

• The Templin-Darley in its entirety evaluates the production of 141 sound elements, including single consonants, vowels, diphthongs, and sound clusters. It is extremely useful as an instrument because it assesses a wider range of articulation performance than any other commercially available articulation test.

• The authors established the validity of this diagnostic instrument by conducting a study of the articulation performance of 150 children, aged 5 to 10 years. The children's performances on selected test items were found to be significantly related to a trained judge's rating of the students' articulation in connected speech samples.

LIMITING FACTORS OF THE TEMPLIN-DARLEY

• The Templin-Darley assesses phoneme production in initial, medial, and final positions within stimulus words. This method of evaluation does not account for the influence of preceding and subsequent phonemes on the articulation of the stimulus sound.

Moreover, in the Diagnostic Test, consonant singles (stimulus sounds and consonant phonemes) are assessed only in the initial and final positions. The authors defend the omission of medial consonants by questioning their validity— on the grounds that all consonants are either syllable-releasing or syllable-arresting in ongoing speech. This premise is shaky. All other commonly used articulation tests evaluate consonants in this position, and it is important to remediate error productions within a word to improve phonemic sequencing skills.

• Judgments of misarticulation on the Templin-Darley are based on general American dialect. No information is given about the effect of geographical variations and foreign dialects on articulation. Provision should have been made for considering such influences when scoring sound errors because these are important considerations for clinicians who are planning appropriate remediation goals.

• The product of the Templin-Darley is knowledge of the specific sounds that a student misarticulates. However, interpretation of these errors in terms of such factors as voicing, manner of formation, and place of articulation must be made independently by the clinician. Information on the distinctive-feature analysis of sound productions and the developmental sequence of phonemic acquistion would have been valuable for interpreting test results and planning therapy.

• Comparison of an articulation performance with the norms presented for a specific subtest will indicate whether the student's sound development is above, equal to, or below that of peers. But to use the normative data provided by the authors, sound productions must be scored as "right" or "wrong." This scoring system fails to account for the severity or specific type of misarticulations exhibited by the student. Placing an equivalent point value on all phonemes does not take into consideration the frequency of a particular sound in the English language. Certainly a student who consistently misarticulates the /s/ and /r/ phonemes is more unintelligible than one who has difficulty with /h/ and /v/.

• The authors report reliability data for only the 50-item Screening Test. Test-retest reliability coefficients ranging from .93 to .99 were obtained for the picture test and from .97 to .99 for the sentence test. Further research appears to be warranted to establish the reliability of the other tests.

• The rapid administration of a picture articulation test depends greatly on the student's recognition of and familiarity with the stimulus items. All but four of the stimulus words in the Templin-Darley appear on the Rinsland Basic Vocabulary list, developed in 1945. (We, the authors, have found that several of the stimulus words are difficult to elicit.) Apparently such an outdated word list includes items no longer relevant to the daily experiences of students. Items like *possum, shredded wheat, sharp, large,* and *help* are particularly difficult for many students to recognize and often can be assessed only on an imitative basis.

• The manual provides a great deal of information that is interesting but not essential for experienced diagnosticians. Instructions for administering the instrument are scattered through the descriptive material and are difficult to follow. In addition, a great deal of practice is required to be able to easily manipulate the record form overlays.

Language Sampling, Analysis, and Training
(Tyack and Gottsleben)

Dorothy Tyack and Robert Gottsleben
Consulting Psychologists Press, 1974, 1977
577 College Ave., Palo Alto, CA 94306

Purpose	To provide a grammatical analysis of a student's expressive language and, through a "resample" procedure, to provide a measure of carryover of these grammatical rules following speech and language training
Major Areas Tested	Grammatical structure of oral language
Age or Grade Range	Not given (most effective with 2–7 years)
Usually Given By	Speech/language clinician
Type of Test	Individual
Scores Obtained	None
Student Performance Timed?	No
Testing Time	60 minutes
Scoring/Interpretation Time	2 hours
Normed On	Not reported
Alternate Forms Available?	No

FORMAT

The *Language Sampling, Analysis, and Training* handbook includes 33 pages of text describing the language sampling, analysis, and training program. A glossary, two completely analyzed language samples, and practice exercise are also provided. With the exception of the Score Sheet for Training Programs, all forms are shown in the manual. They include:

A. Transcription Form
B. Word/Morpheme Tally & Summary
C. Sequence of Language Acquisition
D. Baseline & Goal Data
E. Training Worksheet
F. Score Sheet

All scoring forms must be ordered separately from the publisher.

The initial step in this assessment procedure is to obtain a language sample of 100 sentences. The authors suggest eliciting these utterances through a discussion of a set of pictures taken from *People in Action* (Shaftel and Shaftel, 1970). If these procedures do not suffice, the authors recommend varying the elicitation situation in whatever manner necessary to produce a representative sample.

Transcription of the language, preferably by the same person who gathered it, is the next step. The transcription form provides three lines for each sentence. The first is for response analysis, the second for the child's utterances, and the third for the intended utterance (an expansion).

Child_____ Examiner_____ Date_____

 # 1   **#**

| She sleep on the couch. |
| *is*   *ing* |

 # 2   **#**

| Her won't eat candy. |
| *She* |

 # 3 What's he eating?   **#**

| He eating her hamburger. |
| *is*   *his* |

 # 4 (drops one piece of candy)   **#**

| Oops, I dropped them. |
| *it* |

 # 5   **#**

| Another picture? |
| *That is another picture?* |

 # 6   **#**

| Who's running? |
| |

Tyack and Gottsleben Transcription Sheet, Utterances Noted

Analysis of the language sample involves the following steps:

1. Counting words and morphemes in each sentence. Detailed instruction and illustrative examples for obtaining these words and morpheme counts are provided in the handbook. The counts for the utterances shown in the example here are listed below:

	Words	Morphemes
She sleep on the couch.	5	5
Her won't eat candy.	4	4
He eating her hamburger.	4	5
(Oops), I dropped them.	3	4
Another picture?	2	2
Who's running?	2	4

2. Calculating the "word-morpheme index." Add the mean number of words per sentence to the mean number of morphemes per sentence. Then divide the sum by two. The word-morpheme index for the utterances shown here is four.

3. Assigning the sample to a linguistic level based on the word-morpheme index:

Level I: 2.0–2.5
Level II: 2.5–3.0
Level III: 3.0–4.0
Level IV: 4.0–5.0
Level V: 5.0–6.0

These levels were organized by the authors and are based on the research of Morehead and Ingram (1973), Miller and Yoder (1974), and the author's own research (1974).

4. Identifying the forms and construction types in the sample sentences and sorting them into the categories listed on the sequence of language acquisition sheet. On the transcription sheet, all forms presented in the utterances (or forms substituted) are circled, and the form omissions are checked.

Child_____ Examiner_____ Date_____

 # 1
5-5   (She) sleep on (the) couch.
          is   ing

 # 2
4-4   (Her)(won't) eat candy.
          She

 # 3 What's he eating?
4-5   (He) eating (her) hamburger.
          is   his

 # 4 (drops one piece of candy)
3-4   Oops, (I) dropped (them)
                          it

 # 5
2-2   Another picture?
      That is another picture?

 # 6
2-4   Who('s) running?

Tyack and Gottsleben Transcription Sheet, Forms Noted

Each sentence is then assigned a construction type based on the theory of transformational grammar.

She sleep on the couch.	Noun + Verb + Noun
Her won't eat candy.	Negative–Noun + Modal + Verb + Noun
He eating her hamburger.	Noun + Verb + Noun
(Oops,) I dropped them.	Noun + Verb + Noun
Another picture?	Question–Quantifier + Noun
Who's running?	Question–Noun + Verb

The construction types are written above the sample sentences.

The sequence of language acquisition sheet illustrates graphically the developmental progression of various grammatical forms and constructions. Based on Morehead and Ingram's research (1973), the grammatical criteria (forms and simple sentence contructions) have been assigned linguistic levels of acqusition. Specific lexical categories in this analysis include:

Pronouns	Modals
Prepositions	Copula verb
Demonstratives	Present progressive tense
Articles	Present tense (third-person
Plurals	singular form)
Locatives	Verb particles
Conjunctions	Past-tense verbs

Child_____ Examiner_____ Date_____

 # 1 N+V+N

5-5   (She) sleep on (the) couch.
       is   ing

\#

 # 2 Neg N+modal+V+N

4-4   (Her) (won't) eat candy.
      She

\#

 # 3 N+V+N

4-5   (He) eating (her) hamburger.
     is   his

\#

 # 4 N+V+N

3-4   Oops, (I) dropp(ed) (them)
             it

\#

 # 5 Q quan.+N

2-2   Another picture?
    That is another picture?

\#

 # 6 Q N+V

2-4   Who('s) runn(ing)?

\#

Tyack and Gottsleben Transcription Sheet, Construction Types Noted

Negative and question constructions are listed in order of acquisition, although specific levels have not been assigned to them. Because of the inconclusive research cited by the authors, the order of acquisition of complex sentence structures is not known at present.

The number of sample utterances containing a listed form or construction is entered on the sequence of language acquisition sheet. Columns are provided to indicate where a form has occurred correctly (+), where a form was missing when obligatory by standards of adult English (–), and where one form was substituted for another (X).

5. Entering data on the baseline and goal analysis sheets. These are the final forms in the Tyack and Gottsleben analysis procedure. The baseline analysis lists the forms and constructions used correctly by the student, and the goal analysis lists those needed to bring the student to his or her assigned linguistic level.

STRENGTHS OF THE TYACK AND GOTTSLEBEN

• The Tyack and Gottsleben language-sampling proce-dure provides an extremely thorough assessment of a student's morphological and syntactic competence. It considers a wider range of forms and constructions than most conventional tests of grammar or such language-sampling techniques as Development Sentence Scoring (Lee and Koenigsknecht, 1974). A great deal of useful develop-mental information can be procured by examining the analysis sheets. Because spaces are provided for recording contextual information, some knowledge of the student's semantic competency can also be obtained.

• The authors' handbook is clearly written and relatively inexpensive, and it supplies numerous details and examples of all phases of their method. Unanalyzed language samples are also included for practice purposes. The series of analysis forms provide a concise and graphic method of presenting baseline language behavior and goals of training.

• The authors have increased the usefulness of their handbook by including information about structuring language remediation programs and choosing appropriate therapy goals. Data-taking procedure are also discussed.

• The Tyack and Gottsleben method of language analysis is based on the premise that language-deviant students acquire morphological and syntactic rules in the same sequence as normal students. There are no age norms included, and appropriate remediation goals are based not on chronological age but on the linguistic capabilities and needs of the student. In support of this, research has shown that mean morpheme measure is a more reliable indicator of linguistic development than chronological age is (Menyuk, 1969; Bloom, 1970; Brown, 1973).

• The definition of a sentence as "at least two structur-ally related morphemes" makes this procedure an effective assessment tool with students who exhibit only low-level

language structures. Developmental Sentence Types, described by Lee and Koenigsknecht in Developmental Sentence Analysis (1974), is the only other systematic measure of such immature linguistic forms that is available to speech and language clinicians. However, it does not provide detailed information on choosing appropriate remediation goals.

The information on complex sentences provides a classification system and many examples of each sentence type. This section in the manual helps prepare the evaluator for the job of properly entering the complex sentences into the Sequence of Language Acquisition form.

LIMITING FACTORS OF THE TYACK AND GOTTSLEBEN

• The Tyack and Gottsleben language-assessment procedure is complicated, tedious, and extremely time consuming. Although the handbook presents detailed in-structions, many opportunities arise for errors in transcrip-tion and analysis of the language samples. A clinician who attempts to minimize such errors by transcribing and analyzing his or her own samples may find the time involved to be unrealistic. Futhermore, collecting the 100 utterances suggested by the authors may require several sessions with a severely language-handicapped student.

• This procedure for acquiring and analyzing a language sampling is quite difficult to learn solely from reading the authors' handbook. The analysis forms can be confusing and awkward to handle. A solid background in psycholinguistic theory is necessary for classifying utterances into the forms and constructions listed on the analysis sheet. Thus, if one plans to use this procedure efficiently, attending a language-sampling workshop given by the authors is tremendously helpful.

• The purpose of the Tyack and Gottsleben is to provide data for planning an individualized remediation program, and it should not be considered a diagnostic tool. It does not provide information for comparing one student's perform-ance with others of the same age or grade level. No validity or reliability studies have been conducted, although the basic premises on which the program is based come from years of linguistic and behavioral research.

• The grammatical criteria are based on standard American English. The authors do not provide any informa-tion about assessment of nonstandard dialects or other languages. Clinicians are encouraged to explore the current research on dialectical variations if warranted by their therapy caseloads.

• The speech and language clinician may frequently be asked to evaluate a student whose word-morpheme mean exceeds the limits of Level V. Because the alternate method of language-sampling analysis, Laura Lee's Developmental

Sentence Scoring, also has a ceiling at the 8-year-old level,
no adequate tool for assessing the older child's conversational language is available at present. This is an area
warranting further research.

• This is a syntactic analysis which provides no semantic or pragmatic information to the clinician. Additional data
must therefore be collected and analyzed in order to examine
these other aspects of communication.

Auditory-Visual, Single Word Picture Vocabulary Test—Adolescent (AVSWPVT-A)

Morrison F. Gardiner
Children's Hospital of San Francisco, 1986
Box 3805, San Francisco, CA 94119

Purpose	To determine the depth of an adolescent's single word picture vocabulary
Major Areas Tested	Receptive picture vocabulary
Age or Grade Range	12–17 years
Usually Given By	Psychologist Counselor Special education teacher Speech/language pathologist
Type of Test	Individual Group Self-administered
Scores Obtained	Language age Standard scores Percentile Stanine
Student Performance Timed?	No
Testing Time	10–15 minutes
Scoring/Interpretation Time	5–10 minutes
Normed On	674 students in the San Francisco Bay area ranging in age from 12–17 years
Alternate Forms Available?	No

FORMAT

The Auditory-Visual Single Word Picture Vocabulary Test—Adolescent (AVSWPVT-A) is a picture vocabulary test for adolescents. The test items include pictures of geometric forms, people, action verbs, and abstractions. The materials consist of the manual, containing test rationale, administration and scoring procedures, and norms tables; a spiral-bound book of 75 test plates; and two types of record forms, Examiner's Administration and Self-Administration.

In the individual administration format, the examiner pronounces a word and the student selects the corresponding picture from a series of four line drawings. This is the typical picture vocabulary test format, identical to that used in the PPVT-R and the ROWPVT.

Students are encouraged to guess or use the process of elimination when they are uncertain of a response. Starting points for each age student are indicated on the Examiner's Administration Form. A basal (8 consecutive correct responses) and ceiling (6 out of 8 incorrect responses) procedure allows the student to be assessed over his or her range of ability.

The unique feature of the AVSWPVT-A is that the stimulus word is also printed on the test plate. This feature allows the student who can read to take the test without examiner involvement. The student reads the stimulus word, selects his response, and marks the number of his response on the Self-Administration record form. Students complete the entire 75 items. The examiner determines basal and ceiling levels when the test is scored.

The raw score (number of correct responses) is converted into a language age, standard score, percentile, and stanine.

STRENGTHS OF THE AVSWPVT-A

• The AVSWPVT-A is quick and easy to administer. Administration and scoring procedures are ambiguous. The Self-Administration format allows a quick receptive vocabulary screening for students who can read.

LIMITING FACTORS OF THE AVSWPVT-A

• The AVSWPVT-A has serious theoretical and technical limitations. The addition of the stimulus word printed on the test plate changes the nature of the test from a test of listening vocabulary to a test of reading vocabulary. Even in the examiner-administered format, students read, or attempt to read, the printed word. Students with learning and language problems are often distracted by this process.

• As is noted by the author, the self-administration format should not be used unless the examiner is certain that the student has "adequately developed reading skills, i.e., word pronunciation and word comprehension." No provision is given for assessing a student's reading skills, and no attempt was made to control the readability of the stimulus words. The use of the phonetic key on the self-examination record form is of little value. Very few students know how to use a phonetic key and certainly those for whom it was intended, the poor readers, have no skills in this area. When a student makes an error on the self-administration form, there is no way of knowing whether it was a decoding error, a lack of knowledge of word meaning, or a poor interpretation of the pictures. The addition of a reading pretest or a reading check of items missed would greatly strengthen the AVSWPVT-A.

• Item selection as described in the manual started with a collection of words from dictionaries, texts, teachers, TV, newspapers etc. Attempts were made to exclude words with gender or cultural bias, although these procedures are not clearly described. It is clear that the final selection includes many science and geometry words, penalizing students without coursework in these areas.

• Many of the pictures are quite ambiguous.

• The author states that a picture vocabulary test should measure "vocabulary and intelligence." (Manual, page 16.) Such statements encourage examiners to use the test as an IQ test. At best, the AVSWPVT-A screens a student's receptive vocabulary, and its technical problems make that questionable.

• Technically the AVSWPVT-A has many problems. The sample was drawn from a single geographic area, and no description of the ethnic background of the standardization sample are decribed. No information is given as to the presence or absence of students with reading or language problems in the sample. No test-retest reliability data is reported. Validity data is meager and questionable. The AVSWPVT-A should not be considered anything other than a rough screening test.

• The author states that the AVSWPVT-A can be helpful in comparing an adolescent's English vocabulary with that of his primary language. As no Spanish or other language versions of this test are described, it is not clear how this is to be done.

Boehm Test of Basic Concepts—Revised (BTBC-R)

Ann E. Boehm
The Psychological Corporation, 1986
555 Academic Court, San Antonio, TX 78204

Purpose	To assess mastery of concepts which are fundamental to understanding verbal instruction and essential for early school achievement
Major Areas Tested	Knowledge of basic relational concepts such as more–less, first–last, and same–different as well as concepts of space, quantity, and time
Age or Grade Range	Kindergarten–grade 2
Usually Given By	Classroom teacher Special education teacher Speech/language clinician
Type of Test	Standardized Individual Group
Scores Obtained	Percentile
Student Performance Timed?	No
Testing Time	30–40 minutes (Forms C and D) 15–20 minutes (Applications)
Scoring/Interpretation Time	15–20 minutes
Normed On	Nation-wide sample of over 4,600 children in each testing group; sample weighted to include percentage of large and small school districts in geographic regions representative of current population of U.S.; sample balanced by socioeconomic level, age, and grade
Alternate Forms Available?	Yes

FORMAT

The Boehm Test of Basic Concepts Revised (BTBC-R) is a revised edition of the Boehm test published in 1971. While the basic format and many of the items are the same, the content has been updated and the test completely restandardized.

The materials for the BTBC-R consist primarily of the individual student test booklets and the examiner's manual. The test has two alternate forms, C and D. In each form, the 50 concepts are divided equally into two booklets, Booklet 1 and Booklet 2. The manual includes information on test development and statistical data as well as directions for test administration, scoring, and interpretation.

The revised Boehm is designed as a group test. Instructions are read by the examiner (usually a teacher), and the students mark the correct responses directly in the individual test booklet. ("Look at the toys. Mark the toy that is next to the truck.")

The revised Boehm also includes the Application Booklet. This 26-item test booklet assesses basic concepts. ("Mark all the fish that are long and below the line.") The Applications Booklet is administered in the same way as the rest of the test. It may be used in conjuction with Form C or D or alone. It is intended for use only with first and second grade students.

Upon completion of the test, each student's responses are recorded on the Class Record Form. Each student's correct responses are totaled and converted into percentile scores using tables in the manual. These tables take into account grade level and socioeconomic level. Separate percentiles are provided for beginning and end-of-the-year testing. Separate scores are obtained for Form C, Form D, and Applications. The Class Record Form also allows the teacher to calculate the percentage of students correctly answering each item. Such information is helpful in planning a classroom program as well as in developing local norms. The authors also suggest an optional error analysis system in which the teacher records the following error types: no response, marking all pictures, choosing the opposite concept (top for bottom), and miscellaneous. Such information is helpful in understanding an individual student's performance.

STRENGTHS OF THE BOEHM-R

• The Boehm is an inexpensive way to assess the understanding of space, quantity, and time concepts in young school-aged students. Most young children find it interesting. The illustrations are clear, and the format is well organized. A gross marking response is adequate. A pointing response may also be used if the student is unable to handle a pencil or crayon and if the test is being individually administered.

• The manual is well organized. Information on test administration, scoring, and interpretation is clearly presented. Designed primarily as a group test, careful attention has been given to facilitate group administration with young children.

• The revised Boehm construction included careful attention to item selection and presentation. Items were excluded which were passed by high percentages of beginning kindergarten students. The concepts measured appear frequently in primary-grade curriculum materials. Thoughtfully employed, the test results can be used to assist teachers in recognizing the needs of individual students and classroom groups. The manual provides extensive help in instructional planning.

• The provision of two equivalent forms and separate norms for fall and spring testing make the Boehm-R a useful test for measuring progress.

• The Applications Booklet is a good addition to the test, extending its usefulness with first and second grade students.

• A preschool version of the Boehm Test of Basic Concepts (BTBC-PV) has been developed as a separate publication. This version, standardized on 3- and 4-year olds, assesses the 26 concepts that are mastered by most children entering kindergarten. It is presented in a card booklet format and is individually administered.

• Also available is a Parent-Teacher Conference Report. This form is designed to help teachers present test results to parents. It includes an explanation of the basic concepts, a brief test description, a few sample items, and suggestions for ways in which the parent can help the child learn basic concepts at home. The report can be used with both Forms C and D.

• Directions for the revised Boehm have been translated into Spanish. Spanish-speaking aides or teachers can administer the test using the same picture booklets. However, norms that are specifically for Spanish-speaking students are not provided.

LIMITING FACTORS OF THE BOEHM-R

• As is stated in the manual, the major use of this test is as a *screening* measure. Only one item is included to measure each concept, and factors such as attention and motivation may influence a child's response.

• The reliability data presented in the manual is somewhat low. This may be due to the fact that the range of scores is narrow, especially for older students, or it may reflect the unreliability of group scores with young children. In either case, the data again suggests the need to consider the Boehm-R as a screening instrument rather than as a definitive diagnostic instrument.

• Although extensive research on the original Boehm is reported in the manual, only one, poorly-reported, validity study using the Boehm-R is presented. As this test is easily adaptable to students with various handicapping conditions, research with both normal and exceptional students will probably be forthcoming.

Clinical Evaluation of Language Fundamentals—Revised (CELF-R)

Eleanor Semel-Mintz, Elizabeth Wiig, and Wayne Secord
The Psychological Corporation, 1987
555 Academic Court, San Antonio, TX 78204

Purpose	To provide a practical clinical tool for the identification, diagnosis, and follow-up evaluation of oral language skill deficits in school age children
Major Areas Tested	Word meaning; word and sentence structure; recall and retrieval
Age or Grade Range	K–12
Usually Given By	Speech/language clinician Psychologist Learning disability specialist
Type of Test	Individual Norm-referenced Standardized
Scores Obtained	Standard scores Percentile NCE's Age-equivalent
Student Performance Timed?	No (except for one subtest)
Testing Time	1–1 1/2 hours
Scoring/Interpretation Time	25–30 minutes
Normed On	2,426 students between the ages of 5 and 16; 33 school districts in 18 states were included; students in special education classes or receiving speech therapy were not included; sample was balanced for community size, geographical region, sex, age, race, and educational level of the parents
Alternate Forms Available?	No

FORMAT

The Clinical Evaluation of Language Foundations—Revised (CELF-R) is the revised edition of the Clinical Evaluation of Language Functions (CELF) published in 1980.

The change in name clarifies that the CELF-R is a measure of oral language skills and not language function, or pragmatics. The test is intended to measure language skills in the school-age child, grades kindergarten through twelve. Subtests are designed to assess word meaning (semantics), word and sentence structure (morphology and syntax), and recall and retrieval (memory). The materials consist of an Examiner's Manual, including directions for administration, scoring, and interpretation, as well as norm tables; a Technical Manual describing test rationale, development, standardization, and reliability and validity data; two stimulus manuals containing the pictorial material for each subtest; and individual student record forms.

The CELF-R battery includes 11 subtests; through analysis of standardization data and predictive validity studies, the subtests that best differentiate normal and disordered language were identified by age level. The three best subtests determining a receptive Language Score and an Expressive Language Score for younger and older students are listed below.

Receptive Language

Ages 5–7	Ages 8 and Above
Linguistic Concepts	Oral Directions
Sentence Structure	Word Classes
Oral Directions	Semantic Relationships

Expressive Language

Word Structure	Formulated Sentences
Formulated Sentences	Recalling Sentences
Recalling Sentences	Sentence Assembly

The two remaining subtests may be used as supplementary measures of the student's language, or they may be used as replacement tests if one of the above tests is invalid due to problems in administration. For example, *Listening to Paragraphs* can be an alternate receptive test.

By selecting the appropriate subtests for a student's age level, testing time is used efficiently.

Following the administration of the appropriate subtests, the raw scores are converted to standard scores and percentiles. Such derived scores can be obtained for each individual subtest. Composite scores for Receptive Language, Expressive Language, and Total Language can also be obtained. Confidence levels for each score are given. Age Equivalent scores are given for Total Language only. Information is given on interpreting whether the difference between two subtest scores or the Receptive and Expressive composites is significant. All scores are recorded on the front cover of the Individual Record Form.

The Examiner's Manual includes extensive guidelines for interpretation, including several case studies. Extension testing, the process of evaluating a student's errors, is well described for each subtest. Examples of instructional objectives and curriculum references are given.

STRENGTHS OF THE CELF-R

• The CELF-R is a comprehensive, well constructed battery of subtests to assess oral language competence over a wide age range. The new revision maintains many of the values of the CELF while introducing several subtests with improved content and administration and scoring procedures. The differences between the CELF and the CELF-R are explained in detail in the Technical Manual.

• The Examiner's Manual is extremely well organized; the directions for administration are clear and scoring procedures well explained. Guidelines for extension testing and interpretation of test performance are excellent.

• The Response Booklet is also excellent. Administration is greatly simplified by including the age range, the ceiling procedure, all items, and a place for marking the student's response so that it is immediately scorable. No transference back and forth between the manual and the record form is required. In addition, guides for error analysis are printed following every subtest.

• The format of the pictorial materials is simple and clear. Pages are uncluttered, and it is easy for the student to follow the task from item to item.

• The organization of the CELF-R is greatly improved. By providing a different battery of subtests for younger and older students, the need for a basal procedure is eliminated. Testing time is reduced as a total score can be obtained from six subtests.

• Several features have been provided to aid the examiner in eliciting the best performance from each student. These include demonstration and trial items introducing each subtest, alternating receptive and expressive tests, and providing additional tests in case one subtest is invalidated.

• The CELF-R is a flexible test to use with language and learning disabled students. The examiner is guided toward one of two subtest groupings according to the age of the student. However, if the student proves to be more or less advanced than supposed, the examiner can change levels and still calculate standard scores on the subtests given.

• Many of the tasks contained in the CELF-R battery are unique. There are few diagnostic instruments appropriate for assessing the oral language abilities of older school-age children. The CELF-R tasks and test materials are usually appealing and interesting to this age group.

• The CELF-R diagnostic battery is considered to be an intergral part of Wiig and Semel-Mintz's assessment process, which consists of Screening, Diagnosis, Extension

Testing, Assessment for Intervention, and Assessment for Progress. Based on an error analysis of CELF-R responses, extension or additional testing can be completed. Wiig and Semel-Mintz's book, *Language Assessment and Intervention for the Learning Disabled* (1980), is a valuable resource for criterion-referenced assessment tasks and intervention strategies following the administration of the CELF-R.

LIMITING FACTORS OF THE CELF-R

• The CELF-R is a new test that shows great promise as a clinical assessment tool. Its real value will become clearer with use.

• Although the CELF-R is a comprehensive diagnostic tool, the authors suggest that a standardized measure of receptive vocabulary and analysis of a spontaneous speech sample be included as part of the testing process. Academic and intellectual testing may also be needed to complete an assessment of a school-age child.

• Page numbers or tabs on the Stimulus Materials books would increase ease of administration.

• The test-retest reliability studies reported in the Technical Manual range from low to satisfactory for individual subtests after a period of 4–8 weeks. Scores are reported on only 116 students at three age levels. The authors state that the composite scores—Receptive Language, Expressive Language, and Total Language—are more reliable. However, reliability coefficients for the composite scores are not reported.

• In the Technical Manual several studies are reported concerning the validity of the CELF-R. They appear to support the claim that the CELF-R discriminates between the learning-language disabled student and the "normal language student." The age of students participating in these studies is not reported. As different batteries of subtests from the CELF-R are recommended for different ages, this information is needed to assess the validity of each battery.

CELF-R Subtests

Subtest	Type	Age*	Task	Areas Measured	Comments
Linguistic Concepts (?0 items)	Receptive	5–7	Student executes oral directions requiring logical operations by pointing to a series of six colored lines. *(Before you point to the blue line, point to a red line.)*	Comprehension of concepts related to inclusion, exclusion, coordination, time, condition, and quality.	Similar to Processing Linguistic Concepts on the CELF; assesses critical linguistic concepts to discriminate language disabled from normal students.
Word Structure (36 items)	Expressive	5–7	Student looks at pictures and completes sentences spoken by the examiner. *(Here is a dog; here are two _____ . This girl jogs; she is called a _____ .)*	Knowledge of word structure rules; plurals, possessives, past tense, auxiliary + *ing*, comparatives, superlatives, etc.	New subtest on CELF-R, very similar to the Grammatical Closure on ITPA.
Sentence Structure (26 items)	Receptive	5–7	From 4 choices, student selects the picture which matches the meaning of the sentence read by the examiner.	Receptive morphology and syntax at the sentence level.	Similar to Processing Word and Sentence Structure in CELF; good visual discrimination skills are needed to process pictures.
Oral Directions (22 items)	Receptive	5+	Student executes oral commands ranging in length from 5 to 16 words by pointing to black or white circles, squares and/or triangles in two or three different sizes (Point to the smallest black square).	Comprehension, recall, and execution of oral commands of increasing length and complexity.	Same test as Processing Oral Directions on CELF.
Formulated Sentences (20 items)	Expressive	5+	Student verbally formulates a sentence using each one of 14 words given by examiner. Pictures are used to stimulate responses. In the last 6 items, the student must use two words in a sentence.	Formulation of simple, compound, and complex sentences.	Same test as Producing Formulated Sentences in CELF; extensive examples given to facilitate scoring.
Recalling Sentences (26 items)	Expressive	5+	Student repeats sentences whose length and complexity gradually increase.	Recall and reproduction as a function of syntactic complexity.	Similar to Producing Model Sentences in CELF; however, structurally incorrect sentences have been eliminated.
Word Classes (27 items)	Receptive	8+	In a group of 4 words pronounced by the examiner, the student identifies the two which are related. (before, when, under, after; cliff, hill, house, grass.)	Verbal concept development; vocabulary, association skills.	Similar to Processing Word Classes on CELF. Difficulties in auditory memory can affect performance on this task. For further diagnostic information, the examiner can ask the student why a particular word was chosen.
Sentence Assembly (22 items)	Expressive	8+	The student formulates sentences using key words and phrases. The student must give 2 sentences for each set of stimuli. (on the table, the ball, put, will you.)	Ability to assemble syntactic structures into gramatically and semantically meaningful sentences.	New test, similar to TORC; requiring two sentences is a good diagnostic feature.
Semantic Relationships (28 items)	Receptive	8+	From four possible responses student selects the two correct answers to a question.	Comprehension of comparatives; spatial, passive, and temporal relationships.	Modification and expansion of Processing Relationships and Ambiguities on CELF; elimination of yes-no response is a great improvement.
Word Association (3 items)	Expressive	Alternate test for either age group.	Student produces as many names of animals, transportation, and occupations as he/she can in 60 seconds.	Vocabulary; word retrieval.	Similar to Producing Word Associations on CELF; although responses are scored with respect to quantity (number of words recalled), the evaluation of quality (number of semantic subclasses represented and shifts between various subclasses) is also available.
Listening to Paragraphs (14 items)	Receptive	Alternate test for either age group.	Student listens to paragraphs read by examiner and answers four questions about each.	Auditory comprehension; recall of factual data.	New test; paragraphs increase in length, sentence and content complexity; only factual recall is required; two paragraphs at each age level is a positive feature.

*The subtest is required for the age listed; it becomes an additional diagnostic tool for the other age level.

CELF ELEMENTARY AND ADVANCED LEVEL SCREENING TESTS

At the time this review was written the CELF Screening Tests—Revised were in press. The original screening tests were written by Semel and Wiig and published in 1980 to provide a measure for screening language-processing and language-production in school-age students.

Each screening test contains separate language-processing and language-production sections that can be administered and scored in approximately 15 minutes. The Elementary Level test covers kindergarten through grade 5 and consists of an adaptation of the "Simon Says" game and a set of expressive language tasks (phrase completions, repetition of sentences and polysyllabic words, serial recall, and word opposites). The Advanced Level, spanning grades 5 to 12, involves a series of oral directions using an array of playing cards and a higher-level version of language-production tasks.

The language-processing sections of both screening tests probe aspects of the following:

1. Accuracy in phoneme discrimination
2. Sentence formation rules
3. Interpretation of words and logical relationships among sentence components and linguistic concepts
4. Retention and recall of word and action sequences

Language-production items assess the following areas:

1. Agility and accuracy in phoneme production
2. Ability to recall, identify, and retrieve words and concepts
3. Accuracy in serial recall
4. Immediate recall of model sentences

Both screening tests were standardized in order to identify children who need an in-depth assessment of oral language. Percentile ranks by grade level are provided for the language-processing section, the language-production section, and the total test. The authors suggest that the CELF diagnostic battery be administered to students scoring below the fifteenth percentile on the total screening test or below the tenth percentile on either portion of the test. The same norming population was used to standardize the CELF screening tests and diagnostic battery.

Expressive One-Word Picture Vocabulary Test (EOWPVT)

Morrison F. Gardiner
Academic Therapy Publications, 1979
20 Commercial Blvd., Novato, CA 94949-6191

Purpose	To obtain an estimate of a child's verbal intelligence and the quality and quantity of vocabulary
Major Areas Tested	Expressive vocabulary
Age or Grade Range	2–12 years
Usually Given By	Speech/language clinician Psychologist Special education teacher Counselor
Type of Test	Individual Standardized Norm-referenced
Scores Obtained	Mental age IQ Percentile Stanine
Student Performance Timed?	No
Testing Time	10–15 minutes
Scoring/Interpretation Time	10 minutes
Normed On	1,607 children in the San Francisco Bay Area from 2 to 12 years of age
Alternate Forms Available?	No

FORMAT

The Expressive One-Word Picture Vocabulary Test (EOWPVT) was developed to provide an estimate of the vocabulary a student has learned from the home environment and formal education. The author felt that an expressive format provided more valuable diagnostic information than a receptive test. The materials for EOWPVT include an examiner's manual, picture book, and score forms.

The EOWPVT is individually administered. The student names a series of individual black and white line drawings presented by the examiner. A table included in the manual indicates the starting point for testing, as determined by the student's age. Items are sequenced in order of difficulty, and basal and ceiling levels are provided. Two demonstration items are presented to familiarize the student with the task. All of the student's responses are recorded for analysis purposes.

Stimulus words for the EOWPVT were chosen based on questionnaires sent to parents of children from 18 months to 2 years of age and on vocabulary presented in educational settings in selected areas of the United States. Test items represent four language categories, including general or concrete concepts, groupings, abstract concepts, and descriptive concepts.

Raw scores are determined by the number of pictures appropriately named by the student. Scoring criteria is presented in the manual. Raw scores can be converted to mental ages, intelligence quotients, stanines, and percentiles for students between the ages of 2 years and 11 years, 11 months at six-month and one-year intervals.

STRENGTHS OF THE EOWPVT

• The primary value of the EOWPVT lies in its uniqueness. While there are several standardized measures of receptive vocabulary available to diagnosticians, few tests assess single-word knowledge through the expressive mode. In addition to vocabulary level, examiners can obtain quickly and easily information about a student's word recall and retrieval abilities, speech articulation, and general developmental functioning.

• Since the EOWPVT can be administered so rapidly, it is useful as a screening of expressive language functioning. In addition, when given as part of a comprehensive test battery, the EOWPVT can provide valuable information for contrasting a student's expressive and receptive vocabulary skills.

LIMITING FACTORS OF THE EOWPVT

• The author describes the EOWPVT as a "measure of how a child thinks." This, together with mental age scores and deviation IQ's, implies that the test is a measure of verbal intelligence. However, verbal intelligence is much more comprehensive than the naming of pictures with one-

word labels. The EOWPVT is a measure of expressive single-word vocabulary and should never be used as an estimate of general intellectual ability. In fact, a study (Burgemeister, Blum, and Lorge, 1972) comparing performance on the EOWPVT with the Columbia Mental Maturity Scale (a measure of general cognitive ability) yielded poor coorelations of .29 to .59.

• The size of the sample for children between the ages of 2 years and 2 years, 11 months is very small, indicating that interpretations of performance in this age range should be viewed very cautiously.

• The standardization sample was composed entirely of children from the San Francisco Bay Area. No other description of the sample is given. As vocabulary at a young age is very much influenced by cultural and linguistic background, the racial and ethnic characteristics of the sample need to be well described. The limited geographic area and the poor sample description severely limit the generalizability of the EOWPVT.

• Validity for the EOWPVT was done through an anchoring process, that is, using the PPVT and the CTMM as comparison tests. Each of these tests has serious norming problems.

• Test-retest reliability information is not reported in the manual.

• Knowledge of vocabulary, perhaps more than most other acquired skills, is closely linked with cultural and educational experiences. Therefore, culturally different students can be expected to perform more poorly on such a measure as the EOWPVT when compared with students from the mainstream. In addition, a student might have an excellent fund of vocabulary but perform poorly on the EOWPVT because of severe word recall and retrieval difficulties. The possibility of visual-perceptual problems should also be considered when interpreting a student's performance on this test.

• There is a Spanish version of the EOWPVT that utilizes the same administration and scoring procedures as the English edition. However, only one set of standardized scores is available for both languages, and it was normed on an English-speaking population. Therefore, examiners can use this Spanish version to obtain descriptive information about a student's expressive Spanish vocabulary, but the score should not be reported.

• Examiners should be aware that the EOWPVT does not discriminate well between certain age groups. Scores vary insignificantly between some six-month age intervals.

• The EOWPVT manual suggests that the test be used to determine a child's readiness for kindergarten. Such an important decision requires a reliable instrument with good predictive validity. The EOWPVT can best be viewed as a rough screening test to complement a more extensive language evaluation.

Expressive One Word Picture Vocabulary Test— Upper Extension (EOWPVT-UE)

Morrison F. Gardner
Academic Therapy Publications, 1983
20 Commercial Blvd., Novato, CA 94947-6191

Purpose	To obtain a basal estimate of a child's verbal intelligence
Major Areas Tested	Expressive vocabulary
Age or Grade Range	12–16 years
Usually Given By	Classroom teacher Counselor Special education teacher Speech therapist Psychologist
Type of Test	Norm-referenced Individual or small group Standardized
Scores Obtained	Mental Age Deviation IQ Percentile rank Stanines
Student Performance Timed?	No
Testing Time	10–15 minutes
Scoring/Interpretation Time	5–10 minutes
Normed On	465 students aged 12–16 from the San Francisco Bay Area
Alternate Forms Available?	No

FORMAT

The Expressive One Word Picture Vocabulary Test—Upper Extension (EOWPVT–UE) is the upper level of the EOWPVT. It was designed to be used with students between the ages of 12 and 16 years.

The materials for the EOWPVT–UE consist of the manual, a spiral-bound book of test plates, and the individual test forms. The manual includes directions for administering and scoring the test as well as the norms tables and technical information on standardization, reliability, and validity.

The EOWPVT–UE is usually administered individually. The student looks at a line drawing illustrating a common object or group of objects, an abstract concept (time), a noun participle (flying), and letter symbols (c/o). Entry points are suggested according to chronological age, and a basal (8 consecutive correct responses) and ceiling (6 consecutive errors) process is used so that students are tested over a critical range.

Directions for group instruction are presented in the manual. Group administration requires the students to write their responses. Therefore, this method should be used only for students with adequate writing skills. The basal and ceiling rules are applied when scoring the test. Raw scores of the number of correct responses are converted into mental age, deviation IQ, stanine, and percentile ranks.

STRENGTHS OF THE EOWPVT–UE

• This test was developed to use with adolescents, for whom there are few tests of expressive vocabulary available.

• The EOWPVT–UE is easy and quick to use.

• A Spanish translation is available for use with Spanish-English bilingual students. However, only one set of norms is provided, so scores for Spanish-speaking students are not valid.

LIMITING FACTORS OF THE EOWPVT-UE

• The standardization sample is small, drawn from one geographic area, and not well described as to racial or ethnic composition. All of these are critical variables in vocabulary development.

• No test-retest reliability statistics are reported in the manual.

• Mental ages are calculated by equating a student's scores on the EOWPVT–UE with the PPVT. Therefore, the mental ages are estimates and must be used with caution. This caution is stated in the manual.

• The description of the EOWPVT–UE as a test of verbal intelligence is inaccurate. Obviously, verbal intelligence is composed of many factors, of which picture naming is only one. Use of terms such as "mental age" and "deviation IQ" are quite misleading. The test is best viewed as a rough screening of one aspect of a student's vocabulary development and may lead to a decision to do further assessment in this area.

Peabody Picture Vocabulary Test— Revised (PPVT-R)

Lloyd M. Dunn and Leota M. Dunn
American Guidance Service, Inc., 1959; revised 1965; 1981
Publishers' Bldg., Circle Pines, MN 55014

Purpose	To assess an individual's receptive (hearing) vocabulary for standard American English
Major Areas Tested	Receptive single-word vocabulary
Age or Grade Range	2 1/2–40 years
Usually Given By	Special education teacher Psychologist Speech/language clinician
Type of Test	Standardized Individual Norm-referenced
Scores Obtained	Age level Standard Percentile Stanine
Student Performance Timed?	No
Testing Time	10–20 minutes
Scoring/Interpretation Time	10–15 minutes
Normed On	Carefully selected nationwide sample of 5,028 persons, including 4,200 children, balanced for age, sex, geographic region, socioeconomic level, ethnicity, and community size
Alternate Forms Available?	Yes

FORMAT

The Peabody Picture Vocabulary Test—Revised (PPVT–R) consists of two equivalent forms, L and M. For each form there is an easel book of line drawings printed four on a page and individual student record forms. There is one examiner's manual including administration and scoring procedures and norms tables covering both forms. A technical supplement provides more detailed information on test construction and standardization.

To administer the test, the examiner pronounces a word, and the student selects the corresponding picture ("Show me meringue."). No verbal response is needed because the student can simply point to the correct picture. The vocabulary words gradually increase in difficulty, from such items as *arrow, furry,* and *vase* to *ascending* and *trajectory.*

Although all the items are together in one picture book, the student is tested on only the vocabulary appropriate for his or her age and language development. There are no subtests. Equivalent forms L and M may be given in alternate sessions to increase the reliability of the score, or they may be used as pretests and posttests for evaluating a student's progress. The manual includes detailed directions for administering and scoring, as well as tables for converting raw scores to age equivalents, standard scores, percentiles, and stanines.

The primary changes in the PPVT–R over the 1965 edition include the following:

1. The test was standardized nationwide and the sample was balanced for age, sex, geographic region, socioeconomic level, ethnicity, and community size.

2. The terms "mental age" and "intelligence quotient" were changed to "age equivalent" and "standard score equivalent."

3. Two-thirds of the stimulus items were replaced with new items, and 25 items were added to each form to increase the instrument's sensitivity and reliability.

4. The racial, ethnic, and sex balance in the line drawings was improved.

STRENGTHS OF THE PPVT-R

• The PPVT-R is well designed and well normed. The format of presenting a picture to elicit a pointing response makes it a nonthreatening test that even the young or seriously impaired student can take successfully. It is frequently used as the first in a battery of tests; the easy format makes it a good warm-up for more difficult material. The wide age range covered by the PPVT–R and its alternate forms make it a good instrument for test-retest purposes; it can be administered every year to assess a student's progress in specific language therapy or in general language development. The PPVT–R is relatively quick to administer and interpret. Although it is usually used as a global

measure of receptive vocabulary, analysis of a student's errors can reveal information about the specific nature of a vocabulary deficit. For example, student errors on such items as *filing, assaulting,* and *lecturing* would seem to indicate difficulty with verbs.

• The PPVT–R is available in Spanish. (See Test of Vocabulario en Imagenes Peabody (TVIP).

LIMITING FACTORS OF THE PPVT–R

• The PPVT–R is a test of single-word vocabulary only. The comprehension of spoken language in context is a different skill, and the examiner must not assume that a student's receptive language is adequate simply because he or she obtains a high PPVT–R score. Knowing the meaning of *group* when it is pronounced clearly and represented by a picture of five children is quite different from understanding the word when the teacher says, "First do the group of subtraction problems on page 10, and then do the group on page 14, starting with line 3." In addition, the PPVT–R score may not predict high verbal performance in the classroom. Understanding a word and using it correctly in spoken language are two different skills.

• The PPVT–R does not assess all parts of speech. Only nouns, verbs, and adjectives are included. The understanding of prepositions, a critical skill, is not included.

• The standardization sample of the PPVT–R is greatly improved over the original sample and includes students of various ethnic backgrounds, races, and socioeconomic levels. However, it is still important to consider the effects of different cultural backgrounds on test performance. Students from different cultures or from disadvantaged homes may not have had experience with the pictured items. For a student from a middle-class home and community, a low score may reflect a true deficit in ability to comprehend spoken language, but in a student from a culturally different or disadvantaged background, a low score may reflect lack of language stimulation or experience. The program for developing language skills in these two students would be quite different.

• As in all tests, the student's attention span is a big factor in performance. Low scores on the PPVT–R may be related to impulsive responses caused by an inability to scan four pictures. Or they may result from perseveration—continued pointing to the same position on the page. Such behavior is not unusual in low-functioning children with physical, emotional, or attention problems. A low PPVT–R score therefore may not reflect low vocabulary development but rather an inability to scan and select visual material.

• In the PPVT–R, hearing vocabulary is measured through picture stimuli. Clearly, two processes are involved in doing this: the understanding of the spoken word and the understanding of the line drawings. A low score may not necessarily reflect a problem in receptive vocabulary but possibly a problem in comprehending pictures. For example, a student may know the meaning of the word *exterior* but be unable to interpret which drawing is the *outside* of the house and which is the *inside*. Other measures of receptive vocabulary and picture comprehension are needed to confirm the results of the PPVT–R if a specific definition of the disability is needed.

Preschool Language Scale (PLS)

I. L. Zimmerman, V. G. Steiner, and R. E. Pond
The Psychological Corporation, 1979
555 Academic Court, San Antonio, TX 78204

Purpose	To systematically appraise the early stages of language development
Major Areas Tested	Receptive language, expressive language, and articulation
Age or Grade Range	1–7 years
Usually Given By	Speech/language clinician Special education teacher Psychologist
Type of Test	Individual Criterion-referenced
Scores Obtained	Age level Language quotient
Student Performance Timed?	Yes (some tasks)
Testing Time	20 minutes
Scoring/Interpretation Time	5–20 minutes
Normed On	No norms
Alternate Forms Available?	No

FORMAT

The revised Preschool Language Scale (PLS) materials consist of a manual, a picture book, individual record forms, and the following items supplied by the examiner:

• 12 one-inch colored blocks in a box (red, yellow, blue, green, orange, and purple)

• A small piece of coarse sandpaper

• A set of coins, including a half-dollar, a quarter, a dime, a nickel, and a penny

• A watch or clock with a second hand

The PLS is a developmental inventory with two separate scales: Auditory Comprehension and Verbal Ability. Each scale is administered independently and contains 10 sections spanning the ages of 1 to 7 years. These sections cover six-month intervals from ages 1 to 5 years and two one-year intervals from ages 5 to 7 years. Each interval contains four different items that assess sensory discrimination, logical thinking, grammar and vocabulary, memory and attention span, temporal/spatial relations, or self-image. Consonant articulation is evaluated by word and sentence repetition tasks. References that follow the descriptions of items in the test manual indicate the sources from which these language tasks are drawn. Developmental age-level placement of test items was determined from language research and experience with the original version of the PLS.

The Auditory Comprehension scale is administered first. Testing begins at the point where the child is most apt to succeed, approximately six months below the child's assumed language functional level. A basal age is obtained when all items within an age interval are passed. Testing proceeds until the child fails all items within a single age interval (ceiling age). The Verbal Ability scale is subsequently administered in the same manner, with testing beginning at the basal age obtained on the Auditory Comprehension scale.

A convenient feature of the PLS is the inclusion of identical items at different age levels with varying criteria for passing. For example, in the Verbal Ability section, the child has to correctly repeat a single four-digit series to pass item 25 at the 4-year to 4-year, 6-month level but must reproduce two series to pass item 33 at the 5-year to 6-year level. Therefore, item 25 is administered in its entirety only once, and pass or fail is assigned in both age intervals.

Age levels are obtained by adding 1 1/2 months of credit for each item passed beyond the basal age and 3 months of credit for items from the age range of 5 to 7 years. A more complicated point-credit system may also be used for determining age levels. Auditory Comprehension (AC) and Verbal Ability (VA) ages are calculated separately and can be averaged to obtain an overall language age. Furthermore, quotients may be obtained by applying the formula:

$$\frac{AC \ (or \ VA) \ Age}{Chronological \ Age} \ X \ 100$$

A composite language quotient is calculated by averaging the two quotients.

The authors suggest that any child who scores below age level on the PLS is "at risk" for language problems. Careful examination of response patterns and comparison of performances on the Auditory Comprehension and the Verbal Ability scales provide a more detailed picture of a child's strengths and weaknesses.

STRENGTHS OF THE PLS

• The PLS is a valuable screening tool for young children. The tasks and materials are appealing to most children, the test protocol is simple to use, and responses are easily elicited. The diversity of items enables the examiner to obtain a sampling of performance in several developmental areas in a short time.

• The 1979 edition of the PLS is a revision of the original 1969 form. Modifications in the current version include clearer administration instructions, a simplified scoring system, and the repositioning of some test items to reflect increased knowledge of language acquisition stages. A valuable addition to the PLS is a Spanish translation, contained in Appendix A of the test manual, and Spanish protocols. The examiner may administer the PLS in both English and Spanish to obtain information about language dominance in receptive and expressive areas.

• The "Preschool Language Scale" is a deceptive name. In addition to language, this instrument evaluates areas more commonly considered as "school readiness," such as color recognition, counting, and numerical concepts.

• Various studies reported by the authors demonstrate adequate to excellent reliability and validity. Three studies in which PLS scores were compared with later school success suggest strong predictive validity, an important quality for a preschool screening instrument.

LIMITING FACTORS OF THE PLS

• Effective administration of the PLS requires practice by the examiner—materials vary from task to task, and the manipulation of pictures, objects, and the test protocol can be difficult. Maintenance of a rapid test pace can be important in sustaining the attention of young children.

• Recording a child's performance in chart form can provide useful diagnostic information. However, the value of such a profile on the PLS is diluted significantly by the misrepresentation of several test items. For example: articulation items are listed as tasks assessing memory and attention span; a task involving the discrimination of pictures of a dog and a wagon (1 year, 6 months to 2 years) is considered "logical thinking," while a subsequent item involving the discrimination of playing, washing, and blowing in pictures (2 years, 6 months to 3 years) is omitted from this category.

- The lack of nationwide standardization with a random sample of students severely limits the usefulness of the PLS.

- The authors acknowledge that further normative studies of the PLS are needed. Establishment of means and standard deviations for age intervals covered on the English and Spanish versions would enhance the value of the PLS as a diagnostic tool.

- Speech and language clinicians should be aware of the limitations of assessing articulatory proficiency through imitation of single words rather than through a sampling of connected speech. On the PLS, a child may be able to imitate words that he or she does not articulate correctly on a spontaneous basis.

- No test-retest reliability information is provided in the manual.

Receptive One-Word Picture Vocabulary Test (ROWPVT)

Morrison F. Gardiner
Academic Therapy Publications, 1985
20 Commercial Blvd., Novato, CA 94947-6191

Purpose	To provide an assessment of a child's receptive single word vocabulary based upon what he or she has learned from home and school
Major Areas Tested	Receptive single word vocabulary
Age or Grade Range	2–12 years
Usually Given By	Speech/language pathologist Psychologist Norm-referenced
Type of Test	Individual Standardized Norm-referenced
Scores Obtained	Language age Standard score Percentile Stanine
Student Performance Timed?	No
Testing Time	10–15 minutes
Scoring/Interpretation Time	5–10 minutes
Normed On	1,128 children between the ages of 2 and 11.11 residing in the San Francisco Bay area
Alternate Forms Available?	No

FORMAT

The Receptive One-Word Picture Vocabulary Test (ROWPVT) is a companion test to the EOWPVT, Lower Level. It provides an individual assessment of a child's receptive single-word vocabulary through a picture identification format. The materials consist of a spiral-bound manual containing 100 test plates and individual test forms on which to record the student's responses and scores. Each test plate contains four pictures; the student is asked to select the picture that matches the word pronounced by the examiner. A basal (8 consecutive correct responses) and a ceiling (6 out of 8 incorrect responses) procedure is provided which allows the student to be assessed only over his or her ability range. The correct responses are totaled into a raw score which is converted into a language age, standard score (mean 100; SD 15), percentile, and stanine. As the test is considered a companion to the EOWPVT, it was standardized so that the norms are equivalent. The standard errors of difference are reported at each age level; generally scores on the two tests must be nine or more standard score points apart to be considered significantly different.

STRENGTHS OF THE ROWPVT

• The ROWPVT is quick and easy to administer. The format is identical to that of other picture vocabulary tests. A pointing response may be used so that very young and non-verbal students may be assessed. The test is one on which every student can achieve some degree of success; as such, it is a good test to use first in a battery of language-learning tasks.

• The manual is well organized and presents the necessary information for administration and scoring. Starting points are clearly indicated on the individual test forms. The stimulus pictures are generally unambiguous to children.

• Used together, the Receptive and Expressive One-Word Picture Vocabulary Tests can provide a good screening of a student's hearing and speaking vocabulary.

• A Spanish-language version of the ROWPVT is available and should be administered by a person fluent in Spanish. The Spanish record form lists alternative stimulus words for many items based on geographical differences. The examiner selects the stimulus word that is most appropriate for the dialect of the student.

LIMITING FACTORS OF THE ROWPVT

• The technical aspects of this test are all very weak. The standardization sample is inadequately described. In addition it was drawn from one unique geographical area, San Francisco, so examiners should be very cautious about using the norms with other populations. No test-retest reliability data is reported. The validity data which is reported is very questionable. For example, the ROWPVT is compared to the vocabulary subtests of the Wechsler Intelligence Scale for Children—Revised (WISC–R) and the Wechsler Preschool and Primary Scale of Intelligence (WPPSI). Both of these are tests of expressive vocabulary, yet the author explains the low correlations on the basis of restricted number of items. Due to the poor technical merits of the ROWPVT, the test should not be used for anything other than a rough screening measure.

• Although a Spanish version which is sensitive to dialected differences is available, no norms for Spanish speaking students are provided.

• In the manual, the author has a tendency to state opinions as if they were facts. For example, on page 9 he states, "When possible, testing should be conducted early in the day, since this has been found to be a time when a child is at his best..." No references are given to back up this statement.

Sequenced Inventory of Communication Development—Revised (SICD–R)

Dana Hedrick, Elizabeth Prather, and Anette Tobin
University of Washington Press, 1975, 1984
4045 Brooklyn N.E., Seattle, WA 98105

Purpose	To evaluate development of verbal and nonverbal communication in very young children and to estimate levels of receptive and expressive language functioning
Major Areas Tested	Receptive and expressive communication
Age or Grade Range	4 months–4 years
Usually Given By	Special education teacher Speech/language clinician
Type of Test	Standardized Individual Criterion-referenced
Scores Obtained	Age level
Student Performance Timed?	No
Testing Time	30–75 minutes
Scoring/Interpretation Time	30 minutes
Normed On	252 Caucasian children from the upper, middle, and lower socioeconomic levels in Seattle, Washington
Alternate Forms Available?	No

FORMAT

The Sequenced Inventory of Communication Development—Revised (SICD–R) is a revised edition of the SICD originally published in 1975.

The materials for the SICD–R include a kit of objects used in administering the test, a test manual, an instruction manual, two test protocols (Receptive and Expressive Scales) and four profile sheets (Receptive Processing Profile, Receptive Behavioral Profile, Expressive Processing Profile, and Expressive Behavioral Profile). The manual includes the author's model of communication, information about test standardization, interpretation of test results, several brief case studies, and information about the Spanish translation of the SICD–R. The SICD–R instruction manual gives specific administration and scoring procedures and formulas for computation of communication ages and mean length of response

According to the test authors, the SICD–R was based on a model which represented the processes that contribute to an individual's communicative interaction with his environment. The SICD–R was designed to select behaviors representative of the major avenues of this interaction in the very young child. This test combines a parent's report with direct behavioral observation for the collection of data.

Factors included in the Receptive Behavioral Profile are awareness, discrimination, and understanding. The Expressive Behavioral Profile breaks skills into imitating, initiating, and responding. Skills are documented by observation of motor responses to sounds and speech at home. Examples of the skills evaluated in each area follow. These tasks are passed by 75 percent of the children at the given age levels.

Awareness

Sound: Baby turns to sounds of rattle and cellophane (8 months).

Speech: Baby looks up or smiles in response to "Hi there" (8 months).

Discrimination

Sound: Baby responds to environmental sounds at home, such as phone ringing (16 months).

Speech: Child discriminates between words such as *socks* and *box*, *tree* and *key*, and *bear* and *chair* by pointing to objects (24 to 28 months).

Understanding

Words plus situational cues: Child responds to "give it to me" command (28 months).

Words: Child indicates correct blocks as examiner names colors (36 to 44 months).

Imitation

Motor: Child imitates examiner placing blocks in box (16 months).

Vocal: Child imitates intonation patterns heard at home (20 months).

Verbal: Child imitates common words on request (28 months).

Initiation

Motor: Child uses gestures to elicit labeling response from parent (24 months).

Vocal: Child uses questioning inflection (16 months).

Verbal: Child asks "Why?" (40 months).

Response

Vocal: Child responds vocally to parents' verbalizing (4 months).

Verbal: Child names objects such as car, spoon, and shoe (36 months).

The child's responses or the parent's report are recorded on the receptive or expressive scale form by circling YES or underlining NO for each item. The Receptive scale is usually administered first, followed by the Expressive. The complete test is never given to a child. The examiner begins testing at a level where consistent success is anticipated. A basal is established when three consecutive test items have been passed. A ceiling is obtained when three consecutive items are failed.

The SICD–R yields both a receptive communication age (RCA) and an expressive communication age (ECA). The first step in the computation is to transfer the child's successes and failures as recorded on the test form to one of the corresponding profiles. The numbers of the sequenced items are printed on the profile sheets in the age interval where at least 75 percent of the children in the norming sample passed the items. The examiner circles the numbers of the items passed and underlines the numbers of those failed. The clinician may choose whether he wishes to use one or both profiles. The next step is to determine the precentage of items passed for each level using the appendix in the manual. The assessment of an RCA or ECA is based upon these percentages in comparison with the normative data.

The final portion of the SICD–R includes a 50-response language sample and a traditional develomental articulation profile upon which responses from the Photo Articulation Test are judged. These measures are not factored into the ECA.

STRENGTHS OF THE SICD–R

• The SICD–R is one of a few measures which assesses children's communication skills from 4 months to 4 years of age. The addition of a parent's report to direct observation is therefore a critical component of this measure.

• The use of objects as stimuli helps to maintain the young child's interest in a way that pictorial stimuli could not.

• Interexaminer and test-retest reliability are high. A high correlation between the receptive communication age and expressive communication age would be expected and is reported in the manual. The mean scores obtained by normal subjects closely resembled their chronological age.

• The YES/NO scoring procedure is very simple and the instruction manual very clear, which may allow administration of this test by a wider range of educational personnel.

• Both the receptive and expressive scales of the SICD–R are available in a Spanish translation. The standardization sample was composed of Spanish-speaking students of Cuban background.

LIMITING FACTORS OF THE SICD–R

• This test was standardized on 252 Caucasian children from the Seattle area. Seven subjects were obtained for each age group from three socioeconomic groups: low, middle, and high. The size and standardization of this sample poses serious questions about the reliability of the norms provided and significantly limits the usefulness of the test norms.

• According to the test authors, this test was designed to assess communicative interaction with the environment. However, there is little examination of turn-taking behavior or reciprocity between the child and parent.

• The articulation response form requires coding a simple pass or fail response. This gives the clinician no descriptive information about the child's phonological development and seems a poor practice in light of current linguistic literature.

• The Allen and Bliss study reported in the manual (Allen and Bliss, 1976-80) had two interesting findings. First, the white children in their sample had higher mean scores than black children at all age levels. Another interesting trend was toward higher ECA's than RCA's in all racial groups. As this is not consistent with normal language developmental theory, Allen and Bliss's data suggests that the validity of the SICD–R is highly suspect.

I am also grateful to the reviewers of this book: Janet C. Richards, University of Southern Mississippi; Carol N. Dixon, University of California at Santa Barbara; and Barbara Martin Palmer, Mount Saint Mary's College in Maryland. I appreciate their helpful comments and hope that they will find their suggestions reflected in the quality and content of the text.

To provide illustrations of the current use of journals in the classroom, the author examined journals created by elementary schoolchildren of all instructional levels in a variety of classroom settings. My sincere thanks go to the many students who shared their journal entries with me, and to their parents who permitted this writing and drawing to be shared. I especially appreciate the patience of those students who allowed me to observe and photograph them at work and those who talked to me about how they used their journals for learning.

I would especially like to thank Dick Koblitz, Kathleen Murphy, Emily Grady, Lee Ann Lyons, Nancy Johnson, and Kathleen McDonald at Ralph Captain School in Clayton, Missouri; Claudia Loehring and Susan Schneider at Henning School in Troy, Illinois; Pat Sheahan of Summerfield School in Summerfield, Illinois; Jackie Hogue of Marine School in Marine, Illinois; Sue Wolf of St. Boniface School in Edwardsville, Illinois; and Gail Nave of Tampa Palms Elementary School in Tampa, Florida for sharing their ideas and students' journals with me. Thanks also to Susie Bargiel of Captain School; Susy Drake of Marine School in Marine, Illinois; Christine Lanning and Ingrid Owen of Summerfield School in Summerfield, Illinois; Pam Senjan of Sihler School in Litchfield, Illinois; and Vivian Rohleder of Marie Shaeffer Junior High in O'Fallon, Illinois, for their contributions to the material in Appendix B.

I would like to thank my husband Jerry, whose encouragement and support are without equal; my son Tadd, who loyally reads manuscripts; and my daughter Debora for her suggestions on design.

An Introduction to Learning Journals

Among the various aims we consider important in education, two are especially so. We would like our children to be well informed—that is, to understand ideas that are important, useful, beautiful, and powerful. And we also want them to have the appetite and ability to think analytically and critically, to be able to speculate and imagine, to see connections among ideas, and to be able to use what they know to enhance their own lives and to contribute to their culture.

—Elliot W. Eisner (1997, p. 349)

PREVIEW

1. What is a learning journal?
2. What is the purpose of a learning journal?
3. How do learning journals support the integrated curriculum?
4. What are the theoretical foundations of learning journals?
5. Who are the audiences for learning journals?
6. How do journals help students value their own questions?
7. How do journals encourage language across the curriculum?
8. What is the value of informal language?
9. How do journals assist brain-based learning?

BRIEFLY: Students use learning journals to record and respond to ideas and information related to an integrated theme or a topic in the content areas.

LEARNING JOURNALS: A DEFINITION

Students create learning journals by recording ideas and information from the content areas in a notebook and responding to this material in ways that are personally helpful to their learning. The purpose of a learning journal is to support academic inquiry and to create a history of learning that informs both the student journalist and the classroom teacher. Known variously as *learning logs, response journals, theme books* or *think books,* learning journals are used to record ideas, information, and individual responses to an integrated theme or topics in mathematics, science, literature, language, writing, or the social studies.

Learning journals share certain features with other types of classroom writing, such as diaries or dialogue journals, because they provide opportunities for students to explore ideas, ask questions, and respond personally to their experience. However, they are distinct from these other types of writing because they (a) regard the student as the primary audience for the journal, (b) rely less on a written dialogue between the student and teacher, and (c) focus more specifically on recording and responding to ideas and processes in the academic content areas. Although learning journals involve recording notes from reading, observation, and other experiences, they differ from the ordinary content area notebook because they involve a response from the student, a working out of ideas in a manner that is personally effective for the individual. These are workbooks that are created to be visited again and again, as students grow in their understanding of a topic, use their notes and responses to share ideas with peers, and communicate their learning to the teacher or parents.

Learning journals are intended to help students assume increased responsibility for their learning and to provide teachers with information to assess individual understanding of complex concepts. They provide students with resources that encourage their active participation in group discussions and support informed study for tests. They also help students collect references to assist their learning and ideas or information that can be used to create more polished projects. Initially, learning journals gained popularity in higher education as part of an emphasis on writing to learn or writing across the curriculum, but elementary teachers have discovered that these tools for learning are equally effective for K–8 instruction.

Kinds of Learning Journals

Depending on the particular classroom and grade level, journals may be kept in stapled booklets, spiral or three-ring notebooks, or hard-backed composition books (Fig. 1.1). In some classrooms, students keep journals for each of the content areas and in others, these are combined into a single resource. Entries may be *single entry* (Fig. 1.2), with continuous entries written on each page or *double entry,* with writing arranged in a dialectical format (Fig. 1.3). Students who use the double entry style use

FIG. 1.1. Students record their learning in a wide variety of notebooks and folders.

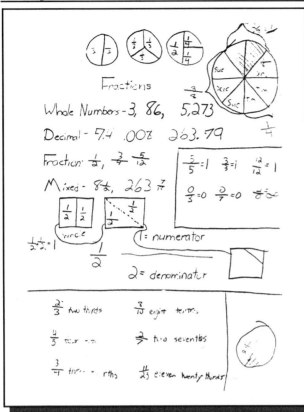

either a two-page notebook spread or one half of a page to create a conversation with themselves, by recording information and ideas on one side of the page and their responses to the subject matter on the other.

Making Thinking Visible

Learning journal entries may be informal and spontaneous, or more carefully organized, depending on the type of entry and the age, development, and personality of the individual journalist. Entries usually involve developmental spelling and grammar, and can include any type of writing or drawing that is helpful to the student in understanding a concept or topic. This writing may be for individual use or shared with others in an informal manner in small groups, to enable students to use

FIG. 1.2. Claire's single entry journal style.

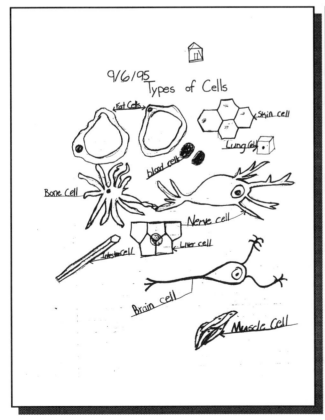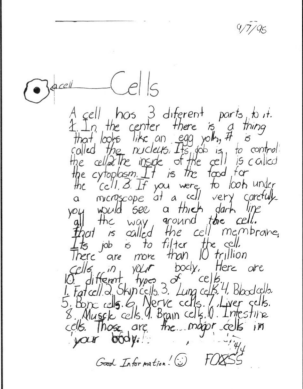

FIG. 1.3. Claire's double entry journal style.

their own ways of speaking and thinking about complex ideas. This kind of informal writing and speaking has been referred to as *exploratory* (Barnes, 1976) or *expressive* (Britton, Burgess, Martin, McLeod, & Rosen, 1975). It helps make children's thinking visible to teachers (Gallas, 1994) because it provides increased opportunities to obtain a more accurate view of students' understanding and skill levels. By periodically examining the contents of learning journals during individual conferences, teachers can identify progress and spot difficulties with concepts that have not been resolved during small group or class discussions. Problems can be noted and dealt with on a one-to-one basis with individual students, or re-presented in a minilesson for students having similar difficulties.

When they review student journals, teachers observe how students use language skills to understand and interpret what they are studying in the content areas. Developmental learners frequently understand more about a topic than they are able to indicate in class discussions or formal projects. Because learning journals offer the possibility of alternative modes of expression, students can write or draw their understanding of concepts to indicate learning that might not be evident with more formal types of evaluation. Conversely, students who perform well with workbooks and standardized tests may give false impressions of the depth of their understanding about a topic. But the process of writing about ideas, explaining them, and relating them to other ideas prompts students to explore concepts in more depth and with added comprehensiveness.

THE PURPOSE OF LEARNING JOURNALS

The goal for either single or double entry journals is to help students work out their ideas in a way that is immediately helpful to them and useful for future learning. Journals encourage elementary students to create a record of their learning that can be periodically reviewed and used as a resource for ideas, information, problem solving, self-evaluation, projects, discussions with other students, and conferences with the teacher.

Academic Purposes

Learning journals also encourage students to examine their experience through the unique perspective of each discipline, and support what Thaiss (1986) described as "language across the curriculum" (p. 2), with an emphasis on all the language arts as tools for learning. As students reflect on what they are learning in terms of their own experience, they begin to observe the unique questions asked and answered by each academic area. Using the processes of each discipline to pose and answer their own questions, students gain appreciation for the explanatory power of each kind of knowledge and methodology. Learning journals encourage students to explore these different ways of thinking and knowing as interesting, helpful, distinct, and interrelated ways to make sense of their experience.

Journals also provide a designated place to record homework assignments, reading, observations, personal responses to learning, questions, problem-solving strategies, learning resources, and terminology associated with a content area. In some classrooms, learning journals replace dialogue journals or portfolios, because they provide similar writing, response, and evaluation functions, without the overwhelming demands of paperwork and time inherent in both. In others, journals directly support the portfolio system. (This is discussed in more detail at the end of chapter 2.)

ACT and REACT

Students use learning journals to respond to ideas from their reading or observation in ways that are personally meaningful to them. The acronym ACTS (ask, connect, transform, share) and its expanded form, REACTS (record, evaluate, ask, connect, transform, share; Popp, 1995), summarize activities of response that assist learning and describe ways that students typically respond to subject matter in classrooms that use learning journals. As students *record* information and observations related to a theme or content area topic, they *evaluate* their experience, responding personally to what they liked, the quality of the material, any difficulties with understanding, and what they agreed or disagreed with. They *ask* questions about what they are trying to understand and make *connections* with their own experience, other knowledge they have about the topic, or other areas of the curriculum. Through drawings, charts, maps, diagrams, a variety of writing forms, or graphic organizers, students *transform* the material in some manner, to help them make personal sense of complex ideas. Then they *share* the information, ideas, discoveries, and strategies in pairs, small groups, with the entire class, or with the teacher in an individual conference. Figure 1.4 is an example of a REACT guideline for exploring a topic in science or social studies.

Example of a record/response entry page in a learning journal

RESPONSE   RECORD

Evaluate: What did you like/dislike?   Five facts from reading
What features of the material were
helpful? (maps, indexes, photos)   1.
Was anything difficult to understand?

1.   2.

2.   3.

3.
                                                4.
Ask: What questions occurred to
you as you read?
                                                5.
1.

2.

3.   Share: List something you
                                                learned about the topic
Connect: What previous knowledge   from each person in your
or experience helped you understand   group.
this material?
                                                1.
1.

2.   2.

3.   3.
Transform: On the back of this sheet,
test your understanding by organizing
the material in a new way. Draw, write,   4.
make a map, graph, timeline or chart
that will help you explain what you've
read to some else.   5.

FIG. 1.4. A model for journaling—sample REACTS guideline.

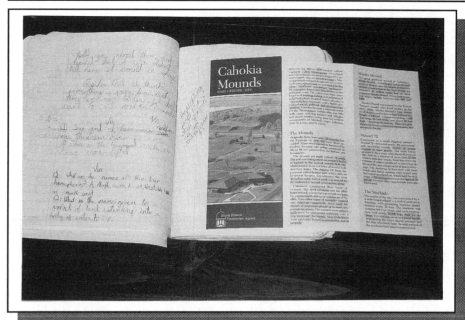

Depending on the subject area, students may also create a resource and reference section in their journals that includes a glossary of technical terms, a personal spelling dictionary, ideas for projects, theme-related articles, pictures from newspapers and magazines, brief annotations of books, and guidelines for working in groups.

FIG. 1.5. Nick keeps records, responses, and resources all in one place.

This all-in-one-place arrangement helps students organize their learning experiences and develop resources to assist future learning (Fig. 1.5).

Getting to Know Students

Although learning journals focus on academic matters, they are not impersonal records. As students attempt to create meaning from information, they struggle with ideas, record their frustration with difficult assignments, make personal connections to their experience, and portray themselves as unique personalities (Fig. 1.6). Many pour their souls onto these pages, permitting teachers to provide support where it is needed and learn better ways of interacting with individual students. Indeed, journals document the quality of the school day from the perspective of individual children in a manner not possible to know by any other means. Teachers periodically review student journals to assess understanding, identify misconceptions, and gain information that will direct their teaching. Many teachers write brief notes to students to clarify ideas, coach, remind, arrange conferences, or provide encouragement and support (see Fig. 1.6).

Student journals may also include entries related to the fine arts and extracurricular activities, such as sports. Many teachers ask students to write what they learned during the day, and these activities are often included. Accounts of success in activities outside the classroom can often provide clues to strong interests and competencies that can be expanded within the rest of the curriculum. Deva, a fifth grader, demonstrated a talent for drawing in her journals, which her teacher encouraged her to use to interpret her learning in a way that made sense to her. Frederick's fourth-grade teacher identified a strong interest in sports from enthusiastic reporting of activities in physical education, and helped him make connections between statistics and mathematical ratios. Jill wrote enthusiastically about drama class and was encouraged to interpret themes in social studies by writing and performing skits and puppet plays.

Visits to special teachers will be full of ideas and experiences to share and relate to the rest of the curriculum. When the music teacher at St. Boniface School introduced kazoos to the fourth-grade class, Clayton made this entry in his journal:

> Yesterday, Mr. Mitchell gave everyone in our class a kazoo. I hummed in it a lot. It's pretty fun. You can hum almost anything. It's kind of hard, because you just don't blow in it, you have to hum in it to get it to work. He also gave us a paper with all the beats to practice. Mine is blue and white. It works by a paper vibrating.

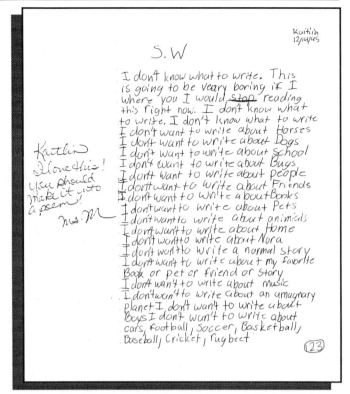

FIG. 1.6. Kaitlin's list of reasons for not writing and teacher response.

This common experience of fourth graders could be expanded into playing patriotic songs together from the time period they are studying in social studies. It also raises questions about how the instrument works, a topic related to experiments in physical science.

JOURNALS AND THE INTEGRATED CURRICULUM

In classrooms that integrate the curriculum, students explore broad themes throughout the content areas. Learning journals provide an organized format for recording ideas, questions, connections, technical terminology, and research strategies that can be used for personal review and sharing with others in study or discussion groups. In departmentalized situations at the intermediate or middle school levels, teachers may focus on study, social, or organizational skills across the curriculum, or rotate emphasis on activities that stress the use of particular cognitive abilities (Gardner, 1992). Students record learning strategies in their journals as they are modeled (Fig. 1.7) and use their notes and experience in one subject area to figure out concepts in others. (See the team-teaching notes for the Grady/Lyons fifth grade in Appendix B for classroom examples.)

When journals are used to explore individual content areas, they continue to serve the goals of an integrated curriculum, as students soon realize that answering their

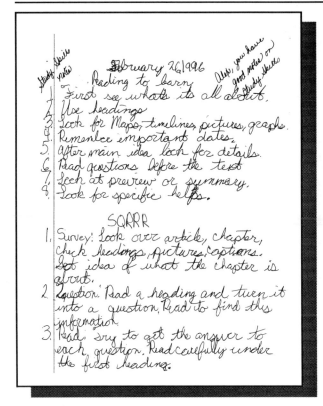

FIG. 1.7. Alex's study strategies.

questions about the world will involve the skills and processes of many subject areas. Each area of knowledge takes on new meaning when students begin to recognize the power of its particular processes to explore or explain phenomena of personal interest. For example, a third grader whose science notes were generally sketchy wrote copious notes during studies of the ear when decibel levels were related to rock music. As Beane (1993) observed:

An integrative curriculum works off the idea that genuine learning occurs as people "integrate" experiences and insights into their scheme of meanings. Moreover, the most significant experiences are those tied to exploring questions and concerns people have about themselves and their world. Thus an integrative curriculum begins with those questions and concerns and brings to bear upon them pertinent knowledge and skill. Through the integrative and continuing process of action, interaction and reflection, people have the possibility of constructing meanings in response to their questions and concerns. (p. 18)

In integrated programs, students may have journals for every content area or they may keep a series of topic- or theme-related learning journals that include everything they are studying. In many classrooms, journals replace workbooks and some textbooks.

THEORETICAL FOUNDATIONS OF LEARNING JOURNALS

The remaining sections of this chapter provide a review of the literature and research that constitutes a foundation for using learning journal activities in the elementary classroom. Some will want to read this material as a preface to the applications that follow in later chapters. Others may decide to read the applications first and return later to explore the theoretical bases for using learning journals in the classroom.

The reading, response, and sharing activities of learning journals emerge from a constructivist view of the learner, which assumes that students create meaning from their experience in terms of what they already know, and that they learn best when they are actively engaged in making sense of their world. Constructivism has its roots in John Dewey's concept of education and Jerome Bruner's view of cognitive psychology. It is also supported by Louise Rosenblatt's reader-response theory, Lev Vygotsky's descriptions of language development, and James Britton's social construction of knowledge. As a methodology, constructivism is further described and defined in the work of educators such as Toby Fulwiler, Christopher Thaiss, Karen Gallas, Peter Medway, Pat D'Arcy, and Donald Graves. The contributions of these and other educators are discussed in the following sections.

Philosophical Foundations: John Dewey

According to Dewey's classic definition, education "is that reconstruction or reorganization of experience which adds to the meaning of experience, and which increases the ability to direct the course of subsequent experience" (Dewey, 1916/1964, p. 76). To say that a person has learned something means first of all that they have done something with an idea or information to make it their own. This reconstruction or reorganization of experience occurs in a school setting when students read, write, listen, observe, or manipulate objects to understand a concept. If the meaning of a student's experience is changed by acquiring new information or ideas, and if the student increases his or her ability to become more autonomous as a learner, then education has occurred. New understanding leads to increased competency as a self-directed learner and provides a foundation for new learning.

Reconstruction and reorganization of experience is one of the key goals of learning journals. Students write and talk about their questions, evaluate their understanding, make personal connections, and transform new ideas and information by writing, drawing, or reorganizing them in a personally meaningful way. Learning journals encourage students to be active participants in their own learning, to develop their strengths as learners, and to create resources for future learning. These activities create a framework for new learning and promote the development of lifelong learning habits, because they enable students to become increasingly autonomous as learners.

Dewey (1916/1964) observed that an "increment of meaning corresponds to the increased perception of the connections and continuities of the activities in which we are engaged" (p. 77). It is important to encourage students to make conscious connections between what they are learning and their personal experience. It is equally important to encourage them to find connections between what they study in one area of the curriculum and other areas, between one topic in a content area and others that have been studied before. For example, a fifth grader used information from an ecology study to analyze the environment depicted in *Island of the Blue Dolphins,* which she was studying in literature. In the context of reading *Charlotte's Web* together, one third-grade class used their journals to research and record information about spiders to enhance their understanding of the main character, respond to the story with evaluations and summaries, locate examples of grammatical constructions in their own writing, and compose a bulletin board, using facts drawn from their journals.

These kinds of connections help create a sense of the interconnectedness of the curriculum and promote a sense of continuity within inquiry. Learning journals encourage this connecting activity throughout the content areas and create a history of learning that students periodically review to make further connections.

Psychological Foundations: Jerome Bruner

According to Bruner (1960), instructing a student in a content area is not a matter of presenting facts and asking the child to commit them to memory. Rather:

> It is to teach him to participate in the process that makes possible the establishment of knowledge. We teach a subject not to produce little living libraries on the subject, but rather to get a student to think mathematically for himself, to consider matters as a historian does, to take part in the process of knowledge-getting. Knowledge is a process, not a product. (p. 72)

As students investigate ideas or processes in literature, language, mathematics, science, or social studies, they ask many of the same questions that occupy the attention of literary analysts, writers, mathematicians, scientists, and social scientists. The reading, writing, problem solving, research, and discussion activities of learning journals provide students with practice in thinking in a literary, mathematical, scientific, or historical manner to find answers to questions they have about their experience in the world.

Bruner (1966) saw the work of the teacher as *activating, maintaining,* and *directing* the academic interests of students. When teachers encourage students to interpret their environment in the context of subject matter content and processes, they help activate students' natural curiosity about the world. Frequent opportunities to translate their observations and reading into writing and talking help maintain student interest and build competence in using the exploratory and explanatory tools of the various disciplines. As students discover that these activities help them build skills to find answers that are meaningful to them, teachers can increasingly provide direction for their research, informing them of resources and helping them move in the directions they want to go. In classrooms where learning journals are used successfully, teachers provide a focus for inquiry and create an environment in which students can obtain information, ask questions, and interact with others to share the results of their inquiry or request assistance.

Bruner (1990) also observed that children use language to structure meaning, as they translate their experience into words and try to make sense of what is happening in the world. More particularly, they develop the ability to use narratives, to create meaning from experience for themselves, and to communicate this meaning to others. As students work with learning journals, they engage in an active use of words (reading, writing, thinking, speaking) to understand their experience. They create, record, and share narratives to describe aspects of experience that draw their interest or concern, and their interpretations of these events. In the process, they construct a history of learning that allows them to return to these responses for further reflection.

According to Bruner (1990), children have an innate will to learn that is exhibited in their natural curiosity, their striving for competence, and reciprocity (the desire to work together with others to solve problems of mutual concern). Learning journals enable students to bring their natural tendencies for learning to bear on school-related tasks by encouraging them to follow their curiosity and make connections to their individual experience. When they work with ideas in personally meaningful and effective ways, they strive for personal competence in their understanding and when they work with others in cooperative groups to solve problems, they give full exercise to their natural desire for reciprocity.

Reader Response Theory: Louise Rosenblatt

According to Rosenblatt (1978), reading is an interactive process, in which readers bring their own experiences, interests, and expectations to what they read, which in turn influences the type and extent of their response.

> The reader brings to the text a reservoir of past experiences with language and the world. If the signs on the page are linked to elements in that reservoir, these linkages rise into consciousness. . . . All readers must draw on past experiences to make the new meanings produced in the transaction with the text. This experience then flows into the reservoir brought to the next reading event. (p. 12)

Rosenblatt (1985) also noted that readers make both efferent and aesthetic responses to literature. *Efferent* responses focus reader attention on "actions to be performed, information to be retained, conclusions to be drawn, solutions to be arrived at, analytic concepts to be applied, propositions to be tested" (p. 70). *Aesthetic* responses focus on "what we are seeing and feeling and thinking, on what is aroused within us by the sound of the words, and by what they point to in the human and natural world" (p. 70). Both types of responses assist student understanding of literature. Analytical responses provide tools for discovering the riches contained in a piece, whereas increased insight and pleasure are gained through aesthetic reflection. These responses to literature are not simply one or the other but rather a predominant stance the reader takes with a particular work. Most responses are a mix of both efferent and aesthetic and arrange themselves along a continuum, according to a reader's primary focus (Rosenblatt, 1991). Consider the mixture of analysis and personal response in Max's entry after reading a chapter in *Johnny Tremain*:

> Every day that he [Johnny] delivers for the British, he reads the notes, so it's kind of like spying. Although one of the officers knocks Rob across the face, they seem nice, and not cruel at all, like the "legend" said. I had a relative, William L. Davidson, that was in the militia. It's exciting to imagine that he was in North Carolina when everything happened in Boston: the Tea Party, the Massacre and everything. . . . Johnny had to *work* to open those chests. I guess it doesn't help that he could only use his left hand to chop. I didn't imagine the Boston Tea Party that way. I thought that it would be more rapid and happen faster. But I wasn't disappointed when it was only like a night of hard work. . . .

Aesthetic response can also be seen as the process by which readers identify with story characters and interpret their reading in terms of their personal experience (Rudell, 1992). Aesthetic response defines what readers bring to reading and defines the processes by which readers enter into reading, whereas efferent reading concentrates on what the reader takes away, in terms of ideas and information. Teachers can assist student responses by exposing them to a variety of analytical and affective questions, and modeling ways that these questions might be addressed (Purves & Monson, 1984).

Learning journals encourage both efferent and aesthetic responses, as students record and analyze ideas, make connections with their own experience, ask questions, and transform new information into a personally meaningful form. Teachers assist a wide range of responses by providing guidelines for response (Fig. 1.8), modeling strategies for problem solving, and encouraging students to experiment with organizational graphics.

The Learner's Sense: Eleanor Duckworth

In her book *"The Having of Wonderful Ideas" and Other Essays on Teaching and Learning,* Duckworth (1987) observed:

> Certainly the material world is too diverse and too complex for a child to become familiar with all of it in the course of an elementary school career. The best one can do is to make such knowledge, such familiarity, seem interesting and accessible to the child. That is, one can familiarize children with a few phenomena in such a way as to catch their interest, to help them raise and answer their own questions, to let them realize that their ideas are significant—so that they have the interest, the ability, and the self-confidence to go on by themselves. (p. 123)

If knowledge is something created by individual students, then teachers can assist students in having "wonderful ideas" in two important ways:

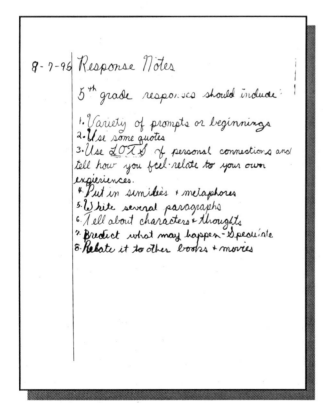

8-7-96 Response Notes

5th grade responses should include:

1. Variety of prompts or beginnings
2. Use some quotes
3. Use LOTS of personal connections and tell how you feel·relate to your own experiences.
4. Put in similes + metaphors
5. Write several paragraphs
6. Tell about characters + thoughts
7. Predict what may happen·Speculate
8. Relate it to other books + movies

FIG. 1.8. Alexandra's guidelines for literature response.

The first is to put students into contact with phenomena related to the area to be studied—the real thing, not books or lectures about it—and to help them notice what is interesting; to engage them so they will continue to think and wonder about it. The second is to have the student try to explain the sense they are making, and, instead of explaining things to students, to try to understand their sense. These two aspects are, of course, interdependent: When people are engaged in the subject matter, they try to explain it and in order to explain it they seek out more phenomena that will shed light on it. (p. 123)

It is clear that learning journals provide a wealth of opportunities for students to record and respond to concepts, to think about their thinking, and to interact with others to share and gain ideas. Journal writing permits students to use their own informal language and drawing to think through difficult concepts and make sense of them in their own terms. It stimulates metacognitive activity by encouraging students to examine and reflect on their entries to find patterns, trends, and relationships in their thinking and to evaluate strategies they use to understand ideas (Fig. 1.9). Journals provide a window into a student's understanding that is often difficult to obtain by other means.

Learning journals create opportunities for children to work with ideas in the curriculum in the same manner that they involve themselves in learning activities outside of the classroom. When students are encouraged to connect new ideas with their own experience and transform them in some way that is meaningful to them, they are more likely to have opportunities to make sense of what they study in terms of their individual strengths of intelligence (Gardner, 1992). If teachers model a variety of ways to connect new information with individual experience and demonstrate many ways to translate learning into different forms, students will develop a variety of ways to respond and have increased respect for the learning styles of others.

AUDIENCES FOR JOURNALS

In traditional classrooms, nearly all student writing is directed toward the teacher as an audience, in the form of answers to questions on tests and assigned reports. Teachers are also the primary audience for dialogue response journals. When students write in learning journals, however, their audience is no longer only the teacher, although it can include this person. Their audience is first of all themselves, and their writing addresses things they want to remember, figure out, puzzle over, and reflect on. The secondary audience is their peers, for whom they record ideas they want to talk over, share, debate, explain, or express. The third audience for the learning journal is the teacher, with whom entries are periodically reviewed. Although this varies from teacher to teacher, this review typically does not involve the correction of ideas or the form in which they are expressed.

For teachers, the purpose of reviewing learning journals is to gain information about levels of understanding that will help direct the course of instruction for

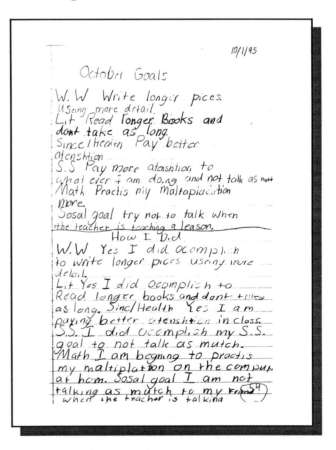

FIG. 1.9. Kaitlin's goals and evaluations of her learning.

individual students and the entire class. Some teachers write brief notes to call students' attention to the need for further research or rereading when they notice a lack of comprehension or a misconception (Fig. 1.10). In some classrooms, students' families are the fourth audience for journals when parents review student work on a daily, weekly, or monthly basis.

Self as Primary Audience

Thaiss (1986) observed that "language is first and foremost our best tool for trying to understand; only secondarily is it a tool for communication" (p. 16). He noted that writing process research suggests that "most of the practical benefit of writing and speaking accrues to the student irrespective of reader/listener comment" (p. 16). Thaiss concluded that too much attention initially to the mechanics of writing interferes with a child's use of language to think with, and that "students tend to write more coherent, fluent pieces as less attention is paid by the teacher to their mechanical use of the language" (p. 16).

Henry David Thoreau once described journals as "of myself, for myself," a place to record and figure out ideas of personal interest. But Stillman (1987) observed:

> What he meant, I think, is that a journal is a fine way to capture life as each of us sees, understands and reacts to it. . . . He also meant that a journal has for its audience the *self*—and this can be the most sensitive and important audience most of us will ever know. (p. 79)

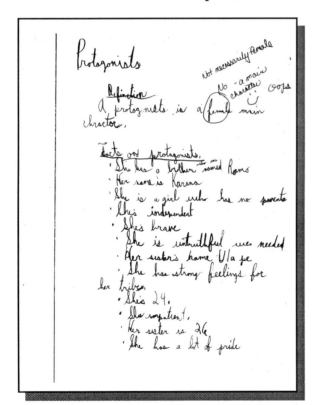

Writing in learning journals begins with students writing or drawing to make sense of their experience, connect new learning with personal knowledge, and record ideas of importance to them. This activity is also complemented by opportunities to talk about these ideas, to expand and enrich them in response to the ideas of others. Summerfield (1987) observed that when we write in journals:

> We withdraw for the long term purpose of re-entering. The ideational work, the reflecting, the speculating, is done so that at some later moment its fruits will be available for the interpersonal work that we inevitably return to, unless we are irreversible hermits. Put it in a nutshell: journals start life as intrapersonal but are directed to long-term interpersonal desires. (p. 35)

FIG. 1.10. Tyrone's interaction with the teacher about the concept of protagonist.

He further noted that "we talk to ourselves primarily in order to talk more effectively to others" (p. 37).

JOURNALS AND QUESTION ASKING

In her book *The Languages of Learning: How Children Talk, Write, Dance, Draw, and Sing Their Understanding of the World,* Gallas (1994) emphasized the importance of encouraging children to explore questions about the world using their own narratives:

> For children, meaning is built into stories; they use narrative to construct mental models of their experience, to make the world they inhabit sensible . . . it seems very important that children have a place where seminal experiences, which occur both in and out of school, move from silent expression into speech. (p. xiv)

Learning journal activities prompt students to follow and value their own questions, a habit that may have been discouraged since they began to talk, when the sheer volume of "why" questions asked of a caretaker may have been discouraged with responses such as "Don't ask so many questions!" At school age, children may learn that it is the teacher and not the students who ask the questions. In some classrooms, teachers further qualify what is asked with prompts such as "Who has a good question?" which can result in artificial or unasked questions. In either case, many students do not feel free to follow the real questions they have when they are presented with new ideas and information.

Teachers can encourage question asking with learning journal activities that prompt students to ask themselves: What do these ideas mean? How does this information touch my experience? What questions do I have as I read (listen to, observe) this? What can I do with this information to help it make more sense to me? What strategies can I use to solve this problem? How can I organize this information to get a clearer picture? Would I be able to figure this out better if I drew a picture, map, diagram, or chart? What ideas, information and strategies do I have to share? What can I learn from this discussion? Journal writing encourages students to explore their questions and periodically review them as tools for learning.

USING LANGUAGE ACROSS THE CURRICULUM

Learning journals help students make sense of what they read by encouraging them to translate new ideas into their own words (Fulwiler, 1987; Healy, 1981). Journaling also provides opportunities for students to ask questions about things they do not understand and to make connections between what they already know and what they are studying. Myers (1984) observed that "students who participate in a writing-to-learn program are likely to learn more content, understand it better and retain it longer" (p. 7). Chittenden (1982) added:

> The learning process is enhanced when kids are surrounded by the language of the unit they're studying: they need to read good works of fiction and non-fiction that deal with the content; they need to be involved in animated discussions in which they ponder and exclaim over the wonder of the content. (p. 37)

Vygotsky (1962) saw thought and language as socially constructed, interrelated, and interactive. According to Vygotsky, the use of language both accompanies and promotes thought, and thought permeates and constructs language. This explains why talking and writing about ideas often lead to a better understanding of concepts and can promote the "deliberate structuring of meaning" (p. 100). Vygotsky also believed that language helps create a distance from experiences that allows us to reflect on them and select those that are useful in a new context.

Britton (1993) saw learning as a process by which learners use language to construct and reconstruct meaning as they interpret and reinterpret their experience. He regarded the activities of reading, writing, and speaking as processes of learning, best used to create meaning from experience, rather than as products to be learned and tested. According to Britton (1993), teachers can assist students' efforts to develop conceptual meaning by providing them with the necessary opportunities to use expressive or informal language to figure out new ideas. This kind of talk and writing is best utilized in a context in which student responses to new ideas are encouraged and valued. He further wrote that:

> When we commit ourselves to paper, the process of shaping experience is likely to be a *sharper* one than it is in talk. The gap between transmission and reception of written language allows a writer, if he needs to, to wrestle with his thoughts, to work and re-work his formulation or projection or transformation of experience. (p. 248)

D'Arcy (1977) viewed expressive writing as a way for students to think aloud on paper, a process that will "allow for the initial sorting out processes which are necessary steps toward assimilating new knowledge" (p. 34). Like Britton, D'Arcy (1989) saw writing as a way for children to bring their ideas into sharper focus. In the process of translating ideas in science or mathematics into words, students increase their understanding of difficult concepts. Bullock (1975) noted that frequent opportunities to write help students practice mental strategies that will be helpful to all of their learning. In his classic *How to Read a Page,* Richards (1958) observed that "writing as a way of knowing lets us represent ideas in order to see further what they mean" (p. 240). Thaiss (1986) saw journals as both experimental and analytical and regarded them as tools toward fluency and deeper insight. He further believed that children understand and remember only what they have the opportunity to talk and write about or respond to in some meaningful way.

THE VALUE OF INFORMAL LANGUAGE

When students talk to their peers or family outside of school, they use informal kinds of language, a comfortable medium in which to think and express themselves. When students are allowed to talk and write in an informal manner in the classroom, they can often figure out the meaning of concepts more easily than if they are required immediately to use complex terminology. This puzzling out in their own terms will eventually lead to the use of technical terms as labels for the concepts they have mastered.

Expressive language provides teachers with insights into students' learning processes and encourages students to connect what they are learning with what they already know. Medway (1980), in his introduction to *Language in Science,* observed:

> The pupil's language, spoken and written, will have to express uncertainty, tentativeness, speculation, argument, sudden insight, patient worrying, "seeing the funny side"—all the states and attitudes to be found in our own heads when we're preoccupied with something unfamiliar. The point is to get it out of the head and into overt language so that those embryonic thoughts and perceptions and questions can be fanned into life and amplified by the stimulus of communicating with someone who is listening seriously and sympathetically to what one has to say. (p. 6)

In *The Climate for Learning,* Torbe and Medway (1981) pointed out that ideas in the content areas are difficult and complex. When students can think, write, and talk about these ideas in their own terms, it helps them focus on their understanding of the concepts involved. When students talk together in small groups, they sort out their responses to what they have read and observed (Barnes & Todd, 1977). These discussions enhance learning because everyone has prepared for them by reflecting in writing about what they have read about and experienced.

When students write about ideas and experiences that have meaning for them and share these ideas with others, they become increasingly aware of the "durable power" of writing (Graves, 1991). Writing becomes a permanent record of things they have experienced or thought about and gives them a sense of personal history. As students practice taking notes about things they have seen, read, or heard about, they begin to understand that information can be stored through writing. When they share their thoughts and ideas in a group, students begin to see themselves as having both a unique and shared perception of the world (Fig. 1.11). They will have ideas and questions that no one else will have thought about; other ideas and questions they will comfortingly have in common.

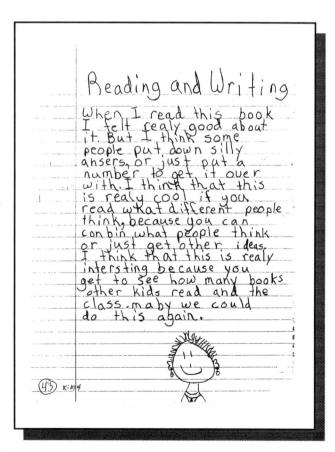

FIG. 1.11. Kimya's evaluation of an activity and participation.

Languages of Learning

Gallas (1994) urged teachers to encourage children to use a variety of languages to respond to their learning. She noted:

> Deep, transformative learning takes place when *language* is defined expansively to include a complex of signs. Children's narratives are not naturally confined to the spoken or written word. From early childhood on they tell stories in dramatic play, in their drawings and paintings, in movement and spontaneous song. (p. xv)

She urged teachers to regard these "enormous number of innate tools for acquiring knowledge" (p. 15) as assets to learning. When children have many opportunities to use a variety of ways to represent their learning, they can more accurately demonstrate what they understand about a concept and conversely, what they do not understand. Gallas regarded talking, writing, drawing, singing, and dancing as alternative languages that enable children to explore ideas and express understanding of their experience. For example, following a discussion about cheetahs in a kindergarten class, students drew pictures to illustrate their understanding. From one child's drawing (Fig. 1.12), the teacher was able to identify an obvious misconception about the cheetah's life cycle.

Learning journals provide opportunities for students to respond to reading, discussion, and observation in a manner that utilizes individual means of expression. In minilessons or workshops, teachers model a variety of ways students can respond to their learning, including all genres of writing, drawing pictures and maps, making

FIG. 1.12. Kristina's egg-laying cheetah.

sketches, and creating diagrams and charts. In cooperative study groups, students share what they have learned and puzzle together over what they still do not understand. As teachers review the individual work in journals and reports of group discussions, they can more accurately assess what students understand about a concept and receive information that helps direct future instruction.

JOURNALS AND BRAIN-BASED LEARNING

Although we know a great deal about the functioning of the brain, all too often this information is not brought to bear on how we support student learning in schools. In many classrooms, school instruction either works at cross purposes with the normal functioning of the brain or seriously underestimates a student's natural ability to learn. The curriculum has been traditionally regarded as a sequential, step-by-step affair, with students cast as passive receptors of information.

In their book *Making Connections: Teaching and the Human Brain,* Caine and Caine (1994) observed:

> Even more neglected and under-used is the innate predisposition of the brain to search for how things make sense, to search for some meaning in experience. This translates into the search for common patterns and relationships. It is a matter of finding out how what is being learned relates to what the learner already knows and values and how information and experiences connect. (p. 4)

Caine and Caine urged teachers to explore what they called "brain-based learning," which "acknowledges and encourages the brain's ability to integrate vast amounts of information . . . allows for the unique abilities and contributions from the learner and . . . acknowledges that learning takes place within a multiplicity of contexts" (p. 9). Brain-based learning, according to Caine and Caine (1995), involves opportunities for students to explore ideas, ask questions, make relationships, work with others, and explore ideas in a context that provides challenge and minimizes stress.

Learning, problem solving, and discovery are ways the brain seeks to understand new experience in terms of what is familiar, and scientists themselves make extensive use of analogy and metaphor when they seek answers to new questions (Churchland, 1995). Churchland observed, "This, after all, is the point of having concepts: to allow us to deal appropriately with the always novel but never *entirely* novel situations flowing endlessly toward us from an open-ended future" (p. 145).

Teachers who encourage the brain to work at school-related learning in the same effective manner that it operates for learning outside the school provide opportunities for students to actively explore objects, events, and ideas. These teachers help students learn to focus attention on what they experience and ask questions about new concepts. Students in these classrooms are encouraged to find patterns in information and ideas and to consciously relate new ideas to those that are already familiar.

Learning journal activities are brain friendly, in the sense that they provide opportunities for students to make the best use of the naturally active and holistic functioning of their brains. Journals encourage students to observe with all their senses, ask questions, connect what they are learning with their own experience, and make sense of new information by actively operating on it in some way. In cooperative study groups, students rehearse new knowledge by sharing what they have learned with others. They listen to their peers' insights and discoveries and consider new strategies. In the process of this interaction, students gain new information, develop new perspectives on the subject matter, and build further connections between new or complex ideas and their own experience.

Using Journals to Explore Ideas and Evaluate Learning

Studies of young learners show that there are few events in their lives when they are required to go back and use previous information of any kind—reread a text, reexamine a math problem, or rethink a social problem in the classroom. . . . Writing in journals, daily reflection, systematic record keeping and interviews contribute to a different view of information than episodic reviews of skills or reading of short stories.

—Donald Graves (1991, p. 50)

PREVIEW

1. How do journals assist learning in the content areas?
2. In what ways does journal writing improve observation?
3. How do journals help students create a history of their learning?
4. How do journals help students relate their experience to new ideas?
5. In what ways do journals encourage self-expression?
6. What is the value of exploratory writing?
7. How do journals provide support for disability or difference?
8. In what ways do learning journals create resources for discussion?
9. How do journals help students evaluate their own learning?
10. How do students use journals to communicate their learning to others?
11. In what ways can teachers use journals to evaluate student progress?
12. How do journals support the portfolio system?

BRIEFLY: Learning journals encourage students to explore ideas in a variety of ways, evaluate their own learning, and communicate their learning to others.

JOURNALS AND CONTENT AREA LEARNING

During the past two decades, teachers have observed that journals assist academic learning in a number of helpful ways. In her conversations with teachers who regularly use learning journals, D'Arcy (1987) found that teachers believe that journals provide helpful information about student understanding and progress, help students generate their own questions, and provide a place for students to collect ideas and information in one place as a resource for writing. D'Arcy's teachers also believe that learning journals help students rediscover information and because of the informal style of writing involved, enable students to develop their writing voice.

Other classroom teachers (Fulwiler, 1987) observe that writing and drawing in journals help students increase their powers of observation and make meaningful connections between what they are learning and everyday experience, with other topics in the content area and other areas of the curriculum. Teachers note that students use the exploratory writing of journals to examine ideas and test their understanding of concepts. They express their personal experience with new ideas and translate them into other forms that will assist their understanding.

Teachers also report that students who use journals for these purposes participate in group discussions and individual conferences in a more active and informed manner. They note that journal writing helps students create a history of their learning that can be used for self-evaluation and to create resources for more autonomous study. Students who face challenges of difference or disability are able to use journals in flexible ways that help them explore ideas with individual strengths and allow teachers to better identify their understanding of concepts. In the following sections, each of these benefits is explored in more detail.

IMPROVING OBSERVATION WITH JOURNAL WRITING

As students begin to recognize and use the specialized languages and processes associated with science, mathematics, literature, writing, and the social sciences, they become increasingly aware of these processes in their everyday experience and they learn to value the explanatory power that each contributes to their understanding and exploration of the world. The following types of questions help students look at their everyday world through the perspectives, terminology, and categories of the content areas or integrated themes:

- *Literature*: Where do you find literary themes (survival, courage) and devices (foreshadowing, parallelism) in newspapers, magazines, TV, or the movies?
- *Language and writing*: Where do you see or hear words (figurative language, puns, alliteration) used in interesting ways in books, movies, TV, newspapers, magazines, at play, at home?
- *Science*: Where do you see biology (metamorphosis), chemistry (oxidation), physics (levers), ecology (interdependence) at home, in nature, in news reports?
- *Math*: Where do you see measurement (odometers, mileage signs), calculation (sports statistics), estimating (crowd numbers), patterns (fences, windows), shapes (buildings, nature) in the world around you?
- *Social studies*: Where do you see history (geography, economics, politics, anthropology, sociology) at home, on vacation trips, at family reunions, in family photograph albums, in the movies, TV, newspapers and books?
- *Integrated themes*: Where do you see examples of systems? Interdependence? Communication? Specialization?

Recording ideas and information in journals also prompts students to observe more closely those things they are writing and drawing about. Questions arise as students work with information in their journals: Does a frog have fingers? Was Gettysburg close to Philadelphia? Did Frederick Douglass live at the same time as Sojourner Truth? Are the window panes squares or rectangles? Is this a simile? Each of these questions sends students back to observations of natural phenomenon, their reading or notes to find details, definitions, descriptions, patterns, or sequences of events that will help them describe their experience more accurately or comprehensively.

CREATING A HISTORY OF LEARNING

Learning journals constitute a continuous record of a student's learning as it happens, recorded in their own language and addressed to themselves. When students examine what they have written, drawn, and puzzled over during the day or over the space of a week, month, or term, they develop a sense of their own history as learners. As they reflect on these entries, they often find that they are able to organize their ideas in new ways, in light of new information or experiences they have had.

Students also review their notes to refresh their understanding of a concept and evaluate the strategies they used to help themselves understand complex ideas. They note the questions they had and the ways they attempted to solve problems or clarify their thinking. When students have the time and opportunity to engage in this type of historical review, they can identify problems and questions that have not been resolved and address them in small groups, class discussions, or individual conferences with the teacher. As they summarize ideas and strategies they have learned from group study or individual conferences, students organize this experience into usable form, creating a record for future reference.

Part of a student's creation of a learning history depends on having notes and responses that can be read or referred to at a later time. Many teachers underwrite developmental writing in journals of beginning writers immediately after they have recorded their thoughts. This not only preserves the student's ideas for later reading and sharing with parents, but it provides an opportunity for students to add ideas as they talk about their writing with the teacher. Some students prefer that these translations not be on the same page as their own writing and set aside blank pages opposite their entries for dictation to the teacher and translation into readable writing.

Older or more experienced writers must often record information and responses in a hurry or under less than ideal writing conditions, such as during lectures, discussions, films, or field trips. These notes may be nearly unreadable, unless they are quickly (within a day) converted to legible writing. In hardback or spiral notebooks, the double entry style provides a place for students to translate and reorganize their quick notes into a form that can be easily read and referred to at a later time. Many teachers provide time during the school day for students to reread and reorganize the entries in their journals. During this time, students may also number pages and list their entries in a developing table of contents (Fig. 2.1). Other teachers may assign this organizing activity as homework.

Journal work gives both individuals and small groups something to share with the larger class. When time is provided for individuals to share writing or research, students can use their journals as reference, and when the sharing occurs immediately after a research period, these notes help students share even more than they have written down, particularly at the primary levels. When groups report out from their joint research, they may decide in advance what to present from their learning, but journal notes will provide a quick reference to respond to additional questions presented by the teacher or other students.

This sharing of entries is valuable to the entire class, because there will usually be information, strategies, and insights that others will find helpful. In some cases the teacher or individual students record new ideas on a KWL chart, which allows everyone in class to benefit from others' research (Fig. 2.2). In other classrooms, small groups use their journal entries as a reference for recording their discoveries on charts, which they present to the class to describe what they have learned (Fig. 2.3).

A first-grade teacher (Winship, 1993) described sharing sessions in her classroom:

Table of Contents	
Analogies Workshop	page 85
reaction	page 86
Jin	page 87
Thyangels	page 88
electrisity	page 89
colems	page 90
Jin	page 91
Reaction	page 92
Vin	page 93
Daily Geography	page 94
Spelling Words	page 95
Race to 1000	page 96
mini Leason	page 9?
The Midnight Mistry	page 98
Math	page 99
How I Did	page 54
math Fractions	page 100
experiments with electricity	page 101
H.W.	page 102
curent event	page 103
Daily Geography	page 104
Curent event	page 105
Jin	page 106
spelling words (cursive)	page 107
England	page 108
spelling words	page 109

FIG. 2.1. Kaitlin's developing table of contents.

FIG. 2.2. A second grade KWL chart on spiders, in progress.

The sharing time sets the tone for learning, because everyone in the classroom is learning about something. Every time a group shares, they teach a science minilesson to the entire classroom. They share their information, share the books they are reading, often introducing new books to their classmates which may be read by some of them at a later date. They "go public" with their writing problems and offer solutions to each other: What to do when you don't know where to start? What to do with too much information? (p. 9)

Students in this same classroom described to an interviewer how they use the information in their learnals (a name for their journals created by a student: learning + journals = learnals) to create a finished piece, in this case an informational book (Winship, 1993):

Interviewer: How did you two decide what information to include in your final piece?

Garrett: We circled the stuff (in the Learnal) we wanted to share and crossed out the stuff we didn't want.

Interviewer: How did you decide what to cross out?

Lindsay: We picked things people already knew, or things that were boring, or things people might not really understand.

Interviewer: Then what did you do with the circled information?

Garrett: We put the circled stuff in order on another piece of paper. We put the parts together that went together. (p. 11)

Some classrooms have "Then and Now" bulletin boards that draw on the resources of individual journals. Students record an idea they held, previous to studying a topic, and list it under a heading such as "I used to think . . . (that roly-poly bugs were insects)." Under the heading of "Now I know . . ." they record their new knowledge ("they are really crustaceans, like lobsters.") These displays draw student interest, as they permit class members to observe both their individual and collective growth of knowledge. The value of creating this history of learning is described by a first-grade teacher (Stires, 1993) who observed:

> Toby Fulwiler once defined writing as visual thinking. When I first heard that, I was struck with the power of those two words. As thinking, writing is clearly a tool for learning because it allows the learner to see his or her thoughts and evaluate them. Since it is visual, it leaves marks like tracks in the snow, identifying the creator and pointing their direction. However, writing is more permanent since it can be preserved to tell the story of the writer's growth. It is a record etched out that allows for review and reflection by the learner and the teacher. Finally, it becomes an artifact to study and celebrate, as its creator moves on as a learner. (p. 19)

RELATING EXPERIENCE TO NEW IDEAS

When students are asked to find examples of science, math, literary devices, figurative language, history, or geography in their everyday experience, they are more apt to remember and be able to use what they have learned. As noted in chapter 1, studies in neuroscience indicate that this is how the brain works, by making connections and detecting patterns in experience (Churchland, 1995). Learning

FIG. 2.3. Sam, Megan, and Tyrone create a discovery chart from their discussion.

occurs when a new experience is connected in some way to knowledge already acquired, to familiar patterns, and to relationships (Hart, 1983). Questions like the following help students become conscious of the way concepts and processes in the content areas relate to questions they have about their experience:

- *Language*: When have you heard someone compared to something in nature? (He runs as fast as the wind; she's as quiet as a dove.)
- *Literature*: What happens at the beginning of your favorite movie that lets you know that it is going to be mysterious? (type of music, setting, character's conversation)
- *Math*: How did Gretzky's (Jordan's, Bettis') statistics change with the game yesterday?
- *Science*: How does science explain all the mosquitoes we are having? (How sneaker lights work? Popcorn pops? Soap makes bubbles? Fielders estimate where a hit ball will land?)
- *Social studies*: Do any of your family members or friends live in the state (country) we are studying? Did anyone in your family come to America from the country (continent) we are studying?

JOURNALS AND SELF-EXPRESSION

One of the most effective ways to make meaningful connections with a subject area is to personalize it. Students are encouraged to respond creatively to information and ideas by drawing, sketching, writing stories, songs, and poems about what they are learning. This permits students to use their favorite modes of expression to work with ideas and it also encourages them to experiment with other kinds of response. Students can be encouraged to evaluate their personal experiences with learning by responding to prompts such as (Eggers, 1995):

Today I had difficulty learning ——————————————————
I used this strategy to help me understand ——————————
I asked —————————— for help to ——————————
They helped me understand ——————————————————

Students can also personalize their learning by finding examples of ideas they are studying in cartoons, TV programs, and movies. This type of involvement in a topic helps make the unknown more familiar and eventually more understandable.

Gallas (1994) saw drawing as an alternative language, a way for students to work out or express their understanding in ways that might not be possible with writing. She believed that this kind of informal translation of ideas from one medium to another helps students increase their understanding of concepts and indicates to them what they do or do not understand. Attempts to draw something often raise questions about details that send students back to sources in reading, observation, or discussion with others. For example, Marina, a fifth grader studying *In the Year of the Boar and Jackie Robinson,* drew the picture in Fig. 2.4, in an attempt to see American children through the eyes of a 9-year old Chinese girl:

FIG. 2.4. Marina's drawing, in response to In the Year of the Boar and Jackie Robinson.

I chose to draw this picture because Shirley said how people's skin was all different: as white as plates to ebony and everything in between. I had never thought of it that way. People are so different in America that it must have shocked Shirley. When she said people's faces were speckled, she must have meant that they had freckles.

JOURNALS AND EXPLORATORY WRITING

When students do exploratory writing, they think about a concept by writing about it. They begin by using their own informal expressions of understanding and experiment with the specialized vocabulary and concepts of the content areas. Like other types of journal entries, exploratory writing does not represent a finished project, but it is a valuable part of mastering difficult concepts in science, literature, language, mathematics, or the social studies. As students increase their understanding of concepts in familiar terms, they begin to use the special languages of the disciplines to ask questions and propose answers (Fig. 2.5).

Just as children learn to read by reading and develop as writers by writing frequently, they develop their ability to assess situations that require scientific, mathematical, or historical tools by thinking and behaving as mathematicians, scientists, and historians. In the process, they begin to observe the

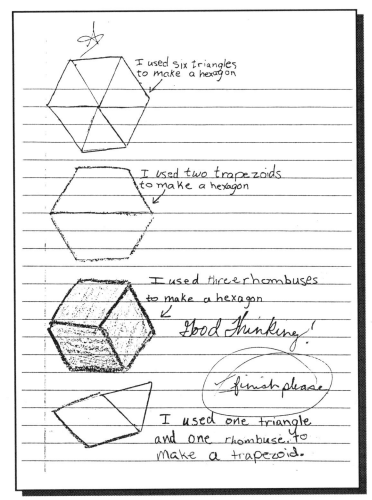

I used six triangles to make a hexagon

I used two trapezoids to make a hexagon

I used three rhombuses to make a hexagon

Good Thinking!

finish please

I used one triangle and one rhombuse to make a trapezoid.

FIG. 2.5. Nora's description of her geometrical figures.

power of these languages to reveal the answers to questions they have about the world, such as: If the sun is so far away, why do we get sunburned? Why does the water going down the bathtub drain look like a tornado? Is this mushroom safe to eat? Why am I so thirsty after I eat potato chips? Why can't I use the medicine I took for a sore throat to help my cold?

SUPPORTING DIFFERENCE OR DISABILITY WITH JOURNALS

Learning journals are especially effective for children who face challenges of disability or differences in language and culture. The informal nature of entries in learning journals allows children to record their ideas and responses in their strongest mode, in their own language, from their own perspective, and at their own rate and ability level. Students who speak little English or who use alternative English grammars can record ideas without the pressures of standardized performance. They can use developmental spelling, draw or cut out pictures, or dictate their entries to a scribe or into a tape recorder.

Students with physical disabilities, such as orthopedic, hearing, or visual impairments, create journals that adapt to their specific needs. Some use specially adapted computer technology to express their ideas, respond to experience, and share their thoughts with others. This type of technological assistance enables students to explore difficult ideas in writing, and it also permits teachers to more accurately observe their levels of understanding. Journal entries often provide teachers with information about a student's interests and difficulties that can direct instruction more precisely. A fifth grader faces the challenge of hearing loss but communicates his understanding of concepts and his intense love of science to the teacher through his writing. Although he often does not hear what other children hear, he has a microscope at home and enjoys looking at all kinds of things that most other people do not see. He takes his science journal home at night to draw pictures of microscopic aquatic life he finds in a pond near where he lives.

In another fifth-grade classroom, a student who has difficulty with reading and writing is a member of a research team in social studies. After one student reads aloud to the group, this student ably extracts the important facts and ideas and dictates them to another student to record in the research journal. This approach capitalizes on the strengths of each student, allowing each to contribute and participate with dignity.

Students who are unable to write legibly or who reverse letters are often successful in recording their thoughts with a word processor. Typing instruction can assist reversal problems, because the letter a student thinks can be immediately translated into print, facing the right direction. The letter "d" is now thought of as a left-hand, third-finger letter, whereas "b" is a letter that the second finger must stretch to a lower level of keys to type.

During the school day, frequent opportunities to record ideas and translate their understanding into writing provide developing readers and writers with helpful practice. When students record and respond to new ideas with pictures, drawings, and developmental spelling, they create materials that help them participate more actively in discussions with the teacher, aide, or other students. Ideas can also be preserved by dictating them to a scribe, so they can be shared with others. Consider, for example, this excerpt from a piece about Martin Luther King, Jr., dictated by Tonia, a fifth grader, who experienced difficulties with writing. Dictation supports and preserves the idealistic thoughts of this young student.

> I'm happy the "n" word is dying in public, but I am sad it still exists. I also dream of not worrying about gang colors in my neighborhood, not playing and hearing gun shots and having to run in the house, less useless killing of animals and no child abuse. The color of skin should not be the issue, but what is on the inside. Today people need more love for life and more love for their religion. Martin Luther King and I share a dream of an equal world. People have changed, but not the world. Because of that, I too have a dream.

Journal writing activities can be easily adapted to accommodate developing or disabled learners in the following ways:

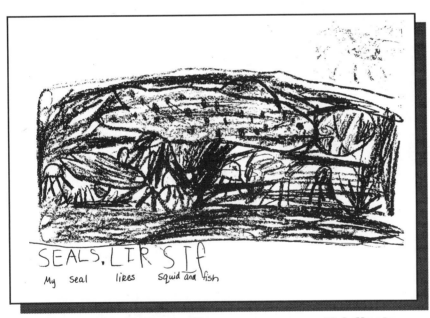

FIG. 2.6. Underwriting preserves Kristina's story about seals.

This report is about the Delaware colony. This colony has an interesting history. In 1609, Henry Hudson was looking for a short cut to Asia when he accidentally came upon Delaware. After a short exploration of the coastal area, Hudson returned to his homeland, the Netherlands. A year later, Samuel Argall from England also accidentally went to Delaware. He named the bay and the river after Lord Le La Warr. Later on people made settlments they all had one governer who made all the desitions. Many governers gave up and left and always a new governer replaced very quikly. Stagly enough people ate the large meal at breakfast, a avage meal at lunsh, and a very small meal at dinner. The colonists even children drank beer, wisky, milk and, tea. Delware had a small population in 1660 the population was 500. in 1690 1500. in 1700 2500. as well as slaves there were hundreds of white indtrud sevants. Poor euapeans came to america payed by weathy americans to come and work for the weathy america for 5 years with no pay and then were free.

FIG. 2.7. George's responses are recorded on the computer and taped into a journal.

• *Recording*: Students draw pictures to record books they are reading. At the kindergarten level, they can also talk about a book with an aide or journal buddy and dictate a caption or sentence for their picture, if they choose (Fig. 2.6). Older children who have difficulty with handwriting can sometimes more easily manage a computer keyboard. They enter their notes directly into the word processor and tape printouts into their journals (Fig. 2.7).

• *Response:* Students should always be encouraged to use developmental (invented) spelling in their journal entries. There should also be an accompanying opportunity for all students to talk about what they are thinking or writing with a partner or in a small group (Fig. 2.8).

- *Observations*: Students can draw pictures or cut out pictures from magazines to describe where or how they see science, math, or history happening in their everyday life. Captions can be added, if desired, by a journal buddy or an aide.
- *Questions and ideas*: These can be recorded with developmental spelling or by dictating them to someone else to record.
- *Minilessons:* Guidelines and strategies presented during instruction can be translated into rebus form for easy reference by developing readers and writers (Fig. 2.9).
- *Discussion*: When students want to record ideas from group discussions or interactions with others, they can enlist the help of a scribe (Fig. 2.10).
- *Reference*: Entries of word spellings or definitions of terms to assist reading and writing can be entered by a journal buddy, an aide, or the teacher. Guidelines or handouts can be taped into journals to assist those who read well but have difficulty with writing.

FIG. 2.8. Bailey talks about her journal entry with others at her table.

FIG. 2.9. During a discussion on bears, Mrs. Loehring codes key words with small drawings.

CREATING RESOURCES FOR DISCUSSION

As students record information, make observations, and work with ideas in their journals, they are also preparing to share what they have learned and thought about with a partner, small group, or the entire class. Depending on the content area and developmental level, students come to these discussions prepared to contribute ideas, questions, sights, research, and problem-solving strategies related to a theme or content area topic. In return, they will receive new information, ideas, strategies, and answers to many of the questions they have. Classroom pair and group activities related to the content areas are discussed in more detail in the individual content area chapters, but might include one or more of the following:

- *Literature circles*: Students meet together in small groups to discuss responses to books they have read, in common, by the same author, or on a theme.
- *Research groups*: Students work together in small groups to find answers to questions about a topic in science or social studies.
- *Math study groups*: Students meet in small groups to share strategies and work on problems together.
- *Laboratories*: Students work with math manipulatives or participate in hands-on activities in science.
- *Writing, reading, science, math, or history workshops*: Scheduled blocks of time for independent work, minilessons, and sharing related to literature, writing, math, science, or social studies.
- *Journal buddies*: Pairs of students in the same class, from the same grade level, or from different grade levels who share entries from their learning journals help each other with ideas and make entries, if requested.
- *Book previews*: A paired, small group, or class activity where students briefly review books they have read and try to interest others in reading them. Students note the ones that interest them in their journals.
- *Individual conferences*: Students meet with the teacher to discuss questions and difficulties they have encountered as they read books, explore ideas, and solve problems.

JOURNALS AND STUDENT SELF-EVALUATION

When students first begin to use journals for recording and response, it is helpful to ask them to reflect on their experience with questions like: How did your writing help you learn? How did your journal writing help you talk about your ideas? Students can also share their responses to using learning journals in a class discussion, listing these on a large chart or the chalkboard. Periodic discussions of this type help students pick up ideas for using their journals more effectively and help them feel less isolated if they are experiencing difficulties. When asked to share ways that journals assist them as learners, students typically say that journals help them:

- Keep a record of things they want to remember or think more about.
- Sort out important ideas.
- Have a place to work with ideas, using their own way of learning.

FIG. 2.10. Brittney talks about her journal entry with Mrs. Loehring.

- Connect new ideas with what they already know.
- Have something to contribute in groups.

Later in the term, when students have used their journals for a longer period of time, they observe that journals provide:

- Ideas and resources for papers and projects.
- Organized information to study for tests.
- Handy references for spelling.
- Reading and writing assistance with glossaries and guidelines.
- A resource for talking to their parents about school.

Sam, a fifth grader at Captain School in Clayton, Missouri, explained the benefits of his learning journal to the author:

Interviewer: What kinds of things do you record in your journal?
Sam: Current events, what you learn, what you enjoyed, what you'd like to do again, procedures for working with equipment, connections between the topic and real life. It's a good reference, too. Let's say I want to remember how to do something that I recorded in the log. I just look it up in the table of contents and find the explanation.
Interviewer: What else do you put in your learning journals?
Sam: When we have guests or visitors that make presentations, we put that information in there, too.

In traditional classrooms, the chief audience for student performance is the teacher. Teachers describe the learning tasks, provide some practice for new concepts or skills, and then rate and rank students according to their performance on tests, papers, drills, and projects. In these classrooms, students are dependent on the teacher's evaluation to tell them how well or how poorly they are learning. In classrooms that adopt a more integrated approach to learning, student self-evaluation is emphasized, and students are encouraged to create goals and assess their performance (Fig. 2.11). Individual conferences with the teacher support this process and provide students with additional criteria for evaluating their work and progress. As Crafton and Burk (1994) observed:

Tucker

1995 - 1996 Goals

Literature: To read different kinds of books by having an open mind and not judging a book by it's cover. I would like to become a better reader. I will do this by looking up words that I don't know, reading at home 30 minutes a night, and reading at school during free time.

Math: To learn division well by having my mom help me. I would like to learn how to do single and double digit division.
Multiplication- I would like to recall my twelves faster. I will practice with my dad.

Social Studies: To learn the states and their capitals. I will use the maps on my computer at home, and I will read a book about the states.

Science: I would like to enter the Science Fair. I will research at topic and conduct an experiment. I will collect data carefully and record the results neatly in my learning log.

W.W.: To improve my cursive writing by writing in cursive more often. I would like to improve my spelling by studying my core spelling list and looking up words I don't know how to spell.

Social: I would like to compromise more because I can be stubborn. I would like to stand up for others. I don't like to see others made fun of. I will try and think of the appropriate thing to say to the people who are arguing.

Study Skills: To work with the television off.

FIG. 2.11. Tucker outlines his learning goals and describes how he will reach them.

> Successful learners do not wait until the end of a performance to think about its effectiveness, nor do they depend wholly on someone else to tell them how they did. They enter the engagement clear about what they value; they use themselves and others as monitors throughout the experience and exit with an altered sense of what to focus on in the future. (p. 4)

A student's learning journal is a portfolio of understanding: a collection of what has been thought, understood, misunderstood, revised, retained, examined, and reflected on. It is a record of thoughts, values, questions, challenges, achievements, and progress. When students review their journals at the end of a day, week, month, or year, they can track the emergence of their own understanding, observe strategies that were successful, and relate past experience to current learning. Because they constantly address the question "How well do I understand this concept (process)?" they take increased responsibility for the direction of their own learning. George, a fifth grader wrote:

> I have not completed my goal of one piece [of writing] a month due to the explorer project. It took up all the time. I have got my projects done on time and all of my rough drafts (which is a mini-miracle, because I have a hundred of each one). My writing is much more in depth and I have thought out my ideas more. I really haven't improved my editing. I can usually find my mistakes, just not know how to correct them. I have improved immensely in journal responses. Before [they] were about three sentences and not good ideas. Now they are at least ten sentences.

Younger children can evaluate their learning by drawing pictures of what they know about a topic before it is studied, and then adding a new picture to illustrate their new understanding. For example, a first grader drew a picture of a butterfly at the beginning of a unit on insects. The butterfly had one large section for its body and two circles for wings. After looking at books about butterflies, seeing a butterfly up close, and talking about them in class, more details began to appear in his drawings, including a segmented body, antennae, and double sets of wings. His pictures indicated an enhanced awareness of butterfly structure and he was able to use the pictures to talk about and assess his own progress.

The writing-to-learn activities of journals encourage students to plan for learning, select information, organize ideas, and review what they have learned. Each of these activities require students to make continuous evaluations, as they decide: (a) what to study, (b) what to select from what they read or observe, and (c) how well they accomplished their learning goals. Typically, students write in content area journals before a presentation, lab, workshop, or research session to identify:

- What they know.
- What they want to know.
- Resources that will help them find the information they are seeking.
- Methods and strategies for finding answers or solving problems.

Teachers facilitate this activity when they model the processes of inquiry in group discussions, create a core of common knowledge with shared information, address misconceptions as they arise, and direct students to helpful resources.

During a study session, students use their journals to record

- Information.
- Responses to ideas.
- Connections with previous experience.
- Answers to their own questions or questions raised in a group.
- New questions that arise as they interact with ideas or others.

The recording and response activities of study sessions require students to decide what information to record from all that they have read about, listened to, or observed. They must also evaluate their own understanding of concepts to decide what they must work with in more depth and what method they will use to increase their understanding.

After a study or work session, students typically evaluate their work by reviewing the information and ideas they have recorded to:

- Identify relationships.
- Find patterns.
- Make connections.
- Identify new questions.
- Draw conclusions.
- Prepare to share with others.
- Refine their notes for more finished writing.
- Plan projects that draw from these collected resources.

It is helpful for students to evaluate group sessions, whether they work in pairs and small groups or participate in class discussions. The following kinds of questions are designed to help students evaluate the quality of the discussion and their own participation:

- How did I help someone understand something?
- How did someone help me understand something?
- What strategy did I share?
- What strategy did I learn?
- What new information did I gain?
- What evidence or ideas changed my mind about something?

COMMUNICATING LEARNING TO OTHERS

Students regularly share their journal entries in small group or class discussions, exchanging information, ideas, strategies, or the results of research. They also use their journals as resources when they want to demonstrate their learning to the teacher or their parents.

End of the Period or End of the Day Reviews and Summaries

It is important to schedule regular periods of time for students to review their journal entries. Many teachers reserve the last 10 minutes of a workshop, lab, literature group, research session, or math study period for students to draw pictures or write notes about what they have learned (see Brandon's end of the day notes in Fig. 2.12). Other teachers ask for brief summaries of what has been learned, which might consist of simple lists from primary children and more detailed summaries from intermediate or middle school students. Response prompts for this review activity might include:

- What did I learn today?
- What do I understand now that I didn't understand before?
- What don't I understand?
- At what point did I get confused?
- What did I like or dislike about class today?

This activity is not a waste of time or busy work. Students are fresh from their interaction with subject matter and this writing helps them organize their thoughts and identify important information. This process assists both comprehension and retention of ideas and provides the teacher with valuable information about individual student understanding. For example, a fifth grader wrote in his journal:

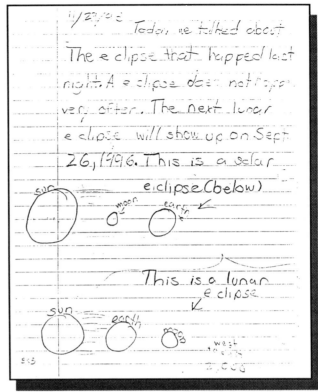

FIG. 2.12. Brandon's end of the day summary of learning about eclipses.

> Today I saw some good gliders. I saw lots of planes that had a lot of speed because of the way the person released it. I didn't get to experience this excitement because when I got down there, nobody would help me. I was going to ask you, but I thought you were too busy. So I just observed. For the gliders, I saw a lot loop. I learned that different planes can do lots of things. I also learned that if you put a point on your plane it will go a little further. (I think).

In response to the student not asking for help, the teacher wrote: "This makes me sad. Always ask!" She wrote an additional note to encourage him to try putting a point on a glider to test the hypothesis he stated in the last sentence. This entry provided the teacher with a view of the student's experience that she could address directly and immediately.

Home–School Communication

In some classrooms students use their journals as resources for writing personal letters home to their families (Fig. 2.13). These daily or weekly notes home describe new information or skills students have learned, as well as their personal responses to class discussions and projects. In primary classrooms, teachers or students may create a classroom journal on a large chart, by listing activities as they are completed. Some teachers create the list in late afternoon, as a review of the day's activities. Students dictate their experiences to the teacher, who records the information in the classroom journal. Older students may take turns being the classroom scribe, and they either record activities on the chart as they occur or list them from their journal notes at the end of the day. However they are created, class journals provide students with ideas for their letters home to parents at the end of the day. In some classrooms, students create a weekly or monthly newsletter, using their individual or classroom journals as resources for ideas and information.

Whether students rely only on their own journal entries or pool their ideas with others, they address one or more of the following questions in their letters:

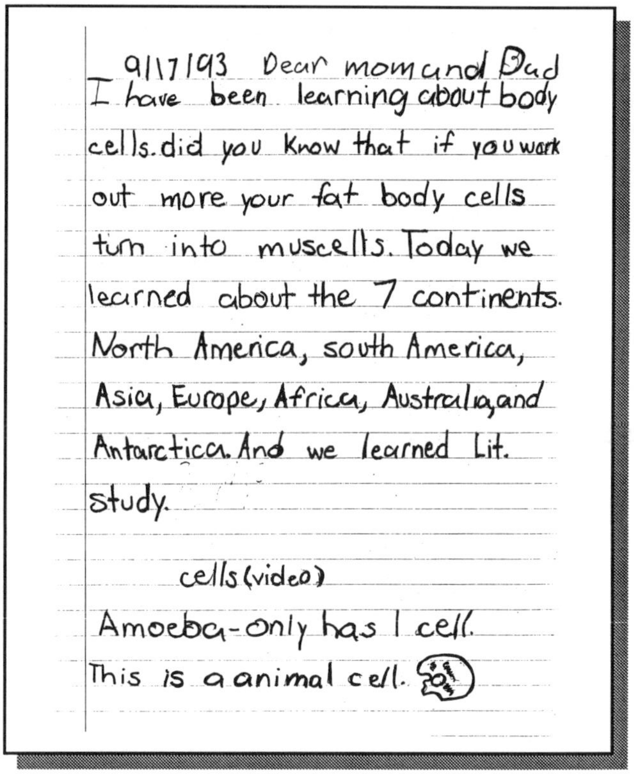

9/17/93 Dear mom and Dad
I have been learning about body cells. did you know that if you work out more your fat body cells turn into muscells. Today we learned about the 7 continents. North America, south America, Asia, Europe, Africa, Australia, and Antarctica. And we learned Lit. study.

cells (video)
Amoeba- only has 1 cell.
This is a animal cell.

FIG. 2.13. Brandon's letter home to his parents.

- What did I learn today?
- What did I like best?
- What ideas interested me the most?
- What problems did I solve?
- What questions did I find answers for?
- How will this information or skill help me find out something I want to know?
- What am I looking forward to learning?
- What might someone at home find especially interesting?

Many teachers send home student journals on a regular (daily, weekly, monthly) basis for review by the parents. In Fig. 2.14, Laura shares an entry in her journal with her mother. Students in her second-grade classroom regularly take their journals home to collect examples of parts of speech and grammatical constructions. When journals are part of home–school communication, parents are encouraged to discuss entries with their children, and either sign them or write a brief note of advice, support, or encouragement. Nick's father wrote:

FIG. 2.14. Laura talks about a journal entry with her mother.

Nick—What I'm particularly impressed by is not simply your ability to use numbers accurately and fast, but also your skill at expressing and explaining what you have done. It's great to see both strengths developing together. Love, Dad

In some school systems, this process creates a three-way conversation that includes the student, teacher, and parent. For example, one fifth grader was having difficulty remembering assignments. At the bottom of the assignment page in his journal, the teacher suggested: "When you don't write down the assignment completely, it's nearly impossible to do it correctly." After the journal went home for parent review, the student's mother wrote back: "All your work is great, but I have to agree with Ms. McDonald about writing assignments down. Why don't you just take a little more time when writing down your homework? Thanks. Love, Mom." At the end of the following week, his mother observed: "It looks like you are writing down your homework assignments better than last week—No comments from Ms. McDonald—Great! Your essay on 'Kids Under 18 Years of Age Voting' was really good. Let's keep up the good work! Love, Mom." The teacher reported that these kinds of cooperative exchanges provided encouragement, coaching, and support that greatly improved the student's academic performance.

Preparing for Individual Conferences With the Teacher

As part of their preparation to meet with the teacher, students review their pictures, notes, and responses to find examples that indicate their understanding of a concept or topic. They also identify successful strategies they have used to solve problems, mark or record questions they have, and note any difficulties they are experiencing. This preparation helps students review their learning and provides a focus for the conference. After the conference, teachers may ask students to write a note in their journals to describe their understanding of what happened in the conference and to enter information about resources, problem-solving strategies, or assignments that were discussed.

Preparing for an End of Term Evaluation

At the end of a topic of study or a grading period, students use their journals to demonstrate their learning to the teacher. In some classrooms, students create final projects, using the resources of their journals. These might be individually or group-prepared reports, books, magazines, newspapers, puppet shows, interviews, TV or radio broadcasts, tapes, murals, exhibits, posters, brochures, experiments, demonstrations, artwork, crafts, dance, or drama. In one third-grade classroom, Isaac, whose family was moving to Israel, researched the country and drew a map to show the class where he would be living. Jessie followed his interest in Abraham Lincoln to research the Civil War. Claire drew from her reading about World War II and a visit to the Holocaust Museum in Washington, DC, to write historical fiction in the form of a young girl's diary. (See chapter 9 for an excerpt from this diary.) A fifth-grade class created a newspaper from colonial times, using individual student research notes as the basis for news stories.

In other classrooms, the journals themselves are presented as evidence of learning. Depending on the age and experience of their students, teachers ask students to review the entries in their journals and mark them to show:

- Growth in understanding.
- A skill they have developed.
- Questions they still have.
- Problems they are experiencing.
- Evidence of problem solving.

Students also identify examples of their best thinking or their best work and justify the selection of these entries (Fig. 2.15), either in writing or orally to the teacher, responding to questions such as:

- How does this show learning?
- Why is this my best work?
- How has your work improved?
- What do I need to learn more about?
- What still interests me about this topic or theme?

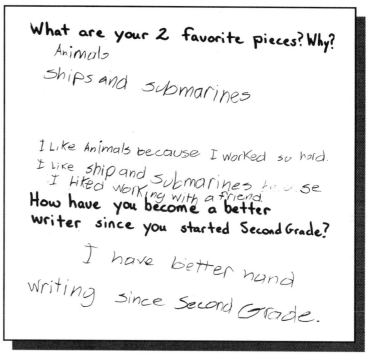

What are your 2 favorite pieces? Why?
Animals
Ships and submarines

I Like Animals because I worked so hard.
I Like ship and submarines
I liked working with a friend.
How have you become a better
writer since you started Second Grade?

I have better hand
writing since Second Grade.

FIG. 2.15. Brandon's (second-grade) evaluation of writing progress.

Depending on the grade level, teachers might ask students to write an introduction to their journal, create a table of contents, summarize their learning about a topic, and write a conclusion that describes the student's development as a learner, including strategies they have discovered, insights they have attained, and the value of the study in general and to them personally.

Some teachers provide end-of-study or end-of-term surveys for students to complete, using their journals as a reference. Students respond to prompts such as:

- List the 3 (5, 10) most important ideas you learned from this study.
- Why are these ideas important?
- What study, research, or problem-solving strategies did you discover?
- What did you most enjoy about studying this topic?
- What things did you find difficult?
- What do you still want to know about this topic?

USING JOURNALS TO EVALUATE STUDENT PROGRESS

In addition to looking at the statements, summaries, notes, and letters that students prepare on a daily, weekly, or monthly basis to indicate their understanding of concepts, teachers may also periodically review learning journals to check comprehension and skill levels, to note any misconceptions, and to identify concepts that need to be reviewed. These evaluations help teachers assess learning progress and permit them to see how well students can evaluate their own learning. Teachers evaluate entries in learning journals for five main purposes:

- To gather information on what students know.
- To note understanding across the class and plan for future instruction.
- To select materials for student portfolios (cooperatively with the student).
- To provide information about progress to parents and supervisors.
- To meet the requirements of local, state, and national mandates.

These purposes can be accomplished in a number of ways, including informal observations of individuals during work periods, individual conferences, and more detailed examination of individual learning journals.

Over-the-Shoulder Observations

The quickest way to see how well students understand a concept or can perform a skill is to watch them informally while they are working with ideas, to observe the following:

- How accurate is the information they are recording?
- How is their understanding reflected in drawings, diagrams, or maps?
- What connections are they making with their personal experience?
- Do they return to a book or observation for more details?
- Are they writing down questions they have?
- Do they have information to share in groups?
- Do they record ideas submitted by others?

Two-Minute Conferences

Several times a week, it is helpful to conduct brief, walk-around conferences with individual students to make personal contact and assess their current level of understanding. Teachers may ask a variety of questions, depending on a student's age level and the content area, such as:

- Tell me about your drawing (map, graph, diagram).
- Tell me what you're working on.
- Can you explain this graph (picture, chart) to me?
- Are you finding everything you need?
- Do you need any help?
- What will you do next? What are your plans for this session?

Group Conferences

When students work in regular groups, it is helpful to sit in on their discussions at least once a week to evaluate the quality of group interaction. If a class has developed guidelines for working effectively in groups, the teacher observes the group in terms of these standards. Depending on the function of the group and the content involved, these guidelines may facilitate discussion or provide directions for doing laboratory work, conducting research, or solving problems. Some teachers take notes on these sessions and discuss their observations with the groups, in terms of how well they meet their guidelines.

Most groups assign different roles to the participants to support the effective functioning of the group and provide all students with the opportunity to develop skill in assuming different roles. Typically, these roles include a discussion leader or facilitator, a scribe who records information produced by the group, a reporter who communicates group discussions to a larger group, and a messenger who collects and distributes materials. In social studies groups there might be a reference expert and science groups often designate persons to set up, clean up, and collect materials for labs. Teachers will want to demonstrate these roles before students meet in groups and periodically review them with group members if there seems to be confusion about what they are supposed to do. More information about the functioning of groups and their relationship to journaling can be found in chapter 3, the content area chapters, and Appendix B.

As they observe groups at work, teachers will also observe how well the students stay focused on a task and suggest ways to prevent or address distractions. It will be evident if students are using their journals as resources for these discussions, if they refer to their journals to:

- Read information aloud.
- Find ideas to discuss.
- Share strategies or provide help to others.
- Argue or defend a point.

Periodic Review of Every Learning Journal

It is helpful to sit down with students at regular intervals to review the entries in their journals (Fig. 2.16). This provides an opportunity for the student to read or interpret entries that might be difficult to figure out and permits the teacher to ask questions that will clarify their understanding of the entries. Conferences are usually conducted on a weekly or biweekly basis, supplemented by more informal observations during work periods. Sometimes teachers review journals on a daily basis, five or more at a time, after school or while students are busy with independent activities. Others use a team folder system, where students file daily individual work and group papers together in a folder for teacher review.

FIG. 2.16. Wendy and Mrs. Johnson discuss entries in a literature journal.

FIG. 2.17. Leya interprets school learning in terms of important events in her life.

What do teachers learn when they review a student's learning journal? One of the most obvious things they discover is an individual student's interest in particular subject matter. When a topic draws attention, students generally write extensively about it, whereas information that does not touch their experience or understanding as intensely will be less fully elaborated. Teachers can also observe the personal connections students make with subject matter. A kindergartner whose family had a new baby incorporated this consuming interest into every response she drew and wrote about during an animal study (Fig. 2.17a–d).

Depending on the grade level and content area, teachers may also observe:

- How well a student can identify main ideas.
- How well they understand key concepts.
- Their informal grasp of spelling and grammar.
- How well they interpret and organize information.
- Preferred ways of working with ideas (writing, drawing, graphic organizers).
- Personal experience and knowledge that forms the basis for new learning.
- Levels of analysis and synthesis.
- Ability to self-evaluate learning progress.

These observations can indicate levels of understanding in students who do not test well or who do not comfortably participate in class discussions. They may also reveal a superficial grasp of concepts by students who are more verbal. Regular observations help direct the teacher's attention to concepts that require review with one student, several students, or the entire class, when there seems to be a general lack of understanding.

At the beginning of the year, students may write very little or they may be confused about what to write in their journals. After a time, however, most students begin to generate longer entries. As they interact in small groups, they observe how others record and respond to ideas. From minilessons and teacher modeling, they learn how to organize information in various ways and become more excited about generating ideas of their own. With time, students write more and risk more, in the types of questions they ask and the responses they make to these questions. For example, early in the school year, a fifth grader wrote about his day in the following manner: "My morning started out by coming in and doing my check-in. (I don't remember what it was). So then we learned a game called Getting to One. We explained the rules and played. It was fun. Then we went to lunch." By the end of the following month, he was writing entries on the computer that extended to three typewritten pages, detailing what he learned, how he learned it, and why he thought his learning might be valuable.

As students become more fluent with their ideas, they may temporarily become less tidy, with writing crossed out or written in the margins. Depending on the student, this may or may not be a problem. Students usually develop improved strategies for recording and organizing from their own experience and from watching others deal with these problems. Some students keep chaotic-looking journals but use them successfully. Teachers can help students evaluate the effectiveness of their journals by asking: "Can you find information easily in your journal? Can you read what you have written at the end of the day or week? What might improve the helpfulness of your journal?"

Obviously, teachers can gain helpful information about what a student understands from examining a learning journal. They can observe enthusiasm for a topic or a particular way of learning and identify points of difficulty. They can also see the particular strategies students use to help themselves learn and gain ideas for instruction. Because students are encouraged to draw, create charts or diagrams, and collect relevant material from their experience to put in their learning journals, these notebooks often present a more comprehensive picture of learning than is possible to gain from tests and formal writing activities.

Sometimes students and teachers write brief notes to each other, to ask questions, request help, or respond to previous notes. Teachers may summarize their experience with students in these notes, offer encouragement and express their pride in student accomplishments (Fig. 2.18). Notice Kaitlin's response to Mrs. Murphy's notes to her in Fig. 2.19.

Many students draw pictures unrelated to a study, make designs, or fill in the margins of their journals with seemingly irrelevant markings. This activity may indicate times when a student is bored, distracted, or in need of an outlet for nervous energy. Designs and drawings may also indicate creativity or talent in this type of expression, which can be encouraged as a medium for exploring ideas in the content areas. In some classrooms, teachers encourage students to set aside scrap pages for doodling or drawing to provide a place for expression that is unrelated to the curriculum. Occasionally these pictures and designs hold clues to interests that can be expanded within a content area study. For example, both interest and ability in fashion drawing is indicated in Fig. 2.20, which might be utilized for researching historical or contemporary cultural dress.

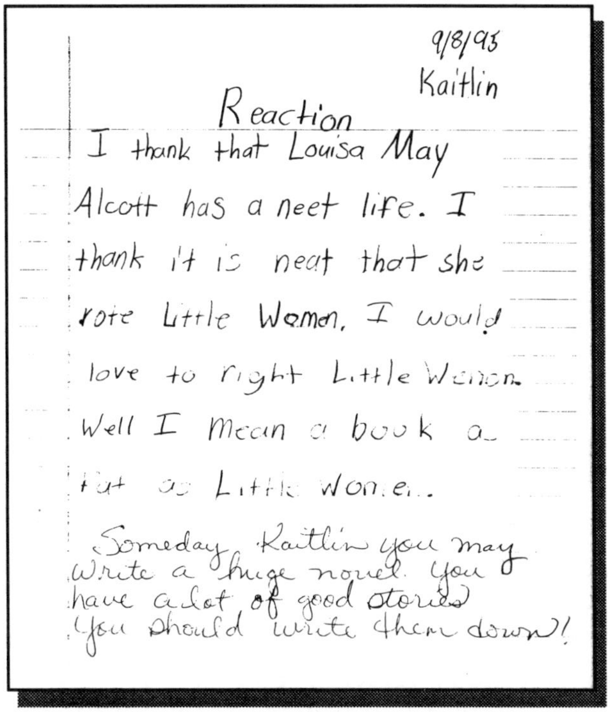
9/8/95
Kaitlin
Reaction
I thank that Louisa May Alcott has a neet life. I thank it is neat that she rote Little Women. I would love to right Little Women. Well I mean a book a fat as Little Women.
Someday, Kaitlin you may write a huge novel. You have a lot of good stories. You should write them down!

FIG. 2.18. Kaitlin's reaction and Mrs. Murphy's response.

JOURNALS AND THE PORTFOLIO SYSTEM

One difficulty with the portfolio system is that it must often serve multiple and incompatible purposes. Part of the value of portfolios is the exercise of choice and the development of self-evaluation on the part of students. It is therefore imperative that students be involved in the selection and justification of materials to be included in their portfolios. At the same time, students may lack the maturity and training required to identify their own best work or progress, choosing more often those pieces that indicate satisfaction with their work, but perhaps not the best of which they are capable. When teachers must use portfolios to show progress to parents or administrators, this creates a dilemma.

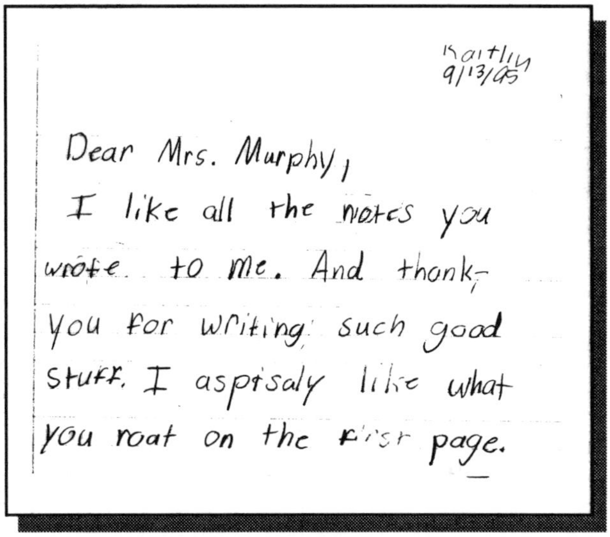
Kaitlin
9/13/95
Dear Mrs. Murphy,
I like all the notes you wrote to me. And thank-you for writing such good stuff. I aspisaly like what you roat on the first page.

FIG. 2.19. Kaitlin's thank you note to Mrs. Murphy.

Like the portfolio, learning journals put response, organization, and evaluation of learning into students' hands, allowing them to demonstrate learning in individual terms. From these entries, teachers can assemble materials that indicate learning or progress in terms of the trained eye. Like portfolios, end-of-term student self-evaluations of learning journals encourage students to identify progress and select examples of their best learning. However, because student and teacher evaluate for different purposes, each is free to choose different items to represent progress.

Teachers may also feel overwhelmed by the time and effort required to manage the materials associated with portfolios. Gomez, Graue, and Bloch (1991) acknowledged the clear value of the portfolio as an assessment tool, observing:

The promise of portfolio assessment is in its collaborative power for students and teachers, providing a common framework to discuss learning and achievement. It also gives teachers a rich opportunity to reconsider their teaching practice by making a tight connection between instruction and assessment. (p. 627)

However, they also noted that "the use of portfolios required significant amounts of both in-class and after-school time to reflect on and prepare for her [the teacher's] next step in teaching" (p. 628) and observed further that portfolio assessment is often added to other forms of assessment and that "the responsibility of making this restructured assessment work falls squarely on the shoulders of already burdened teachers"(p. 628).

FIG. 2.20. Marina's fashion drawing.

Many elementary teachers who value the goals of portfolios find that learning journals provide a more manageable way to meet these goals. In some ways, the learning journal is really a portfolio in a book, an all-in-one-place collection of a student's experience in a content area or with a theme that allows students to demonstrate growth, show their best efforts, and get to know themselves as learners. In addition, a comprehensive learning journal can provide the benefits sought in the portfolio system, such as informing instruction, providing an authentic and multidimensional view of student learning, emphasizing what the student does well, and providing opportunities for collaboration and reflection.

In the following interview conducted by the author, Sam and Brandon reflected on the relationship between learning logs and portfolios in their school:

Interviewer: What do you do with your learning logs at the end of the year?

     Sam: We take two things out of each learning log to put in our portfolios. [In this class, students keep a series of logs throughout the year. Because the class is team taught, there are both morning and afternoon journals.] We keep these from year to year. Would you like to see mine? [Sam produces a large, sturdy, plastic-bound, three-ring notebook from a nearby bookcase.] We keep portfolios to show our growth in grades 2–5, saving a few pieces from each year.

Interviewer: How do you decide what to put in your portfolio (a collection of work from grades 2–5 that is sent on to the middle school)?

     Sam: The teacher gives us guidelines, such as including our explorer piece and something from our government unit. I saved my tests, too, because they're so good. I like these kinds of tests—we write everything we know about government and everything we know about science. We share all our stuff by putting it on display in the cafeteria. [This activity is called The Buffet Table at this school.] Other kids can read what we've written. Then they write their comments on sticky notes and put it on our writing, so we can see what they liked.

Interviewer: Do you choose items to include in the portfolio?

Sam: We put two writing pieces of our own choice in the portfolio, something we're most proud of or did well on. They can be from things other than what we did in class, like from an extracurricular project. [The school sponsors extracurricular classes that meet before and after school, where children explore literature, computers, foreign languages, and other projects.]

Interviewer: Do you use these portfolios in any way?

Sam: We can refer back to them when we're studying something similar. They're here in this cabinet for us to use. [He points to a tall cabinet that provides easy access to portfolios.] Our teachers encourage us to use them for reference. They use them for parent teacher conferences too. They show how your thoughts work.

Another student observed Sam taking the portfolio from the cabinet and sat down to enter the conversation.

Brandon: I used my portfolio today. We had a lesson on microscopes in third grade and I looked back at some information to help me understand some things we're looking at today.

Brandon offered to bring his journals from earlier grades to show his progress as a student. Excerpts from these journals are included throughout the book.

In schools where portfolios are encouraged or required, learning journals can provide excellent support because they create a daily record of learning progress and provide resources for creating writing and other projects to be placed in the portfolio. More formal papers can show a greater depth of understanding and organization when ideas have been worked out in an informal manner in the journal. The use of learning journals encourages a continuing process of evaluation and provides opportunities for the metacognitive activity associated with portfolios. When students respond to ideas and then reflect on their responses on a daily basis, they begin to see patterns and relationships in their own thinking. Journal writing creates a history of learning that provides students with insights into their strengths as learners and helps them develop habits of reflective thought that will permit them to explore increasingly complex ideas.

Journal Formats, Guidelines, and Activities

Intelligence cannot develop without matter to think about. Making new connections depends on knowing enough about something in the first place to provide a basis for thinking of other things to do—of other questions to ask—that demand more complex connections in order to make sense. The more ideas about something people already have at their disposal, the more new ideas occur and the more that can coordinate to build up still more complicated schemes.

—Eleanor Duckworth (1987)

PREVIEW

1. What kinds of writing formats are used for journal entries?
2. How are graphic organizers used in learning journals?
3. How does reading and writing poetry help students increase their understanding of content area concepts?
4. What kinds of guidelines are helpful to beginning writers?
5. What materials are required to construct a learning journal?
6. How are entries arranged in a learning journal?
7. What kinds of classroom activities are supported by learning journals?
8. How do special-use journals strengthen the home–school connection?

BRIEFLY: When students practice making journal entries in a variety of writing formats and in response to generic prompts, they create a repertoire of ways to explore their experience, respond to ideas, and express themselves.

WRITING FORMATS FOR JOURNAL ENTRIES

Teachers can help students move toward more autonomous and flexible responses in their learning journals by providing them with a variety of models for responding. Writing promotes thinking about a topic and different formats encourage students to think in different ways. For example, summaries help students identify and sequence the major ideas of a topic, whereas essays, diagrams, and matrices promote analysis, synthesis, evaluation, or elaboration of ideas. Different formats can be introduced and practiced in writing workshops or demonstrated in minilessons that are part of content area instruction. As students become familiar with different kinds of entries, they can be encouraged to select those that are most comfortable for them. Notice how Robert, a fifth grader, was assisted in his learning by participating in a variety of recording and response activities in his classroom.

> *Interviewer*: What are you most proud of in this journal?
> *Robert*: My picture of a tulip dissection. We looked at all the parts of a tulip with a magnifying glass and took notes from the teacher. [He checks his table of contents and finds another page.] These are my notes on genes, and this is a list of how we can react to what we learn. [The list includes: What did you learn? What did you like or dislike? Do you understand the information? How do you feel about your learning?]

Robert displayed his handouts on types of microscopes and the rules for using them, and explained how the teacher taught them to draw what they see. He described how he used his table of contents for his own reference or to show the teacher a particular entry. Other entries in his journal included a report from a field trip to the arboretum and a prediction he had written before the trip. He explained that he took his notebook along to sketch and take notes so that he could remember what he had seen and learned.

Most teachers allow students to choose their own form of response but might encourage experimentation with new forms as they are modeled. Because the purpose of these entries is to encourage fluency and follow immediate thought, they will be of an exploratory, informal, and developmental nature and may include spelling, punctuation, and grammatical errors. From these entries, students often take away a new understanding and helpful organization of ideas, which can then be translated into more finished projects.

As noted in chapter 1, recording and response entries may be recorded sequentially in single entry style, or placed on opposite sides of a folded page or on facing pages of a notebook, in a double entry (dialectical) format. Resource and reference entries may be kept together in one section of the notebook or recorded separately, according to the practice of a particular classroom. (Note: Examples from student learning journals for the types of entries described in the following can be found at the end of this chapter.)

Recording and Response

• *Notes*: These are one of the simplest kinds of entries. Numbered or unnumbered, notes record individual pieces of information gleaned from reading, research, observation, discussion, conferences, and other experience. Notes may also include opinions, questions, or ideas about a subject area.

• *Essays*: These are longer entries, written in paragraph form, that attempt to organize or analyze information, or develop an idea in a more comprehensive way. These may involve comparison and contrast, cause and effect, or persuasion. Essays written in the different genres of literature may be included in literature or writing journals.

• *Outlines*: Many students find that organizing information into major topics and subtopics helps them get a clearer picture of the relationships in a study.

- *Quick-writes*: Students write briefly (5 minutes) about an assignment as a warm-up exercise at the beginning of class, preparation for class discussion, a brainstorming technique to generate ideas about a topic, or as an evaluation activity to summarize what has been learned during a session. A quick review of this writing gives teachers a thumbnail sketch of the levels of understanding in the class.

- *Inquiry writing*: Teachers may provide students with a list of questions about a topic, or these questions might be developed by individuals, small groups, or the entire class. Entries are intended to be shared with others.

- *Diary entries or dialogues*: Students write diary entries for historical or fictional characters or create dialogues between contemporary or historical persons, characters in a book, or a combination of these. This kind of writing helps students identify with characters and events in literature or history.

- *Practice or fictitious letters*: These are written to a person or organization related to a current study. They may be practice for sending an actual letter or letters that are directed to imaginary or historical persons. Letters help students think about a topic with a specific audience in mind.

- *Quotes or excerpts*: Students record favorite phrases, sentences, or paragraphs from their reading in a content area and respond to them. This response may state an opinion, evaluate literary quality, or note a personal connection with the quoted material.

- *Maps*: Visual representations of locations under study help students develop a sense of place and spatial relationships. These are often used in connection with literature, science, or the social studies.

- *Semantic maps*: Often called *clusters* or *webs,* these maps are visual illustrations of categories and relationships related to a concept. Maps are organized around a key idea or question that is supported by subtopics that explain the concept. These subtopics are often written inside balloons and are connected to the main topic by lines. Subtopics may also be described by strands that contain additional details. In more complex webs, subcategories may be connected by lines to show relationships among them.

- *Data banks*: At the beginning of a study, teachers may distribute lists of terms related to a topic to provide support for reading, writing, or research, or students may create these lists of words themselves and group them into categories. As students encounter related words in their reading or discussion, they add new words to the bank in the appropriate category. For example, students might create a data bank of words related to seasons, holidays, historical events, weather, or a particular selection of literature.

- *Magazine articles or pictures*: Students photocopy or cut out magazine pictures and tape them into their journal to use as resources for a particular study. Beginning readers and writers often cut out letters or words to practice the alphabet or to illustrate drawings. Students may also use cut-out pictures to illustrate books they have read, math problems, and concepts in science or the social studies.

- *Drawings*: Labeled or unlabeled representations of stories, characters, processes, events, or objects help students translate their understanding of a topic, event, or thing into graphic form. Drawing requires attention to detail and often increases observational skills.

- *Diagrams*: Frequently used in science journals, these are labeled sketches that show the parts of something or show how something works. Lines are drawn from labels to show where parts are located or how they work.
- *Charts and matrices*: Organizing information in labeled columns provides students with a structured place to record information in categories and identify patterns and relationships that otherwise might not be apparent.
- *Graphs*: This type of organization of data includes bar, line, circle, pie and scatter graphs. They help students display information, make comparisons, show relationships, draw conclusions, and explain their ideas to others.
- *Poetry*: Students create their own verse or collect poetry related to a theme or topic in a content area study. Writing original poems encourages students to synthesize what has been learned about a topic by translating it into a different form and expressing it in more precise terms.

Resource and Reference

- *Lists*: Students list titles of books that they have read or that they want to read. They may also make lists to record assignments, steps for solving a problem, materials required for a project, procedures for labs, guidelines for responding to reading, or rules for working in groups. Lists may be numbered or unnumbered.
- *Photographs*: Original or photocopied photographs of people, places, events, or things related to a content area study or theme help students illustrate an idea.
- *Cartoons*: A favorite of students, these may be original or cut out from newspapers or magazines. In some classrooms, teachers feature a cartoon sharing time each week for students to display and talk about the cartoons they have found that relate to a topic of study.
- *News articles or pictures*: These may be used to illustrate concepts or to support or extend research in the content areas. Articles in local papers often help students make connections between what they are studying and their immediate environment. These are shared as current events on a regular basis with small groups or the class.
- *Glossaries*: These are lists of terms related to a study that provide a quick reference for students when they are reading or writing about a topic. Students generally write the definition of the term and include the pronunciation, a synonym, or an example, if these are helpful to their understanding.
- *Personal dictionaries*: Students record the correct spelling of words they use frequently, but spell incorrectly. Dictionaries may be kept in a separate section of the journal or merged with the glossary. Some students keep separate spelling journals that are used both for reference and practice.

USING GRAPHIC ORGANIZERS

Graphic organizers represent knowledge in a visual way, helping students think about and organize information so that they can better understand, add to, or remember it. Researchers have found that students realize the greatest instructional benefits from using graphic organizers when they are trained how to use them and have opportunities to construct their own (Dunston, 1992). Teachers model the use of graphic organizers by using a variety of forms to introduce or build concepts in science, math, literature, or the social studies (Fig. 3.1). As students practice using the different graphic forms in group situations, they begin to find them useful for exploring ideas on their own in their journals.

Graphic organizers help students focus on key elements of information and organize their thinking about a topic. As visual representations of information, they often provide structure for identifying relationships among persons, places, objects, and events that might otherwise not be apparent. Graphic organizers encourage students to integrate what they already know about a topic with new ideas and create places to put new information. They also help them look for characteristics of a concept and encourage them to create categories. When students meet together in small groups, graphic organizers help focus discussion on main ideas. Because these representations help students depict the main ideas of a topic and identify patterns and relationships, they also provide students with helpful ways to review concepts and serve as resources for writing, discussion, tests, and further research.

There are four major types of graphic organizers: hierarchical, sequential, conceptual, and cyclical. *Hierarchical* organizers are top-down, general to specific structures that create categories to explore a topic. For example, Fig. 3.2 illustrates the pyramid of life that begins with energy from the sun. *Sequential* organizers help students order events with information that involves time, processes or cause–effect relationships. Time lines and flowcharts are examples of sequential organizers. *Conceptual* organizers help students compare and contrast ideas, events, objects or persons by displaying information that supports a main idea. Venn diagrams, Vee maps, matrices,

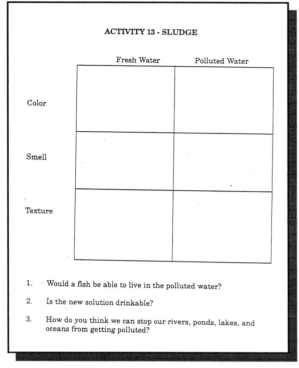

FIG. 3.1. Model organizer from a third grade theme journal.

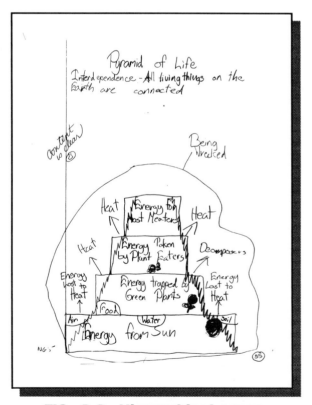

FIG. 3.2. Hierarchical organizer—Nick's pyramid of life.

graphs, charts (Fig. 3.3), and semantic maps (clusters and webs) are examples of conceptual organizers. *Cyclical* organizers are used to portray a continuous series of events, such as systems, life cycles, seasons, precipitation, and chemical processes (Fig. 3.4). The uses of graphic organizers are described in more detail in the individual content area chapters.

Graphic organizers are equally valuable to teachers for evaluating student learning and the effectiveness of their teaching. Not only do these visual representations assist a student's learning, they can also indicate their level of understanding and the ability to identify patterns and relationships. Teachers can often assess comprehension more quickly and accurately by observing students' graphic organizers than by administering more standard kinds of tests.

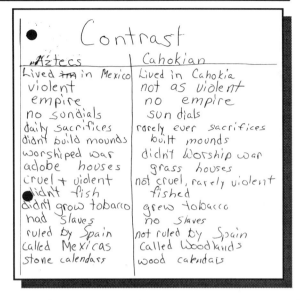

FIG. 3.3. Conceptual organizer—Abbie's contrast of Indian cultures.

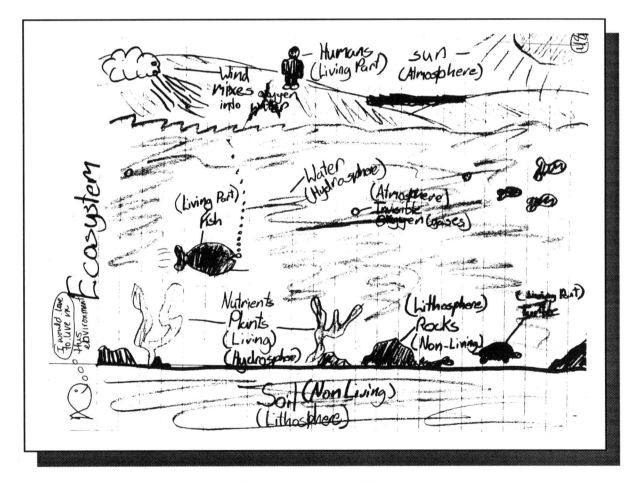

FIG. 3.4. Cyclical organizer—Nick's ecosystem.

RESPONDING WITH POETRY

Poetry with themes from science, math, geography, or history provides students with interesting and entertaining models of precise expression about topics that often seem remote, forbidding, or complex. Content-related poetry cuts to the essence of concepts, provides insights into the nature of things, and creates models of response that students can adapt to their own experience and feelings. For example, after listening to Carl Sandburg's "Arithmetic" (1982), students in one class created their own definitions of arithmetic to explore the way they relate to math and to express frustration or joy about this relationship. In the poem, Sandburg wrote that "Arithmetic is where numbers fly like pigeons in and out of your head," and "Arithmetic is numbers you squeeze from your head to your hand to your pencil to your paper till you get the answer." Students defined arithmetic in the following ways:

- Arithmetic is like the air—it's all around us.
- Arithmetic is like a bad cold—it never seems to go away!
- Arithmetic is randomness; you either pick it right or you don't.
- Arithmetic is sweaty hands working to find an answer.
- Arithmetic is like walking. . . . You take one step at a time.
- Arithmetic is shapes, lines, and angles, and if you're not careful, will get you in a tangle.

One of the best ways to encourage children to respond poetically to what they are learning is to read all kinds of poetry to them on a daily basis: narrative, lyrical, descriptive, concrete, poetry from all cultures, poetry that rhymes, and poetry that does not rhyme. It is also helpful to point out examples of the precise use of words and the figurative language characteristic of poetry. Many teachers write selected poems on the board for students to copy into their journals and encourage students to find others of their own to share with the class.

With a little encouragement, some students make spontaneous poetic responses to the ideas they are studying. Thoughts or feelings recorded in a journal may have poetic qualities, even though they might not be written in poetic form. As teachers review these entries they become aware of descriptive abilities students possess and can alert them to the possibilities of different kinds of expression. Consider Tucker's poetic entry in his fourth-grade learning log:

> When I want to get away from it all, I can really go anywhere, as long as I have my imagination with me. I can go anywhere. I can do anything. I can gallop down long grassy fields on my horses. I can fight the most wanted killer and become famous.

How can poetry be used to respond to content area studies? A boy who expresses himself frequently or fluently in poetry might be encouraged to pretend he is Columbus, trying to convince Queen Isabella that his proposed voyage deserves financing, or he might use poetic form to describe the metamorphosis of a butterfly or the flight of a bird. Students who reveal talent in this area will often work with great persistence to communicate their understanding of a topic in poetic form.

At the early primary levels, students still see themselves as poets, but intermediate-age and middle school children may be hesitant to use the poetic form to think about ideas or express their understanding of concepts. For the reluctant or aspiring poet of any age, the poetic forms described in the following provide a framework for expression that can enhance observational skills and the ability to analyze, synthesize, and evaluate experience.

• *Haiku* (HIGH-coo) is an unrhymed poetic form developed by the Japanese. It often has a nature theme, is just three lines long, and contains 17 syllables. The final line may describe a response to the observations of Lines 1 and 2.

Line 1—Five syllables
Line 2—Seven syllables
Line 3—Five syllables

Southeast Indians
hunted deer, turkey, and fish.
Kept tails for good luck. (Steve, 5th)

Southeast Indians
Drank tea for strength in battle
To defend their land. (Andy, 5th)

• *Cinquain* (SIN-kane) from the French word for "five" is a five-line poem created around specific ideas and certain numbers of syllables in each line.

Line 1—Subject (two syllables)
Line 2—Description of subject (four syllables)
Line 3—Action of the subject (six syllables)
Line 4—Response to the subject (eight syllables)
Line 5—Another word for the subject (two syllables)

A snake,
Cold-blooded brown,
Slithers toward me through grass,
Hollow sounding warning strikes fear,
Rattler! (James, 6th)

• *Diamante* (dee-ah-MAHN-tay) The name of this seven-line poetic form means *diamond*. It helps students create a contrast between persons, places, things, and events. The first and last words in the poem are opposites, such as fission and fusion, Jekyll and Hyde, or wealth and poverty. Requirements for each line include:

Line 1—One word subject, a noun that is the opposite of the noun in the last line
Line 2—Two adjectives that describe the subject in Line 1
Line 3—Three participles (-ing or -ed words) that describe the subject in Line 1
Line 4—Four nouns: the first two related to the subject in Line 1; the last two related to the subject in Line 7
Line 5—Three participles that describe the subject in Line 7
Line 6—Two adjectives that describe the subject in Line 7
Line 7—One-word subject, a noun that is the opposite of the word in Line 1

Sunlight
Bright, yellow
Warming, moving, revealing
Trees, flowers, mushrooms, moss
Cooling, calming, hiding
dark, gray
Shadows (Amy, 7th)

- *Two-word poems* can be any length and express ideas about any topic, but they are limited to two words per line.

Tyrannosaurus rex
Mighty tyrant
Huge appetite
Sharp teeth
Little arms
Big legs
Now gone
Nothing left
But bones. (Frank, 3rd)

- *Limericks* generally have humorous themes, with a twist at the end, but some students enjoy using the form to express ideas of a more serious nature. Limericks have five lines. Lines 1, 2, and 5 rhyme and Lines 3 and 4 rhyme. Lines 3 and 4 are shorter than the others.

The Indians were very religious
All of their food was nutritious
Their main crop was corn
Which grew in a swarm
And tasted so very delicious. (Elizabeth, 5th)

Doing drugs is bad for your health
If you buy drugs it takes all your wealth
You'll drop out of school
And won't be so cool,
So do not do drugs, for yourself. (Rachel, 5th)

- *Concept poems* focus on color, shape, texture, sound, taste, and smell and help students look more closely at their surroundings. They also help students identify patterns in their observations and encourage them to relate new information to their own experience.

Springtime
It is springtime
One by one
The flowers pop out of the ground
All kinds of baby plants are born
School is near the end
Summertime is near. (Rolf, 4th)

Fall
I'm looking out my window
Watching the leaves quietly but swiftly
Falling to the ground.
People are raking leaves into a pile,
Other children are jumping into them.
In the background I can see a
 beautiful sunset of
 many colors.
And that's all I can see from my
window. (Tucker, 4th)

These kinds of poems are especially useful for students to organize and describe events and objects in nature or to draw their attention to features of the classroom they may not have noticed. Students might respond to questions like:

- What do you see that is green?
- How do things you have touched feel?
- What different kinds of sounds can you hear?
- What did you taste in the cafeteria today?
- What shapes can be found in the classroom?
- How did the botanical garden smell?

Different colors, shapes, textures, and sounds can be compared to each other or compared to other things using similes or metaphors. Students can also describe their personal responses to observations by telling how different colors, shapes, textures and sounds make them feel. Tucker recalled being allowed to drive his father's truck:

Driving the Truck

Feel—The rubber covering of the steering wheel. The car going up and down from the bumps. My dad sitting next to me. The furry car seat beneath me.

Feel (emotions)—Proud that my dad trusted me to drive his truck. Happy that I was staying on the road.

See—The rocks beneath the car. My dad's wide-eyed face. The birds sitting most still on the branches of the tree. The long stems of flowers beside the truck.

Hear—The birds singing their most delightful songs. The car running over the rocks beneath us. The huge engine roaring like a lion.

Smell—The exhaust coming from the muffler. The leather of the steering wheel. The clean fresh air of nature.

Taste—The dirt flying through the open window.

This exercise in exploring the sense experiences in a moment of time creates material that can be used for reflection or further writing. As Calkins and Harwayne (1991) observed:

Once a writer has found and reflected upon beautiful language, puzzling lines, anecdotes that reveal something bigger . . . then what? Where does the drumroll lead? It leads to insight. It leads to questions, to memories, to discovering feelings we didn't know were there. It leads us to uncover layers of meaning around the bits of life we collect. (p. 65)

GUIDELINES FOR BEGINNING JOURNAL WRITERS

When students first begin to write in learning journals, it is helpful to provide them with response guidelines. These are questions that model different ways of thinking about ideas and experience, and should be as generic as possible to encourage students to express their own ideas. Students copy guidelines from the board, list them word for word from lecture, or rephrase them in terms that are personally meaningful. In some classrooms, guidelines are printed on handouts, which are punched and inserted into journals contained in three-ring binders, placed in divider pockets, or folded in half and taped into spiral notebooks or journals in hardback composition books. The following examples can be used sequentially in single entry journals or organized, as they are here, for double entry journals:

Right-Hand Page Entries

- What did you observe (see, hear, taste, smell, touch) related to the study?
- What did you read? (title, author, pages)
- What ideas did you discover? (new information or strategies)
- Who did you interview, and what did you learn?
- What problems are you working on?
- What experiment or demonstration did you set up?
- What did you learn from your discussions with a partner or group?

Left-Hand Page Entries

- What questions do you still have?
- What difficulties did you experience?
- How will you change what you do as a result of this experience?
- What comments or reactions do you have?
- What did you enjoy? (about reading, research, interaction, process)
- What did you dislike? (same as above)
- Can you translate what you have learned into a drawing, graph, diagram, map, data bank, web, or cluster?
- What connections can you make with your experience, other ideas about this topic, or other areas of the curriculum? (at home, in reading, math, science)

Guidelines can be remembered easily by students if they use the ACT (ask, connect, transform) or REACT (record, evaluate, ask, connect, transform) models for response. Initially, teachers might ask students to respond to a number of different kinds of questions related to a content area study, but gradually offer them the opportunity to select questions and formats from a list of possibilities. Eventually, students might select their own forms of response and their own questions from the types they have practiced. Suggestions for content-specific response guidelines can be found in the chapters that describe the use of learning journals in the individual content areas.

CONSTRUCTING A LEARNING JOURNAL

Kindergarten and Early Primary

At the kindergarten and early primary levels, learning journals are most frequently used as part of a theme study. Some teachers prefer using large, unlined spiral notebooks, whereas others provide students with folded pieces of newsprint that have been stapled together into a book of four to eight pages. When students complete journal drawing, writing, or cut-and-paste activities related to a topic, they date their entry with a library stamp and place their journal entries in personal files. These files can be easily accessed when students want to review their work or find information they have stored in a previous journal.

Individual newsprint journals are periodically bound together during an extended study, so that students can use them for reading practice and as resources for writing. Some teachers punch the daily sheets and have students attach them with fasteners into a growing journal. These can be stored on Big Book racks, rolled up in cubby holes, pinned over a clothesline, or filed in a tall box. At the end of a theme or topic study, these sheets are bound together with a cover decorated by the student to send home or to keep at school for reference and review.

Other teachers staple construction paper covers onto several sheets of plain or lined paper, for students to keep daily records of a month's activities. In some school districts, thematic booklets include information about the topic being studied, which are bound together with blank sheets of paper for student response (Fig. 3.5). This format allows students to share information about their study with their parents and to use key words from the material in their writing.

Late Primary, Intermediate, and Middle School

At the late primary, intermediate, and middle school levels, students may use a variety of notebooks for journaling. In classrooms that encourage students to use journals extensively

FIG. 3.5. Opposite a printed page about bears, Michael draws and writes his own story.

for reference, jour-
nals are kept in
hard-cover compo-
sition books. Infor-
mational handouts,
homework assign-
ments, and tests are
folded and taped
into these books
(Fig. 3.6). Several
pages at the begin-
ning of the journal
are reserved for a ta-
ble of contents. As
students add entries
or materials, the ti-
tle of the entry is re-
corded, along with
the page number

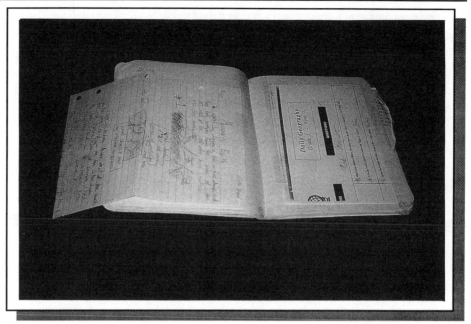

FIG. 3.6. Supplementary writing and handouts are taped into a journal.

and date. This allows students easy reference to materials they want to review or refer
to. Students in other classrooms may use either an ordinary spiral notebook or a
three-ring binder for their journals. Spiral notebooks are easy for students to manage
and they are frequently used in classrooms where several content areas are explored
with journals (Fig. 3.7). Bound notebooks that feature easy removal of pages are not
as desirable, because the pages fall out with repeated use.

Looseleaf binders are often preferred by intermediate and middle school teachers
who integrate ideas or methodology across curriculum areas. The looseleaf format
permits students to add pages, expand individual sections, remove pages for review by the teacher, or file them in portfolios. Duplicated materials such as guideline questions, problem-solving strategies, lab rules, protocols, calendars, schedules, quizzes, or tests can be punched and easily inserted into a reference section.

In some classrooms, teachers review the daily

FIG. 3.7. In some classes, students keep multiple content area journals.

work of cooperative teams by asking them to place individual and team papers into a table folder. When they have been examined by the teacher, they can be easily replaced in individual journals. If a three-ring binder is used, sections should be divided with tabbed index divider pages, allowing 10 to 15 pages for each section. More pages can be added as sections develop. Many students prefer to use section dividers with pockets to have a convenient place to store handouts. Others like to punch handouts and insert them directly into the binder in the reference section.

At the kindergarten and primary levels, students usually place their journals in a designated place at the end of the school day. Depending on the physical setting, this may mean stacking notebooks in the center of tables or in a designated area on a shelf or countertop. This provides the teacher with easy access to the journals for review, and they are available in the same place to students the next day. Journals kept in folders are filed in a place where they are accessible to both students and teacher. Compilations of student work that are used for reference may be stored in large binders, labeled with the students' names.

Primary students often attach a pen or pencil to the journal in some fashion, so that it is immediately available for making entries. Some students tie a colorful shoelace around a pen and fasten it to a spiral or tie it to one of the metal clips in the looseleaf binder. Others thread pencils through the spiral part of the notebook or fasten their pens by the clip to the cover or to the first few pages just inside the notebook.

If journals are used for more than one content area, students may use looseleaf notebooks with tabs for different subjects or they may store a collection of spiral notebooks in a three-ring binder. Binders can also be used to store a series of notebooks in a single content area to keep journals accessible for use as reference or resource. In many classes, students use computer word processors to record their journal entries, and print them out daily or weekly to store in a three-ring binder. Primary age students, particularly those who experience difficulty with the mechanics of handwriting, may fold printouts of their entries in half and tape them into their journals.

Where the technology is available, students create electronic learning journals by communicating with each other on cooperative research projects through e-mail. On a larger scale, students create cooperative journals through participation in interactive learning environments on the Internet. They record their work on joint projects, asking and answering questions, sharing and responding to information related to a topic in the content areas. Programs such as CoVis (O'Neill, 1996) have provisions for three different kinds of notebooks, which include (a) private journals, which are accessible only to the individual author, (b) group project notebooks, which allow a variety of permitted authors to read and contribute information, and (c) group discussions, open to any member of the CoVis community. The CoVis Project also pairs science students at the middle and high school levels with adult mentors who have expertise in science or technology.

ORGANIZING A LEARNING JOURNAL

Single Entry, Sequential

Students arrange their entries in journals in a variety of ways. Some record assignments, homework, exercises, information, and responses on successive pages and create a continuing table of contents to keep track of entries. Other journals are organized so that there are specific places to record information in several categories, depending on the grade level and specific needs of particular classrooms or students.

Double Entry, Multiple Sections

Recording Entries.   Students use one side of a folded notebook page or a page on one side of an open notebook to record assignments, notes from reading, problems to solve, observations of phenomena in everyday life, observations of science demonstrations, or experiments and experience with manipulatives. Recording entries might also include ideas from books read aloud and notes from classroom visitors, interviews, field trips, or other experiences related to a theme or content area study.

Response Entries.   On the opposite side of the folded notebook page (or on the page opposite the recording entries), students respond to their learning experience by commenting on ideas from their reading, discussion, or observations. Using the ACT or REACT acronym as a guide, they express personal likes and dislikes about subject matter or information, state opinions, ask questions, and relate information to personal experience or other areas of knowledge. Responses may include drawings, pictures, strategies, essays, poetry, maps, charts, graphs, and diagrams that help students understand new ideas. They might also include notes from conferences or discussions, and comments entered when students review their learning at the end of a period, day, week, or term. Recording and response entries can be used as a basis for writing, theme projects, workshop discussions, research or study groups, individual conferences with the teacher, and letters written to parents.

Resource Entries.   This section contains a collection of materials related to a topic of study and might include poetry, articles and pictures from newspapers or magazines, brochures, editorials, cartoons, or quotations related to a subject area. Resource sections may also include lists of books related to the study and the names, addresses, and phone numbers of persons or institutions that are available for help with themes or topics.

Reference Entries.   Depending on the subject area, this section might include one or more of the following: a daily or weekly schedule; a weekly, monthly, or year-long calendar; a glossary of terms used in the content area; lab rules; a personal spelling dictionary; strategies for solving problems; mathematical or scientific conversion charts; grammatical rules, genre definitions, and publishing guidelines; directions for using reference materials, the computer, or the library. Some students reserve part of the reference section to record assignments.

USING JOURNALS TO SUPPORT OTHER CLASSROOM ACTIVITIES

A major goal of using learning journals in the classroom is to help students increase their understanding of the world. Writing in journals and sharing what they discover encourages students to explore their own strengths as learners and to gain skill in using mathematics, literature, writing, science, and the social sciences to make sense of their experience. Teachers who use learning journals as part of their classroom program believe that students increase their understanding of concepts when they are encouraged to write and talk about them. They assume that students bring knowledge, skills, and experience to school that can benefit the understanding of all learners in the classroom. Activities prominent in classrooms that integrate language learning across the curriculum (Popp, 1996) are both supported and enhanced by using learning journals.

Reading aloud from both fiction and nonfiction books related to the content area introduces new ways of looking at subject matter. Good stories involve mathematical or scientific concepts in integral and intriguing ways and historical fiction provides an excellent introduction or enrichment for historical studies. Informational books for children often provide very clear explanations and examples of topics under study. Reading aloud from more difficult texts helps make information accessible to children, in terms of concepts that they can understand but might not be able to read about on their own. This practice also provides common experiences for the class and encourages discussion (Fig. 3.8).

Book previews take only a few minutes each day and help develop interest in theme or topic-related books. Teachers hold up a book and tell the title, author, and a little about its features. They read a short passage, describe the kinds of information students can find in the book, and share a few illustrations when these are prominent in the presentation. Students can also share books in this fashion, telling what they especially liked about them or how they were helpful. Teachers encourage students to note any books that draw their interest in the resource sections of their journals.

Independent reading that is part of a daily schedule permits students to explore a wide range of literature and other printed material. Referred to by various acronyms such as SSR (silent sustained reading) or DEAR (drop everything and read), this practice involves a set time for students and the teacher to explore books of their own choosing, for a period of 10 to 20 minutes (Trelease, 1995). Everyone reads, no one talks or is interrupted in their reading, and there are no assignments associated with the reading. This is a time when students often make connections between the focus of a content area topic and other types of literature. They find science in fantasy, mathematics in sports novels, and history in compelling biographies. When students find books related to a theme or content area study, they use their journals to record titles and page numbers. Because

FIG. 3.8. Mrs. Cook reads aloud to her first graders.

independent reading time is set aside for reading only, teachers may provide a few minutes afterward for students to jot down notes about books that draw their interest. Many teachers also schedule book preview times either before or after independent reading.

Minilessons are brief instructional presentations used to introduce information about a content area or to demonstrate a skill or strategy. Students practice using the information from these presentations immediately, by relating the content to something they are studying or want know. The content for minilessons is derived from teachers' observations of students at work, interactions during individual conferences, and examination of entries in learning journals. Teachers may also present minilessons to provide students with tools they will need to explore a new theme or a particular topic in a content area (Fig. 3.9). Topics might include strategies for problem solving, graphic organizers, prewriting techniques, and ideas for conducting research, interviews, or experiments.

If students are using single entry, sequential journals, they record the information and strategies presented in minilessons in dated order in their books and list it in their developing table of contents. For example, a fifth grader learned how to create a literature web as part of a study of *Island of the Blue Dolphins.* She recorded the reference for these pages in her table of contents as WEB, *Island,* which allowed her to find an example of a web or to refer to her work on this particular book. If students use multiple sections in their journals, strategies, graphic organizers, and procedures are recorded in the reference section for future use in reading, writing, research, or problem-solving assignments.

Cooperative study groups involve students meeting in pairs or small groups to share and explore ideas together. Depending on the content area, they may read aloud to each other; respond to guideline questions; work on problems; share problem-solving strategies; evaluate each other's work; set up and conduct labs; encourage each other as readers, writers, problem solvers, and researchers; or create a group project. In each instance, learning journals permit individuals to make significant contributions to group activities and provide a place to record new ideas that emerge from group discussions. Journaling helps students prepare for study groups productively and provides opportunities for students to get immediate answers to simple questions or to enlist the help of others

FIG. 3.9. Mrs. Parker demonstrates the use of a web to fourth graders.

to explore more complex issues. Student competence and self-confidence are enhanced by opportunities to think about ideas at an individual pace before they are shared with others.

In math study groups, students work on problems and activities together, following brief presentations by the teacher. Members of science study groups share information from reading, interpret observations, set up demonstrations, and conduct experiments together. In social studies, students may research a topic together, conduct interviews, construct graphics, and work on projects to share information with an audience. Literature groups meet together to study books they are reading in common. Part of a writer's workshop involves students meeting together in pairs or small groups to share their writing and receive feedback and support for their efforts. When instruction is integrated around a theme, small groups permit students to share ideas and conduct research together.

Workshops in writing, reading, math, science, or the social sciences provide opportunities for students to write, read, solve problems, and conduct research during extended blocks of time. Workshops involve individual, group, and class activities and feature a sharing component where students may bring writing or research in progress to a group for comments and evaluation. The workshop concept assumes that students benefit from uninterrupted periods of time to develop skills and pursue information of interest to them. Learning journals provide places for students to record ideas and information from reading or observation, suggestions from group discussions, strategies for research or problem solving, and ideas to share with others.

Individual conferences in reading, writing, or a content area feature a one-to-one meeting between the teacher and an individual student to discuss books, writing projects, problem solving, or progress with research in a content area. Students prepare for these conferences by recording their connections, comments, questions, and problems about learning in their journals. This preparation helps focus the conference interaction and permits the teacher to more accurately assess a student's knowledge, skill or progress.

Journal buddies involve the pairing of students from the same or different grade levels to share entries from their journals, such as books they have read; stories they have written; pictures, graphs, or charts they have drawn; and other entries as they choose. This activity encourages students to talk about what they have written and thought about. During these sessions students can assist each other where it is appropriate and welcomed, by taking dictation for buddies, making entries in their journals, or recording ideas with the computer word processor. Older or more proficient buddies can also record words in personal dictionaries that their partners want to use in writing.

In return, buddies who receive help with writing can listen to and comment on entries from their partner. In journal buddy sessions one frequently hears students asking each other: "What do you think of this? Do you think this idea would make a good story? How do you think I could set up this project? Can you think of some examples of . . . that I could use? Where do you think I could find a good picture to scan into this report? Do you know how to use the computer search?"

Journal buddy programs, like the book buddy programs that feature students sharing books and reading to each other, provide opportunities for students to interact positively with each other. More proficient writers model habits of thinking and response, and in return, their partners provide them with opportunities to refine their ideas. Regardless of developmental level, each student can read and share what they have written and thought about. They can talk to each other about books they have read, ideas they have recorded, and things they have thought about. Each student gets practice translating what they have recorded and learned into speech, and each gains a new appreciation of the thinking, observations, and ideas of another person.

THE HOME-SCHOOL CONNECTION AND SPECIAL USES OF JOURNALS

In most classrooms, journals are sent home for periodic review by parents and there may be occasional assignments that are recorded from work completed at home. For example, kindergarten students draw pictures and write with developmental spelling to record the activities of their weekend. First graders find examples of geometric shapes at home and record them in a chart. Fourth graders estimate the dimensions of familiar objects at home, such as beds, tables, windows, and chairs, then compare their estimates with the exact measurement of these objects. Fifth graders take home journals to record their exploration of the layers of soil in their yard and middle school students record interviews with family members for a genealogy study.

In some classrooms, students keep a separate homework journal to record assignments and report any difficulties encountered with the work. This provides parents with a clear idea of what is expected in terms of study at home and helps remind students of work that must be completed by a specified time. These journals are dated, and may include strategies for study, goals for learning, and student self-evaluation of learning. They may also provide a means of communication between teacher and parent, with notes exchanged concerning a student's progress (see Nancy Johnson's description of this use of journals in Appendix B).

Students with special learning challenges may use homework journals to practice specific skills at home, such as handwriting, spelling, identification of words and letters, or math. Both beginning and developmental learners can benefit from practicing handwriting at home and recording their efforts in a writing journal. Combined with exercises that involve writing in the air and trying to identify letters written on one's back, students may practice a particular letter each evening in their journal. These entries usually feature practice of letters that present difficulty and are combined, when appropriate, with sentences copied from a favorite book or original writing that uses the letter under study. Students date the entries and return their journals on a weekly basis for teacher review.

Developmental readers may record several words in their journal and look for these in their favorite books at home. They might record examples of mathematical processes that pose particular challenges and practice these at home by drawing pictures to illustrate them, or creating stories that involve specific types of problem solving. Most parents are eager to support efforts to help their children improve their learning skills and these "take-home" practice journals provide some direction for their assistance. Many kindergarten and early primary teachers also send home stuffed animal mascots and a journal in a backpack with a different child each night. Students and parents together write about the adventures the animal has in their home, and these accounts are read to the class the next morning. Other teachers regularly send home a sheet of paper, crayons, and a pencil in a zip bag with a book to be read aloud, either by the parent or student. The student then responds to the book by writing or drawing a picture to bring back to school the next day.

EXAMPLES OF ENTRIES FROM STUDENT JOURNALS

Figures 3.10 through 3.27 are examples of the different types of entries students create in learning journals.

FIG. 3.10. Amy's dated journal entry.

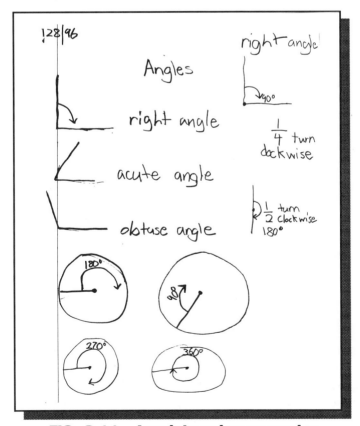

FIG. 3.11. Jessie's notes on angles.

Camouflage

Camouflage means to disguise or blend in with your saroudings. For example a cameleon can change color to match any-thing.

Many animals camouflage to protect them from enemies. Other animals hide to cach food and when they see there anext meal they poue on it. I happens in war too people camouflage their clothes so there enemy will not see them.

FIG. 3.12. Claire's essay on camouflage.

Letter to Ms. Verderber

Dear Ms. Verderber,

Thank you for coming and talking to us about your disability. Some people are shy to talk about their disability. We are glad that you came back to explain. Your car was really neat. You were absolutely right, technology can really help people for different reason different. Well, thanks again.

Sincerely,
Tyrone Gordon

FIG. 3.13. Tyrone's practice letter to a classroom visitor.

10-25

Mystery of the Dead Fish →

What is the environment?
everything around us

What are the 3 parts?
a. non-living
b. living
c. energy

What is an ecosystem?
a community of plants and animals and how they work together

The non-living parts are:
rocks - lithosphere
water - Co2
air is made of gases - oxygen clouds, dust

FIG. 3.14. Brandon's inquiry writing.

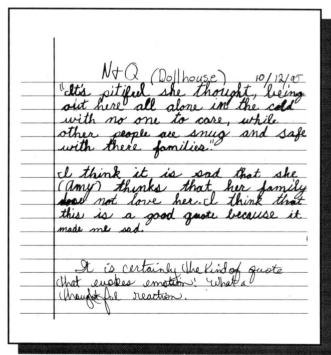

N+Q (Dollhouse)   10/12/95

"It's pitiful she thought, being out here all alone in the cold with no one to care, while other people are snug and safe with there families."

I think it is sad that she (Amy) thinks that her family does not love her. I think that this is a good quote because it made me sad.

It is certainly the kind of quote that evokes emotion! what a thoughtful reaction.

FIG. 3.15. Nora's response to a quote she has chosen.

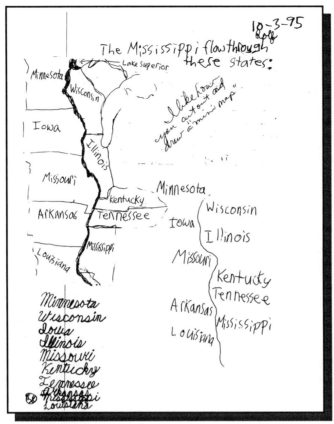

FIG. 3.16. Rolf's map of the Mississippi River.

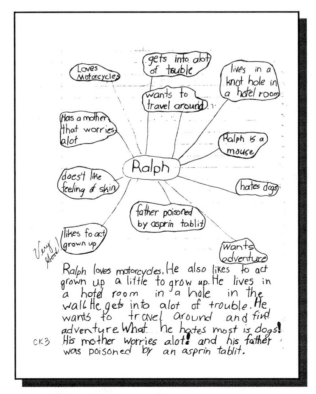

FIG. 3.17. Claire's web of Ralph, the mouse.

Seasons

spring
returning birds
blooming flowers
budding trees
warn days
hibernatioin ending
animals reproduce
green grass
rainy days

summer
hot days
picnics in the park
vacation
colorful
swimming
Forth of July
watermelons
camping outdoors

autumn
Halloween Thanks-giving football
trees turning colors
fire prevention week
cooler days
pumkins and apples
hunting season
school beging
birds migrate
raking leaves

winter
Crismas/Hanukka
cold days
snow
hockey
basketball
sleding
hibernating animals
sledding/skiing
hot soup
sitting by the fire
new years

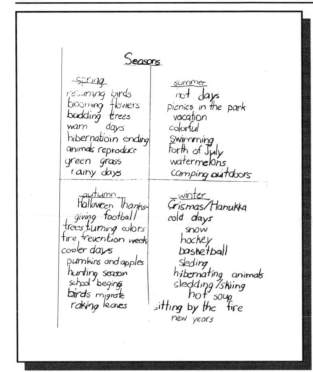

FIG. 3.18. Claire's data bank of seasonal concepts.

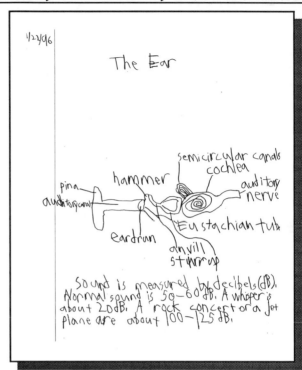

FIG. 3.19. Evan's drawing of the ear.

U.S. Prarie

Plants	Animals	People
Grasses	prairie chicken	Native Americans
big bluestem	bison	-Siaux
switch grass	prairie dog	
indian	snakes	cowboys (1820)-(1880)
cordgrass	quail	settlers
	hawks	overlanders (1840)-(1860) (settlers)
Wild Flowers	insects	
sneezeweed	owl	miners (1849)-(1860)
gentian	deer	trapers (1820)-(1840)
prairie dock	badger	
pasque flower	3 lined squirrel	
shooting star	horned lizard	
cone flower	cotton tail	
compass	jack rabbit	
butterfly	mice	
milkweed	bees	
senative briar	spider	
	grasshoper	
	butterfly	
	pronghorn	
	coyote	
	ferrit	

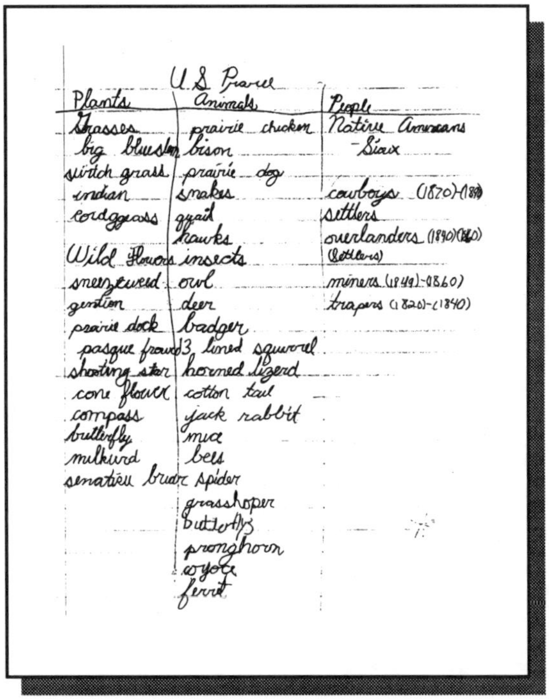

FIG. 3.20. Claire's chart of the U.S. prairie.

Timed Writing 8/29/95

Winter Time

Snow falling to the ground,
Children playing all around.
When I look out my window I see
a blanket of
snow has coverd the grond.
The trees with out leaves star at you
constently.
The children are making snow angles,
Drinking hot cholete,
And breeting in the cold frozen air.
As I'm looking out the window I relise
Chrismis time is near.

I love this poem!
(I underlined the strong phrases that really grabbed me)
♡ mom

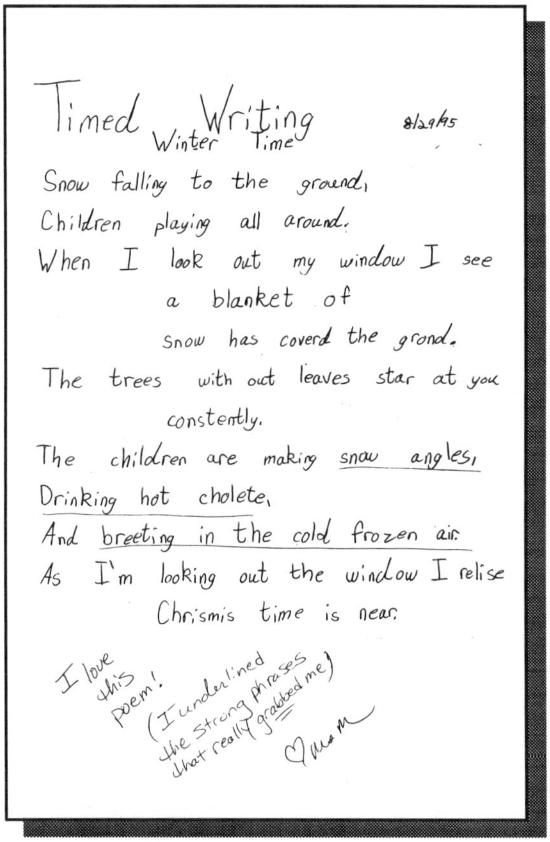

FIG. 3.21. Tucker's poem about winter.

9/6/95

Reading Family Stories   49
Rechenka's Eggs-
Patricia Polacco

Grandpa's Face-
Eloise Greenfield

Grandfather Tang's Story-
Ann Tompert

Chicken Sunday
Patricia Polacco

Uncle Jed's Barbershop-
Maigeree King Mitchell

The Great Pumpkin Switch-
Megan McDonald

FIG. 3.22. Marina's list of books about families.

My grandmother me and my sister at the zoo.

Me Tony, Reggie, Ashlee, and me in my Backyard at my old house.

FIG. 3.23. Robert's photographs of his family.

10-9-95

Super Hero   Rolf
I would be Carattie Cat
Caratie Cat:
1. Keeps mice out of people's homes.
2. Gives alley cats a nice, new home.
3. Picks up trash.

AAA A Mouse

I'm comming

FIG. 3.24. Rolf's cartoon.

Current event

9.21.95
Rolf

John Costello, a former Cardinals relief pitcher, now lives in Grover and is a rookie with the St. Louis County Police.

St. Louis and Atlanta are places that former pro athletes find very hospitable after the games have ended, or when they've been traded to teams in other cities, says Maria Costello.

She's late of Oceanside, N.Y., and the wife of John Costello, a former Cardinals middle relief pitcher, now a St. Louis County cop. They live in Grover, now part of the far-West County community of Wildwood, with their two small children, Heather, 5, and John Michael, 3. It's a long way from Long Island Sound.

Maria Costello keeps in contact with a network of players' wives, including Jamie Worrell and Laurie Van Slyke. They live nearby, and their husbands now play for teams in other cities — reliever Todd Worrell in Los Angeles and outfielder Andy Van Slyke in Philadelphia.

Most baseball players play untill they are too old to play. When they are too old to play they usualy become a manager or something else that still has something to do with baseball. I wonder why he wanted to be a cop. He is the first person I've ever heard of that switched from pitching on a baseball to a police officer. *That is unusual! Your reaction is well written & includes personal response. Good job!* ⓐ⁺

FIG. 3.25. Rolf's response to a news article.

3 propertes of matter

Smushed together: hard	(drawing of circles packed together)	Solid: ↙
Are more spread oux that the solid, but are able to attracteachother	(drawing of spread circles)	Liquid ↙
They float ar-ound very fast + cannot attract each other.	(drawing of scattered circles)	Gas: ↙

FIG. 3.26. Alexandra's chart of the properties of matter.

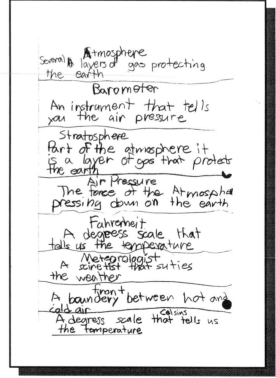

Several Atmosphere
layers of gas protecting the earth

Barometer
An instrument that tells you the air pressure

Stratosphere
Part of the atmosphere it is a layer of gas that protects the earth

Air Pressure
The force of the Atmosphere pressing down on the earth

Fahrenheit
A degrees scale that tells us the temperature

Meteorologist
A scinetist that suties the weather

front
A boundery between hot and cold air

Celsius
A degress scale that tells us the temperature

FIG. 3.27. Jessie's glossary of weather terms.

Introducing Learning Journals to Students

In what I call the language-rich, learning-intensive classroom, a spirit of experimentation, of play . . . will reign. The teacher will be more a listener than a talker, and most of his or her talk will be in response to the children, either as questioner, to help the children take their thinking in new directions, or as one source (not the source) of information. Writing will contribute to this experimental spirit through emphasis on its great value as a tool of discovery and as a tool of imagination.

—Christopher Thaiss (1986, p. 7)

PREVIEW

1. Why is it helpful for teachers to create their own learning journals?
2. How are journals introduced to kindergarteners and developing learners?
3. How are journals introduced to primary children?
4. How are journals introduced to intermediate level students?
5. How are journals introduced at the middle school level?

BRIEFLY: At every instructional level, journal writing is best learned through teacher modeling, peer interaction, and many opportunities to respond to information and ideas in a variety of ways.

CREATING A TEACHING JOURNAL

When teachers plan to introduce learning journals to their students, the most helpful preparation they can make is to create a journal for themselves. The experience of using a journal to explore a topic provides teachers with firsthand information about using a journal as a learning tool, allows them to anticipate difficulties that might arise, and helps them be more realistic about their expectations from students. As Brandt (1991) noted, "Thinking deeply about what we are doing leads us to ask better questions, break out of fruitless routines, make unexpected connections, and experiment with fresh ideas" (p. 3).

Students observe adults carefully and tend to assign value and status to activities that draw adult interest. No matter how enthusiastically journal writing is championed as an important learning activity, a teacher's own regular use of a journal will prove to be the strongest convincing statement. In addition, from their personal experience with the various writing formats and responses to generic prompts, teachers can provide their students with a model for the different types of entries possible, and demonstrate how to use these entries to record, respond to, and reflect on things that are important to them (Fig. 4.1).

A teacher's learning journal may be centered around a particular theme or topic he or she plans to teach, or it might be organized around a content area, particularly if the teacher's main assignment is in the departmentalized teaching of language arts, science, mathematics, or social studies. Teachers' journals may also have a more general theme and may be used to record ideas and information for teaching across the curriculum. As tools for reflective practice, journals prompt teachers to look closely at what they do in the classroom to help them decide if these practices agree with their beliefs and knowledge about teaching (Sparks-Langer & Colton, 1991). A journal is a record of interactions and activities that are successful (or that do not go as expected) that creates the opportunity for examining events more closely to see why things might have happened in a certain way. This narrative inquiry provides helpful clues to teachers who want to improve their instruction (Wellington, 1991).

FIG. 4.1. Mrs. Hogue examines student writing to plan for the next day's instruction.

The main deterrent to this type of reflective practice is time, already at a premium with increased demands from inside and outside of the classroom. On the other hand, journals can be time savers if they reveal ways to accomplish instructional goals in more efficient ways or help put into perspective the inevitable frustrations that contribute to professional fatigue. It is also helpful to have an established place to jot down ideas as they occur, so that a periodic brief review can provide either information or inspiration at the appropriate time. The time taken to record the name and page number of an article that has a good idea for a social studies project, or to jot down the idea itself, saves the time and frustration involved in either relocating or rereading the reference in the future.

Because elementary teachers tend to be great collectors, they listen for ideas everywhere: university classes, fellow teachers, students, textbooks, trade books, nature, home, family, friends, magazines, journals, newspapers, TV, radio, and movies. When they use journals, there is a designated place for ideas from all of these sources. Journals are also good places to record reading and research in a subject area, jot down ideas for lessons, make notes about schedules, ponder concerns about students, think about their teaching, and collect resources for future use.

One Teacher's Journal

The following notes are excerpts from a fifth-grade teacher's journal. Jackie Hogue used the narrative style, recording her thoughts and reactions in a continuing story of her classroom experiences. She responded to what she read, tried out new ideas, and observed how her own attitudes and thinking changed in the process. Note that she observed both the responses of the class as a whole to new activities and the responses of individual students for whom she might have particular concerns. She has found journal writing to be helpful, both as an immediate reference and as a longer term resource, and periodically reviews her entries to locate successful practices or to gain a perspective on her history as a teacher and learner.

Entry: Today we talked about how chapters end in such an exciting way that it makes us want to read on. That's called a cliffhanger. They [the students] wrote a prediction in their journals for the next chapter. Adam said he had included some cliffhangers in the story he is writing.

Entry: At the end of our reading/study time we did a whip. The kids shared one thing they had learned that day about colonial life. It is exciting because then they want to read books that their friends are reading.

Entry: We took a day away from the New England study on February 12th and studied Lincoln. After I read a book to them about Lincoln, we brainstormed the kind of person he was and webbed the stories to match his personality. For example: Humor—He kept important papers in his top hat and turned kids upside down so they could walk on the ceiling and leave footprints.

Entry: In reflecting on my role as a teacher, I have noticed that when I engage with the kids, they stay more on task. For instance, during SSR, when they read, I read. When they write in their journals about their readings and thoughts, I also write. When they share their writings with the class, they want me to share, too. This, in a sense, is also demonstrating.

Entry: (Reflecting on an article she had just read) I like the idea that students must try to spell a word or look in the dictionary before I spell it for them. I will do that tomorrow! I also like the idea of a peer giving spelling strategies. I will show them how to make a personal dictionary. That way, each student can keep his own words in a book for reference.

Entry: After reading the article on Buddy Journals, my student teacher and I modeled on the board. We wrote why we liked or disliked the books we were reading. I wrote about *Maniac Magee* and Dustin said that he wanted to read it! I think this will promote interest in other books. They wrote so much today and didn't want to stop.

Entry: In the "Great Teachers: Carol S. Avery" article, I was interested in the math-writing lesson. I want to try that when I introduce a new concept. She gave the kids a problem and told them to try to work it. She asked them to write how they solved it, or why they couldn't.

Entry: I've noticed an increase in self-esteem when I focus on the child's strengths rather than weaknesses. I have found that since my attitude towards learning and how children learn has changed, that discipline problems occur less often.

Jackie's journals over the years have contained a record of her teaching, the responses of students to particular activities, charts to organize information, new ideas to try, anecdotal material on students, student observation check lists, and check list records of student work completion. She has recorded ideas from books, videos, and other teachers, descriptions of units, projects, classroom visitors, and field trips. She also included events that have affected her and her students. For example, in an early journal she wrote about how her class received the news of the discovery of a child who had been missing from her home in St. Louis County. Students used their journal responses as the basis for writing letters to their congressmen. An example follows Jackie's entry.

Entry: My kids were so upset on the day Cassidy's body was found. That's all they wanted to talk about. We wrote in our journals how we felt and some decided to write Congress to pass stricter laws. Several read their journals from the author's chair. I found addresses for Paul Simon and Dick Durbin [U.S. Senator and State Senator in Illinois at the time] and many are writing letters.

Student Letter: I am a 10-year-old student at Marine Grade School in Marine, Illinois. When we heard about the police finding Cassidy Senter's body, we decided to write a letter to you. In my class we said that the laws we have are not protecting girls and boys like us. . . . Some kids are afraid to sleep in their own bedroom, or walk to a friend's house, since this has happened. . . . [We] should not have to feel this way. Please help our parents and our schools find ways to help keep us safe.

Teachers often find that students include things they are worrying about in their journals, regardless of the topic. As students evaluate their experience with academic subject matter, they may confide their difficulties, frustration, or disappointment. Accounts of group work turn up problems with group dynamics or feelings of isolation. This kind of information directs the teacher to sit down and listen to what is happening in a group, to schedule individual conferences with students who are experiencing difficulty in an academic area, or to be more understanding of student behavior when it reflects stresses from outside the classroom.

The narrative style of journal keeping is helpful for some teachers, because it allows them to tell the story of their experience in a familiar and comfortable way. Others prefer to jot down lists, notes, comments, and ideas in a variety of formats that are helpful to them as individuals. Many teachers keep an ongoing record of their experience in the back of their lesson plan books, listing ideas for activities, revising presentations, or making notes about what seems to be successful or unsuccessful with a particular class.

Teachers at the intermediate and middle school levels may find it helpful to use the double entry format, with one or more of the sections described in the following. It should be noted that these entries are usually brief, but having several sections allows entries to be classified when they are recorded, makes information easier to find, and ultimately saves time and effort.

Recording and Response.   On one side of an open notebook, teachers record information and ideas from a content area topic or theme; ideas for setting up science labs, exhibits, displays, or demonstrations; and pictures, maps, charts, and diagrams for explaining concepts to students. Teachers may also include observation check lists in this section to evaluate student work and progress. Comments, observations, or anecdotes about particular students can be recorded on the page that faces the check list. Some teachers write comments on self-adhesive notes as they observe students at work and stick them to these pages for later transfer into written entries.

Response Section. On the page opposite the recorded information, teachers respond with ideas about how to present content to students, ways to connect instruction with other areas of the curriculum, comments about how well an idea worked in class, and ideas for changing presentations. This section is intended to stimulate reflection on teaching and may contain notes for helping particular students with difficulties they are experiencing. It might also include labeled drawings and ideas or insights that occur in response to reading, discussion, or reflection. Elementary teachers often use these left-hand pages to record ideas for integrating art, music, and physical movement into a study and suggestions for involving parents, other classes, school personnel, and the broader community.

Resources. This section might include ideas from graduate study, lists of topic or theme-related books to read aloud and brief annotations of fiction and nonfiction books related to a particular study, sketches of ideas for room arrangements, art projects, interesting displays observed in other classrooms and schools, ideas for theme-related activities prepared by other teachers, instructions and sketches for projects seen or read about, interesting classroom arrangements; classroom management ideas, class and school projects, and content-area related materials, such as articles and pictures from newspapers, magazines, or journals, editorials, cartoons, essays, poetry, and quotations related to a subject area.

Reference. Depending on the subject area and experience and background of the teacher, the reference section might include one or several of the following: a personal spelling dictionary; a glossary of terms used with a theme or in a content area; curriculum requirements; standards and mandates that must be considered in instructional planning; field trip guidelines; possible places to visit related to a theme, content area, or topic of study; student rosters; lists of parents' names and phone numbers; names and phone numbers of persons and institutions that provide resources and speakers to schools; and guidelines for using the library, computer, and audiovisual equipment.

INTRODUCING JOURNALS
TO DEVELOPING LEARNERS

At the kindergarten level, most journal writing will be in response to whole group activities, books read aloud, or manipulative math play. With the entire class, teachers can model an ACT (ask, connect, transform) of learning for a topic being studied (see chapter 1 for a more detailed description of ACT) by asking for questions, encouraging students to relate the study to their own experience (or other things they are studying), and modeling ways to transform the information in a helpful way. Some classes keep class journals of theme studies, which are dictated to the teacher and bound for class reference.

When students ACT on their learning as individuals, they draw or cut out pictures to signify questions and connections or use developmental spelling to write responses. There should be frequent opportunities for students to work with a partner who can assist them with making entries, if this is something they choose. Some classrooms have journal buddy programs that pair more proficient writers with those who are developing their skills. Buddies take dictation and make entries for students who tire easily from writing or who have disabilities that prevent them from writing.

It is always the most desirable situation for children to make their own entries in their journals, because it creates a sense of ownership in writing. Children who face muscular or vision challenges can often be assisted with specially equipped computers that feature oversized keys, large print on monitor screens, or sound systems that read screen print aloud. In the absence of this equipment, however, journal buddy arrangements are often very successful. Children with physical challenges that interfere with reading or writing can listen to journal entries read aloud by their partners and provide informative feedback, in exchange for writing or reading assistance from their buddies. Teachers, aides, and parent volunteers may also take dictation from children. In some classrooms, students talk into a tape recorder and the tapes are transcribed into print.

It is important to note that not all children will be responsive to these kinds of writing assistance. Many believe that only the words or marks they write themselves constitute their own writing, even if it is their ideas that are being written down. Peto-Ostberg (1992) described an intermediate activity for beginning writers. As a first-grade teacher, she noticed that some children became discouraged with writing because their hand and finger muscles had not developed, and they became easily tired. While they gradually built up strength, she provided an activity that helped supplement their writing efforts, so that the physical act of recording their ideas did not interfere with what they wanted to say.

She asked children to draw several pictures of their story, one picture to a page. These pictures were then placed in order on a long mat. Students stood on the mat beside the first picture and began telling their story, moving forward to the section beside the next picture to continue. As they moved down the mat, talking about their pictures, their story was recorded onto a cassette. Later, the cassette was played to their reading and writing group, and children could see and hear the stories of their peers. These tapes were added to the listening center and could also be taken home to share with families.

This activity can be used to record ideas from field trips, visitors to the classroom, science observations, and interviews. Students can also record their problem-solving experiences and strategies for math to share with small groups. Older ESL students can draw their understanding of a concept and record their ideas on tapes. This supplementary activity helps students develop confidence in their ability to communicate through words while they develop muscular maturity or experience with written language. It also convinces students that their ideas are worth saving and sharing.

When students are just beginning to read, guideline questions and ideas for types of entries can be indicated with pictures, symbols, and rebuses. For example, stickers that represent different kinds of entries can be placed on the appropriate notebook or attached to file folders when children use newsprint journals. Pictures can also be cut out of magazines or students can create a coded filing system with their own small drawings. Some teachers create instructions for making entries, combining pictures with a few easily recognized words. A library stamp should be available in the writing center or near the place journals are stored, so that children can date their entries. Dating helps create a record of development in writing and conceptual learning that is informative to both the student and teacher.

Kindergartners can usually manage two or more learning journals, depending on their level of development. Some teachers use general content-related journals, such as math, science, and social studies, whereas others use learning journals to help students focus on themes, such as seasons, months, animals, families, or holidays. Others integrate both content area and theme studies with reading and writing journals. Each kind is briefly described in the following paragraphs, and more information can be found in the individual content area chapters.

Math Journals. At the kindergarten level, students draw pictures to illustrate play with manipulatives or record math stories, using number symbols to describe their play. At the beginning of each math period, teachers often encourage students to draw pictures of a math concept they have observed, such as patterns, shapes, or numbers. Students may also draw pictures or write number stories about things and events in the classroom, or record observations from outdoor math walks. Math journals are an effective means of recording experiences in such programs as *Math Their Way* and the Marilyn Burns math series, both of which are described in more detail in chapter 7.

Science Journals. Students draw pictures or write sentences about classroom exhibits, informational books, or demonstrations. Science journals encourage students to observe carefully, notice details, and make relationships between what they know and new learning events. As they attempt to draw pictures of objects and living things, such as the spider in the class aquarium, their hamster at home, an insect they find in the yard, or an interesting rock on the playground, students discover the need to revisit the object of their drawing for more details about shape, size, or movement. They may also choose to write captions on their pictures and describe them in writing. Special terminology may be recorded in glossaries at the back of their journal or rebus descriptions can be distributed and taped into the inside covers.

Social Science Journals. Students draw pictures of their family and write about them, using captions or developmental writing. They draw maps of their room, house, or neighborhood and pictures of community helpers who visit the classroom. Drawings and writings about field trips and classroom visitors are also included in these journals. In some classrooms students keep calendars and document the daily weather conditions. Journals for each month may feature holidays, school events, and seasonal changes.

Reading and Writing Journals. Students use these journals to record responses to books they have read, gradually adding writing in the form of captions and descriptive sentences. Later in the year, students can copy the titles of books they have read and rate them with stars. The back of the journal is reserved for personal dictionaries, lists of favorite words, and words students can read or want to learn how to read.

Theme Journals.   When there is a theme study, teachers write key words on the board that students might want to use to write or talk about their ideas. Some teachers provide sentence prompts, such as "I saw. . . . I heard. . . . It was. . . . I liked. . . ." and children respond from their own experience. In connection with a theme study, teachers might ask children to examine something closely, such as the shape, size, color, and habits of an insect and to record what they have observed.

Classroom books, demonstrations, exhibits, visitors, field trips, and other events all provide occasions for students to write and draw about things they have seen and done. Students might also illustrate something they saw or heard, related to a theme study, such as characters or events from books read aloud, a movie, or TV show. They might draw a map of their room or create a simple graph of ice cream preferences in their family. Records of these out-of-school activities can either be reentered in their journals or taped into them.

It is important to give students several opportunities during the day to write and draw in their learning journals. Journal writing at the beginning of the day allows children to record their ideas about experiences they have had outside of school. Children typically arrive in the morning with many things to tell the teacher and their classmates. Journal writing helps them organize their ideas and experiences by drawing and writing about them. Teachers follow this activity with a sharing session, where children can show pictures and talk about their writing.

INTRODUCING JOURNALS
TO PRIMARY (GRADES 1–3) STUDENTS

At the primary level, students will increasingly use writing to record information and responses in their learning journals, but they should also be encouraged to make drawings and other graphics to illustrate their understanding of concepts. To keep expression fluent, students should use developmental spelling (when necessary) for their entries, periodically reviewing their journals for frequently misspelled words to enter in their personal dictionaries. As children develop the muscles of their fingers and hands and can write without tiring easily, they should also be encouraged to create narratives to express their understanding of mathematics, science, and social studies. When students write stories to explain phenomena they wonder about, it helps them think analogically and develops appreciation for the special explanatory powers of the academic disciplines (Gallas, 1994).

One first-grade teacher (Wollman-Bonilla & Werchaldo, 1995) introduced literature journals to her students by reading aloud to them and then modeling a response, telling what she liked or thought about the story. On the third day, she provided sheets of 9" × 12" picture-story paper stapled between a manila paper cover and asked her students to write about the story. She offered prompts and invited them to illustrate their responses. Those who experienced difficulty dictated their ideas to the teacher and then copied them into their journals. As the children wrote, the teacher circulated throughout the room, inviting them to share their responses, asking questions, and recording both the question and response in the student's journal. Later in the year, she demonstrated more response options and encouraged students to write why they responded in a particular way with prompts such as: "What I liked or did not like, what I wished had happened, or what the book reminds me of."

Primary students can usually manage several learning journals. In some classrooms, children keep a series of theme-related journals, in addition to a literature or language journal. In other classrooms, there may be a learning journal that includes several different content areas. In either case, it is important for students to understand that these journals are their books, a place where they record ideas and information that interests them, and where they can explore these ideas with a variety of writing and drawing activities. Students should be encouraged to examine pictures for information and to pick out interesting facts to record. In some classrooms, an aide or parent volunteer is available to read aloud to students from books that have information they seek but are too difficult for them to read (Fig. 4.2).

Primary REACT

It is helpful to provide a dated stamp or ask students to write the date of each entry as they react to new information.

FIG. 4.2. Mrs. Skingly reads research information aloud to Heather.

Older primary students can create a developing table of contents to record the date, title of entry, and page number where it can be found. In their entries, students respond to one or more of the following:

- *Record*: Write down 2, 3, 4, 5, 6, 7, 8, 9, 10 (circle one) things you learned from reading, listening, or observing.
- *Evaluate*: What did you like? What caused problems?
- *Ask*: What questions do you have?
- *Connect*: What did you already know about this idea or topic?
- *Transform*: Draw or write something to help yourself understand these ideas better or to show someone else what you have learned.

In some classrooms, primary students work independently to record ideas about a topic or theme, whereas in others they work in pairs or small groups, sharing the tasks of research. Depending on the skills and preferences of the researchers, one child may read aloud to the others from books, another might decide what to record about what they have learned, and still another student records what they decide. When individuals or small groups have finished working with ideas on their own, they meet together in a larger group to share information and strategies. Older primary students can create their own glossaries and personal spelling dictionaries to use as references for writing and learn how to review journal entries to get ideas for projects, reading, and writing.

Beginning in the primary grades, students learn how to skim books for information, how to use the index and table of contents, and how to scan a page for specific information. They can practice taking notes and learn how to write down important ideas, list questions they have, record sources, paraphrase information, create outlines, and make short summaries. In minilessons or content-specific instruction, teachers introduce primary students to a variety of ways to translate their understanding of concepts into other forms, including drawings, diagrams, charts, webs, graphs, and maps. These and other entry formats are described in more detail in chapter 3.

Primary Reference

Journals provide primary students with a place to keep informational handouts about a particular study. Depending on the subject area, guidelines are distributed for using the library, computers, encyclopedias, dictionaries, atlas, or thesaurus. Some teachers provide their students with pages that list guidelines for research, the parts of a book, literary genres, measurement guides, grammatical rules, punctuation hints, and lab procedures. Journals are good places for students to keep a calendar of activities, homework assignments, and holidays. All of this material can be placed in the pockets of spiral notebooks, punched and placed in the reference section of a three-ring binder, or folded and taped into composition notebooks.

When primary students begin to create glossaries for a topic or theme study, they may want to include a formal definition, but they should also describe complex terms in their own words. This process is both immediately helpful in transforming information into a useful concept and in later providing a reference that is readily accessible. In addition, students may want to create an example, compare and contrast a term with familiar words, and find a synonym, if this is appropriate. Working with an unfamiliar word or a difficult concept in this way provides practice that helps make it more familiar.

A Typical Day With Journals

Students at the primary level may keep journals for several different curriculum areas, or they may keep all entries in a single notebook. Entries for a typical day in a primary journal might include the following:

Check-In or Academic Warm-Up Activity

1. Editing grammar and spelling from sentences written on the board.
2. Math activity.
3. Responding to a creative writing topic related to current events.
4. Research practice on geography or history facts or concepts.
5. Free writing—poetry, essays, drawings, sketches, personal notes, and opinions.

Math

1. Students record assignments, work on problems, draw pictures, diagrams, charts, and graphs.
2. Students work cooperatively to solve problems and discuss solutions.
3. Handouts and tests are folded and taped into journals.
4. Previous entries are reviewed for information in problem solving.

Literature

1. Students take notes on their reading and respond to guideline questions.
2. Students draw pictures, maps, and diagrams that illustrate their reading.
3. Students share ideas from their reading and discuss answers to questions in small groups or with the entire class in a literature circle.
4. Students record titles of books they read independently and recommend them to other readers.

Learning Log/Journal

1. Students record information from minilessons in science, health, and social studies.
2. Students draw pictures, make maps, and create charts to assist their understanding of science or social studies concepts.
3. Students fold and tape into their journals brochures from field trips, handouts, guidelines, and ideas for projects.

INTRODUCING JOURNALS TO INTERMEDIATE (GRADES 4-6) STUDENTS

At the intermediate school levels, students use journals for each content area or create a series of journals that integrate the curriculum around successive themes. Many teachers introduce learning journals to older students by showing them journals created by students in previous years. If there are sufficient numbers of these, students browse among the entries or a single journal is displayed and discussed using an overhead projector. The journal format can also be drawn and displayed on the chalkboard or on a large newsprint tablet. Depending on the age level and purpose of the journal, teachers present either the single or double entry format and talk about the different kinds of entries that students will be making in their journals. When double entry journals are introduced, teachers use a topic being studied to rehearse this format and enlist ideas from students about the kinds of entries that might be placed in each section.

Intermediate REACT

The REACT model for response is especially helpful to students of this age, because it provides a helpful structure for exploring increasingly complex ideas in the content areas. Guidelines for this level include:

- *Record*: Write down five (or more) facts or ideas from your reading (presentation, experiment, video, discussion, field trip) that you feel were important or interesting.
- *Evaluate*: What did you like about this learning experience? What did you find difficult?
- *Ask*: What questions occurred to you as you read, listened, experimented, or observed?
- *Connect*: How does this new knowledge connect to things you already knew or experiences you have had?
- *Transform*: Use another form to express what you have learned or what you are trying to understand (map, drawing, sketch, diagram, essay, chart, web).

Most intermediate teachers take several days to introduce the recording function of a learning journal, using a series of minilessons to demonstrate each type of writing (see chapter 3 for examples). This is most helpfully done in the context of the theme or content area study, so that students can see how this kind of focus will help them better understand what they are studying. Some teachers provide their students with duplicated sheets that describe the different ways to record and respond to information, whereas others place this information on a chart in the room or write it on the chalkboard or overhead for students to copy into the reference sections of their journals.

It is helpful to provide students with generic guidelines for evaluation responses: What did they think of the book they read? Did they enjoy, dislike, or were they disappointed by a learning experience (book, field trip, project)? What caused them difficulties? How did they address the problem? What was the most interesting idea they found in their research? How did the new math strategy help their problem solving? Where might they look next for information on a topic in science?

Opportunities to ask questions about what they are studying is vital for students at all age levels, but it is particularly important in the intermediate grades, where children may become increasingly hesitant to reveal their level of understanding of concepts. Writing down questions about subject matter, exploring these questions in small groups, and learning new strategies for finding answers are all supported by journal activity. In over-the-shoulder observations and 2-minute conferences, teachers can often identify difficulties by reviewing the questions students record as they work with new ideas and information.

Whether a learning journal is organized around a theme or a particular content area study, making connections with other knowledge or experience is one of the most important features. Students make sense of new information by relating it to their own experience and current knowledge. By consciously making these connections, they learn how to use their own resources to gain understanding. Students should also be encouraged to look for patterns and relationships between what they are studying and other areas of the curriculum. This helps them gain an appreciation for the interrelatedness of all knowledge.

When response entries are introduced, students should have time to practice transforming their understanding of a concept into writing, drawing, or graphic organizers. It is important to introduce or review a number of response forms so that students can experiment with them and choose those that best support their individual learning styles. Suggestions for working with ideas in a wide variety of ways are described in chapter 3, but include essays, summaries, opinion pieces, maps, pictures, drawings, sketches, diagrams, or any other form of response that individual students find helpful or personally meaningful.

It is important to remember that the optimal use of learning journals at all grade levels requires opportunities for students to share what they have learned with others in pairs or small groups. This helps them clarify and expand their own ideas and modify what they know in terms of the ideas and information that other students bring to these sharing sessions. When students meet together to discuss literature, work on math problems, set up experiments, or do research in any area, their learning journals provide them with resources for discussion, problem solving, planning, and decision making. These opportunities for students to share what they have written and thought about allow them to engage in the exploratory talk necessary to build their understanding of difficult concepts.

Preserving Student Privacy

Unless a direct assignment requires students to create something to share with others, all other writing in a journal should be shared at the student's discretion. At the intermediate level and above, students sometimes use their journals as places to record strong feelings about personal experiences. At the same time, they have begun to treasure their privacy, and may not want certain entries reviewed by the teacher. This can be handled in several different ways. In some classrooms students are given time to make entries in daily diaries, where they can think out problems and difficulties they are having. These are not shared with anyone else. Other teachers encourage students to tape together pages they want to keep private, or to remove them from spiral notebooks or three-ring binders before they are submitted for teacher review. If a teacher is conducting over-the-shoulder reviews, students can lay out a black bookmark on the desk to indicate that they are recording private thoughts.

Intermediate Level References

Depending on the content area, the reference section of an intermediate level learning journal will include lists of books, lab rules, problem-solving strategies, grammar rules, parts of speech, literary devices, genre descriptions, a glossary of terms, and a personal dictionary related to the theme or content area study. Strategies might include ideas for analyzing reading, conducting research, or solving problems in math. Difficult or technical terms are recorded in the glossary, along with pronunciation (if necessary), a definition (in the student's own words), and an example. Personal dictionaries include alphabetical lists of words students use frequently and want to spell correctly. In some classrooms, students keep a separate language journal for spelling, punctuation, grammar rules, word study, and reading strategies. In others, these topics are incorporated into a writing journal or integrated within the content area reference sections.

Some students find it helpful to use pocket folder dividers in their three-ring binders to hold duplicated guidelines, such as formats for journal entries, guideline questions for the content areas, prewriting techniques, and check lists for revising, proofreading, and publishing. Others prefer to punch these and put them directly into the binder. In some classrooms this information is displayed on posters or listed on charts around the room. Students copy these guidelines into the reference sections of their journals or tape duplicated information to pages in their spiral notebooks or hardback composition books.

Student Description of Journaling

Alexandra, a fifth-grade student, described the value of her journal and told how she assembled it so that it would be useful to her:

> A journal keeps me from losing things I might need. It's a good collection of things and keeping one makes you proud of your work. A journal also lets other people know all the hard work you did.

> I leave a number of pages blank at the beginning of the journal for a table of contents. This helps me find what I need to know or to show something to someone. Each time I make an entry, I enter the topic in the front, along with the page number. Then I can find it easily. For example, if I want to know how to do an SQ3R [Survey, Question, Read, Recite, Review], I can find it by looking in the table of contents.

> We also keep our check-ins in the journal [daily warm-up exercises students perform when they first enter the classroom in the morning. These include working with geography terms, writing reactions to current events and math practice.] I also tape handouts, brochures from field trips—I highlight interesting information with a marker—and tests into the book so I can refer to them.

INTRODUCING JOURNALS
TO MIDDLE SCHOOL (GRADES 6–8) STUDENTS

Teachers at the middle school level introduce journals in much the same way as they are introduced to intermediate age students. It is important for students at this age level to understand the purpose of the journal, as a place to work out their ideas in their own words and in their own way. Procedures for review by the teacher should be explained. Most teachers do over-the-shoulder, 2-minute conferences or periodic reviews once or twice a month. If the journal is to be evaluated in some way as part of a final assessment, guidelines for this evaluation should be distributed, so that organization can begin immediately. In most subject areas, it is helpful for students to create a continuing table of contents and use either a three-ring binder with section dividers or a series of spiral notebooks for individual themes or subject areas.

It is equally important at this level for students to see themselves as the primary audience for their journals and to regard this writing as a conversation with themselves. They should be able to use spelling and handwriting that is comfortable and relaxed for them, without concern at this stage for correct or final form. This is a practice manual, a workbook that allows them to wrestle with ideas in a manner that is comfortable and productive for them as individuals. As such, it is also a resource for more polished and complete works. Journals created in this manner allow teachers to see how a student thinks and where to aim instruction to assist individual and class development.

Response Forms

Depending on the subject area, students should be introduced to a variety of graphic organizers and response guidelines that will help them explore concepts. The REACT model described in the previous section is equally helpful for middle schoolers, because it encourages students to explore subject matter in a comprehensive manner, but also supports differences in cognitive development that are increasingly apparent at this age level. This model also prompts students in integrated curriculum settings to make conscious connections between subject matter areas and permits teachers to observe the extent to which students are making these critical relationships.

In the middle school literature, teachers propose a number of ways for students to use journals and logs to assist individual learning and participation in groups. Tomlinson (1993) suggested that students keep a process log, to record their thoughts and activities:

> They can write about how they developed their topic, ideas they gained as they did background research, ways in which their thinking changed over time, problems they encountered and how they solved those problems, how they dealt with frustrations and how they felt when things were going really well. The log may include sketches, photos, journal entries, etc. Such a log not only helps students become more aware of their thinking processes, but also helps students understand what transpired in creating a product whose appearance may belie its actual scope. (p. 58)

For both group and individual work, Hough and Donlan (1994) suggested the use of participation guides to help students explore texts. These guides should be developmental, beginning with simple responses and moving gradually to the more complex, until students can develop their own guides for response. They encourage the use of graphic organizers, mapping, and summarization, and believe it is valuable for students to meet in a variety of learning groups, to discuss books and ideas. As part of an integrated strategy to help middle school students maximize their learning, Hough and Donlan believed:

> Discussion clusters, guides, and writing activities are three strategies that can help students respond to text. Each of the three strategies can be sequenced in a series of steps to insure that the students can gain independence in reading and learning from text. Integrating instructional strategies can help students formulate independent responses, allowing teachers to reach a wider variety of student interests and abilities. (p. 35)

Anita Graham (1994) introduced learning logs to her middle school students as places to respond and reflect on their learning. She saw learning logs as:

> a collection of writings of many different types, written for many audiences and purposes. . . . Learning logs help students "find meaning in the world by exploring it through language—through their own easy talky language, not the language of textbook and teacher" (Fulwiler, 1987 p. 1). (p. 7)

When her students began a study of Michael Shaara's *The Killer Angels,* Graham asked them to respond in their learning logs to the following: What is a tragedy? When is an event tragic? What tragic event could you write about? This exercise helps students connect the novel to their own experience and to think about it as both history and dramatic tragedy. Through the year, Graham provided students with response prompts for their journal writing, asking them to write a description of the Europeans in the New World from the natives' point of view. She asked students what they learned about the Puritans from the literature they had studied or if they would recommend that students the following year read the same books.

Graham asked students to create entries in their logs that reflected on their progress as learners. After tests, they considered their strengths and weaknesses and suggested ways to improve their performance. At the end of a grading period, students submitted their logs for final evaluation. They created a table of contents and submitted their work for two grades: one for completing all activities and the other for any entry they chose as a favorite. Graham asked the students to justify the choice of this work, which prompted students to reflect on the quality of their own learning. Other suggestions for evaluating journals can be found in chapter 2 of this book.

5

Exploring Literature With Learning Journals

The teacher of literature, then, seeks to help specific human beings discover the satisfactions of literature. Teaching becomes a matter of improving the individual's capacity to evoke meaning from the text by leading him to reflect self-critically on this process. . . . The teacher's task is to foster fruitful interactions—or, more precisely, transactions—between individual readers and individual literary works.

—Louise Rosenblatt (1983, p. 46)

PREVIEW

1. What is a literature learning journal?
2. What levels of response can be expected in literature journals?
3. How are literature journals constructed?
4. What kinds of guideline questions encourage responses to literature?
5. What kinds of response formats are used in literature journals?
6. How do literature journals support individual reading conferences?
7. How do journals support literature groups?
8. What if students do not like a book they are reading?

BRIEFLY: Students use literature learning journals to record individual responses to literature and to prepare for group discussions or reading conferences with the teacher.

LITERATURE LEARNING JOURNALS: A DESCRIPTION

Students use literature journals as they read to write down ideas that interest or puzzle them, make connections with their own experience, and record any questions they have. When they finish reading, students evaluate their experience, noting any difficulties they had with understanding and what they enjoyed or disliked. If appropriate, they draw pictures or create graphic organizers to help increase or communicate their understanding (Fig. 5.1). Students may also respond to generic questions that model ways to examine books in more depth. This response activity prepares them to meet with a partner, in a small group, or in a reading workshop with the entire class to share ideas and information from their reading. Literature learning journals are also a resource for individual reading conferences with the teacher, because students can refer to notes, questions, and responses as a basis for this conversation.

In some classrooms, students respond in journals to books that are read aloud to them by the teacher. Although this practice is more common at the kindergarten and primary levels, intermediate and middle school students enjoy being read to and appreciate the opportunity to communicate their questions, comments, and comprehension more privately to the teacher in journal entries.

Kindergarten children respond to literature primarily with drawings, captions (titles of their pictures), descriptive words, or several sentences. They might also cut out pictures from magazines to illustrate or interpret their understanding. At the early primary level, students record the titles, authors, and illustrators of the books they read, along with a sentence or two about the story. Late primary, intermediate, and middle school students write more extensive responses, but students of all ages draw pictures of story events and favorite characters, or create story maps to get a sense of setting or plot sequence.

FIG. 5.1. A first grader responds to literature in her journal.

Teachers usually provide students with guidelines for their responses, which may be generic or specific to particular books. Literature journals are excellent places for students to explore the genres of children's literature and to describe various literary devices and techniques used by authors. These journals then become a reference for future reading and writing, as students explore new books in a genre or try their hand at writing in these forms.

When students read for enjoyment on their own, they usually record the title and author of the book in a special location (resource section) in their journal, with a brief note about its contents. These notes help remind students of books they especially liked and want to recommend to others during book preview time. Students may also record titles in this section that the teacher or other students have recommended in book preview sessions or during reader's workshop.

TYPES OF RESPONSES TO EXPECT FROM STUDENTS

What kinds of responses can teachers expect to find in children's journals? Purves and Monson (1984) analyzed children's comments about literature and observed that they:

1. *Describe*: This is a book about rabbits. Their names are Flopsy, Mopsy, Cottontail, and Peter. The illustrator used watercolors to make the pictures.

2. *Analyze*: Every page has another story in the margin. The story is told from the cat's point of view.
3. *Classify*: This book is a survival story and it's realistic fiction. It's the second book the author wrote about this character.
4. *Respond personally*: I liked this book, because it reminded me of the summer I spent with my grandparents.
5. *Interpret*: This is really a story about holding on to your values, no matter what.
6. *Evaluate*: This really isn't very well written historical fiction because many of the historical facts are not correct.

Purves and Monson also identified characteristic responses of children at different grade levels, observing that primary children tend to focus on retelling the story, whereas intermediates identify with the characters and find personal connections with their experiences. At the middle school level, students begin to respond with increased empathy to characters and look for deeper meaning in the stories they read.

Wollman-Bonilla and Werchadlo (1995), however, found that first-grade students were capable of responses beyond the typical retelling when there were opportunities for them to write personal responses in journals and elaborate on them in discussions with each other or the teacher. This interaction helps the teacher better understand and appreciate the thinking of individual students, and to evaluate their level of comprehension. Journals encourage students to reflect on what they read or listened to and their writing creates a springboard for discussion. When teachers ask students to elaborate on their responses by asking them why they have commented in a certain way, this prompts students to comment more thoughtfully and extensively in subsequent responses. Wollman-Bonilla and Werchadlo observed:

> Further, the journals were useful in assessing individuals' thinking and were particularly important as windows on the thinking of those children who rarely spoke in class. At the beginning of the year, because all were responding to a book read aloud, the journals also allowed the weakest readers to reveal their complex thoughts and their appreciation of a challenging text [*James and the Giant Peach*]. (p. 569)

Wollman-Bonilla (1995) developed a system to categorize students' responses, which she described as being either text centered or reader centered. *Text-centered* responses included retelling, understanding characters, asking questions, and making predictions. *Reader-centered* responses were personal reactions relating to the experiences in the story and finding oneself in the story. (Compare these categories with Rosenblatt's descriptions of efferent and aesthetic response in chapter 1.) Wollman-Bonilla found that, initially, the majority of responses were text centered, but as the year progressed, the number of reader-centered comments increased, as the teacher modeled these kinds of responses and encouraged students to respond personally to what they read.

CREATING A LITERATURE JOURNAL

When students use learning journals to explore literature, they may record their responses on consecutive pages in single entry style or create a dialogue with themselves by using the dialectic or double entry format. In some classrooms, students set aside several sections in a notebook to record a variety of entries. Depending on the age and ability of the student, these sections might include pages for recording and response and a section to record or collect materials for resource and reference. The REACT model can be used to structure entries for both single and double entry styles. The recording section of a literature journal might include:

- Assignments and guideline questions.
- Information from reading workshops, conferences, and discussions.
- Ideas and information from reading.
- Page numbers of passages or pictures they especially like.
- Notes about the author or illustrator.
- Background information about the story's events or setting.

In single entry journals, recording and response are intermingled. In the double entry format, students use the opposing page or side of a page to help themselves make sense of their reading. In either format, these responses will be personal and highly individual, and may include some or all of the following:

- *Evaluation* of the reading experience: A personal response that includes what they liked or disliked about a story; comments and opinions about characters, plot, events, or style; and difficulties they experienced with understanding any part of the reading.
- *Questions* about the reading: New vocabulary; difficult concepts; unfamiliar people, places, things, events, and settings.
- *Connections* with personal experience, previous knowledge, and other curriculum areas.
- *Transformations* of the reading, to interpret ideas or assist understanding. These include writing of all kinds, drawings, collages of cut-out pictures, sketches, maps, diagrams, tables, graphs, or graphic organizers.

When students create a continuing table of contents for their journals, resources and references may be merged with other entries. In other instances, students create a separate section for materials they plan to use for resource or reference in their reading. These resources for thinking, writing, and sharing with others might include definitions of vocabulary words; strategies for reading; examples of literary devices from movies and television; articles about books from newspapers or magazines; quotes and cartoons with themes related to books in general, specific books, or literary themes.

Some students also record jingles, quotes, advertisements, or dialogue from TV shows or movies related to literary characters or themes. When separate journals are not kept for writing, students may include poems, newspaper articles, and story ideas that could be adapted for their own writing and trial sketches for illustrating responses to literature. Many students also make lists of books they have read, with brief annotations of content. These can be used as a reference for previewing books for other students or they can be classified by topic for use in other studies. In some classes, students collect a favorite poem from their reading each week to share with the rest of the class.

Students in the upper grades often create a separate reference section, or even a separate section for each of the following. Others merge these functions in the same section and identify them with headings on separate pages.

- *Glossary*: A list of annotated terms to assist reading and writing, such as descriptions of genres or unfamiliar words and concepts encountered in reading.
- *Book list*: Lists of books the student wants to read, derived from their own browsing, those by favorite authors or illustrators, books read aloud, or recommended by the teacher or by other students during preview sessions.
- *Personal spelling dictionary*: A quick reference for words that a student has looked up for spelling or definition, and words that the student uses frequently and wants to learn to spell. Most students reserve a page for each letter of the alphabet.
- *Guidelines*: These include guidelines for literature groups or preparing for conferences, rules for using the library or the computer, and generic or specific guideline questions for literature exploration.

GUIDELINES TO ENCOURAGE RESPONSES TO LITERATURE

Guidelines for responding to literature are usually generic and are designed to help students explore the meaning of what they read in more depth and detail. Included in this section are examples that teachers have used successfully at all levels of elementary instruction. Although a number of suggestions are included, most teachers begin by selecting only one or two in each category. This offers students experience with a number of different kinds of responses before they are asked to select several from each type on their own. Both generic (appropriate to the exploration of most books) and specific (particular to a certain genre) examples are listed. These questions can be used as guidelines for individual study, preparing for individual conferences with the teacher, or as preparation for paired, small group, or class discussions.

Most teachers distribute a set of the generic prompts to students at the beginning of the school year and then provide additional sheets with genre-specific questions as they are introduced in minilessons or reading and writing workshops. These can be punched and inserted into the reference section of three-ring journals, kept in divider pockets, or taped into spiral or composition notebooks.

Kindergarten and Beginning Levels

At the kindergarten or beginning reading levels, students draw pictures or cut out pictures, letters, and words from magazines to express their responses to the prompts. Teachers can also construct posters with rebus pictures to provide ideas for responding to literature. These can be posted somewhere in the room and used by the teacher, an aide, a parent helper, or a Book Buddy to prompt discussion about a book. For example, students might choose two or three of the following:

What did you like about this book? (happy face)
What is your favorite picture in this book? (stick figure)

What is this book about? (question mark)

Did you learn something new? (plus sign)

Did you already know something about the topic? (star)

Did you find any words you didn't know? How did you figure them out? (puzzle)

Have you read another book like this? (two open books)

Have you ever had an experience like this? (light bulb)

Do you want to read another book like this? Another book by the same author? (open book with happy face on it)

Draw a picture of your favorite part of the book. (crayon)

Make a collage that shows what you liked or learned. (scissors)

Write your favorite word. (pencil)

Write your favorite sentence. (pencil writing)

Make up a poem about this book. (several wavy lines)

Primary, Intermediate, and Middle School Levels

The following sets of prompts can be adapted for use at any elementary level. At the primary level, one or two questions in each category are appropriate. At the intermediate and middle school levels, students may consider several in each category. Offering students a choice of responses in each category gives them practice with all aspects of analysis, but does not force responses of a personal nature, which might invade their privacy.

Evaluation prompts help readers explore their responses to literature and gain insight into the behavior of the characters in the story. Responses in this category will help teachers assess a student's preferences in literature and their identification with characters, the situation, or values.

What did you like about this book?

What about this story interested you?

Who was your favorite character?

Who did you most admire in this story?

Why do you think this character acted the way he or she did?

Why do you think this character changed beliefs or behavior?

What do you think of this character's behavior?

Could this character have done things differently?

Would you have reacted the same way?

What values were important to the main character? Other characters?

Do you share or disagree with these values?

Would you read another book of this type or by this author?

Connection prompts help students relate personally to the ideas they are reading about and help them connect their reading in one area of the curriculum to other content areas.

Did you learn something new by reading this book?

Have you ever traveled to the place where the story is set?

Has anyone you know ever been to this place?

Has anyone you know ever been to this place?
Did any of the characters remind you of someone you know?
Have you or anyone you know ever had to face a similar challenge?
Can you relate anything about this book or story to other things you are learning?
Have you read any other books like this, or by the same author?
Did any previous knowledge or experience help you understand this writing?

Comprehension prompts help students develop skills of literary analysis as they look for the main idea of a story, make inferences, interpret the behavior of characters, assess the author's purposes in writing, and identify genres, literary techniques, and story elements.

What kind of story is this?
What elements of this story helped you identify the genre?
What was this story about?
Briefly tell the story.
What is the story really about (in one word or sentence)?
What happened at the beginning of the story, the middle, and the end?
What do you think is the theme of this story?
What is the meaning of this story?
What was the author trying to say?
Why do you think the author wrote this story?
What do you think the author wanted you to feel when you read this book?
Did this story have a message?
What do you think the main character learned?
Why do you think this character did this?
What would have happened if the character had acted another way?
What ways did the author use to tell you about this character?
Would it have made a difference if the main character were a boy instead of a girl?
How would this story change in a different place or time?
How did the setting affect the story?
What important decisions did the main character have to make?

Strategy questions help students use word analysis or reading techniques to figure out the pronunciation or meaning of words that are unfamiliar.

Does this word look like any others you know?
Can you tell what it is by reading other words around it?
Can you figure it out by looking at the pictures?
What sound does the word start with? End with? Sound like in the middle?
Does it make sense if you just go on and read around it?
Where can you find out what this word means?
Does this word have more than one meaning?
Should you put this word in your glossary?
Where can you find out more about this person, place, time, author, or book?
What pictures, illustrations or graphics tell you more about the story?
How did you figure out words you didn't understand or couldn't pronounce?

How did you figure out sentences or paragraphs that were difficult to understand? What special features helped you understand the reading better? (indexes, glossaries, pictures, maps, graphs, photographs, or diagrams)

RESPONSE FORMATS FOR LITERATURE JOURNALS

Teachers model a variety of ways to respond to literature in reading workshops, during guided reading sessions, or in separate minilesson presentations. Students should be familiar with enough models to permit them to respond in ways that are comfortable for them to use and that reveal the level of their understanding. Each kind of format should be tried out at least once, when this is appropriate. Instructions for writing in these forms are recorded when they are introduced or a printed description of the forms is distributed to students at the beginning of the year. In either case, these guidelines are included in a reference section for easy review.

Students should be encouraged to experiment with alternative forms of response, with the goal of finding a variety of ways to make sense of what they are reading. They may discover additional and unique ways to respond on their own, which can be shared in small groups or with the entire class. The following are ideas that have been used successfully in elementary classrooms:

• *Notes*: Beginning readers record their favorite words or sentences, or write a summary word or sentence about their reading. Older students use either the REACT or ACT acronym as a model or respond to guideline prompts suggested by the teacher. They take notes on ideas they want to remember, write the page numbers of favorite illustrations or significant passages, and record ideas for responses that occur to them as they read.

• *Essays*: This form is used to respond in more detail to guidelines that ask students to summarize a story; analyze a character; compare and contrast characters in the book; compare the characters, story, or setting of two books on the same theme or different books by the same author; or contrast treatment of a topic by two different authors or in two different genres of literature.

• *Drawings*: Many students express their understanding of a story by drawing pictures of their favorite character, the setting, or a scene in the story. Some find pictures or photographs to represent these elements in magazines, which they cut out and tape into their journals.

• *Maps*: When maps are not part of a story, it is sometimes helpful to draw one from the information given to get a better idea of the setting. Story maps are helpful when location and movement through space is critical to the understanding of a story, such as those found in complex fantasies, historical fiction, or informational literature.

• *Diagrams*: Students create labeled sketches or Venn diagrams to help them make better sense of what they are reading, to demonstrate their understanding to someone else, or to enable them to more easily explain ideas to another student.

• *Charts and Tables*: These help students sort out characteristics of characters, organize events, or permit them to discover relationships among groups of places, persons, or things in a story or informational book.

- *Quotations*: Students select a favorite sentence or brief passage to comment on and describe its significance to them or to the story.
- *Character descriptions*: These can be created in the form of a conceptual map, a brief essay, or a list of characteristics. Students also create character webs or describe a character through the eyes of another person in the story.
- *Data banks*: These are lists of terms that are critical to the understanding of the story. Specialized terminology, historical terms, geographical locations, slang, or foreign language used in the story might be included in a data bank. Lists may be provided by the teacher or developed by students.
- *Graphic organizers*: These visual representations help students organize ideas from their reading and discover relationships among persons, places, and events. Time lines, comparison diagrams, and semantic maps (clusters and webs) are among the most popular with students.
- *Interviews*: Many students enjoy conducting mock interviews with characters in a book. This response form also helps students adopt different perspectives, as they interview characters with conflicting values and ideas.
- *Letters to characters*: Students write letters to characters in a story, giving them advice, asking questions, and sharing problems. They might also write letters between two characters in the same or different books.
- *Diaries*: Students make entries in a diary for a day or longer, pretending that they are a character in the book.

JOURNALS AND INDIVIDUAL READING CONFERENCES

In classrooms where students select their own books to practice reading comprehension and word analysis skills, teachers meet regularly with individual students to evaluate their progress. These meetings provide teachers with information about a student's reading development and allow them to observe literacy skills in action. This is also a time when teachers can identify strong interests in reading and recommend supplementary materials that will enhance the appreciation of a particular book.

In many classrooms, the books discussed in conferences are chosen by the student, although they may be required to select from a particular genre. In this event, genre-specific guidelines help students explore the special features of the genre. For example, when picture books are read, students might respond to prompts like:

- What was your favorite picture in this book?
- What kinds of materials did the artist use to illustrate this book?
- How did the artist use line, color, shape, or texture to add to the story?
- What additional pictures do you wish the artist had created for this story?
- Illustrate your favorite part of the story.

In a similar fashion, students might respond to other genres:

Historical fiction
- How did this book make you feel like you were really there?
- What did you learn about a historical person, setting, or event?

Biography
- What anecdotes about this person gave you insight into his or her character?
- What influences in this person's life helped him or her succeed?

Realistic fiction
- Do you agree with how the main character solved his or her problems?
- Have you ever had to face a similar problem?

Modern fantasy
- What made this story seem like it could happen?
- What do you think is the message of this story?

Multicultural literature
- What new thing did you learn about this culture?
- What experiences were similar to your own? Different than your own?

Traditional literature
- What elements of a folk tale (legend, tall tale) did you find in this story?
- What virtues are emphasized in this story?

Students prepare for individual conferences by selecting a favorite illustration to talk about and/or a favorite passage to read aloud. In their journals, they respond to prompts suggested by the teacher or chosen from a list of possibilities. Students use these questions to analyze what they have read, explore ideas in more depth, and make connections between literature and their own experience.

Teachers use the same guidelines to direct the conversation, beginning the conference with questions like:

- Tell me about your book.
- What did you like about this book?
- Why did you pick this book to read?

They ask the students to talk about their favorite passages or pictures and listen while they read aloud from a passage they have practiced. Students anticipate these questions and refer to their journals for page numbers. As the conversation continues, the teacher will ask additional questions, using the same guidelines the student has used to prepare for the conference. Students may refer to their journal entries to respond, or they may show the teacher pictures, diagrams, maps, charts, or other materials that demonstrate their skill or understanding. Many teachers use checklists to keep track of skills they observe in these conferences. Collected information from conferences creates a profile of reading skills across the class that enables the teacher to plan minilessons for small groups or the entire class (Fig. 5.2).

The learning journal format encourages students to use a variety of ways to explore literature and develop their skills of analysis and comprehension. Their preparation for the conference helps them focus on questions and difficulties they are experiencing, which enables the teacher to provide direct and effective help to the student during the one-on-one session. Students anticipate and enjoy this time alone with the teacher, which gives them the opportunity to talk about their favorite books and share personal responses to literature.

As the conference draws to a close, the teacher will comment positively about the session and provide time for the student to make brief notes about strategies that have been discussed. There might also be an assignment that links a favorite book with skills to practice or literary elements to explore. If students are experiencing difficulties with comprehension, interpretation, or word analysis, the teacher might assign them to a small task group to work on a particular skill.

Many teachers conduct over-the-shoulder reviews of literature responses while students are writing, or brief 2-minute conferences to check on comprehension (Fig. 5.3). Others review journal entries by chapter on a regular basis to track student response and identify misconceptions. For example, after reading the first chapter of Gulliver's Travels, Nick wrote:

FIG. 5.2. Mrs. Sheahan tracks second grade language skill development with a checklist.

> From this first chapter I learned that Lemuel Gulliver lived in the late 1600's and early 1700's. I figured that out because he put in a request for sailors in 1699, so that must mean that he either took the job or was interested in it. I can tell from the things he put in his first diary entry and the tracings that he had many strange adventures.

It is evident from Nick's response that he has sufficient comprehension skills to continue reading the story.

On the other hand, the following entry signaled that a student was having difficulty with making inferences as he struggled to make sense of his reading in In the Year of the Boar and Jackie Robinson. In the story, Shirley, who is newly arrived in America, meets her new principal on the first day of school. The principal winks at her, as a friendly gesture, but Shirley interprets the winking to be an American custom that

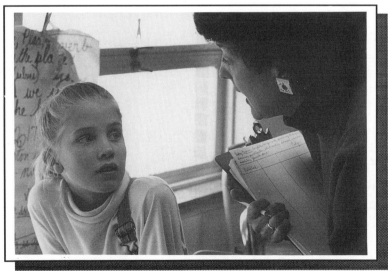

FIG. 5.3. Mrs. Hogue conducts a 2-minute literature conference with Nancy.

should be responded to in kind. Later, she blinks both her eyes at her teacher, who then believes that Shirley may need to have her eyes examined and sends home a note to her parents. The student wrote, "I wonder why Mrs. Rappaport thinks Shirley is sick, but it must be serious because she sent a note home." His teacher responded: "Did you understand today when we talked about the winking?" and opened up the chance to talk about the misunderstanding.

USING JOURNALS TO SUPPORT LITERATURE GROUPS

Literature study groups, sometimes called literature circles, feature small groups of students who meet together to read and discuss the same book, books by the same author, or books on a common topic or theme. Four students seem to be the optimal number to participate in these groups. When numbers do not come out evenly, it is better to form several groups of three, because smaller groups help promote better participation. Teachers usually provide these small discussion groups with generic or specific prompts that model a variety of ways to explore the meaning of literature. These questions can be used by students individually, as they read and respond to literature, and as the framework for discussions with a partner, in small groups or with the entire class. In some primary classrooms, students meet as a whole group to share their responses (Fig. 5.4).

As students read, they record their personal responses, interpretations of their reading, and strategies for understanding in their learning journals. Some groups read and discuss books a chapter at a time, whereas others read the entire book before discussing it. When they read together, students lay out a colored bookmark when they have finished reading and responding to a chapter to indicate that they are ready for discussion. This frees faster readers to continue reading and does not penalize those who read more slowly. What is important is that each individual has time to read, think about, and respond personally to a book in preparation for sharing ideas and strategies with others. Some groups assign themselves chapters to read outside of class and save the in-class time for discussions and artistic responses to books.

As students discuss the meaning of a book together, they take notes from these discussions to add to their own individual responses. Insights and information gained from discussions that increase appreciation or understanding of literature can be added as a new entry in single entry jour-

FIG. 5.4. Dr. Koblitz and his third-grade class discuss a book together.

nals, or added to the response side of the double entry style. Some teachers encourage students to adopt rotating roles for participation in literature groups, which include the following:

- *Facilitator,* who reads the response questions, focuses the discussion, and makes sure that everyone participates.
- *Recorder,* who takes notes on significant ideas that everyone might want to include in their journals. In many classrooms, the recorder provides a summary of the group's discussion for the teacher's review at the end of a meeting period.
- *Reporter,* who reports small group discussions to the larger class group. In groups of three, this role is assumed by the recorder or messenger.
- *Messenger,* who obtains, distributes and collects materials used by the group or handed in to the teacher. If team folders are used, this person files all materials in the folder.

In some classrooms, students meet together to discuss literature in reading workshops that involve the entire class. Students take notes on their reading and create entries in their journals as resources for participating in the discussions. The basis for this discussion may be a combination of ACT, REACT or guideline questions provided by the teacher. Students may also use journals to record ideas or information provided about the book by the teacher or other students. Additional ideas for using cooperative groups to study literature can be found in Appendix B, which describes the ways these groups function in specific classrooms.

JOURNAL SUPPORT WHEN STUDENTS DISLIKE A BOOK

A key feature of the literature learning journal is that it provides a place for students to record what they like or dislike about their reading. In programs where students self-select books, teachers usually suggest that they read at least three chapters of a book (three to five pages in a picture book at the kindergarten and early primary levels) and perhaps sample some pages in the middle before deciding not to complete it. In systems where the school or district requires the reading of certain books, journals provide an outlet for students to record their unfavorable responses as they work to understand and appreciate the author's style or point of view. It is frequently the case that students may dislike a story in the beginning, but later become very enthusiastic about it.

For example, a fourth grader just beginning to read *The Doll House Murders* (Wright, 1983) wrote a brief response, "I think there is not anything exciting in Chapter One and Two. I don't think this book is going to be that interesting to me." Two days later, he wrote:

> I think this book is finally getting exciting. I wonder what's going to happen next? I wonder what they're going to do at the double birthday party. I can't believe that the dollhouse is exactly like the real house. The dollhouse even has candle sticks.

[His teacher responded: I'm glad you are enjoying *The Doll House Murders*. Sometimes it takes a while to get into a book.]

When he finished the book a week later, he concluded:

I really really really like this book. I hope *Christina's Ghost* is as much fun. I rate this book a 10, because it got very very interesting. . . . At first I thought this book was going to be boring, by looking at the cover and the title. But it was very very very good. [His teacher responded: I'm so glad you got a lot out of this book. Isn't it funny how our attitude about a book can change? I felt like you did when I read *Hatchet*.]

Journal entries provide a history of the process by which students are pulled into the story, which is often comforting to review if they encounter new books that seem unattractive or difficult to get in to. Occasionally, students encounter books that they dislike from beginning to end. Sometimes the genre of the book is new to the student, plots vary in the amount of action, or the character does not make a connection with an individual reader. One student wrote in his journal that he did not like it when the author hinted at things that were going to happen in the story. For him, the technique of foreshadowing gave away surprises. He worked to analyze the story, however, and acknowledged that other readers might enjoy the book using criteria other than the ones he used. In contrast, the same student was enthusiastic about a survival story, where he enjoyed the action, identified strongly with the main character, and could imagine himself trying to face similar challenges. In both instances, the student increased his awareness of what he liked in literature and was able to articulate his reasons.

When students have difficulty moving into a story, small group discussions often help them observe details that they might otherwise not have noticed. For example, when fifth graders in one class studied *In the Year of the Boar and Jackie Robinson*, students generally understood and enjoyed the book because of its humor, school setting, the strong sports theme, the main character's persistence, or their own experience moving to a new school or entering a new culture. A few students, however, expressed frustration with the story in their journal responses, which indicated problems with understanding the customs of another culture, making inferences (see the previous section), and identifying with the main character. As they discussed what they liked, disliked, or found difficult about the story in small groups, these students gained new enthusiasm for the story and were able to identify more strongly with the main character. Journal entries helped the teacher track the increase in comprehension that resulted from these discussions and enabled her to provide information or assistance as it was necessary.

EXAMPLES OF STUDENT ENTRIES
FROM LITERATURE JOURNALS

Figures 5.5 through 5.10 are examples of entries from student literature journals.

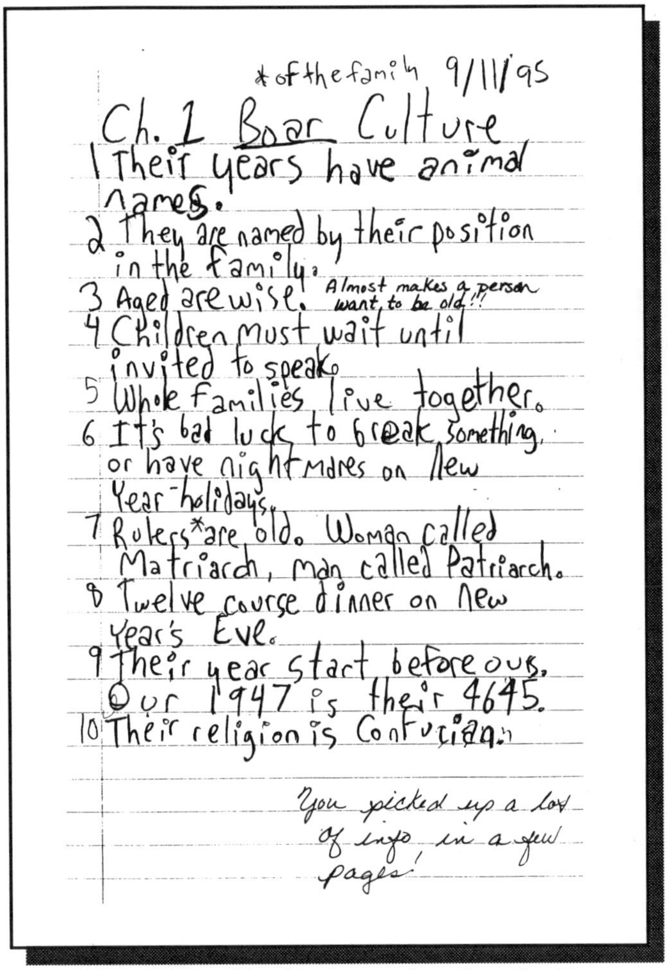

* of the family 9/11/95

Ch. 1 Boar Culture

1 Their years have animal names.

2 They are named by their position in the family.

3 Aged are wise. *Almost makes a person want to be old!!*

4 Children must wait until invited to speak.

5 Whole families live together.

6 It's bad luck to break something, or have nightmares on New Year holidays.

7 Rulers* are old. Woman called Matriarch, man called Patriarch.

8 Twelve course dinner on New Year's Eve.

9 Their year start before ours. Our 1947 is their 4645.

10 Their religion is Confucian.

You picked up a lot of info in a few pages!

FIG. 5.5. Marina's notes for In the Year of the Boar and Jackie Robinson.

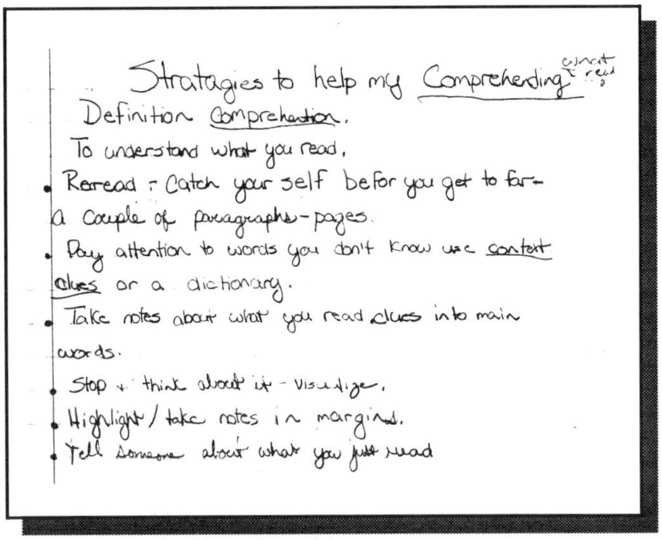

Stratagies to help my Comprehending *cant read?*

Definition Comprehention.

To understand what you read.

- Reread - Catch your self before you get to far- a couple of paragraphs-pages.
- Pay attention to words you don't know use **content clues** or a dictionary.
- Take notes about what you read clues into main words.
- Stop + think about it - visualize.
- Highlight / take notes in margins.
- Tell someone about what you just read

FIG. 5.6. Robert's strategies to assist comprehension.

FIG. 5.7. Rachel drew a scene from Berlioz the Bear.

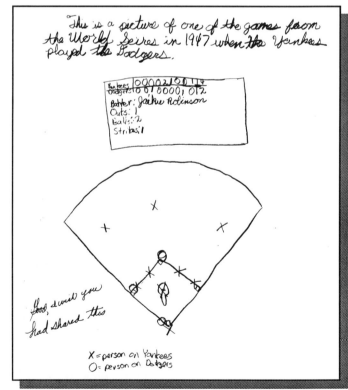

FIG. 5.8. Alexander's drawing of the Dodgers' baseball field from In the Year of the Boar and Jackie Robinson.

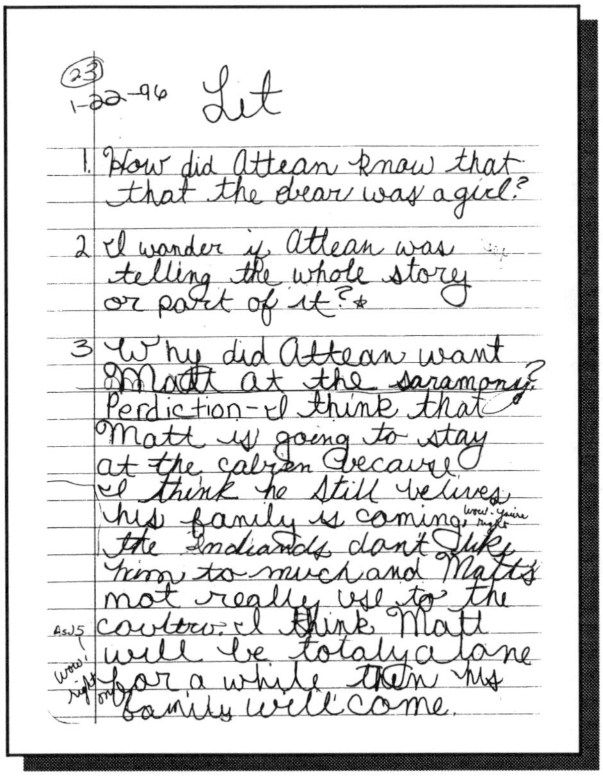

23
1-22-96 Lit

1. How did Attean know that that the bear was agiel?

2. I wonder if Attean was telling the whole storey or part of it? *

3. Why did Attean want Matt at the saramony? Perdiction- I think that Matt is going to stay at the cabin becaure I think he still belives his family is coming, the Indiands dont like him to much and Matts not really use to the cowtrw. I think Matt will be totaly alone for a while then his family will come.

FIG. 5.9. Ashley's questions about Sign of the Beaver.

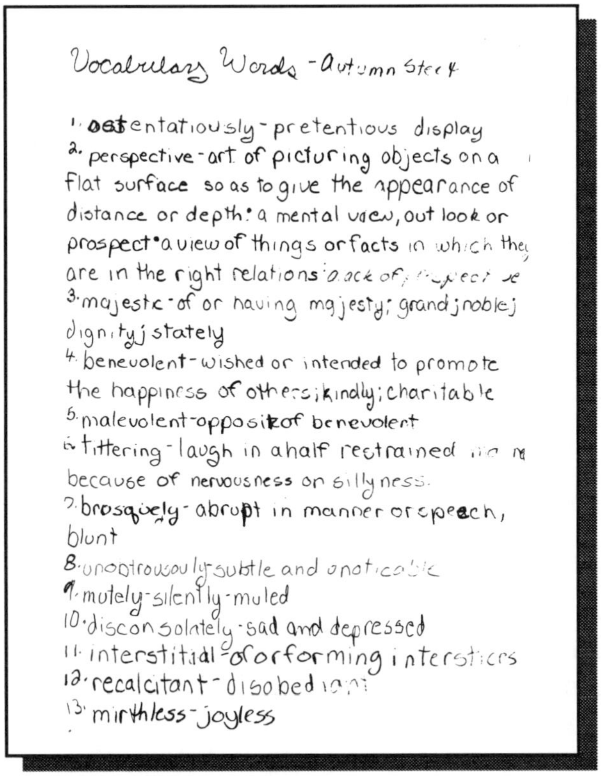

Vocabulary Words - Autumn Street

1. ostentatiously - pretentious display
2. perspective - art of picturing objects on a flat surface so as to give the appearance of distance or depth: a mental view, out look or prospect: a view of things or facts in which they are in the right relations: a ack of p... ...
3. majestic - of or having majesty; grand; noble; dignity; stately
4. benevolent - wished or intended to promote the happiness of others; kindly; charitable
5. malevolent - opposit of benevolent
6. tittering - laugh in a half restrained ... because of nervousness or sillyness.
7. brosquely - abrupt in manner or speach, blunt
8. unootrousouly - subtle and unoticable
9. mutely - silently - muted
10. disconsolately - sad and depressed
11. interstitial - of or forming interstices
12. recalcitant - disobedient
13. mirthless - joyless

FIG. 5.10. Alexandra's list of vocabulary words from Autumn Street.

6

Exploring Writing With Learning Journals

Children need to know that as writers, we run our hands over and over and over the bumpy fabric of our work. . . . And so, in share sessions—and in minilessons, conferences, and alone at the desk—we look back at the trail of our thinking in order to see what we have said, to hear tunes and rhythms in our language, to feel the power of an idea, to see how one insight links with another and another and another, to gather momentum for more writing, to notice, to be surprised, to marvel, to listen.

—Calkins and Harwayne (1991, p. 61)

PREVIEW

1. What is a writing journal?
2. What kinds of entries are found in writing journals?
3. How do journals support developmental spelling and handwriting?
4. How do journals support writer's workshops and peer conferences?
5. How do journals support individual writing conferences?
6. How do journals provide students with resources for writing?
7. Of what value is literature that depicts children as writers?

BRIEFLY: Students use writing journals to experiment with language, reflect on their experience, collect resources for projects, assemble grammar or spelling references, and practice handwriting.

WRITING JOURNALS: A DESCRIPTION

Every journal described in this book is a writing journal in the sense that writing is used as a tool to explore ideas and information in the content areas. However, writing is also a content area in itself, one that concerns itself with helping students develop ways to use language to communicate effectively and express themselves creatively. This chapter describes the many ways journals support and encourage student writing in classrooms that feature writing workshops and those that are organized in the more traditional manner. Additional ideas for writing activities are found in chapter 3, the annotated resources of Appendix A, and the other content area chapters.

In more traditional classrooms, journals support instruction and practice in the separate elements of writing—composition, grammar, spelling, and handwriting. Students record information from English lessons, create personal dictionaries to assist spelling, and construct glossaries of terms used in the content areas. In more holistic classrooms, writing journals contain successive drafts of original compositions, a record of students' thoughts about experiences they have had, problems they are experiencing with their writing, and ideas for future pieces. In some classrooms, writing journals integrate the several purposes of both traditional and holistic journals to provide a place for student writers to:

- Record ideas and resources for their writing.
- Work on these ideas in an exploratory way.
- Review their work to get ideas for more finished pieces.
- Create graphic organizers to represent and develop their ideas.
- Explore the elements of language and genre.
- Create a personal spelling dictionary.
- Construct a glossary of terms used in the content areas.
- Record grammatical rules and protocols.
- Practice the essentials of handwriting and graphic lettering.

The number and kinds of entries in a writing journal will vary, depending on the particular classroom situation and the age, experience, and developmental level of students. Each type of entry is introduced over a period of time so that students can practice and become familiar with it. Although students may use fewer or more types of entries than those just listed, the major purpose of the journal is to provide students with a place to record their ideas for writing, practice the elements of writing, and create references for correct language use that can easily be accessed.

Experienced writers know that ideas often come to them at odd moments, which accounts for the fact that more than one good idea has begun its life on the back of an envelope. Writing journals provide places for students to record ideas for writing as soon as they occur to them. They also create opportunities for students to experiment with these ideas, to make character sketches, or list words they find particularly intriguing.

KINDS OF ENTRIES FOUND IN WRITING JOURNALS

Perhaps the most important function of writing journals is to provide a place for students to write in an exploratory way about ideas of interest to them. Some of this writing activity will help them sort out their thoughts in much the same way as writing in a diary. Other kinds of writing will help them examine and organize their ideas as a way to prepare for writing. In either case, exploratory writing allows students to separate the creative and editing phases of writing and express their ideas without initial concern for grammatical construction or spelling. This first draft or working-out-of-ideas stage may be discarded or used as a resource for a more polished piece. Initial unedited writing helps students develop fluency and voice in their writing, as they express their ideas first and then pay attention to form.

Koblitz (1995) pointed out that when children use writing throughout the day to explore ideas and express them to others in writing, they gain valuable experience with the sounds and conventions of language. He observed that, unlike the days when spelling instruction was primarily a testing activity, the teaching of spelling is now an all-day activity, integrated into all areas of the curriculum. Research shows that young children who use invented spelling use a greater variety of words in their writing (Gunderson & Shapiro, 1988; Stice & Bertrand, 1990). Clarke (1988) and Stice and Bertrand (1990) also found that first graders who were allowed to use invented spellings typically scored as well or better on standardized tests than children who could use only correct spellings on first drafts. Clarke (1988) also found that young children who used invented spelling seemed to develop word recognition and phonics skills sooner than those not encouraged to spell the sounds they heard in words.

When children write in great quantities and attempt to use all the words they can talk and think with, there will appear to be more nonstandard spelling. As students share their writing or review it on their own, they become increasingly aware of the importance of correct spelling and grammar to communicate their ideas. When they struggle repeatedly to read their own handwriting or find that others are unable to read what they write, students pay greater attention to form and legibility.

Many students create personal spelling dictionaries as part of the reference sections of their writing journals. Words that are used frequently and are regularly misspelled are entered in a special section of their journal. Most students assign a page for each letter of the alphabet, with the exception of less frequently used letters, such as X and Z. These dictionaries are a convenient reference for students and can be used to support individualized spelling programs. In kindergarten and early primary classrooms, words that children want to use for writing may be recorded on charts that are displayed around the room. Many teachers create class chart dictionaries of frequently used words, words that are not phonetic, rhyming words, and those drawn from theme studies, field trips, seasons, and holidays.

The reference section of a writing journal contains information to assist the student writer, such as grammatical constructions, illustrations of figurative language, spelling rules, peer and teacher conference guidelines, and instructions for prewriting, revising, editing, and publishing. Depending on the grade level, this section might also include an outline of paragraph form, formats for process writing, forms for creating graphic organizers, and models for writing for different purposes or in different genres. Other types of entries might include guidelines for note taking, outlining, interviewing, discussion, and the use of reference materials such as dictionaries, the thesaurus, encyclopedias, the computer, and the newspaper. These can be copied from the chalkboard, overhead, or charts following a minilesson, or teachers may distribute printed handouts to be folded and taped into bound journals or punched and inserted into three-ring binder journals.

Students may also use their writing journals to record their ideas, observations, opinions, and experiences with language. Where do they notice different kinds of language being used? Do they hear or see particular parts of speech, figurative or persuasive language, bandwagon lingo, jargon, grammatical errors, mispronunciations, or misspellings in their everyday experiences, on signs, on TV, in newspapers, or on the radio? Examples can be entered in the journal to be shared with the rest of the class. A student in one fifth-grade class found examples of bandwagon speech in a newspaper editorial, and another found a sign that read "Sale on Tee-shirt's," demonstrating the common confusion between possessive and plural forms. Still another noted the irony of seeing crushed cans of crushed pineapple on the grocery shelf.

In addition to their own firsthand experience, students also collect resources for writing from books or materials found in newspapers and magazine articles. Ideas from reading are copied into the resource section and articles, pictures, cartoons, and advertisements are either photocopied or taped in their original form onto individual pages of the journal. Particularly good clippings may be photocopied in quantity for distribution to the class. Many students create a bibliography of books that contain ideas for writing or publishing. Older primary and intermediate students include lists of books about language, such as Heller's (1987, 1988, 1989) colorful, poetic series on parts of speech or interesting examples of alphabet books (Base, 1986; Johnson, 1995; Sandved, 1996). They might also record rhyming words or create data banks of words associated with holidays, seasons, the content areas, or thematic studies. Some students reserve a section of their writing journals to collect words that look or sound interesting to them.

Word books or skills notebooks are frequently used in more traditional classrooms and feature lists of words developed by students to use in their writing. In classrooms that use writing workshops, the function of these word books has been incorporated into the writing journal as a glossary. Devices such as alliteration, idioms, metaphors, similes, personification, and foreshadowing are introduced and practiced in minilessons or as part of a reading or writing workshop. Students make entries in their glossaries by listing a part of speech, grammatical construction, literary device, or type of figurative speech that has been highlighted in the minilesson. Individually or in small groups they search favorite books for words, sentences, or phrases that illustrate the construction they are studying. In this way, these forms become resources for future writing, unlike those presented in workbooks or ditto sheets, where completed pages are either discarded or never referred to again. These word collections help students become aware of the uses of language in their reading or everyday life and build resources for their writing. In many classrooms, this function of the writing journal replaces English textbooks and related workbooks or duplicated material.

SUPPORT FOR DEVELOPMENTAL SPELLING AND HANDWRITING

Most student journals contain a mixture of sloppy and neat handwriting, standard and developmental spelling. Writing journals are not intended to be a repository of polished, reader-oriented essays, but rather a place where the raw materials of thinking and experimenting are recorded. The key questions are: Can the journal writer easily read his or her own notes? If first drafts of writing are submitted to a peer or teacher, is this person able to read it without undue effort?

Emerging Writers—Kindergarten and Early Primary

Kindergarten and first-grade teachers are the most likely to see the widest range of marks that children identify as writing. Sulzby (1992) observed that children display a variety of emergent writing forms on their way to conventional orthography, including scribbling, drawing, nonphonetic letterstrings, and invented spelling. From her extensive study of children's writing, Sulzby concluded that children write with many forms before they write in a manner that both they and another person can read from conventionally. She also pointed out that "the sophistication in children's ideas of composition and the nature of written language is not always reflected in their choice of writing forms" (p. 294).

For this reason, it is helpful to underwrite what a child has written in an emergent form, to emphasize the act of writing as communication to share with others or to reread oneself. Some teachers refer to this underwriting as "reading" writing, so that it can be saved to read later. In response to a class discussion about bears, Dennis drew a picture of a bear and wrote about the picture, using a combination of letters to represent what he wanted to say. In a conference with his teacher (Fig. 6.1) he dictated what he had written and she recorded his words beneath the letters. Sometimes children do not want others writing on their paper, but accept notes written on an opposing page or self-adhesive notes placed in one corner. Other suggestions for supporting developing writers can be found in chapter 4 of this book.

When young children first begin to make writing-like marks, they may scribble, make up-and-down connected lines, or a series of shapes, usually circles. This kind of writing may fill up a page or be used to caption a picture. As letters are learned, they are drawn like pictures and will appear next to a picture as a label. Later, a nonphonetic string (a series of letters that do not make a word) represents the ideas of the writer or describes a picture. Interestingly, long strings may translate into brief remarks, whereas short strings might say a great deal when they are interpreted to a listener. This may happen when children see letters as part of their drawing and not remarks about the drawing. The important thing about this translating activity is that children observe that their talk can be changed into writing and that their writing can be read by others.

Children generally draw capital letters first, perhaps because these are the ones that are modeled for them by adults. As instruction in the formation of lower case letters progresses (or children observe the writing of older friends and siblings), these will be mixed in with the capitals. At all stages of development, letters may be reversed and there may be a mixture of letters and numbers. Many students also incorporate their names into these strings or other words they have learned to write.

Favorite words or phrases are practiced frequently and words that may have been originally underwritten by the teacher are adopted by the student and used to label pictures or write new sentences. As students begin to create words from sounds they can hear, they

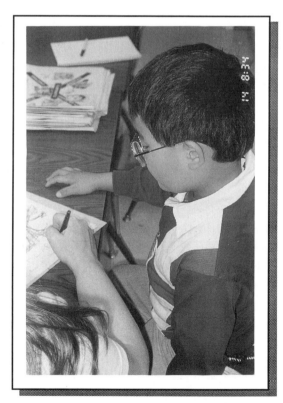

FIG. 6.1. Mrs. Loehring underwrites Dennis' developmental writing.

will write an initial letter to stand for the word, then several letter sounds they can identify, mixing them with words they have copied or already know how to spell. Eventually all words are written out in a mixture of developmental and standard spelling and handwriting.

As children struggle to express themselves in terms that others can understand, they may revert to simple descriptive sentences that lack the sparkle of their dictated writing. Kindergarten teachers experimenting with journals for the first time frequently report feeling discouraged at their students' initial writing efforts. But with time, experience, encouragement, and developing muscle strength, most regain their unique voices and are able to express their ideas as fluently and interestingly in standard writing as they previously did through talking or drawing. To assist this emerging skill, teachers often encourage students to create lists of words they use frequently in their own personal spelling dictionaries, which may be contained in a separate journal or written on the inside cover of individual theme journals. In some classrooms, words that individual students want to learn to spell comprise their own individual spelling programs, whereas in others, these lists complement a standard list mastered by everyone in the class.

If teachers create folded newsprint journals for kindergarten students and developing learners, these should include both lined and unlined paper to provide students with the option that is personally most helpful to them. Some students find that lined paper provides the necessary structure for them to draw letters, whereas others find it overwhelming to create a letter's shape and also get it to perch on a line or between two lines. In many classrooms, teachers construct journals from paper that is lined only on the bottom, which leaves the top free for drawing pictures. These pages are stapled together inside construction paper covers that are decorated by the student.

Developmental Writers—Late Primary and Above

Models for the appearance and construction of letters are provided to students throughout the elementary grades to help them develop their writing in a manner that will help them communicate effectively with others. In addition to the manuscript or cursive letter displays that line most classrooms, students may also keep a copy of model letters in the reference section or inside cover of their journals. In kindergarten, primary, and early intermediate grades, time may be reserved each day for students to practice manuscript or cursive writing, or handwriting may be practiced in the context of expressing ideas about a theme study. In either case, when students record these efforts in their journals, they create a history of their writing that allows them (and the teacher) to observe their own progress and evaluate their best work.

It is helpful for students above third grade to be able to write legibly in both manuscript and cursive styles. In some classrooms, students practice spelling words in both styles. As a general rule, cursive writing allows students to record ideas more quickly, whereas manuscript is preferable for artistic work and labeling drawings, maps, diagrams, and graphs. For some students, however, writing in both styles may not be a possibility. A small proportion of students may continue to experience difficulties with the mechanics of handwriting at the intermediate and middle school levels. If teachers notice that a student's manuscript writing is consistently more readable than their cursive writing, they may encourage them to make their entries in manuscript. If difficulties are severe and the technology is available, students may create their entries on a word processor and keep the printouts in a three-ring binder or tape them into a spiral notebook. As noted in chapter 2, more serious writing disabilities may require dictation or the use of computer technology to assist written expression.

JOURNALS, WRITING WORKSHOPS, AND PEER CONFERENCES

Writing workshops provide students with extended blocks of time to write, edit, and prepare to share their work in more polished form. Teachers might begin writing workshops with a minilesson on grammatical use or writing in a specific genre and then provide time for students to practice the information or skill that has been introduced. Minilesson presentations may: (a) address difficulties the teacher has observed in students' writing, (b) describe techniques for writing, or (c) introduce the elements of writing in a particular genre. At the kindergarten and early primary levels, workshops often follow presentations related to a theme, observations of scientific phenomena, play with math manipulatives, a classroom visitor, a field trip, or books read aloud.

In some classrooms, reader's and writer's workshops are combined, and students use the literature they are studying as models for creating works of their own. In other classrooms, students use their journals to brainstorm ideas for writing in a variety of formats, such as newspapers, magazines, letters, brochures, posters, advertisements, and books with special themes, such as books of advice, cookbooks, and informational books of all types. In still others, students follow their own interests in writing and create a variety of pieces that meet specific criteria.

The writer's workshop also provides a time for individual students to share completed work or works in progress. Typically, they sit in a special place, called the *author's chair,* to read their writing aloud. Other students are encouraged to respond to the writing with positive comments and suggestions, which have been modeled by the teacher. It is important to encourage students to comment on each other's writing in terms of what they liked (*"I liked* the way you showed how Lincoln had a sense of humor") rather than to comment negatively about the fact that the piece is too brief or does not include enough information. Constructive advice that addresses problems with a piece, such as too little information, can be offered by asking questions, such as "Could you tell me more about Lincoln's life in Springfield?" "What are you going to include to show how Lincoln felt about the war?" or "I wish you'd tell more about the part when he visited the battlefront during the Civil War." At the kindergarten and early primary levels, teachers model prompts such as "Tell us about your picture," "Tell us about what you've written," or "Can you tell us anything more about your picture (story, event)?"

Teachers also model ways to respond to another's writing with comments that reflect how a piece of writing affects them as a listener or reader. These kinds of statements might include comments such as "You really had me scared, with that scene in the vacant building," or "I can't wait until you finish the next chapter!" Questions such as "Tell me more about how you get the saddle on the horse," or "I'm not sure I understand her writing, talk about it in response to the questions, and then move on to revise or extend the original piece.

The writer's workshop may also involve *peer conferences,* where students meet together in pairs or small groups to talk about problems with their writing, ask for suggestions, or try out their first drafts on a listener. They read their work aloud to each other and ask questions such as: How could I make this introduction more interesting? Do you think I have enough description of the tepee? Where do you think I should put this stuff about the ghosts? Writing journals provide a good place to record comments, suggestions, and ideas that occur during these conferences. These can be recorded on set-aside editing pages, between the lines of double-spaced copy, or on opposing pages of double entry journals. Entries are then available for review at a later time for consideration by the writer. In some classrooms, journal buddies read silently from each other's journals and respond to what they read in the margins of the journal, on an editing page, or the blank page opposite the text in double entry journals.

Writing workshops provide a good context for students to develop familiarity with ways to think about their writing, organize their ideas, and identify patterns and relationships as they emerge. For example, in one fifth-grade class, students constructed story maps and wrote character descriptions to assist the development of stories. Erin created a chart to build ideas for her story, *Annamarie, the Friend Thief,* an adventure about a young girl detective. She recorded the characters' names, what they wanted, hindrances to what they wanted, and how she planned to resolve their dilemmas. She also created a character profile by analyzing the main character, Lucy, in terms of education; ethnic, religious, social, and economic background; residence; hobbies; special interests; appearance; personality; hopes; and philosophy of life. As mentioned in chapter 3, these ways of thinking about writing and organizing ideas are more likely to be used by students when they have observed their value in class demonstrations and have participated in their construction in a cooperative setting.

In an extension of the author's chair, students at Captain School in Clayton, Missouri, display their writing on tables in the cafeteria in an activity known as The Buffet Table. They take turns reading each other's writing and make brief comments in response. Students wrote to Nick about his autobiography:

- "It must have been cool in England."
- "I didn't know you lived in England for a year. That must have been fun!"
- "Your baby picture and your picture in a Three Musketeers suit are so cute!"
- "Your time line is great. Why did your dog die?
- "How did you break your leg in Colorado?"
- "I think this is really good and I can tell that you put a lot of time in this."
- "You have a lot of details."
- "Dear Nick, I did the same thing. I went through the mist at Niagara Falls too."
- "Was England fun? I went there when I was 7. I loved it! Good time line."

Nick's teacher wrote: "Dear Nick, Your baby picture is darling, you look so peaceful. It is also impressive that your first word was 'gently.' I was sad to read that your dog, Jessie, died. I'm happy that you are getting another dog today, because you seem excited." The comments are positive and reflect questions or personal connections that readers have made with his writing. This is a popular activity with students and one that helps build confidence in young writers.

Individual writing in learning journals supports all elements of the writer's workshop. When students have recorded their thoughts, practiced working with ideas, and collected resources for their writing, they have something to share with others. When they exchange buddy journals, read their writing aloud in peer conferences, or present their work from the author's chair during writing workshop, students gain information from the responses of others that will help them develop their skills as a writer. Over a period of time, students delight in each other's unique perspectives and writing styles and help each other develop a sense of voice and audience. As ideas are shared in small groups, students often gain inspiration and direction for their own writing. They also learn how their writing affects others and what is required to communicate clearly and effectively.

JOURNALS AND INDIVIDUAL WRITING CONFERENCES

It is important for teachers to spend some time briefly with each student to talk about their writing. Writing for many kindergarten and early primary children may involve captioned pictures and developmental writing. Some encouraging prompts for discussion include:

- Tell me about what you've drawn (written) here.
- What else did you see (hear, think about)?
- Is there anything else you would like to write? (Fig. 6.2)
- What would you write about this new thing?
- Would you like to write some more about this?
- Who (what else) is in this picture? Would you like to write their names?
- Is there anything else you'd like to put in your story?
- Is there anything you'd like me to write down for you?
- Where would you like me to write it?
- Would you like me to print what you've written in reading words?

At the intermediate and middle school levels, Atwell (1987) suggested that teachers go to the students' desks, make eye contact, and ask a question about their writing. A good lead is "How is it going?" or "Tell me about this piece." When problems are presented, ask "How do you plan to work this out?" encouraging stu-

FIG. 6.2. Bailey thinks of something new to add to her story.

dents to solve their problems on their own. A good closure question is "What are you going to do next?" or "What are your plans for the rest of the session?" It is helpful to make brief notes about recurring difficulties and use these as a basis for minilessons or more extended individual conferences.

For specific problems with writing, Atwell suggested questions that will help direct the writer's attention in a productive manner. For example, when a piece is unfocused, the teacher can ask students what they are trying to say, or to identify their favorite part and tell how they might build on it. If there is not enough information about the topic, students might be asked what else they know about the topic, or where they could find out more about it. When teachers respond in writing to journal entries, it is important to respond in ways that (a) build on what the author has achieved, rather than on what has not been accomplished; (b) indicate how the writing affected the listener and avoid judgments and generalized statements such as "good" or "very good"; and (c) reflect a desire to understand what the writer is attempting to communicate.

Some entries are a mixture of organized notes and evaluative comments. During a workshop on poetry, two students neatly recorded a class discussion on the characteristics of poetry, but when asked to write how they felt about writing poetry, one responded, "I really like to read good poetry but I don't like to write it because it seems so hard. If it is easy than [sic] I think that I might write it." The other wrote: "I like to read it, but I don't like to write it. I have a mental block that it has to rhyme. I'm not very good at it, and I just plain don't like it." These are valuable responses for the teacher, who now knows that although the students have recorded notes that will eventually provide good reference to them for writing poetry, they will require some success experiences to help them respect their potential as poets. (See chapter 3 for ideas to help students experiment with poetic expression.)

CREATING RESOURCES
FOR WRITING

Writing in learning journals is intended to be exploratory. Although the double entry format may provide some organization, it can be expected that journals will be somewhat messy. Students record their thoughts and responses using developmental spelling, the grammar of everyday language, personal abbreviations and less than tidy handwriting. However, this informal collection of thoughts, information and insight is the raw material of more finished writing (Fig. 6.3). Once an idea is recorded, it becomes a resource of many possible uses. Stu-

FIG. 6.3. Claire reviews the rough copy of her historical fiction diary.

dents return to their thoughts, to expand, change, or dismiss them, in light of a particular project. A particularly well-described scene might encourage a poetic response from a young writer, or an interestingly drawn character sketch may support or stimulate an idea for a short story.

Most students create a table of contents to help them keep track of their writing, but some also code individual pages for future reference. One student created a page index for his journal by recording the topics of his writing in one corner of the left-hand pages of his journal. For example, one right-hand page contained a short description of his grandfather, a few lines of poetry about music and an idea for a report on the Aztecs. In the upper left-hand corner he wrote: "grandpa, music poem, Aztecs." This key word index helped him quickly identify ideas for longer works when he reviewed his writing journal.

In the resource and reference sections of a writing journal, students may have lists of words related to a theme and examples of figurative language they have found to be interesting. These words and phrases can provide ideas for poetry and descriptive passages in stories. Data banks, maps, and graphic organizers represent ideas that have been worked out more fully and can be translated into reports, essays, or presentations for a group. It is helpful for students to periodically review the entries in their writing journals, to remind themselves of projects they have begun and ideas they have recorded in an informal way. Teachers should encourage their students to record their incomplete thoughts so that they will not be lost for some future consideration. This encourages students to value their ideas and to see their experience as a reservoir for creative response.

CHILDREN AS WRITERS IN LITERATURE

Books that depict children as writers provide models for a student's own writing and often supply inspiration for students to begin recording their own experiences. The theme of children writers occurs in all the genres, including picture books, historical fiction, realistic fiction, fantasy, biography, autobiography, and informational literature. Letter writing is used as a narrative device in *Beethoven Lives Upstairs* (Nichol, 1994), a fictional description seen through the eyes of a young boy whose mother rents the upstairs of their home to the great composer. *Letters From Rifka* (1993) by Karen Hesse chronicles the perilous trip of a young Russian immigrant girl to America in the early part of the century through notes written in the end notes and margins of a book of poetry. *Dear Mr. Henshaw* (Cleary, 1983) is a collection of letters written by a young boy who is trying to deal with his parents' divorce.

Diaries are featured in *A Gathering of Days: A New England Girl's Journal* (1979) by Joan Blos and the eyewitness account of the Holocaust in *Anne Frank: The Diary of a Young Girl* (Frank, 1961). Photographs of her family and pages from her diary add authenticity to *Zlata's Diary: A Child's Life in Sarajevo* (Filipovic, 1994), a touching account of the Bosnian conflict, seen through the eyes of a young girl. Birdie's diary in *Catherine, Called Birdie* (Cushman, 1994) chronicles the life of a young girl in the Middle Ages and Avi uses a diary to tell the story of a young girl who is kept captive aboard a ship in *The True Confessions of Charlotte Doyle* (1992). Avi also uses a boy's diary, a teacher's letters, and administrative memoranda to describe the injustices wrought to innocent persons in *Nothing But the Truth* (1991). Jean Little's (1986) *Hey World, Here I Am!* chronicles the joys and sorrows of growing up through the journal entries of a contemporary young teen.

Three Days on a River in a Red Canoe (1981) by Vera Williams is a good example of a journal that includes a variety of record and response entries, as is her *Stringbean's Trip to the Shining Sea* (1988), which is told on a series of postcards written home by the travelers. The journey of Columbus is compellingly portrayed in a fictional cabin boy's journal in *Pedro's Journal: A Voyage with Christopher Columbus, August 3, 1492–February 14, 1493* (Conrad, 1991) and the odyssey of a young boy who runs away to live in the woods is interestingly recorded and illustrated in Jean George's *My Side of the Mountain* (1988). James Gurney's *Dinotopia* books (1992, 1995) are full of drawings, memorabilia, maps, charts, and diagrams that chronicle a father and son expedition on a lost island where dinosaurs and humans live productively together. Harriet the Spy (1964) by Louise Fitzhugh details the problems a young girl faces when a journal she is writing is discovered by persons she has unflatteringly depicted on its pages.

EXAMPLES OF ENTRIES IN WRITING JOURNALS

Figures 6.4 through 6.12 illustrate the types of entries found in student writing journals throughout the elementary grades.

FIG. 6.4. At the beginning of kindergarten, Amy uses a letter-string to write about picture of a swing set.

FIG. 6.5. A month later, Amy uses developmental spelling to draw a picture in response to reading Donald Crew's Freight Train.

FIG. 6.6. In December, Amy is writing sentences with a mixture of standard and developmental spelling.

FIG. 6.7. By the end of kindergarten, Amy is recording her own stories.

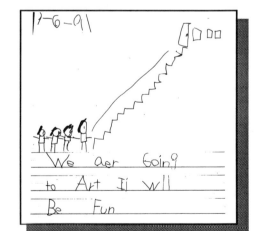

FIG. 6.8. Brandon anticipates a visit to art class (first grade).

berry berries
fairies
strawberries
cherries
babies
bodies
worries
panties
pennies
marries
canaries
blueberries
burles
bunnies
flies
stories
cities
pennies
funnies
hurries

FIG. 6.9. Jackie creates a list of plural words to use in writing (second grade).

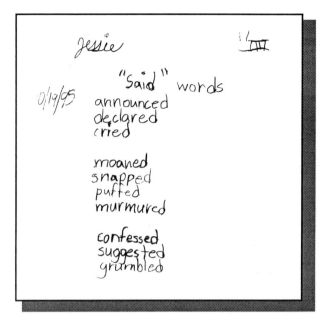

Jessie

0/19/95

"Said" words
announced
declared
cried

moaned
snapped
puffed
murmured

confessed
suggested
grumbled

FIG. 6.10. Jessie makes a list of words to use instead of "said" (third grade).

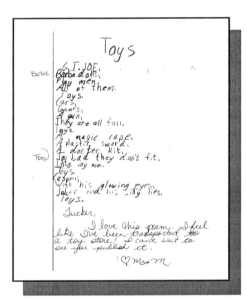

Toys

Barbie G.I. JOE,
Barbie dolls,
Play men.
All of them.
Toys.
Cars,
games,
guns,
they are all fun.
Toys.
A magic cape,
A plastic sword,
A docter kit,
Too bad they don't fit,
Into my room.
Toys,
Caspen
with his glowing eyes,
Joker and his silly lies.
Toys.

Tucker,
I love this poem, I feel
like I've been transported
a toy store! I can't wait to
see you publish it.
♡ mrs M.

FIG. 6.11. Tucker creates a poem about a toy store (fourth grade).

I WANT TO GO HOME TO ......

I just can't do it! I can't bear the idea of going to an American school. I don't even know one word of English. What if the kids at school laugh at me? What if they tease me like the way Chen Gao teased me back in China? I just wish I could be in my old school back in China. How I long to be there! What with my best pals, the language I was born to speak (Chinese) , and the fun activities like art and music. I bet in this new school there aren't any subjects. You probably just sit in a desk and listen to the teacher, and I wouldn't know what she was saying and nobody will translate for me and .... Suddenly my Mom interrupted my thoughts.

" Chen Lu, why aren't you eating your breakfast? You need a good breakfast to start your new and exciting day!" I started moaning.

" But Mom, I'm worried. What if the kids don't like me?" My Mom gave one of those looks that meant: stop moaning, it'll be alright. I settled down, but I still had that feeling that I wasn't going to be alright. Inside my stomach I could already feel a knot forming bigger, bigger, and bigger until suddenly it will explode and burst me into millions of pieces.

" Now here's your lunch. Have a good day!" I waved back trying to put a smile my face and convicing myself that I would have a good day like Mom had said. since I was walking to scnool ,I tried to seek out things that I could remember, so I wouldn't get lost on my way home. My dad had driven me to school on Saturday, but I still wanted to be sure of my route. I was walking by myself because my Dad had to go to work right away and my Mom had to stay home and unpack the boxes that were left. Anyway she told me that this was a big opportunity to walk by myself since there weren't a lot of people in this thes new country. In China you couldn't walk by yourself without getting kidnapped. The kidnapped part was just a thing Mom made up to cheer me. I saw a bush of roses in a big yard leading to a big tall white house. That, I thought would be a great target. By now I could see my new school, a two story brick school. It wasn,t ugly though. It looked well built and it was big compared to my old school. I was standing by the door now, Will I thought here I go. I was greeted by a warm gust of air extending to an empty hall. There was a clock on top of a door that had strange symbols printed on a nameplate. I could only understand the clock. It read 8:30. I wasn't late, so why weren't there any people around? A lady came out of the door with the clock above it. The lady looked at me. I recognized her from when my dad had registered me.

" Oh!" she said, " You must be Chen Lu. You're a little early." Then seeming that I didn't understand what she said, except for my name, she

FIG. 6.12. Wendy writes realistic fiction that is semiautobiographical (fifth grade).

7

Exploring Mathematics With Learning Journals

Finding, describing and understanding patterns is central not only to math, but to the human experience itself. It is through this process of identifying interconnections and regularity that we make sense and meaning of our lives. Our understanding of a natural occurrence, such as the weather we experience, is based upon the identification of the patterns we observe and then put into some meaningful and useful form. The same is true of other life occurrences such as human relationships, reading, and mathematics.

—Richard McCallum and Robert Whitlow (1994, p. 3)

PREVIEW

1. How do learning journals support the study of mathematics?
2. What are the theoretical foundations of math journals?
3. How are math journals constructed?
4. What kinds of guidelines are helpful for individual or group study?
5. How are math journals used at different levels of instruction?
6. How are journals used to evaluate mathematical learning?

BRIEFLY: Learning journals help students explore mathematics in terms of their own experiences and current skill levels, make meaningful connections with other mathematical ideas, and share their discoveries in problem-solving groups.

USING JOURNALS TO EXPLORE MATHEMATICS

Mathematics is a specialized language used by mathematicians, scientists, engineers, and space explorers. It is also a language we use every day to measure time and other things that are important to us. We use the language of mathematics to reason with and to describe objects, solve problems, and make decisions. The study of mathematics permits us to observe and explore the world in a manner distinct from other disciplines. Mathematical learning journals encourage and support this specialized way of seeing and analyzing experience. They also provide opportunities for students to use and develop skills of thinking, reading, writing, speaking, and listening as they record, respond to, and reflect on mathematical experiences.

Students use math journals to record their experience with mathematics, both inside and outside of the classroom. Outside of class, students look for instances and occasions that illustrate mathematical concepts, applications of mathematics, and mathematical reasoning. In class, they record their experiences with problem solving, make connections among concepts, and share strategies with others in pairs or small group settings. A mathematical learning journal creates a history of skill development that can be used to demonstrate achievement to the learner and progress to the teacher.

For students who are apprehensive about math, the opportunity to work in cooperative groups to solve problems and to use a variety of individual ways to explore mathematical concepts provides the type of support that eases math anxiety and gives students a sense that they can master mathematics. Using journals individually and in small groups helps students figure out complex ideas in their own terms, using tallies, pictures, graphic organizers, and writing to increase their understanding (Fig. 7.1). As they work in small groups, students have

FIG. 7.1. Haley uses tally marks to figure out how many animals accompanied Rooster in Eric Carle's (1987) Rooster's Off to See the World.

additional opportunities to rehearse key ideas, compare procedures, learn new strategies, make new relationships, refine their ideas by explaining them, and receive support and encouragement from other members.

Math journals can also be excellent reference tools, providing students with resources for solving new problems and creating a history of their learning that enables them to observe their own progress. Math journals typically include several of the following features:

- A *record* of the student's problem solving and experiences with ideas, observations, predictions, and hypotheses about math; notes and strategies from individual and group problem-solving sessions.
- *Personal evaluative* responses to mathematical experiences that include notes on difficulties with concepts and comments about what students like or dislike.
- *Connections* between new mathematical ideas and the student's own experience, between new concepts and those that are familiar, and between topics in mathematics and other areas of the curriculum.
- *Questions* that occur during reading, hands-on work, or problem solving.

- *Transformations* of understanding that might include drawings, tallies, webs, graphs, charts, maps, time lines, and diagrams that help students organize, interpret, or practice mathematical concepts.

Students may also keep a *resource and reference section* in their math journals that includes:

- *Resources* for thinking, writing, and problem solving, such as pictures and articles from newspapers and magazines, quotes, cartoons, billboard signs, sports statistics, and advertisements.
- *Reference* materials that may include a glossary of new or difficult terminology; lists of math-related books for reading or sharing; algorithms; procedures for group problem solving; and measurement guides, geometrical figures, conversion charts, and mathematical formulas.

THEORETICAL FOUNDATIONS
FOR USING MATH JOURNALS

Current thinking about mathematical learning stresses the importance of grounding understanding of mathematics in real experiences, with an emphasis on helping students develop a view of math as a functional tool for describing, explaining, and exploring real-life experiences. The National Council of Teachers of Mathematics (NCTM) has established standards for the teaching of mathematics that urge an increased emphasis on understanding the operations of mathematics and the use of thinking and problem-solving strategies.

According to NCTM standards, teachers should provide opportunities for students to ask questions, connect mathematical concepts with everyday experiences, look for patterns and relationships among mathematical ideas, discuss and solve problems in cooperative groups, and integrate mathematical learning with other areas of the curriculum. Learning journal activities address each of these standards, with provisions for students to work together in cooperative groups, develop learning strategies, ask questions, interpret their learning in a variety of ways, and make connections between mathematics, their personal experience, and other areas of knowledge.

Elementary teachers interviewed for a math-themed *Curriculum Update* (Willis & Checkley, 1996) observed that when their students write about mathematical problems, they are more able to find out what children are thinking as they problem solve and why they misunderstand concepts. They also noted the importance of being patient as students learn to express their understanding in words or pictures. Initial efforts may falter, but with experience and modeling by the teacher and other students, all children come to see writing as a process that helps them better understand mathematical ideas. Students are also better able to communicate their understanding to the teacher. One teacher observed that when she reads student journals, she may see several different ways of solving a problem that can be shared with the class. She also noticed that "students will write things they wouldn't say out loud—that they feel frustrated, for instance, or are not 'called on' often enough. Thanks to the journals, 'no child is invisible'" (p. 7).

Journal activities support the various learning strengths that students bring to mathematics. Using the categories of multiple intelligences developed by Gardner (Armstrong, 1994), learning journals encourage students to express their understanding of mathematical concepts by providing opportunities to:

- Draw—Visual/spatial.
- Write—Verbal/linguistic.
- Create poetry—Musical/rhythmical.
- Measure—Bodily/kinesthetic.
- Reflect on ideas and make personal connections—Intrapersonal.
- Compute and solve problems—Logical/mathematical.
- Talk about mathematical concepts in small cooperative groups—Interpersonal.

Vacca and Vacca (1993) saw journal writing as an effective method of teaching mathematics because it encourages students to make concepts meaningful for themselves, and later to communicate this understanding to others. Evans (1984) observed better retention of information when students had worked with it in a journal entry. Stix (1992) found the multimodal process of using pictures, words, and numbers helped students use a variety of ways to understand concepts and reduced their math anxiety.

Learning journals also build on the idea of the developmental learner. Mary Baratta-Lorton, a pioneer in developing successful mathematics learning activities for young children, created a program based on developmental stages. This program for primary children, called *Mathematics Their Way* (M. Baratta-Lorton, 1994) and its intermediate counterpart, *Mathematics, A Way of Thinking* (R. Baratta-Lorton, 1994), emphasize the building of conceptual understanding with number experiences. Beginning with the experiential or concept stage, students count and sort familiar objects, developing one-to-one correspondence and a sense of number or process. Manipulative play continues into the connecting stage, where students begin to use picture representations of real objects and may use process signs and numerals in connection with their talk and drawing about mathematical experiences. In the symbolic stage, students use numerals and signs to represent quantities and processes.

Recording and talking about mathematical experiences is a key component of Baratta-Lorton's developmental approach, as it is with math journals. Developmental learners are encouraged to draw pictures or tallies to work with number concepts and to express their understanding. Students talk to each other about what they are learning, share ideas, and work together to solve problems. Mathematical understanding is regarded as developmental and mathematical concepts are pictured in terms of everyday experiences that involve time, comparisons, and measurement.

Students of all ages benefit from working and talking together about mathematical concepts. When students work in small cooperative groups, they receive assistance and encouragement from each other, but they also acquire other skills. For example, McCallum and Whitlow (1994) observed that "students who can identify a geometric pattern, but who do not have a term to describe that shape can, through discussion and interaction with others, acquire the language of mathematics" (p. 21).

Marilyn Burns, who developed the *Math By All Means Series* (1991–1995) for Grades 2 through 4 and *A Collection of Math Lessons, From Grades 1 Through 3* (Burns & Tank, 1988), *From Grades 3 Through 6* (Burns, 1987), and *From Grades 6 Through 8*

(Burns & Humphreys, 1990), connected language and literature with mathematics in creative and productive ways. Students are encouraged to talk, think, and write about mathematics and share problem-solving tasks. Like *Mathematics Their Way* (M. Baratta-Lorton, 1994), this developmental approach to mathematical learning emphasizes the use of manipulatives and authentic tasks to introduce and build mathematical concepts. Both Burns (1992) and Whitin and Wilde (1992, 1995) saw mathematics as a language for describing the world. They suggested that teachers read aloud from books that involve mathematical concepts and provide additional books that involve mathematical themes for student reading. Suggestions for math-related books to use at the various grade levels are found in a later section of this chapter and in the annotated resources in Appendix A.

Math journals are consonant with and supportive of mathematical programs in most classrooms. They encourage students to explore concepts using a variety of means, work together to solve problems, and keep records of their work and strategies. Journals encourage students of all grade levels to use the language of mathematics to observe and describe their world. The record and response activities of learning journals also provide opportunities for students to respond to math-related literature in creative and productive ways by drawing pictures, making tallies, and creating charts, graphs, or diagrams to work out ideas and communicate their findings to others. Teachers may encourage students to keep lists of math-related books in the reference sections of their journals for their own use and for sharing with others.

CONSTRUCTING A MATH JOURNAL

The record and respond sections of math journals can be set up in both single and double entry style. Work may be entered on consecutive pages or students can create a double entry format by recording problems and their solutions on one side of an open notebook spread and using the opposing page to work problems, evaluate their experience, jot down notes from discussion, and make drawings or other graphics that help them figure out assignments. Some students create sections for recording and response by folding a notebook page in half vertically or by drawing a line in the middle to divide the pages in half horizontally. With this arrangement, problems and solutions are recorded in the top section, or right-hand side of the page, and the lower half, or left-hand side, is used for working out the problems. Some students color code these entries, using different colored pencils for problem solving and solutions.

Assignments may originate with a student text, minilessons, or from assignments created by an individual or group. Students are encouraged to keep a record of their work with new concepts, including difficulties they experienced, strategies they tried and comments about what they felt they understood. They also transform mathematical ideas into drawings, webs, tallies, charts, graphs, maps, or diagrams to assist their understanding or explain ideas to others. If worksheets are used, these are folded in half and taped into hardbacked journals or punched and entered into three-ring binders. Entries in this section might also include questions about the problems, connections with other topics in mathematics or other areas of the curriculum, and examples from everyday life. These entries provide teachers with a quick and fairly comprehensive idea of how the student is thinking about a problem or process and permits a more focused instructional response.

Students may also create a section for reference in the back pages of the math journal. These entries might include a glossary of mathematical terminology and descriptions of computational processes, signs, and symbols. For example, a primary student draws pictures to illustrate the process of division, whereas a fourth grader illustrates the terms *divisor* and *dividend* by creating a problem and labeling its parts. Older students might use both of these methods to help themselves remember how to solve equations or prove a theorem. Students of all ages can use the reference section to record successful strategies for problem solving and list books with mathematical themes. In some classrooms, students keep pencils, calculators, and measuring instruments, such as rulers and protractors, in plastic pockets at the back of their math journals.

GUIDELINES FOR INDIVIDUAL OR GROUP STUDY

Teachers usually provide students with both generic and specific guidelines for writing about their problem solving. A quick response guide might consist of only three questions:

1. What was the problem?
2. What did you try?
3. How did it work?

Responding in writing to these three questions helps students use language that is familiar to them to explore the sometimes more difficult language of mathematics. Teachers may also select questions from more comprehensive guidelines, such as those listed in the following. All can be adapted for use from the primary grades through middle school.

Analyzing the Problem
- Can you draw a picture or map of this problem?
- Would a graph, diagram or table help make sense of this problem?
- What numbers are a part of this problem?
- Underline the numbers in this problem.
- What words tell you what to do with these numbers?

Following the Process
- What process do these words suggest?
- What words will the answer need to tell about?
- What will you do first? Next? Next?
- What steps did you follow in solving this problem?

Using Strategies
- What difficulties did you experience?
- How did you address these difficulties?
- What knowledge did you already have that helped you?

- What questions do you have about this problem?
- What seems to be difficult to understand?

Using Resources
- What does this problem remind you of?
- What else do you know about these numbers or this process?
- Do you know how to solve part of the problem?
- Is there any information in your reference section that might help?
- Can anyone help you answer these questions? (For later reference)

Evaluating the Process
- Describe what you did.
- How did you figure out this problem?
- What difficulties did you experience with this task?
- How did you handle these difficulties?
- What resources helped you solve this problem?
- Did anyone give you helpful ideas?
- What did they say or do to help you?
- What do you understand now that you did not understand before?
- How did writing or drawing help you understand the problem better?
- How did you decide which process to use?
- What did you learn that will help your group next time?

MATH JOURNALS FOR ALL LEVELS OF ELEMENTARY INSTRUCTION

Kindergarten

At the kindergarten level, students use journals to record their experiences with mathematical concepts: (a) in whole class settings, (b) with books, (c) with manipulatives, and (d) outside of class. Teachers encourage students to draw pictures of things they see happening in everyday life that are related to mathematics. Students also draw pictures of objects they count, shapes they see, and computational problems they create with objects. Students might record patterns they see in objects, shapes, or numbers and write number stories as they are able. Many teachers take "pattern walks" where students look for repeated patterns in fences, buildings, sidewalks, and natural plantings.

Students enjoy working together in pairs or small groups to measure, estimate, count, create number stories, and find patterns or shapes. Their findings can be recorded in their individual math journals or entered as joint entries in a continuing journal they keep together as journal buddies. Many teachers encourage math exploration with blocks and toys, and ask students to record their play in some way in their journals. Students draw pictures of their experiences, use tallies, or cut out colorful pictures from magazines to illustrate their work. One kindergartner cut out pictures of his favorite cars to create a counting story. Another drew pictures of sorting experiences with an old key collection, showing how she had classified the keys into groups according to their notches. Still another recorded the movements of fish as they appeared and disappeared into tank sculptures in the class aquarium.

Kindergarten students are also encouraged to draw pictures of real or imaginary events associated with math. One student drew a picture of a house and a very lively engagement between a Tyrannosaurus rex and six Triceratops. He dictated this story problem onto a tape:

> It was exciting when a Triceratops came to my house and then another one. The house was getting bursting full, but there were four more that came, because we were having pizza and it smelled so good. "Help, help," my mother said, "the house is falling down with all these dinosaurs busting the walls." So then a big Tyrannosaurus rex heard my mother and came and ate three of the Triceratops. My mother said this was bad manners and chased him away. Now how many Triceratops were left to eat pizza?

Other children enjoy hearing these stories and solving the problems. The storyteller benefits from this exercise because it requires translating number concepts into another form. Students who are encouraged to observe mathematically will often include numbers as part of pictures drawn to explore themes in the content areas.

Teachers also read aloud from books with mathematical themes, such as *The Very Hungry Caterpillar* (Carle, 1969) or *The Doorbell Rang* (Hutchins, 1986), and they encourage students to draw pictures to demonstrate their understanding or add to the story in creative ways. Many teachers use Marilyn Burns' (1992) *Math and Literature (K–3)* as a resource for lessons to introduce and extend the understanding of mathematical concepts using children's literature. (For a more detailed description of these materials, see the annotated bibliography in Appendix A.)

Primary

Students in Grades 1 through 3 use math journals to assist the transition from concrete to symbolic forms of representation. Problems can be entered in the journal in the form of drawings or tallies and then translated into symbols, or a symbolic problem may be translated into pictures to assist understanding. Students meet in small groups to work on problems, share strategies, explain computational processes to each other, and create examples to help themselves and other group members understand mathematical concepts.

Primary students also enjoy creating narratives to illustrate math concepts. They may begin by drawing pictures in their journals to assist their understanding of a process, and then write a story that involves the process in some way. Or they might initially write a story and draw pictures to illustrate their ideas. Math stories may also emerge spontaneously, as one first grade teacher (Stires, 1993) described:

> One day I wore mouse earrings to school, and Kate, a great animal lover, noticed them at the beginning of math class. She then said, "I found a nest of five baby mice, but three of them died right away, and, even though we fed them with an eye dropper, the other two died a couple of days later." I recorded her story in words, and then we translated it into number sentences with the correct student-identified operation, subtraction. I abandoned my previous plans for the class, as the

students launched into the telling of a plethora of mouse tales, using both addition and subtraction, as well as fact and fiction. I asked the students how we could remember the tales, and they rushed for the papers and pencils to author their story problems. Later they shared a selected problem for the class to solve. (pp. 17–18)

Primary students can usually record instances of math in their everyday environment with notes, sketches, diagrams, and drawings. They are also able to conduct simple surveys and construct graphs to illustrate their findings.

Group work is a popular activity for the upper primary grades. Students enjoy working together in pairs or small groups of three to collect data, measure, estimate, and solve problems; create maps, graphs, or graphic organizers; and share stories, pictures, and strategies for problem solving with each other. One group of first graders recorded the length of their table in books, shoes, and lunch boxes. In a second-grade classroom, students created a graph to summarize data collected during a theme study on Native Americans. Students in a third-grade class met to work on a chart that would help them analyze data about sports statistics. One student demonstrated how she would make the chart, and the others agreed to try her approach. When difficulties arose, they modified the first plan and continued. A boy who spoke little English, pointed out a problem with the chart and showed how he solved it. The others were delighted with this contribution and patted him on the back. The sum of their knowledge about creating charts was then obviously more than the parts they originally brought to the group meeting.

Primary students enjoy listening to math-related books read aloud, such as David Schwartz's *How Much Is a Million?* (1985), Jerry Pallotta's *The Icky Bug Counting Book* (1992), and Malcomb Weiss' *Solomon Grundy, Born on Oneday: A Finite Arithmetic Puzzle* (1977). They find interesting concepts in these books to discuss in small groups or as a class and create extensions to the stories in their journals with drawing and writing. The books and lessons in the Marilyn Burns material are also quite popular with primary students, because they encourage active participation and sharing of ideas within a group. If teachers make them available, students enjoy exploring books with math themes on their own during independent reading. For annotated lists of quality books that involve math concepts, see the description of Whitin's books in the annotated bibliography in Appendix A.

Intermediate Level

Students in the intermediate grades continue to use journals as a place to practice difficult mathematical concepts. They use drawings, charts, graphic organizers, diagrams, and tables to translate mathematical ideas into a form they can best understand. Students at this level also benefit from using manipulatives and figuring out concepts in small study groups. They use their journals to record the work they do with problem solving in these groups and new strategies they may discover as a result of this interaction. Instructions for math-related games provide a reference when game playing is used to teach concepts or practice computation.

Guidelines from the previous section are helpful for intermediate level problem solving. The following format, which is an adaptation of the REACT model, can also be used by students of this age to help them analyze and solve mathematical problems.

1. Write down the problem.
2. What do you already know about this kind of problem that might help you solve it?
3. What is your plan for solving this problem?
4. Make tallies or draw a picture, chart, graph, numberline, or other graphic that might help you better understand the problem.
5. Record your solution.
6. Describe how you arrived at this solution.
7. Evaluate your problem solving. Was it effective? Was the problem difficult or easy?
8. What questions do you still have about this problem?
9. Share your findings with a partner or group. How does your answer compare with theirs? Did you learn something from someone else? Did you teach something to someone?

Many intermediate teachers read books aloud to their students to introduce a concept or enhance understanding of difficult mathematic concepts. Children's literature can often provide the necessary bridge between complex ideas and familiar experience. Math-themed literature may also stimulate students to interpret their experience with mathematics in creative ways. In *The Math Curse* (Scieszka & Smith, 1995), the protagonist experiences an entire day in mathematical terms. This clever and humorous story can be used as a prompt to encourage students to see their own experience in terms of mathematics. Intermediates enjoy the challenge of imagining their own day in a similar manner, recording their efforts in their journals and sharing them with the rest of the class.

Students at both the intermediate and middle school levels are impressed with the power of binomial sequencing when they listen to David Birch's *The King's Chessboard* (1988) with calculators in hand. The book *What Do You Mean by Average?* (James & Barkin, 1978) describes a school election and sparks interest in the concept of mathematical averages. It can also be used to create interest in collecting and analyzing data.

Middle School

Middle school students continue to use learning journals in much the same way that they are used by younger elementary students. Math journals are particularly effective with students at the middle school level because cooperative groups are an established part of the instructional approach. Both the format for problem solving described earlier for intermediates and the more expanded group inquiry discussed in a previous section are effective for this age level. Working with manipulatives and other hands-on approaches to learning are as effective at this level of instruction as they are in the early grades and journals provide a helpful structure for recording these experiences. Writing, drawing, and organizing new ideas and information in individually meaningful ways also assists students in making sense of more abstract concepts at this time of widely differing cognitive development. Because the middle school curriculum is often integrated in some fashion, learning journals encourage students to find patterns and identify relationships between topics and themes in different subject areas.

Hanselman (1996) suggested using brainstorming webs with middle school students to help them collect the ideas they have about a concept and to develop their thinking strategies. For example, she may begin by asking students to tell her what they know about a centimeter. As students remember where they may have seen the term or used it to measure something, the web builds with their responses, such as, "A centimeter is smaller than a meter," "A centimeter is smaller than an inch," and "My little finger is about 1 centimeter wide" (p. 769). As Hanselman pointed out, "The open-endedness of webs allows a teacher to begin with what the students know and use that knowledge to extend their learning" (p. 769). This is particularly helpful with students who experience difficulty with mathematics, because these kinds of learning problems are built on years of misunderstanding and a lack of helpful dialogue. Webs provide remedial students with strategies other than guessing or memorizing.

This kind of brainstorming can begin with individual students recording their ideas in their journals, then adding to them as they brainstorm in small groups. Group ideas are shared with the larger class, to continue the conversation and create the conditions for expanding their understanding further. Graphic organizers of all kinds can also begin as an all-class activity, with individual students adding what they know about a concept and recording this information in their journals.

Because graphic organizers reach out to include relationships among many mathematical concepts, they build on meaning and are not narrowly focused on specific problems. This extended understanding of what a problem means assists students in figuring out new problems, because it allows them to use what they know to figure out what they do not know. If students understand that multiplication is repeated addition, they can use their certain knowledge of one multiplication fact to find another. If they cannot remember the product of 6×4, but remember 6×2, they can add sixes to find the answer.

In addition to the math-themed picture books used at other elementary levels, students at this age enjoy listening to or reading biographies of famous mathematicians, the history of mathematics, and pop math, such as *Zero to Lazy Eight: The Romance of Numbers* (Humez, Humez, & Maguire, 1993), which blends interesting and outlandish trivia with real mathematics. Older students may enjoy excerpts read aloud from *Flatland: A Romance of Many Dimensions* (Abbott, 1884/1992), a satire that describes a two-dimensional world in which the classes of society are various geometrical shapes. Lower class men are isosceles triangles, middle and upper classes are equilateral triangles, nobility are hexagonal, and the priestly class are circles. Women of all classes are straight lines, an interesting social comment from this book written in Victorian times, which is bound to stir discussion. *How to Lie About Statistics* (Huff, 1954), another favorite for this socially conscious age level, reveals how information is often distorted by the ways in which it is collected and presented.

Middle school students enjoy creating their own math-related stories or poems, particularly after they have listened to those with mathematical themes. This writing opportunity often allows students to exhibit their understanding in unexpectedly creative ways. It also helps them express frustration or anxiety about work with mathematics. Martha Eggers of McKendree College provided the following samples of student work from her middle school math methods class that reflect both the joys and challenges of mathematical experience.

> Grandma made me a big apple pie
> And I knew that I ought to share.
> Three big brothers, my dad and I
> Maybe a piece or two to spare.

First I divided it right down the middle
  One half was on each side.
Surely one half was not too little
  So I took out one half to hide.
One half of a pie cut into four
  One-eighth of a pie for each man.
Until I tripped over a toy on the floor
  The four-eighths lay face down in the pan.
I still had half of a pie left for me
  But I couldn't have eaten it all
So I cut it in five pieces equally
  One-tenth of a pie was enough for us all.
           RaLynne

If math were an animal . . .

It would be a vulture in a tree. If you act dead, it will pounce on you and eat you. If you become alive, it will be your friend.

It would be a lion. It looks all soft and cuddly from outside the cage, but once you go inside the cage, it displays the fact that it isn't very nice, after all. Lions can also be tamed and made to do what you want them to do. Math can also be tamed. Once it is, it is your friend for life.

It would be a camel. With math, you store up lots of information, like the camel stores water in its hump. Then you can use this knowledge for a long time.

It would be a dog, because sometimes it's fun to play with, times when you don't understand it, times when you know what to expect and times when you just can't stand it.

It would be a giraffe. Math can take one to great heights, but can also bend down to touch the earth, for a foundation to build.

USING JOURNALS TO EVALUATE MATHEMATICAL UNDERSTANDING

Because students keep a record of their interaction with mathematical concepts in the form of writing, drawing, tallies, and other graphic responses, teachers have a better idea of what they do or do not understand about an idea or process. Recording their questions, comments, connections, pictures, or graphic organizers to interpret a mathematical concept sometimes allows students to communicate their understanding to teachers in ways that are not reflected in symbolic problem solving.

Writing prompts that encourage students to explain concepts, processes, and computation provide the teacher with excellent information on a student's understanding, and help children organize what they have learned into general principles and specific examples. Questions designed to help teachers evaluate understanding might include:

- Describe this process in words (Without using numbers, explain 2/3).
- Draw a picture of this concept (What does 2/3 look like?).
- What does this concept, process, or computation mean (What is a fraction?)?

It is helpful for students to write what they know about a concept or process at the beginning of a unit. This allows teachers to determine a student's present level of understanding and direct their instruction more precisely. During the work sessions, when attention is not required for particular problems, most teachers walk around the room, making over-the-shoulder observations of student's problem-solving and response efforts. Whether students work individually or in small groups, teachers may ask them to submit end-of-session notes or summaries of their work. These summaries will generally include the student's perception of what has been learned, along with questions, comments, and personal concerns about the session. Small groups may file individual work sheets and team problem-solving papers in a file folder, which can be collected and reviewed on a daily basis by the teacher. This information helps teachers assess the progress of individual students and the learning dynamics of particular groups, which provides information to direct further instruction.

EXAMPLES OF ENTRIES IN MATHEMATICAL LEARNING JOURNALS

Figures 7.2 through 7.11 are examples of entries students make in learning journals used to explore mathematics.

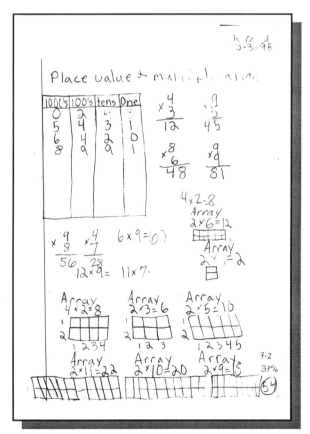

FIG. 7.2. Kimya's notes and graphics for place value and multiplication.

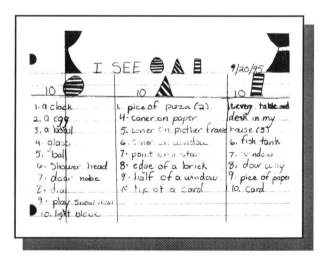

FIG. 7.3. Nora identifies objects at home with geometrical shapes.

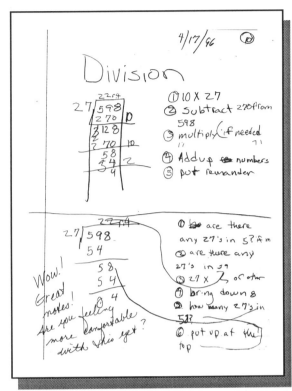

FIG. 7.4. Leah describes how to divide two different ways.

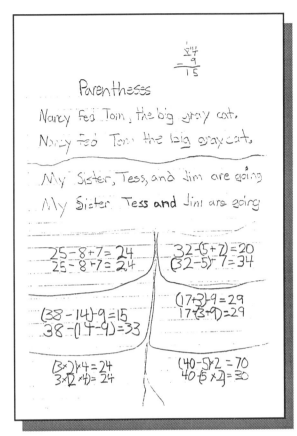

FIG. 7.5. Jessie compares the functions of commas and parentheses.

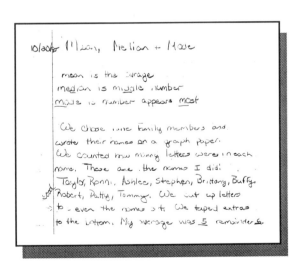

FIG. 7.6. Robert describes a group activity using mean, median, and mode.

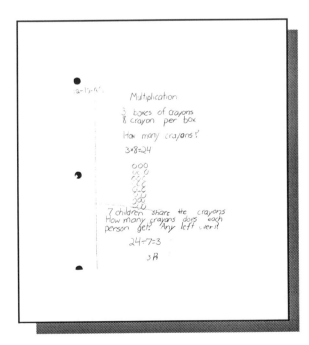

FIG. 7.7. Claire creates two problems and solves them.

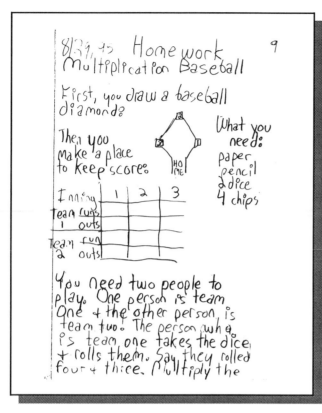

8/29/95 Homework
Multiplication Baseball   9

First, you draw a baseball diamond?

Then you make a place to keep score?

What you need:
paper
pencil
2 dice
4 chips

Inning	1	2	3
Team runs 1 outs			
Team run 2 outs			

You need two people to play. One person is team One & the other person is team two. The person who is team one takes the dice & rolls them. Say they rolled four & three. Multiply the

FIG. 7.8. Marina's notes on the rules for playing multiplication baseball.

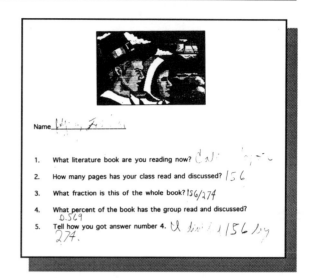

Name _____

1. What literature book are you reading now? _____
2. How many pages has your class read and discussed? 156
3. What fraction is this of the whole book? 156/274
4. What percent of the book has the group read and discussed? 0.569
5. Tell how you got answer number 4. I divided 156 by 274.

FIG. 7.9. Jeffery's warm-up exercise creates a math problem from literature study.

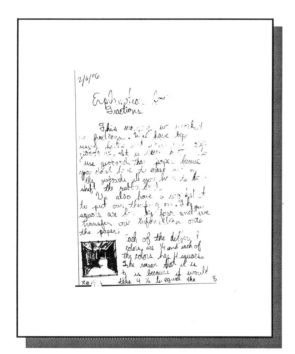

FIG. 7.10. Brandon describes the use of geoboards to understand fractions.

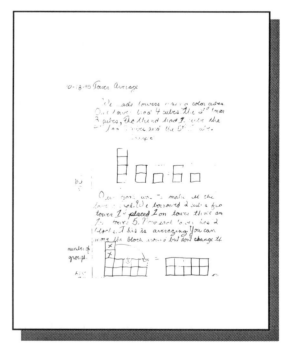

FIG. 7.11. Alexandra described an averaging exercise in words and pictures.

8

Exploring Science With Learning Journals

I have learned that the questions children ask often reflect a very deep effort to understand their world, and that their ability to form theories about difficult questions far surpasses my expectations. Through the medium of science talks and science journals, I have seen children develop ways to make their thinking visible in narrative. In doing so, they were more able to clarify what they knew and created an expanded readiness for new information and new insights.

—Karen Gallas (1994, p. 77)

PREVIEW

1. How do journals help students explore ideas in science?
2. What are the benefits of exploratory talk and "speaking science"?
3. How do students use the resources of their science journals?
4. How do teachers introduce science journals to their classes?
5. How do kindergarten, early primary, and developmental learners use science journals?
6. How do older primary, intermediate, and middle school students use science journals?
7. How are science journals used to study a theme or topic?
8. What are the benefits of using science journals?

BRIEFLY: Science journals provide students with opportunities to explore their experiences with science and address questions they have about themselves and the natural world.

EXPLORING IDEAS IN SCIENCE WITH JOURNALS

All children try to make sense of the world they live in. From the time they are born, they experiment with their environment, wonder about natural phenomena, and ask many questions. When children are encouraged to record their questions about science and seek answers by observing, thinking, reading, writing, and talking, they learn to value their questions and begin to see science as a meaningful way to explore their experience. Journal activities help students learn how to use the language and processes of science to REACT to information and ideas, by recording what they read and observe, evaluating their experience, asking and answering questions they have about the world, making connections between new ideas and what they already know, and transforming these new ideas into new forms that increase their understanding. These entries create resources for sharing new information with others or create a record of experiences shared together in labs and research.

Recording

Depending on the grade level and individual development, students use science journals to record notes from their reading, observations, lectures, mini lessons, and discussion. The composition of these notes will vary from student to student, depending on the ideas that draw their particular interest and the way they organize what they are learning. For example, when third graders recorded information for a discussion on bison, Jessie drew a picture of the animal and wrote facts about its physical description. Evan recorded interesting facts about the geographical range of bison, and Claire emphasized how it was used for food, clothing, and shelter by Native Americans.

In addition to listing facts and ideas, students also record citations for the sources they consult in trade and reference books. For example, in second grade, Brandon used an entire page to document a source for his research on civets. He listed the *Science Encyclopedia,* volume number, and page for the reference and followed this with information he found at this source: how large the civet is, where it lives, what it eats, its color, type of animal, and habitat. As he progressed through the grades, these citations became more detailed, but information recorded at this level documented his facts and could be shared with others.

Students use their journals to record observations and experiments outside of class. For example, as an outside-of-class assignment, Nick described in his journal how he dug down into the soil layers in his yard and drew pictures of what he found. Students also record reports from field trips, presentations by classroom visitors, descriptions of demonstrations, setups for experiments, experimental results, and predictions or hypotheses related to a topic. These records often indicate the level of enthusiasm a student has for an experience, in addition to the learning that has taken place. For example, after a trip to the arboretum, Teddy, a fifth grader wrote:

> I learned that there are many kinds of specks (molecules) such as air, water and soil that go from one item to another. Like the air specks that I'm breathing right now could have been breathed by Thomas Jefferson or someone else famous. . . . I learned that all the plants munch on the sun for energy, and little animals or insects eat the plants for energy and bigger animals may eat the little animals, and that's how the munch line (food chain) works.

Evaluating

Students react to new information and experiences in their journals by recording what they liked or disliked about the experience and noting things that were difficult to understand or perform. One student expressed frustration with the members of his group, who seemed less than serious as they worked on experiments together. Another student felt that information he needed to complete an assignment had been presented too quickly for him to understand.

Students also record what they believe to be positive about experiences and they indicate enthusiasm about particular learning activities. For example, Nick liked to learn from firsthand experience, which is evident from the entries he typically made in his science journal:

> I think that just letting everybody experiment with microscopes was a much better way to get people used to using the microscopes than reading books and directions about how to use them.

> I liked the way the teacher told us about each animal and then showed us the animal, because then we could get a chance to see some of the adaptations he had told us about.

Information from these evaluative entries helps teachers identify interests, learning preferences, difficulties, and concerns. They also provide clues to teachers about the quality of individual learning experiences with field trips, group study, video presentations, and guest speakers. Student evaluations of their experiences create resources for discussions to fill in the inevitable gaps that occur as a result of individual differences in student background knowledge and the quality of presentations.

Asking Questions

As students read, observe, listen, discuss, and experiment, they ask questions about what they are experiencing. These questions can be brought back to small or large group discussions or become the focus of individual research. A primary student reading about whales asked:

- Do whale babies nurse near the surface or deep under water?
- How big is the whale baby when it's born?
- Do whales swim different places at different seasons?

Some of these questions became the focus of her individual research and one became the focus of a shared inquiry within her small group.

Connecting

As students are presented with new concepts, they try to connect these ideas with others they are familiar with, which might include (a) personal experience; (b) information they already know about the topic; or (c) related concepts, processes, or themes in other areas of the curriculum. The third grader who was studying whales (previous section) wrote that she knew what blubber and flensers were from reading Judy Blume's book *Blubber* and that she had heard tapes of whales singing. A fifth grader beginning a study of chemistry tried to connect what she knew about everyday examples of chemical elements, observing that pennies are made of copper, gold is used to make jewelry, tungsten is used in electricity, and helium is used to inflate balloons.

Transforming

Students respond to new information and ideas by translating what they are experiencing in reading, discussion, mini lessons, observations, experiments, and demonstrations into drawings, summaries, diagrams, charts, examples, tables, graphs, semantic maps, poetry, stories, and songs. For example, a student who was researching whales created a perspective on the size of the blue whale by drawing it beside an elephant and a dinosaur. A fourth grader wrote poems to describe the seasons, a second grader created a simple concept web to illustrate the kinds of penguins she was researching, and a sixth grader demonstrated his understanding of the principle of levers by drawing pictures of levers found in his home.

Resources and References

Students may also include a section in their journal for resources and references related to a study. These might include the following topic-related elements: (a) lists of books and magazine articles; (b) lists of words; (c) a glossary of technical terms; (d) a personal dictionary of words used frequently in writing; (e) laboratory procedures; (f) observation and research guidelines; (g) ideas for projects; (h) recording procedures; and (i) materials related to a topic in science, such as articles from newspapers, magazines, and journals, quotes, pictures, photographs, cartoons, or editorials.

EXPLORATORY TALK AND SPEAKING SCIENCE

When students are encouraged to explore questions they have about the world, respond to new information in a personal way, and think about their learning reflectively, they maintain the natural curiosity they have used to figure out the world since they were born. Often, students learn to suppress the questions they have or dismiss them as not valuable. Science journals provide places to record questions and work through them in a way that is personally satisfying and effective.

As students gain experience with writing, drawing, and talking about scientific concepts, they become more confident in themselves as learners. Although inquiry about things scientific will naturally include ideas from other disciplines, the focus on science helps students became increasingly aware of the particular power of scientific inquiry to answer questions they have about their experience.

When students record ideas of significance to them and respond to them in ways that are personally meaningful, they are also creating resources for interacting and sharing with others. Discussions in small groups help students clarify their ideas and work out difficult concepts. Barnes (1976) believed that when students engage in collaborative talk, they are better able to work through complex ideas. These discussions, which are highly informal in nature and use students' everyday language, are an example of *exploratory talk,* in which students interact to examine ideas together. Britton (1990) similarly believed that the use of informal language among peers (which he called *expressive language*) helps students work through new ideas. He suggested that students should use their own language to talk about scientific ideas before they are labeled with technical terms.

Lemke (1990) compared science talk to learning a foreign language and observed that fluency develops when students have to put words together to make sense. This requires practice in *speaking science,* an activity promoted and supported by using science journals, as students shape questions, debate ideas, generalize, hypothesize, and predict, using the terminology of science.

When teachers encourage students to begin the study of a topic by drawing, writing, or talking about what they already know, they are helping students activate their schema for the concepts to be explored. Students become more immediately involved in a study as they relate it to their personal experience and current knowledge. These spoken, written, and drawn representations also assist teachers in identifying misconceptions and provide direction for future instruction.

USING THE RESOURCES OF SCIENCE JOURNALS

Students use the materials collected in science journals in a variety of ways. As individuals, they use their recorded observations to think about their experiences in scientific terms, responding in ways that are personally helpful to them by creating pictures, charts, graphs, diagrams, poetry, or stories. They also use these resources to communicate with others, to share ideas, and to demonstrate their learning.

Projects

In the process of recording and responding to information about a topic, students collect, organize, and transform ideas that can be used as resources for writing reports, creating projects, and planning future research into areas of interest. Glossaries of scientific terminology assist students as they explore new sources of information or write about complex ideas.

Sharing

As students work out their personal understanding of scientific concepts, they also prepare to share what they discover with others. This sharing might include information from personal research, such as resources and references related to a particular study. They will also share ways they have attempted to make sense of complex concepts and use their experience to explain their understanding to others.

Communicating Learning

Journal activities help students evaluate the progress of their learning and communicate this progress to the teacher. In 2-minute conferences or over-the-shoulder observations, teachers examine the ways students are figuring out ideas through their note taking and individual responses to information (Fig. 8.1). They may also periodically collect pages from the journals or schedule individual conferences to assess student understanding more closely. In many classrooms, students use their journals as a resource for writing informational letters to their families about what they have learned during the day or at the end of a week (for more information about this practice, see chapter 2).

FIG. 8.1. Mrs. Murphy checks with fourth graders who are observing and recording the characteristics of various minerals.

INTRODUCING SCIENCE JOURNALS TO STUDENTS

At every level of instruction, it is helpful to provide students with a science journal as a model, preferably one that the teacher has constructed for personal use (teacher's journals are described in chapter 4). Teachers may also ask students from previous years to display their journals and talk about their usefulness. If double entry journals are introduced, it is helpful to use a large mock-up or an overhead projector to demonstrate this split page or opposing page format. This approach permits the teacher to demonstrate how specific kinds of entries are made and allows students to ask questions about this particular way of recording and responding to ideas in science.

Kindergarten and Early Primary

Science journals at the beginning or early primary levels are often general in nature and may be used to record students' thoughts and questions about anything that draws their interest. Teachers may introduce science journals at this level as places to write or dictate stories about things or events that puzzle them. When a specific science theme or topic is studied in class, teachers may ask students to look for related information in their own experience. Journals then become places to draw and write what students see, hear, think, and read about in their everyday experience that is related to the topic being explored. Students may also list the titles of books they have read and draw pictures to record observations, demonstrations, classroom visits, or field trips related to the study. (See the final section of this chapter for using journals in a specific study.)

Later Primary, Intermediate, and Middle School

At the later primary, intermediate, and middle school levels, teachers may provide students with printed guidelines for constructing a science journal, including sample entries. In minilessons, or as part of a science workshop, teachers introduce students to note taking and graphic organizers that help the students work with ideas and build their understanding of complex concepts. Students are encouraged to relate their exploration of topics in science to mathematics or social studies and to look for examples of scientific thinking in fantasy and science fiction. Journals at the intermediate and middle school levels support a wide variety of cooperative group experiences, such as research teams and laboratory sessions. Guidelines for group interaction should be discussed before students meet together, and these should be a part of the reference section of each student's journal. (There is additional discussion of cooperative group activities in chapters 2, 4, and 9 and a description of journaling in a specific topic in the final section of this chapter.)

SCIENCE JOURNALS FOR BEGINNING AND DEVELOPMENTAL LEARNERS

Students at every instructional level use science journals to better understand their experience. They draw and write to interpret new information to themselves and connect it with previous learning. They also practice using new terms and concepts related to a topic in science by talking about them with others. These interpretative and interactive functions of a science learning journal are especially important for beginning readers and writers, who may be better able to convey their understanding of ideas through drawing and discussion.

Gallas (1994) described how first graders use science journals to draw and write about their ideas, make sketches and diagrams of something they have read or seen, and write poems and stories about scientific ideas. She saw journals as places for students to ask questions and try to answer them, to make up stories about something that interests them, to record observations and to "think consecutively about one subject" (p. 81). Gallas underlined the importance of science talks to complement journal writing:

> Where the journal is an individual, introverted activity that prods each child to formulate his or her notion of what important questions and ideas might be, the talk is directed at group or collaborative thinking and requires the child to alter his or her language in order to converse with a group. (p. 83)

Gallas believed that these discussions provide opportunities for children to explain their thinking, revise and modify it with increased information from others, and work toward a better understanding of complex ideas.

Drawing and Talking

Drawing that is followed by discussion helps students refine their ideas and prompts research or observation. When Haley drew the picture at the top of Fig. 8.2, she explained that this was a picture of a ladybug and that it had "lots of legs." After several experiences counting legs in Eric Carle's (1977) *The Grouchy Ladybug,* she discovered that ladybugs have six legs. Listening to Jerry Pallota's (1992) *The Icky Bug Counting Book,* she learned that all insects have six legs. The following day Haley observed an ant on the playground, but could not catch it for a close look. She did see that the ant had three sections, and drew six legs on each section, "because it's an insect and has six legs" (middle drawing in Fig. 8.2). A verbal or written test on insects would not have provided the same information to the teacher about her understanding, because she would have been able to reply correctly to the question: "How many legs does an insect have?" in spite of her misconception.

Later in the week, Haley captured several ants, a ladybug, and a butterfly and observed that six legs were the total for the entire insect. The following week, she drew a ladybug with six legs, more defined spots on the wings, and antennae (bottom drawing in Fig. 8.2). In the process of observing, drawing, talking, and reading about insects, Haley's concept of a ladybug became more complex, as revealed by her drawing. It developed from a generic "bug" to a more well-defined insect, with particular characteristics.

It should be noted that just as the drawing of the insects indicated something about her understanding, discussion can reveal even more and is vital for accurate assessment. For example, in the weeks that followed the anatomically correct ladybug, Haley occasionally drew colorful, many-legged creatures. When asked to talk about her pictures, she explained, "These are pretend insects. You can tell they're pretend, 'cause they've got more than six legs. I draw them that way because they look better with lots of legs."

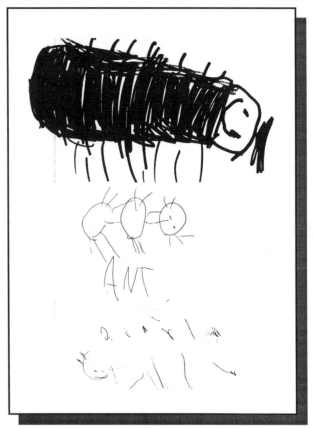

FIG. 8.2. Haley's developing concept of an insect (Pre-K).

Interest and Experience

Individual interests and experience with a topic can also affect interpretation of information. After a study about snakes, Dusty portrayed a confrontation between predator and prey. The snake was drawn long and thin, its tongue flickering and its movement toward the birds depicted by an undulating form. The birds looked down at the snake from the tree, facing off their predator, and "Snakes bite," was the cautionary caption. In contrast, the snakes in Tricia's picture were less fierce in appearance and revealed an interest in the family group: "Mom snakes have tons of babies," she wrote. Indeed, a multitude of intertwined snakes can be seen to the right of the picture and two have crawled over the hill to greet their mother. As the teacher reviewed the pictures drawn from this study with her students, she developed a more comprehensive view of their understanding and interests, and was able to direct reviews and further instruction in a more productive way.

Other Kinds of Entries

What other kinds of entries do beginning readers and writers typically make in science journals? The following is a list compiled from the entries of developmental learners in special education, ESL, kindergarten, and first-grade classrooms:

- Drawings and labeled sketches of observations.
- Pictures cut out from magazines and newspapers to illustrate ideas.
- Stickers of scientific interest and student-written labels.
- Words and sentences related to the topic they are studying.
- Drawing and writing about ideas from discussions.
- Pictures or titles of books the student has read about a topic.
- Original stories that attempt to explain scientific phenomena.
- Poems about science-related experiences.
- Questions about things that interest or puzzle them.

Most of the entries in these journals are made by the students themselves, although some may be dictated to other students, an aide, a parent helper, or the teacher. In a number of journals there are transcripts of tapes dictated by students and computer printouts of material entered by a journal buddy. Beginning writers may want to create a "stepping story" by drawing pictures of ideas, experiments, and observations and describing them on tape. (This procedure is described in more detail in chapter 3.)

Science Stories

Kindergarten and primary teachers usually provide time for students to tell and write stories to answer their own questions about objects, living things, and events. This is a natural process for children, who explain things to themselves in terms of familiar concepts. As Einstein noted, imagination is a powerful tool for scientific theorizing. Jonas Salk (1995), who developed the first successful polio vaccine in 1955, described his own approach to problem solving:

> Very early in life, I developed a way to examine my experiences by imagining myself as the object in which I was interested. After I became a scientist, I used this system to imagine myself as a virus or a cancer cell, for example, and to sense what it would be like. I would also imagine myself as the immune system to reconstruct what I would do if engaged in combat with a virus or a cancer cell. After I played through a series of scenarios on a particular problem and acquired new insight, I designed laboratory experiments accordingly. Based on the results of these experiments, I would then know which questions to ask next—until I went as far as I could go. When I observed phenomena in the laboratory that I did not understand, I would ask questions like, *Why would I do that if I were a virus or a cancer cell or the immune system?* Before long, this internal dialogue became second nature to me. I found that my mind worked like this all the time. (p. 13)

When children make up stories to try to explain phenomena, they are making critical connections between complex ideas and their own experience. Young children regularly use metaphors or analogies in their stories to explain scientific phenomena to themselves or others. This use of figurative language is actually a sophisticated process that requires children to simplify ideas and transfer their understanding into another context.

In Thaiss' (1986) book *Language Across the Curriculum in the Elementary Grades*, Hauser described the use of learning journals as her third-grade classroom observed the hatching of eggs:

The children kept journals in which they recorded what we talked about each day as well as the observable development of the embryos. Most of the children's journals became a record, not only of their study of the embryology of chickens, but also of their growth as active participants in class discussions. This was not a "hands-on" unit like our science units; what the children learned was mostly from class discussions. When questions were asked that no one could answer, we checked our books. At times, we could only speculate on the answers, using information we knew to be true in order to guess. (p. 31)

Because children in this classroom met together to share ideas, they could help each other locate resources and provide peer responses to writing. The stories they created to explain what they observed helped them think about their observations and stimulated the thinking of others.

The creation of stories utilizes students' personal experience and knowledge and provides them with familiar images they can think with and manipulate. Opportunities for students to respond creatively to their experiences allow them to work with their natural curiosity, express wonder, ask compelling questions, and try to understand how the world works. Young children are not afraid to ask difficult questions, nor are they intimidated by trying to answer them. Journal writing supports and encourages this process of inquiry, and creates a record that can be reviewed and used as a resource for discussion and further research.

JOURNALS FOR OLDER STUDENTS

Students in the late primary grades and at the intermediate and middle school levels can read, conduct research, and participate in lab experiences on a more independent level. In classrooms that use science workshops, journals provide a place to record information from reading and observation and to gather resources for sharing with others. They also provide a place to plan and record experiments and demonstrations.

In a fifth-grade classroom at Captain School, students gathered around their teacher to collect samples of animal hair to compare with their own. Jerry held his journal close behind his microscope to draw what he saw (Fig. 8.3) while others observed first, then recorded what they had seen on a grid they drew in their journals. Some students worked alone, but most worked in small groups to compare notes and observations. The teacher went from table to table, checking the drawings and asking questions to help clarify entries. At the end of the session, students created discovery charts in small groups (Fig. 8.4) listing what they learned and creating visuals for whole group discussion.

When older students first begin to use science journals it is helpful to provide them with guidelines for journal activities. Each type of guideline might be presented as a part of a series of minilessons, designed to acquaint students with the procedures of inquiry. The following guidelines are generic and provide ideas for responding to observations, thinking about what is observed, conducting research, setting up labs, and working with information.

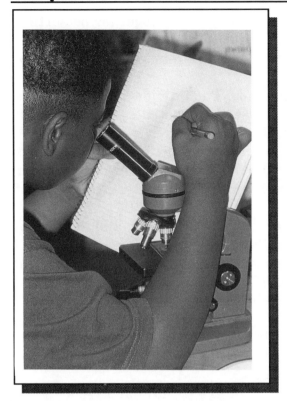

FIG. 8.3. Jerry carefully records what he sees in his journal.

FIG. 8.4. Chris, Brandon, and Michael create a discovery chart to record what they have learned.

Observe and Record

- *Focus carefully* on what you are observing. Look, listen, touch, taste, or smell, as appropriate and possible.
- *Observe* from different perspectives (close up, at a distance, from above or below) to see new features. Imagine that you are observing as a different person, a plant, an animal, or an object.
- *Record* what you are observing, using notes, drawings, sketches, diagrams, charts, and maps. Check your drawings and sketches for relevant details.
- *Use eye drawing* by following the lines of an object and drawing it with your eyes. Try free drawing by looking at something and sketching it without looking at your paper.
- *Circle your fingers* or roll a sheet of paper into a tube and look at an object or scene through it, focusing on details.
- *Think about* cause and effect: Why did this happen? What do you think will happen? Look for more than one cause or effect. Look for a chain of causes and effects; observe how one event can cause another, which in turn causes another. Is there an underlying cause, as well as a direct one?

Classify, Compare, and Connect

- *Compare and contrast* objects and processes. List ways things are alike, then ways they are different. List features that can be compared, such as size, color, habitat, skin, animal type, food source, hardness, distance, and habitat.

- *Classify ideas,* objects, and observations by grouping them together or sorting them out. This will help you to identify, understand, and explain them. Can you classify what you are observing or reading about in different ways? Can things belong to more than one class?
- *Begin with a topic and divide it into two subtopics.* Then divide these subtopics into others. Find features that are alike and use these as categories. Make a category chart, listing entries under major features.
- *Order information.* Look for key words (first, second, next, then, before, after, last, finally). Ask questions: What happened next, what happened then? Does the order make sense? Draw a time line or a sequence chain to help you see the order of events.
- *Use graphic organizers* (charts, graphs, semantic maps, pictures, and diagrams) to identify and describe differences and similarities, create categories, depict cause–effect, and describe systems and processes. Make a list and write down the parts you find. Make a chart that shows the different parts and how they relate to each other. Create a web or cluster. Draw a diagram and label it.
- *Ask yourself questions:* What happened next? Why did this happen? Show the steps in a process in the order in which they occur. Make a numbered list or a sequence chain. These visual representations will help you organize information, see patterns and relationships, and draw conclusions.
- *Analyze your observation.* Break down an object or event into parts. Ask: What are the parts? What is it made of? How is it divided? What does each part do?
- *Look at material creatively.* How might you solve a problem associated with the properties of what you are observing?

Read and Research

- *Decide* what you want to know or what problem you want to solve. What do you need to do or find out?
- *Talk to others* to get more information. Read and take notes. Go to the library, use a computer search, and interview people.
- *Observe* anything that has to do with your idea. Use your senses, measure, and think about how things related to each other.
- *Describe* what you observe, draw pictures, and write down details. Draw diagrams to help organize and develop your ideas.
- *Write down* where you find information, so you can find it again, share it with others who are interested, or create a citation for a report.

Plan and Experiment

- *Plan.* What materials will you need? What equipment will be used? How much time will you need? Can materials be handled without supervision? If supervision is required, who can help? What safety features need to be considered? What are the steps in the demonstration or experiment? If you are working with others, who will be responsible for each part of the setup? Draw a picture of the equipment, list the materials, and describe the processes.

- *Conduct*. What do you want to know? What do you think will happen? Describe what happens at each step. Observe carefully and write down or draw pictures of what happens.
- *Conclude*. Examine the evidence and decide what you know. Do you have enough examples? Enough facts? What do the facts mean? Does the evidence fit the conclusion?

USING LEARNING JOURNALS TO EXPLORE SCIENCE THEMES

The following descriptions of a week's activities at different levels of elementary science instruction suggest how science journals can provide a framework for exploring scientific ideas. Keep in mind that the activities listed for each day assume the large blocks of time reserved for exploration in an integrated curriculum setting. The same general activities can be adapted for science classes that meet for shorter periods of time daily or every other day.

Kindergarten—Life Cycles

- *Monday*. Teacher and students talk together about how living things grow and change. As they talk, the teacher writes key words on a chart: eggs, hatch, chicken, spin, leaf, cocoon, caterpillar, butterfly. In the classroom terrarium, students observe eggs and cocoons with a magnifying glass. They draw pictures of their observations in their folded newsprint journals and some label their drawings, using words from the chart. Over a period of weeks, they will observe and draw the metamorphosis of the egg through the larval, pupa, and butterfly stages.
- *Tuesday*. The teacher reads Eric Carle's *The Very Hungry Caterpillar* (1969) aloud and children use individual student copies as a reference for drawing pictures of the four stages of the butterfly's life cycle in their journals. Some children examine other books about butterflies that the teacher has displayed on the chalkboard ledge to find pictures and words that describe the metamorphosis.
- *Wednesday*. The teacher asks students to predict what the caterpillars in the aquarium might look like when they hatch from the eggs. Students draw pictures in their journals to record their predictions and write stories about what they think is happening inside the egg.
- *Thursday*. Students write stories about what they think is happening inside the cocoon. Some students dictate their stories to their fourth-grade journal buddies. Buddies write on separate pieces of paper so the kindergartners can copy their stories into their journals. Others ask for their stories to be entered directly into their journals. Some buddies work at the word processor and get a printed copy of the story to tape into the science journal. A few students draw pictures and dictate their stories into a tape recorder to create a "stepping story" (see chapter 3).
- *Friday*. Students write poems about their expectations of the metamorphosis, and use their pictures, words, and stories to write letters home to their families, describing the class study and what they are learning.

As the egg hatches and the caterpillar creates a cocoon and then emerges as a butterfly, students predict, observe, make hypotheses, and draw pictures of what is happening. At the end of the study they will each have a record in their journal that creates a history of their learning.

Primary—Dinosaurs

- *Monday.* The teacher reads aloud from an informational book about dinosaurs to introduce the topic. Students record guidelines for research in the reference sections of their journals. The teacher hands out a sheet of names of dinosaurs and a pronunciation guide, which students fold and tape into the reference section of their journals. Several trade and reference books about dinosaurs are previewed and students list these titles in their journal resource sections. Students also record interesting facts they learned from the book read aloud and choose a dinosaur to research on their own or with a partner.
- *Tuesday.* Research continues. Students take notes from the books they are reading about the particular dinosaur they are studying. On pages in their journals that they mark with a T for transformations, some students draw pictures of dinosaurs and their environments to help themselves understand their reading, whereas others create time lines of the various periods involved or charts that compare size statistics and food preferences. Students who have difficulty reading pair up with another student or request help from the aide. When students have questions about their reading, they record them on the opposite side of the page, next to a capital A, for Ask. Someone notes that dinosaurs lived millions of years ago and records this next to a C for connections, because the class is studying the concept of large numbers in math. Others note that they have seen large dinosaur skeletons or models in museums or movies. The teacher moves around the room, interacting briefly with each student, observing their notes and assessing their understanding and progress. Trouble spots and questions are addressed in a class session that follows the research period. At the end of the period, each student shares an interesting fact or discovery, which is recorded on a chart.
- *Wednesday.* Research continues. At the end of the period, students meet in small groups to share their research. One student is having difficulty finding information on a particular dinosaur, which another remembers seeing in a book. He looks in his reference section for the title to share. They share general information about dinosaurs and record ideas that interest them or that relate to their own study. They try to answer each other's questions or share ideas about where to look for answers. They share the connections they've made and record ones they hadn't thought about. Individual students write notes to the teacher, using their journals as a reference to share significant ideas and unanswered questions from their research.
- *Thursday.* Using the notes as a guide, the teacher presents information to the entire class or small groups that share similar questions. Students review their notes, responses, resources, and references to think about how they will present the information they've gathered about their dinosaur. They consult a reference sheet about possible projects and choose one that will demonstrate their learning. Several students or small groups may work together to create larger projects, such as a mural, class museum, newspaper, play, panel discussion, or TV program.

• *Friday.* Students continue working on their research projects. Some work on informational reports that will be gathered together into a class book. Others draw illustrations for the book, and still others participate in creating the large class mural. At the end of the period, all students write letters home to their parents about their study, describing their individual research and class activities. During the following week, all projects will be shared with the entire class and visitors from other classes.

Intermediate/Middle School—Earth Science

• *Monday.* As a homework assignment, students record what they already know about rock and earth formations in their journals, along with five questions about what they'd like to learn. They share their knowledge during class discussion and the teacher creates a composite of their questions on a learning chart. As students find answers to these questions, they will be entered on the chart and in their journals during whole class sharing sessions. The teacher hands out pages that describe lab procedures for demonstrations and experiments, which students punch and put into the reference sections of their journals. Students choose an area to research and form small groups with those who have similar interests. They meet together and decide on what they will individually research within their topic.

• *Tuesday.* Students explore their questions in the science textbook, trade books, and reference books, taking notes in their journals. On the response pages they evaluate their reading, noting materials that are especially clear and could be used later for reference. They record any questions they have as they read and connections they make with their personal experience or ideas in other curriculum areas. Some students draw pictures of rock formations or mountain ranges, and others make cross-section diagrams of volcanoes. Several students create graphs, charts, or webs to organize and think about information they are exploring. Technical terms and their definitions are recorded in the reference section of their journals. The teacher walks around the room, observing the note taking and responses, offering suggestions, and answering questions. At the end of the period, students meet in their small groups to share what they have learned and exchange ideas about where to find resources. In a whole class session, each student shares an interesting fact they have discovered. They begin to plan their experiments and demonstrations.

• *Wednesday.* Students paste or tape geology-related newspaper and magazine articles in their journals and list the titles of trade books that they find helpful in the resource reference section of their journals. They share these resources in the larger class discussion and use the notes from their group discussions to share the progress of their research. Experiments and demonstrations are set up, diagrammed, observed, and recorded, along with questions that emerge in the process.

• *Thursday.* Students use their collected resources to begin working on individual or group projects. One group decides to create an all-class project and asks everyone to contribute a page to a Geology Alliteration book. They list key terms from the study and ask students to choose one and write an alliterative sentence that gives information about a particular thing. They give an example: "Paula proposed that pyrite probably puzzled prospectors." Students are also asked to draw pictures to illustrate their sentences. Other groups plan projects that include a model of an erupting volcano, a three-dimensional model of the process by which mountains are formed, and an exhibit of minerals found locally.

• *Friday.* Students meet together to address the original questions of the study and record answers that various groups and individuals have found. Several students are planning a newspaper, "The Hard Rock Times," and ask for contributions of articles. Most students will have plenty of information from their research, experiments, and collected resources. Others will create original stories, poems, and drawings from the information in their journals. Another group is writing a television show, "Real World Flintstones." Research and work on projects continues. At the end of the work period, students use their journals to write letters home to their families, telling about the study and what they have learned.

EXAMPLES OF ENTRIES
FROM SCIENCE LEARNING JOURNALS

Figures 8.5 through 8.10 are examples of entries that students make in science learning journals.

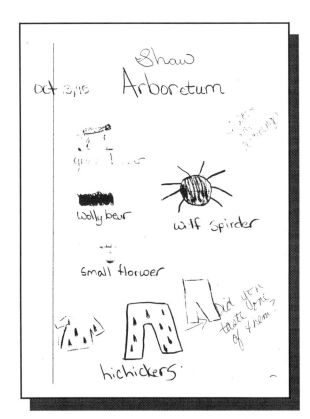

FIG.   8.5. LaToya's   field drawings from a trip to the Arboretum (fifth grade).

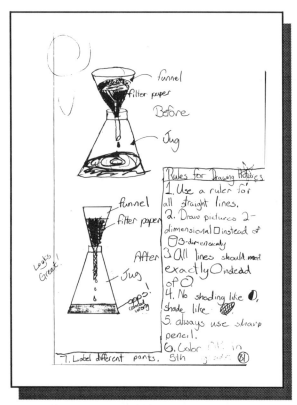

FIG. 8.6. Nick's drawings of lab equipment and drawing instructions (fifth grade).

Current Event
I think the artecal on Giganotosaurus Carolinii is very intrestean. I never thought they would descover a predicter bigger than T. Rex. I wonder what it would be like to descover the biggest carrnevore man has ever seen. I wonder what it would be like to be a dinosaur I bet their life was much much much much much different from ares. I think whoever found this dinosaur is very very exsited.

Move Over, T. Rex: New Fossil Find Is A Beast

Compiled From News Services

NEW YORK — The fearsome Tyrannosaurus rex has been toppled from its perch as the largest meat-eating dinosaur, replaced by an even bigger predator found in Argentina: a 42-foot-long, 6- to 8-ton behemoth called Giganotosaurus carolinii.

The first bones of the new king of the prehistoric beasts, which lived about 100 million years ago, were found in 1993 by an amateur fossil hunter, Reuben Carolini. The creature's skull, backbone, pelvis and leg bones were later excavated by two Argentine paleontologists, who described the find in a report published today in the journal Nature.

The report says the titanic preda-

FIG. 8.7. Tucker's current event in science (fourth grade).

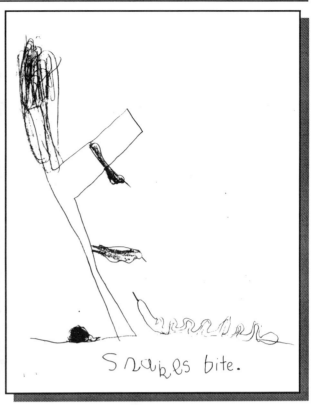

Snakes bite.

FIG. 8.8. Dusty's depiction of the predator-prey relationship (kindergarten).

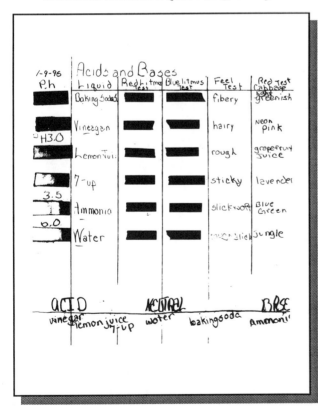

FIG. 8.9. Alexandra's litmus chart of acids and bases (fifth grade).

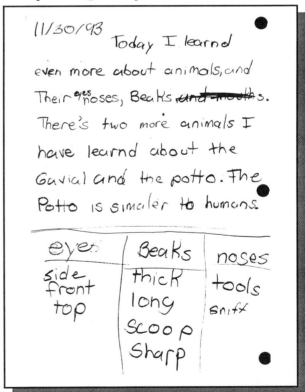

FIG. 8.10. Brandon's notes about what he has learned in science. Notice the chart he creates to classify eyes, noses, and beats.

9

Exploring the Social Studies With Learning Journals

Children need not discover all generalizations for themselves, obviously. Yet we want to give them opportunity to develop a decent competence at it and a proper confidence in their ability to operate independently. There is also some need for the children to pause and review in order to recognize the connections within what they have learned—the kind of internal discovery that is probably of highest value. The cultivation of such a sense of connectedness is surely the heart of the matter. For if we do nothing else, we should somehow give to children a respect for their own powers of thinking, for their power to generate good questions, to come up with interesting informed guesses.

—Jerome Bruner (1966, p. 96)

PREVIEW

1. How are learning journals used to explore social studies?
2. What kinds of entries do students make in social studies journals?
3. How do journals support individual study and response activities?
4. How do social studies assist group inquiry?
5. How do journals support the use of textbooks and trade books?

BRIEFLY: Students use learning journals in the social sciences to record and respond to information, share ideas with others, and create resources for projects, research, and reports.

USING LEARNING JOURNALS TO EXPLORE THE SOCIAL STUDIES

Children are social scientists from the time they are born. They express interest in the people, places, spaces, and things of their environment by observing them and asking questions. As sociologists, they watch people in their families and neighborhoods and try to figure out why they behave as they do. They observe the specialized work of community members and quickly become aware of the political power in their families and neighborhoods. Spaces in their homes and neighborhoods are explored in detail, as children develop a geographical sense of where things are in their environment. Economics become a consideration as they compare their possessions with those of others, are told there is not enough money to buy things they want, or try to manage an allowance.

Children are natural historians. They tell stories about events and create their own interpretations. They develop a sense of their own history as they look at baby pictures and hear stories about themselves and accounts of events that happened before they were born. They wonder over different clothing and hair styles from previous eras and become aware that certain cultural and religious practices of their families are not shared by others. Teachers build on these experiences to help students extend their natural social interests into the broader world around them.

In many classrooms, social studies are explored within an expanding world framework, such as myself, families, neighborhoods, communities, American history, and world cultures. At the kindergarten level, concepts of time and celebration are explored, with themes such as holidays, seasons, and months of the year. In other classrooms, social studies center around broad ideas like resources, work, survival, friendship, freedom, and equality, or all of the subjects in the curriculum may be used as tools of inquiry in theme cycles to explore questions students have about their environment. Students may also focus on the individual disciplines of history or geography in a workshop format.

In each of these organizational arrangements, learning journals assist students with their individual inquiry and cooperative work with others. Students record information about a topic and respond to it in ways that are personally effective to their learning. They collect resources related to their study and create references that assist their writing and research. Teachers may use some form of KWL inquiry (What do we know? What do we want to know or what do we wonder about? What did we learn?) to introduce and explore a social studies theme with a class. They ask students to share what they already know about a topic to begin creating a core of common knowledge for the class. In small groups and with the entire class, students continue to build this knowledge core by searching for answers to questions developed by the group and recording what they discover in their journals (Fig. 9.1). Students also share resources, such as titles of helpful informational books, names of persons who can be interviewed, and strategies for finding resources. Many teachers provide time at the beginning of a research activity period for individual students or groups to share this kind of helpful information with the entire class (KWL is described in

FIG. 9.1. This group of fifth graders records information for a topic they are studying together.

FIG. 9.2. Jessie records information about the Civil War in his journal.

more detail later in this chapter).

Activities associated with keeping a journal support many of the goals of social science instruction. The recording and response activities provide practice for processing information, making generalizations, and integrating new information into developing systems of knowledge. As students interact with information in their journals, they write their understanding of concepts (Fig. 9.2), draw maps, and create graphics to organize and interpret what they are learning. As individuals and as participants in a variety of groups, students reflect on what they are learning, create hypotheses, make comparisons, draw inferences, and consider alternatives and consequences. They develop interpersonal skills and learn to see other points of view. As part of long-term objectives, journal-related group activities provide experience with the kinds of cooperative problem solving and decision making that are necessary for effective participation in a democratic society.

TYPES OF ENTRIES USED IN SOCIAL STUDIES JOURNALS

Entries in a social studies journal can be arranged in a variety of ways. Some create sections for their entries, including a section for recording and responding to information and one that includes resources and references to support inquiry and projects. Students at the intermediate and middle school levels may separate the resource and reference functions into separate sections. In some classrooms, students use an ACT or REACT organization for their recording and response organization, whereas others record all information sequentially and create a continuing table of contents to permit easy reference to entries. This section describes the four general functions of social studies journals, but it should be noted that classrooms vary in the way journals are assembled. The next section expands the discussion of the kinds of entries usually found as part of the record and response function.

Recording Entries

Students take notes in their journals to record ideas and information from reading or other media such as videotapes, computer programs, and TV. These notes may be numbered or later organized into short paragraphs or summaries. Students also record information gathered from classroom visitors or experiences on field trips. Interviews may be recorded verbatim or summarized. Johnson and Ebert (1992) suggested that students keep a record of their thoughts in a theme journal as they read trade books related to a topic. Journals might be specific to a particular study and consist of writing and/or drawing paper stapled together with a construction paper cover that the student decorates appropriately.

Many children have difficulty with time relationships. It is helpful for them to date each of their journal entries to establish a history of their work and document their learning (Fig. 9.3). Children enjoy seeing how their ideas change over time, and dating provides information for evaluation of progress. Primary and developmental learners benefit from reading strategy lists that encourage them to notice key words, such as *first, second, next, then, before, after, last,* or *finally.*

Students may be encouraged to draw a time line or create a sequence chain to help them see the order of events. They might also review their reading to respond to the following: What happened first? What happened next? What happened then? Does the order make sense?

FIG. 9.3. Sameetra reviews what she has written and drawn in her October journal.

Response Entries

Teachers encourage students to draw their understanding of concepts for several reasons. Not only do these representations help teachers better assess what students understand, but the effort to draw requires that students pay close attention to details and critical relationships. When students attempt to draw a map, diagram, or illustration, they must often return to their reading or observation to find additional information about things they are trying to represent. One fifth-grade teacher observed that a student who wrote little in response to social studies topics could eventually write at length, if she were allowed to draw a picture of what she was studying first. Both she and the teacher discovered that if she could draw a concept, she could write about it.

Depending on the age level and the focus of social studies in the classroom, teachers help students observe how the social studies are a part of their own experience by asking them to identify examples of history, geography, economics, anthropology, politics, or sociology in their everyday lives. When students are encouraged to search the newspaper for articles of interest to them, they often find strong connections between their own lives and events happening in the world. Rolf, a fourth grader, chose an article about a hurricane, noting:

> I chose this article because one of my uncles flew to Florida last week. He flew from Germany. He called once before the hurricane, but he hasn't called since. Although no death has been reported, my family is concerned, because according to the newspaper, two people are missing.

His teacher responded by expressing concern about her own family and friends in the Florida area and encouraged him to share the article in class for discussion.

This kind of assignment might also follow discussion about a specific topic being studied or an examination of one of the particular disciplines of the social studies, such as economics or history. Students can look and listen for words or concepts related to particular disciplines or topics as they walk home from school, play with their friends, talk with their family, watch television, read periodicals, or listen to the radio.

Students may also view and evaluate videotapes or special presentations on television related to a social studies theme. Journal responses might include considerations such as: How was the theme presented? Whose perspective was adopted? Was the topic treated fairly? What questions do you still have? As a regular part of their at-home interaction with media, students can also be encouraged to evaluate and record what they see through the perspective of the social studies: What concepts in economics do they observe as they watch or listen to commercial advertisements? What cultural themes and values are addressed or expressed in commercial programming, movies, popular literature, or tabloid newspapers?

Graphic Organizers

Students use these visual representations to organize and interpret ideas and information. Graphic organizers help students display relationships, develop categories, depict cycles, and portray cause and effect. As mentioned in chapter 3, students learn how to use these graphic forms on their own by helping to create them as a part of a group. When teachers demonstrate the use of time lines, flowcharts, graphs, maps, matrices, diagrams, and webs as part of a class inquiry, it is likely that students will adopt several of these forms as tools for exploring the social studies.

Creative writing in response to reading and research can have limitless forms, but teachers help students increase the range of their responses by demonstrating ways to explore historical persons, events, or settings; critical social or political issues; cultural practices; economic problems; or geographical concepts using the following:

- Biographical sketches of famous persons.
- Imaginary journal or diary of an explorer or politician.
- Anecdotes about famous persons.
- Descriptive sketches of famous persons, places, ideas, or events.
- Real letters to civic leaders or the newspaper.
- Imaginary letters to historical or contemporary persons.
- Imaginary letters between historical and contemporary persons.

- Editorials commenting on social, political, or economic issues.
- Responses to editorials.
- Newspaper stories about historical, contemporary, or future events.
- Songs, ballads, and poetry.
- Folk tales that portray the values of a culture.
- Poster designs to advertise historical or contemporary locations and events.
- Reviews of books, films, tapes, or TV programs related to a topic.
- Directions to reach a remote geographical location.

Catie, a fourth grader, pretended she was an early American settler and wrote an entry that reflects what she is beginning to learn about this historical time period and her own experience with younger children:

> I am Samantha Smithston, an early American settler. Today I went to pick berries with my younger sister. Instead of putting the berries in the basket, she put them into her mouth. After that, she was too full to eat dinner and mother blamed me. But secretly, I think she just didn't want to eat her green beans.

Students who experience difficulties with writing can dictate notes and responses to a scribe. These can be handwritten or entered into a word processor, printed out, and taped into a journal. The following is an excerpt from a letter dictated by Tonia, a fifth grader who experienced difficulty with writing. She imagined that she was a young girl living in South Carolina in the late 1600s, writing to her cousin back in England. It is evident that she absorbed a great deal of information about the topic through listening and discussion. She told her cousin about the work she had to do and about a recent purchase of slaves. She also wrote:

> We grow a lot of different crops in South Carolina, such as tobacco, corn, indigo and cotton. The indigo plant makes a very pretty dye. Ma dyed two of my white dresses. She said if I get them dirty, you can't tell as much on the colored dresses. . . . Last week, we had a town frolic. It's kind of like a hoe-down dance. We had a few fiddlers, and we danced and played to the music. Afterwards, we had a corn shucking bee where we shucked corn until someone found a red ear of corn. The older men played a game where the first one who found a red ear got to kiss the prettiest girl.

Her letter continued, and in the midst of news a young girl would write to her cousin in England, she revealed knowledge about the crops, how cotton is grown, entertainment, and customs and religious practices of the time. She concluded her letter: "Ma is calling me. I need to dip some more candles. Write me back soon. Send my love to little Joe."

Resource Entries

Students should be encouraged to explore newspapers and magazines to find words or discussions related to topics of themes they are exploring. They can also collect words or ideas they hear or see on radio, television, or the movies. Some classrooms augment text and trade books with projects such as *Newspapers in Education* and school book club newspapers such as *Scholastic News* or *Weekly Reader*. Both of these activities generate opportunities for students to write and respond to ideas in their journals.

Students can also be encouraged to collect information about a topic or theme from their parents and relatives and to record these interviews in their journals to share with the rest of the class. Wendy, whose family moved to the United States several years ago, told about her family's history, complete with anecdotes about a near tragedy with a babysitter when she was small and an adventure her mother experienced as a young girl:

> My Dad came [to America] in 1991 and my Mom and I came in 1992. We all came from Cheng Du, China. My Dad is the oldest here [in America] that I could interview. . . . When my mom was 16, she and her other four friends went to a river. There was a whirlpool in the river and my Mom and her friends got whirled in, but fortunately one of her friends stayed ashore and when she saw that her friends were going up and down in the water, she quickly called some men close by in the river so that they could be saved.

All families have stories to tell and connections to make with geographical locations and historical events. Books such as *How to Tape Instant Oral Biographies: Recording Your Family's Life Story in Sound and Sight* (Zimmerman, 1992) provide helpful tips for interviewing, questions that encourage people to share their experiences, and ideas for recording information. Students might also interview friends or pen pals from other schools to get ideas for projects and record these in the resources section of their journals for future reference. Students who have access to the Internet can browse for project ideas on children's websites devoted to specific topics.

Reference Entries

The reference section of a social studies learning journal may contain a glossary of terms used in the study, a personal spelling dictionary, reference guidelines, printed location maps or journal maps constructed by the student, and a bibliography of books or resources consulted as part of research.

Glossary. This section includes lists of topic-related words that either the teacher or student judges to be critical to the understanding of a topic. An initial list may be provided by the teacher, with additional terms added by students as they are encountered. The amount of information necessary for these entries will vary from student to student, but teachers will want to model the possibilities, which include:

- The term, divided into syllables.
- Pronunciation cues or phonetic spelling.
- A synonym or definition.
- An example, if it is a general category.
- Its use in a sentence.

Personal Spelling Dictionary.   Although most students are encouraged to write without concern for correct spelling in their journals, they are usually aware of words they are spelling incorrectly. Teachers may provide time on a daily basis to collect words that students are attempting to use in their writing and list their correct spelling on a chart for students to copy into their personal dictionaries. As they see words that others have requested, students often add these to their own dictionaries for future reference. Others circle words that are frequently misspelled in individual journals and students add them to their dictionaries, or look them up as preparation for more polished drafts of writing projects.

Guidelines.   These may include directions for using the library, working in groups, making journal entries, accessing the Internet, or using equipment and materials such as the computer, interactive video, programs and searches, CD-ROM, encyclopedias, dictionaries, atlases, almanacs, and reader's guides.

USING THE REACT MODEL
TO RESPOND TO SOCIAL STUDIES

Recording and response in social studies journals usually includes two or more of the types of entries described by the REACT model: record, evaluate, ask, connect and transform (see chapter 4 for additional description of the REACT model). Depending on a student's age and developmental level, entries in a social science journal might include the following.

Record

- Notes from reading, discussions, observations, and interviews.
- Information from class visitors or field trips.
- Data from research or surveys.
- Information to use for debate.
- Ideas from film, video, radio, newspapers, magazines, and multimedia programs.
- Cut-out pictures.
- Warm-up or check-in exercises in history or geography.

Evaluate

- Comments and opinions.
- Problems encountered.
- Likes or dislikes.
- Difficulties with reading or understanding.
- Assessment of an experience.

Ask

- Questions about new ideas and information.

- Questions about a presentation.
- Questions from reading or research.
- Questions about an experience.
- Predictions and hypotheses.

Connect

- Connections between the topic and personal knowledge.
- Connections between the topic and personal experience.
- Connections between a current and a previous study.
- Connections between the topic and other curriculum areas.
- Connections between the topic and current events.

Transform

- Summaries or essays.
- Drawings or sketches.
- Review of notes.
- Location maps.
- Graphs, time lines.
- Tables, matrices, charts.
- Venn diagrams.
- Letters to fictional, historical, or contemporary persons.
- Diaries.

Resources for Writing, Thinking, Research, and Discussion

- Newspaper and magazine articles and pictures related to the study.
- Editorials, cartoons, and advertisements related to study.
- Poetry and quotations related to the study.
- Names, addresses, and phone numbers of resource persons and organizations.
- Ideas for projects, such as posters, plays, newspapers, and displays.
- Brochures or printed material from community resources.

References

- Procedures or guidelines for projects.
- Personal dictionary, with the correct spelling of frequently used words.
- A glossary of technical terms used in a particular study.
- Instructions for using reference sources: encyclopedia, computer, library.
- An annotated bibliography of trade books and other sources of information.
- Procedures for organizing information.

Using individual journal entries as resources, students meet together in small groups, or as a class, to share what they have learned. From these discussions they find answers to questions they have from their own reading or research and decide on individual or group projects.

At the kindergarten and early primary levels, recording and response entries will feature more drawings and pictures cut out from magazines or newspapers to illustrate what students are learning. Students at this level can create and illustrate time lines and draw or fill in simple location maps. As they participate in teacher-assisted class creations of graphic organizers such as charts, graphs, and webs, young children begin to experiment with these forms on their own. Students of this age can create additional records of their learning by dictating information or responses to their parents, the teacher, an aide, or a journal buddy. They might also create audiotapes to share ideas with others or to review their own thinking about a topic.

At the late primary, intermediate, and middle school levels, journal writing provides an excellent resource for papers and projects because students:

- *Work* with ideas from their reading in a personal way, to organize and interpret what they have learned.
- *Collect* additional current information from newspapers, magazines, interviews, and observations.
- *Explore* key ideas with others, which provides them with additional insight and interpretation to challenge, modify, or confirm their thinking.
- *Create* reference material, in the form of dictionaries, glossaries, guidelines, lists of resources, and bibliographies that will support research and writing about a topic.

Bibliographies will be more detailed at the intermediate and middle school levels, with brief annotations, publication information, and page numbers of material students may want to use in written reports. Students can draw from these resources to synthesize their learning into limitless projects, including research papers, essays, diaries, letters, stories, brochures, posters, panels, newspapers, TV and radio programs, game shows, plays, and murals. When tests are associated with a particular study, journals provide an excellent way to review what has been learned.

At all instructional levels, social studies frequently provide themes that integrate the exploration of other content areas or develop skills and processes that can be used for inquiry across the disciplines. Students can also review their learning journals periodically to identify processes in mathematics, science, writing, or literature that will be helpful to inquiry in the social studies, such as graphing, observational techniques, recording notes, expressing ideas, or analyzing reading material. Within the integrated curriculum, the connecting response becomes more prominent, as students are encouraged to look for patterns and relationships within and among the topics they study.

Linquist (1995) described how she used social studies journals in her fifth-grade classroom to create links with characters and events in literature. She read a chapter aloud from a theme-related book, then students completed reading the book on their own. As they read, they selected words, phrases, or paragraphs that appealed to them in some way. These were recorded on one side of a double entry page and their response to the passage was written on the other side. In Kathleen Murphy's fourth-grade classroom, students record a quote they have chosen from their reading at the top of the page, and a response at the bottom, leaving room for the teacher to respond to the entry. Rolf, for example, recorded a quote from a book about Sacajawea that described the rather arrogant demands of Charbonneau (the main guide on the Lewis and Clark expedition). He responded with outrage at Charbonneau's behavior and then expressed relief that the conflict was resolved.

SUPPORTING GROUP INQUIRY WITH LEARNING JOURNALS

As students record information and ideas about a topic in their journals, they examine what they are studying in light of their own experience, organize it in some way that helps them better understand it, and prepare to share what they have learned with a partner, a small group, or the entire class. This individual drawing, writing, and thinking activity helps students participate effectively in group inquiry, because they have worked through the material on their own and are more aware of what they do and do not understand. They can share effective ways of thinking about or organizing a topic and get answers to their questions or ideas about where to look for answers.

Teachers often help students organize and direct their research into a theme or topic with a class KWL interaction, an approach to inquiry with a number of variations, described in the following section.

KWL

This is the simplest form and it is used to help students prepare for and carry out research into a topic or theme. Teachers ask students to create lists of things they already know about a topic or theme in their journals and an additional list of things they want to know. This activity helps teachers identify both current knowledge and misconceptions about a topic that can help direct instruction. It also reveals the particular interests students have that could be followed and shared with the rest of the class. For example, when a fourth-grade class began a study of England, Kaitlin's list of things she knew and wanted to know centered on sports, whereas Tucker expressed an interest in clocks, particularly Big Ben. This type of inquiry to find out what others know and are interested in enriches the knowledge and experience of everyone in the class even before the study is begun.

In some classrooms, teachers ask students to complete this pretopic survey assignment during a study period, whereas other teachers prefer that students take the assignment home to provide sufficient time to think about it and to involve the parents. Some teachers assign a brief topic-related reading assignment in a text or trade book before this discussion begins, so that everyone has something to contribute. As students share their ideas in class, they are recorded on a large chart for future reference. The class decides on ideas they want to research and responsibility for finding information about specific questions is assumed by individuals or small groups. As answers are found, students share what they have learned with the entire class and the teacher records this information on the question-and-answer chart. In some classrooms, students record research information from their journals on large charts as soon as it is found (Fig. 9.4).

As students research topics, they encounter discrepancies in the information they find, such as different interpretations of historical persons and events. Johnson and Ebert (1992) suggested that this experience should provide the basis for discussion in class, as students compare information from various sources. From these discussions, students learn to look for and record the credentials of writers as they read, closely observe publication dates of materials, identify the point of view of the author, and note the supporting evidence for claims made in writing.

Variations of KWL involve additional features:

- *H—How* will we find the answers to our questions? This question helps children begin to think about resources for information, and may involve minilessons to describe or demonstrate the use of reference materials and resource persons.
- *C—*What *connections* does this study have with other things we have studied or are studying? This consideration helps students begin to see the interrelatedness of knowledge.
- *Q—*What new *questions* were generated as a result of your research? This feature is usually included in theme cycles (Altwerger & Flores, 1994), where the intent is to demonstrate that inquiry about ideas is continuous and never really ends.
- *P—*What *projects* demonstrate and share our learning? Artwork, writing, plays, demonstrations, exhibits? Will there be individual or small group projects? Will the project be the joint effort of the entire class? With what audiences will they be shared? Classmates, other classes, the entire school, family, community?

Students should also be encouraged to write their responses to group presentations. These entries allow teachers to assess the content of learning, ideas that need clarification, and a student's enthusiasm for a project. For example, Brian, a third grader who often did not write extensive responses, wrote at length to evaluate a unit on Egpyt, which he especially enjoyed. Tyrone, a fifth grader, responded to a map activity by writing:

> I was shocked to see how many things happened from 965 to 1587. I learned that if two people claimed the same land, they would have a war. Some of the other things that interested me were the different lands the countries claimed. It interested me because I wanted to know which land claimed which. Even though this assignment was long, it was informational. And it would be good if we did it again.

Nick, a fifth grader, wrote about a simulation of the Dred Scott trial at the Old Courthouse in St. Louis. He described the room, drew a picture of the courtroom, and observed:

FIG. 9.4. Abbie adds to the research recorded on group learning charts.

If I had been Dred Scott, I would have been very scared. Because if I lost the case, then the Emersons would probably have treated me badly because I had sued them. I would also have thought about quitting the case if I had to go back to court five different times.

Photographs and Pictures

To help students begin to think about a topic or theme, teachers may introduce the study of a historical period, country, or culture by posting pictures or photographs related to the study on a chart or bulletin board. At the kindergarten level, the teacher will invite oral responses and record these in a class journal. At the primary and intermediate levels, students write responses directly in their own journals. Students are asked to speculate on the persons, places, or events shown and to give reasons for their answers: Where do you think this picture was painted or where was this photograph taken? What is happening in this photograph? What are these people doing? What might they be saying? Where might they be going? Teachers also invite students to create their own questions about pictures and to attempt to answer them as part of their research.

Strategies

Teachers help students make useful notes about their experience by modeling strategies for active listening, a skill that helps students focus on the content of oral presentations of all kinds. TQLR (Irvin & Rose, 1995) is similar to KWL and features a four step process that encourages students to:

- *Tune in*—by briefly recording what they already know about a topic.
- *Question*—by considering what they might learn as they listen.
- *Listen*—and write down key words and ideas.
- *Review*—notes, mark answers to questions, and summarize.

Because students may encounter reading material associated with a study that is difficult to read or understand, it is helpful to introduce and model techniques for active reading. Practice with the *insert method* helps students interact with new reading in a productive way. Students use a coded response to mark passages of a duplicated handout, placing a check mark beside paragraphs they understand, small circles beside new information, question marks for words they do not know or ideas they find confusing, and stars beside obviously important information. To adapt this method to the learning journal, students record page and paragraph numbers where they experience difficulty with reading or concepts. As they continue reading, they often figure out these difficulties on their own, or they can be brought to the teacher or a group session for discussion. This technique gives students a sense of what they understand about even the most difficult passages and focuses attention on terms and ideas that require more study.

Another effective way to draw attention to key words and ideas in a study is to ask students to consider what kinds of questions someone should be able to answer if they were knowledgeable about a topic. Students can either ask and answer their own questions as individuals, create and answer them in small groups, exchange questions with other groups, or create a question bank that is addressed by the entire class. Students can also be asked to speculate about terms and create a before and after chart of their predictions.

JOURNALS, TEXTBOOKS, AND CHILDREN'S LITERATURE

In more traditional classrooms, social studies texts are the centerpiece of instruction, although most teachers supplement the information in these texts with additional materials of their own. In other classrooms, teachers may use the text as one of many resources for information and rely more heavily on trade books and other media for their own information and student research. Journal activities can be used effectively to support both the exploration of social studies texts and topic-related trade books.

Textbooks and Learning Journals

In classrooms where texts are still used, teachers may use them as one of many resources to:

- Provide a broad overview of a topic.
- Outline the important ideas and events associated with a topic.
- Illustrate how information is organized.
- Demonstrate the use of ancillaries, such as maps, glossaries, and indices.

To begin a study, teachers ask students to explore a specific chapter in their textbook that deals with the topic. Students make note of titles, topics, and questions at the end of the chapter, then record what they think they know on one side of a folded page in their journals. After reading the chapter, they record what they learned on the opposite side of the page, indicating misconceptions that were cleared up and questions they still have about the topic.

Students can also examine their textbooks to identify helpful resources (maps, glossaries, pictures, indices, charts, and graphic organizers) that can be listed for future reference by page number in the reference sections of their journals. It is helpful for students to look for additional strengths in particular texts. Perhaps there are organizational charts, a particularly interesting map of Colonial Williamsburg, well-drawn pictures of clothing styles during the Renaissance, vivid photographs of Civil War battlefields, or a glossary definition of latitude that is clear and understandable. Textbooks may also list related reading in trade books or suggest reference sources that students find helpful. Some teachers keep copies of older texts for student reference use. One fifth-grade teacher found copies of political documents, letters from slaves and slave owners, and newspaper accounts of historical events in a set of discarded social studies texts, which she laminated and put in a file for her fifth-grade students to use as resources for studying U.S. history.

Trade Books and Learning Journals

Social studies trade books offer several advantages to students. Moss (1991) noted that whereas textbooks are frequently written above the level for which they are intended, well-written trade books on individual topics are available for many reading levels. Complex terminology is better explained in trade books and they are, on the whole, better written and more appealing to student readers. Information is generally more current, and because trade books can focus on a limited number of concepts, the treatment of these concepts is more intensive.

Trade book literature explores topics in the social studies in a variety of forms. Well-written and beautifully illustrated or photographed picture books with social studies themes are available for use at all elementary levels. Award-winning historical fiction gives children a sense of being present for critical events in history and well-written biographies provide insight into the lives and motivation of key players in history. Students can use series, such as those created by Ann McGovern (. . . *If You Sailed on the Mayflower in 1620*, 1970), Jean Fritz (*Will You Sign Here, John Hancock?*, 1976), or David Adler (*A Picture Book of Thomas Jefferson,* 1990), as models to create a scenario of their life if they had lived during a particular historical period. Salesi (1992) pointed out that informational books provide students with models for their own writing, such as indices, authors' notes, and bibliographies. These books also demonstrate how authors make ideas clear to an audience, by using visual material, printing new words in italics, and using precise descriptions. Similarly, Jaggar, Carrara, and Weiss (1986) found that children tend to incorporate words, content, and structure from literature they encounter into their own writing.

Both historical fiction and biography can offer students new and multiple perspectives on historical events when they are portrayed from the viewpoint of minority participants. Quality informational books are available at every reading level for each of the concepts explored in the social studies, including time, space, culture, social issues, economics, politics, government, history, geography, and anthropology. Many of these topics are also interestingly and sensitively explored in contemporary realistic fiction, picture books, poetry, and the traditional literatures of cultures around the world. Refer to Appendix A for annotated lists of quality children's books and materials that describe the use of literature to extend and enhance the social studies.

Learning journals are a helpful support to students as they explore trade literature for information. The riches of these books tend to be more effectively mined when students record their questions as they read, make connections between what they are reading and their personal knowledge or experience, and work with the material in some way with maps, drawings, charts, or graphic organizers to increase their understanding. At the end of their reading, students will have a list of significant or interesting ideas available for further reflection, analysis, and synthesis. For example, in a fourth-grade study of England, Kimya used a Venn diagram to compare King Arthur with Superman, recording their obvious unique characteristics in separate areas of overlapping circles and noting that they both helped people, had certain powers, were heroes, had enemies, were brave, wore capes, were smart, and fought for good. She also observed that both heroes' stories had been made into movie and television shows.

Max, a fifth grader, indicated a growing interest in the American Revolution as he followed the adventures of the main character in *Spies on the Devil's Belt*:

> I could really picture what Jonathan looked like when he was described. But it took me a while to figure out why he was running in the rain. He decided to join the Army! He's only 14, although I guess the Army is the place to go when you don't care if you die. [The teacher responds to this entry: "I wonder why a kid would feel that way?"]

He added questions: "How did Gracy know that Jonathan didn't kill his friend? And how does Gracy just put that death behind him so fast?" He also evaluated the quality of the book: "The foreshadowing keeps me, literally, on the edge of my chair. I found it hard stopping after Chapter 4." He made connections with his own experience: "He [Jonathan] was very pressured to take a swig of the India rum. If I were him, I wouldn't have done it, (well, maybe). I can't wait to see what happens next." Obviously, history has taken on a new excitement for this young reader, who continues to respond enthusiastically to the book in subsequent entries.

EXAMPLES OF ENTRIES IN SOCIAL STUDIES LEARNING JOURNALS

Figures 9.5 through 9.12 are examples of entries students make in learning journals used to explore the social studies.

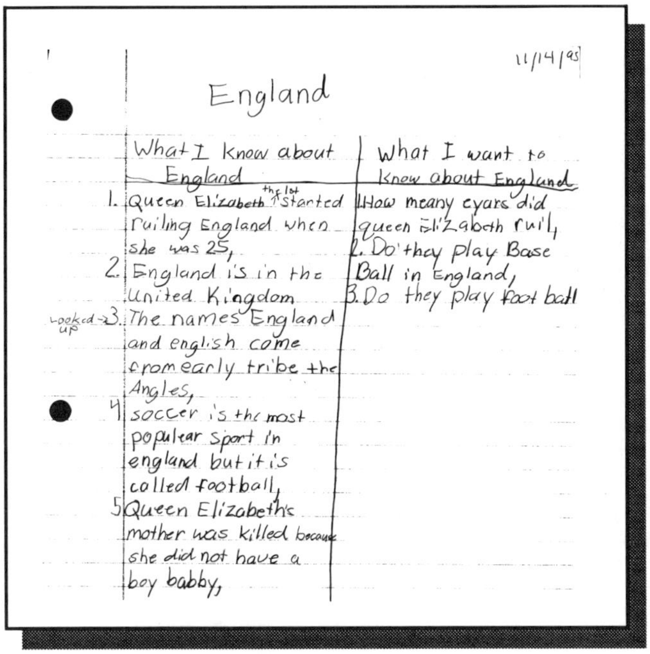

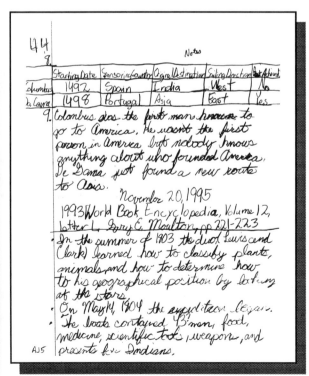

FIG. 9.5. Kaitlin's KWL.

FIG. 9.6. Alexander's chart.

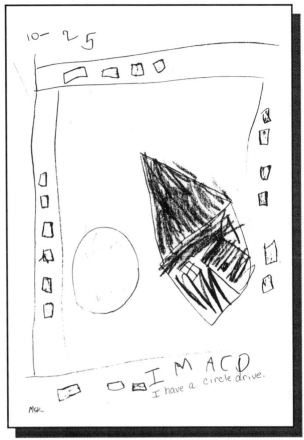

FIG. 9.7. Molly's map of her neighborhood.

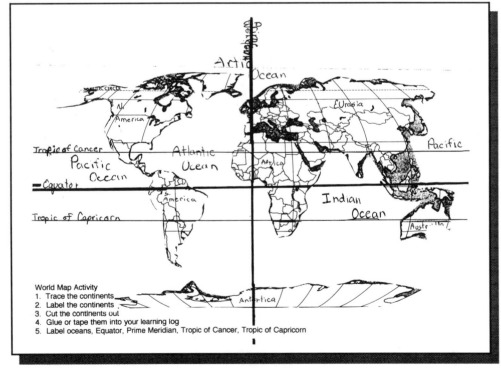

FIG. 9.8. Alexandra's map of the world.

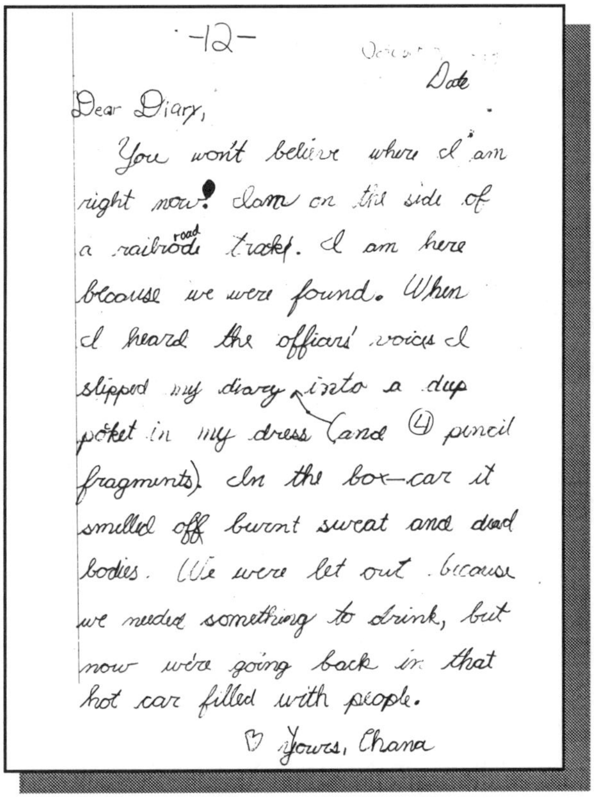

-12-
Date

Dear Diary,

You won't believe where I am right now! I am on the side of a railroad tracks. I am here because we were found. When I heard the officers' voices I slipped my diary into a deep pocket in my dress (and 4 pencil fragments) In the box-car it smelled off burnt sweat and dead bodies. (We were let out because we needed something to drink, but now we're going back in that hot car filled with people.

♡ Yours, Chana

FIG. 9.9. Using diary entries, Claire creates the character of Chana, a young German Jewish girl who lived and died during the Holocaust.

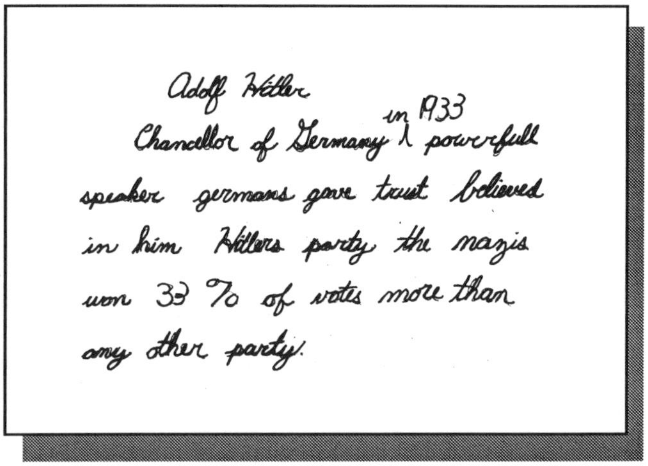

Adolf Hitler
Chancellor of Germany in 1933 a powerfull speaker germans gave trust believed in him Hitlers party the nazis won 33% of votes more than any other party.

FIG. 9.10. Claire records information on Hitler as a resource for her writing.

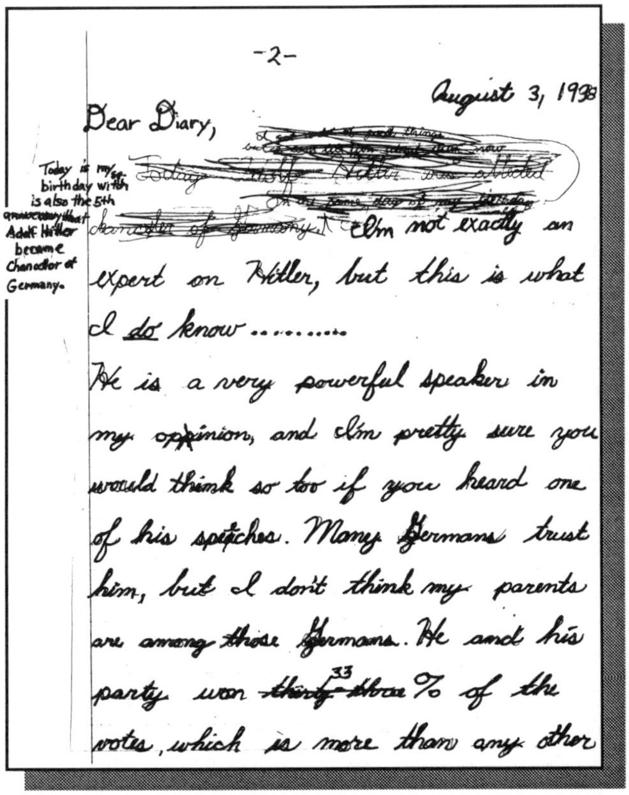

-2-
August 3, 1938

Dear Diary,

Today is my birthday with is also the 5th anniversary that Adolf Hitler became Chancellor of Germany.

I'm not exactly an expert on Hitler, but this is what I do know..........
He is a very powerful speaker in my opinion, and I'm pretty sure you would think so too if you heard one of his speeches. Many Germans trust him, but I don't think my parents are among those Germans. He and his party won thirty-three % of the votes, which is more than any other

FIG. 9.11. Claire uses the notes on Hitler to create a diary entry.

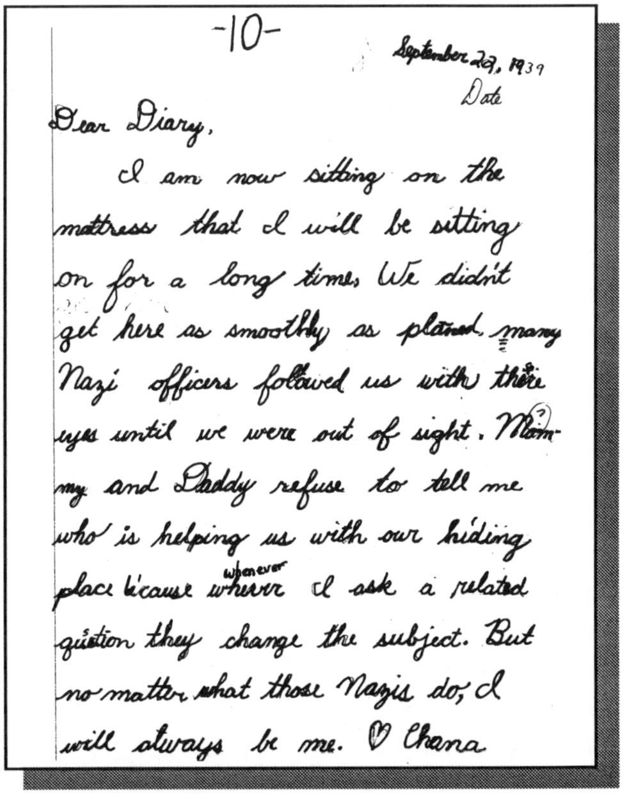

-10-
September 29, 1939
Date

Dear Diary,

I am now sitting on the mattress that I will be sitting on for a long time. We didn't get here as smoothly as planned, many Nazi officers followed us with their eyes until we were out of sight. Mommy and Daddy refuse to tell me who is helping us with our hiding place b'cause whenever I ask a related question they change the subject. But no matter what those Nazis do, I will always be me. ♡ Chana

FIG. 9.12. Claire's character reaches her hiding place. The fictional diary is finished by a friend, after Chana dies in a concentration camp.

APPENDIX A

Annotated Bibliography of Teaching Resources

GENERAL RESOURCES

The Journal Book (Fulwiler, 1987) is a collection of articles that describe the use of learning journals across the curriculum, at instructional levels from early primary through university graduate studies. These first-person accounts contain helpful ideas that can be adapted to almost any level.

Journaling: Engagements in Reading, Writing, and Thinking (Bromley, 1993) is an easy-to-use handbook that describes 13 different kinds of journals that can be used in elementary classrooms, including the double entry, draw and tell, buddy, and home–school journal. This how-to-do-it manual uses the stories of 25 classroom teachers to describe these journals and illustrates each with examples of student writing.

Graphic Organizers: Visual Strategies for Active Learning (Bromley et al., 1995) is a practical handbook for using graphic organizers in the content areas. The authors provide examples of each kind of organizer and illustrate their use with excerpts from conversations among real students.

Starting Early With Study Skills: A Week-By-Week Guide for Elementary Students (Irvin & Rose, 1995) is a compendium of ideas for helping students locate, analyze, and organize information. Included are techniques for promoting active reading and listening, taking useful notes, making and using maps, writing reports, and test taking. This book can be used as a teacher reference for minilessons and there are more than 90 reproducibles for students to use or keep for reference.

The Languages of Learning: How Children Talk, Write, Dance, Draw, and Sing Their Understanding of the World (Gallas, 1994) details the author's experience in helping children respond in a variety of ways to information and ideas in the primary curriculum. Classroom accounts illustrate the power of narrative to create a sense of community in the classroom, describe students' interaction with ideas in science, and show how art provides opportunities for students to communicate their understanding of ideas.

Using Non-Fiction Trade Books in the Elementary Classroom: From Ants to Zeppelins (Freeman & Person, 1992) is a collection of articles that describe the use of nonfiction to support learning in the content areas. Included are suggestions for evaluating nonfiction, ways to use informational books to develop reference skills, and ideas for using nonfiction literature in theme teaching.

Language Across the Curriculum in the Elementary Grades (Thaiss, 1986) describes how to make the elementary classroom "language rich" by helping students explore the curriculum through reading, writing, and talking about ideas. The first two chapters provide a theoretical base for the observations in five classrooms where teachers use language as a tool for learning in the content areas.

LITERATURE

Grand Conversations: Literature Groups in Action (Peterson & Eeds, 1990) describes a literature-based reading program that involves students meeting together in small groups to discuss books they have read. This helpful book contains ideas for selecting books and describes ways to introduce literary techniques. The presentation is organized around the conversations of real students.

Literacy Through Literature (Johnson & Louis, 1987) is a collection of creative ideas for responding to literature. Although it is directed to teachers of primary children, many of the ideas can be effectively used at the intermediate and middle school levels. Included are directions for creating story ladders, literary report cards, passports, wanted posters, letters, journals, book awards, sociograms, news reports, interviews, poetry, songs, and dramas.

WRITING

The Writing Corner (Cheyney, 1979) is a collection of practical and creative ideas for classroom writing that can be easily adapted to the journal format. Included are suggestions for creating poems, stories, outlines, family trees, newspapers, cartoons, stories, diaries, journals, logs, letters, and radio or television shows.

Teaching Writing: A Workshop Approach (Fiderer, 1993) describes the use of writing notebooks to develop ideas for writing and to practice writing skills. This helpful book contains practical ideas for integrating writing, thinking, reading, and discussion and provides suggestions for minilessons to introduce the elements of writing.

Writing Workshop Survival Kit (Muschla, 1993) describes the writing process and contains many helpful ideas for setting up and managing a writer's workshop. Included are 100 minilessons that describe types of writing, literary techniques, and writing mechanics. Also helpful are tips for teaching students how to revise, edit, and publish their writing.

In the Middle: Writing, Reading, and Learning with Adolescents (Atwell, 1987) traces the author's experience with setting up and conducting writing and reading workshops at the middle school level. Included are guidelines for minilessons, group sharing, peer conferences, teacher conferences, classroom management, and a wealth of anecdotal material. Of particular help are Atwell's suggestions for responding to young writers and her conference guidelines (pp. 95–96). An appendix contains reading and writing surveys, favorite adolescent fiction, and strategies for introducing the writing process.

Living Between the Lines (Calkins & Harwayne, 1991) provides an account of children's struggles to understand themselves and the world through their writing. In addition to ideas for reading and writing workshops, there are guidelines for writing memoirs, using picture books, and conducting research.

Lasting Impressions: Weaving Literature Into the Writing Workshop (Harwayne, 1992) describes the use of writer's notebooks to collect impressions and ideas. This book contains suggestions to help students improve their writing by examining literary techniques and genres. There are also ideas for minilessons, conferencing, and response groups.

MATHEMATICS

Writing to Learn Mathematics (Countryman, 1992) describes the use of journals, learning logs, letters, and autobiographies to investigate mathematics. Examples show how writing about mathematics improves reasoning abilities of students at all grade levels.

Linking Mathematics and Language: Practical Classroom Activities (McCallum & Whitlow, 1994) describes activities for integrating language and mathematics to help students explore patterns, logic, categories, measurement, numbers, estimation, geometry, graphs, and statistics.

Language in Mathematics (Bickmore-Brand, 1993) is a collection of articles that describe how to use literature to teach mathematics and how to use language to explore mathematical concepts.

Language in the Mathematics Classroom: Talking, Representing, Recording (Griffiths & Clyne, 1994) contains ideas for using the language arts to extend students' understanding of mathematics.

Books You Can Count On: Linking Mathematics and Literature (Griffiths & Clyne, 1991) by the same authors, contains many ideas for teaching primary mathematics through literature.

Read Any Good Math Lately?: Children's Books for Mathematical Learning, K–6 (Whitin & Wilde, 1992) describes how math-related children's literature can be used to help students investigate mathematical concepts and relationships. Annotations are provided for books with mathematical themes, including fiction, nonfiction, poetry, games and puzzles, and books with multicultural elements. Topics presented in this collection include place value, estimations, large numbers, geometry, measurement, fractions, classification, and computation.

It's the Story That Counts: More Children's Books for Mathematical Learning, K–6 (Whitin & Wilde, 1995) is a follow-up to *Read Any Good Math . . . .* It features additional math-related books, along with children's work samples that illustrate how children's literature helps students think mathematically. Annotations of books and suggested activities support instruction in measurement, the number system, statistics, and probability. Interesting features include a bibliography of 300 new books arranged by category, a Top 20 list, ideas for encouraging a multicultural perspective, and a chapter for grown-ups.

Math and Literature (K–3) (Burns, 1992) uses themes from literature to continue the exploration of a mathematical concept. Drawings, such as tallies, pictures, and markers are used to represent the elements of a problem and give children images to think with. There are 10 lessons that use children's books, with suggestions for using an additional 21. *Math and Literature (K–3): Book Two* (Sheffield, 1994) is a sequel to the Burns book, and contains new lessons for linking literature and writing with mathematics. It contains examples of students' work and real classroom experiences.

SCIENCE

The Astonishing Curriculum: Integrating Science and Humanities Through Language (Tchudi, 1993) is a collection of articles written by practicing teachers that suggest ideas for integrating the curriculum with group discussions, journals, hands-on activities, and research. The articles feature classroom anecdotes, examples of student dialogue, and samples of student work.

Science and Language Links: Classroom Implications (Scott, 1993) addresses the ways language supports science learning and describes activities that use science to develop children's language skills.

Science Workshop: A Whole Language Approach (Saul et al., 1993) contains helpful ideas for creating science workshops and suggests ways to integrate science and language learning. This helpful book also features an appendix of resources for teaching science and a collection of useful reproducible forms.

SOCIAL STUDIES

History Workshop: Reconstructing the Past With Elementary Students (Jorgensen, 1993) is a workshop approach to the study of history. This adaptation of the writing workshop describes history-related reading and writing conferences and includes examples of student work and classroom dialogue.

Connecting With the Past: History Workshop in Middle and High Schools (Brown, 1994) contains many good ideas for adapting the workshop concept to the study of history. Chapter 6 is of particular interest, because it describes the components of the history workshop, with attention to journal writing and group discussions.

Cooperative Learning: Getting Started (Ellis & Whalen, 1990) describes how to set up and facilitate work in cooperative groups. The authors also provide a rationale for cooperative learning, outlining both the social and academic benefits.

Constructing Buildings, Bridges, & Minds: Building an Integrated Curriculum Through Social Studies (Young, 1994) describes a classroom program designed around inquiry in the social sciences. Because writing is used as a tool for exploration, there are many interesting ideas that can be adapted to the journal format.

The Story of Ourselves: Teaching History Through Children's Literature (Tunnell & Ammon, 1993) is a collection of articles by writers and educators that provide helpful ideas for using trade books to support instruction in the social studies. Included are classroom examples of literature-based history programs, ways to use historical fiction, ideas for using trade books to teach about the Holocaust, and a list of American historical books for young readers.

Seeing the Whole Through Social Studies (Lindquist, 1995) describes an integrated approach to teaching the social studies, with "how-to-do-it" suggestions for integrating the content and processes of the content areas. There is an excellent description of how to use journals to record, respond to, and reflect on reading and an appendix full of activities and ideas, such as ABC organizers, little books, books of knowledge, storyboards, storyladders, interior monologues and a Civil War perspective newspaper. Also included are forms and illustrations of organizers that can be used for student research or evaluation.

Children's Literature & Social Studies: Selecting and Using Notable Books in the Classroom (Zarnowski & Gallagher, 1993) is published by the National Council for the Social Studies and features ideas for using quality children's trade books to support inquiry in the social studies. This book also includes classroom illustrations and an annotated bibliography.

How to Tape Instant Oral Biographies: Recording Your Family's Life Story in Sound and Sight (Zimmerman, 1992) is a great "how-to-do-it" book for getting students interested in their family's history. Interviewing techniques and questions are designed to build bridges between generations, and to be rewarding to both the subject and young biographer. A "Guide for Educators" section provides good ideas for incorporating oral biographies into the classroom program.

JOURNALS

Professional journals in curriculum and content areas frequently address issues of writing to learn and writing across the curriculum. Increasingly, these articles promote journals as tools for investigating concepts, sharing ideas, and assessment. Many of the current articles related to learning journals are referenced as part of the text of this book, but interested readers will want to follow new ideas for journaling as they are introduced in professional resources such as the following:

- *Language Arts*—National Council of Teachers of English.
- *Primary Voices K–6*—National Council of Teachers of English.
- *The Reading Teacher*—International Reading Association.
- *Science and Children*—National Science Teachers Association.
- *Social Education*—National Council for the Social Studies.
- *Educational Leadership*—Association for Supervision and Curriculum Development.
- *Middle School Journal*—National Middle School Association.
- *Teaching Children Mathematics*—National Council of Teachers of Mathematics.
- *Arithmetic Teacher*
- *Mathematics Teaching in the Middle School*

APPENDIX B

Interviews With Teachers Who Use Learning Journals

Journals are used in a wide variety of ways in classroom programs. The interviews and classroom descriptions included in this appendix are intended to provide the interested reader with an idea of how journals are used across the curriculum by teachers who follow both integrated and more traditional programs.

RALPH M. CAPTAIN SCHOOL, CLAYTON, MISSOURI

At Captain School, students use a variety of learning journals and logs throughout the elementary grades. At the lower primary levels, students keep monthly or themed journals, using split page drawing and writing paper stapled between construction paper covers. In later primary grades, journals are kept in folders or spiral notebooks. At the intermediate levels, many classes use hardbacked composition notebooks, because their booklike sturdiness helps them better withstand frequent and heavy use for recording and reference in the content areas. Additional materials, such as handouts, tests, science experiments, homework, and field trip notes are folded and taped onto individual pages in the journal. These pages are titled, numbered, and listed in a developing table of contents.

Third Grade—Dr. Dick Koblitz, Captain School

In Dick Koblitz's third-grade classroom, students keep individual journals for literature and math, and a general learning log to record information and ideas related to science or social studies. They also use bound construction paper journals provided by the district as a resource for exploring topics in the curriculum. These usually include (a) information about the topic; (b) ideas for student research; (c) location and semantic map outlines; (d) charts to help organize ideas, poems, and games; and (e) space for written responses. Students use these logs to explore a topic by interacting with ideas presented in class and responding with writing and drawing that assists the development of understanding.

A supplementary learning log provides a place for students to record additional research about topics in science and social studies and creates resources for projects and reports. Although a separate literature log is kept for recording responses to stories, students may use their learning logs to research topics related to literature they are studying. For example, as part of reading *Charlotte's Web,* students research information about spiders and record facts about penguins in their learning logs when they study *Mr. Popper's Penguins.*

At the end of the year, students review their journals for ideas to research topics on their own. From a favorite study or an intense personal interest, they develop a project that uses the skills they have developed during the year. For example, Jessie became interested in the Civil War after studying Abraham Lincoln and used his journal to record information for an independent project. Notes, drafts, and a bibliography were recorded in the journal and a final draft was produced on the word processor. Claire researched the Holocaust and created a diary, as it might have been written by a young girl at that time (see chapter 9 for an excerpt from this diary).

Third Grade—Susie Bargiel, Captain School

Students in Mrs. Bargiel's class use reflective journals, literature logs, math logs, and learning logs to explore the curriculum. Mrs. Bargiel believes that logs and journals help students

> organize and solidify learning, structure communication of ideas to others, and help them reflect on and revisit concepts addressed in class as a whole or in small group work. Logs and journals help document growth over time, so they may be used by all "stakeholders" (kids, teacher, parents) as evaluational tools.

She also believes that journals assist both instruction and evaluation, which she sees as interconnected and reciprocal activities, and observes:

> As I respond to logs, new ideas are explored within the context of meaningful communication. For example, sometimes kids share log entries within small groups or with the whole group, or I respond with my perceptions or ideas in writing or in conferences with individual students.

Fourth Grade—Kathleen Murphy, Captain School

Students in this fourth grade keep a general learning journal that includes reactions to and reflections about their learning experiences. The teacher provides them with prompts to help them with this reflection, such as: What part of the unit did you like best? Why? What helped you learn? Why? What would you change? Why? Math entries include definitions and illustrations for the concepts students are learning. Students cut out current events from the newspaper and write about them to share with the class. Journal entries that use drawings, sketches, and maps show what students have learned from field trips. Geography questions are part of a daily morning warmup and involve questions and research related to physical features of the earth. These exercises are taped into the journal, along with reactions to field trips, lesson presentations, practice exercises, and original poems and drawings. As students make entries in their journals, they create a developing table of contents.

Mrs. Murphy reviews five journals a night, which enables her to look more closely at every student's responses at least once a week. Her responses are encouraging and include suggestions to help students improve their learning. She asks questions to elicit additional learning and directs their attention to progress they have made. Journal entries are shared on a daily basis in the classroom to help students see new and different ways to respond to ideas and information.

Fifth Grade—Nancy Johnson, Captain School

Students use logs to record learning in every subject area in Mrs. Johnson's fifth grade. Entries in these logs are used for discussions between two students, for peer review, and for teacher review. Logs are also sent home for review and they provide a helpful resource for communication between parents and the teacher. Mrs. Johnson summarizes the value of journals to her students and herself as a teacher:

> Students have a record of their work and growth in one place. They automatically know everything is written in their logs, unless specific directions state otherwise. When they write their accomplishments for a quarter, everything (all the data) is right there. They clearly see their own growth, or lack of it. Because learning logs are a collection of student work, they provide an opportunity for me to look back over their work to see growth.

> I can also check to see if I have written notes to them about something they specifically need to focus attention on. It keeps me focused on the child—their abilities and progress. Logs are the best record of growth I've ever used. They are a wonderful tool to use in conferences. When I say a student has shown significant progress in an area, the proof is right there.

Tonia, who experiences difficulty with reading and the physical process of writing, listens to material read aloud and dictates ideas and understanding of content areas to a scribe. Tests and reports are completed this way, allowing the student to demonstrate her understanding of information and her own synthesis of the material presented. Other students in this class who can read, but who experience writing or attention difficulties, record their understanding of a topic on the computer and tape the printouts into their journals. Informational handouts are also folded and taped into the learning log for future reference.

At the fifth-grade level, students can study a topic in social studies by selecting any books they wish, but must record the titles of books read, respond to their reading, complete a certain number of projects, and share them with the class. Whole class discussions provide background knowledge and help students share and organize information. The teacher begins the discussion with a key topic and students add to the discussion from their reading. The remainder of class time, students do independent reading and response activities. A learning journal helps students be accountable for their reading and allows them to respond in individual ways.

Each student receives a set of unit guidelines. Included in these guidelines is the requirement that students read at least 30 pages per day in their books and keep a book with them to read at all times. They create a journal for each book, where they make a daily record of their feelings, thoughts, and reactions to what they are reading (see chapter 9 for Max's responses to his reading). During the course of the unit, each student completes two projects, based on a book they have read, and these projects are shared with the entire class.

Fifth Grade—Kathleen McDonald, Captain School

In Kathleen McDonald's classroom, students use a basic learning log that includes entries about all subjects except science, which is kept in a separate composition notebook. Ms. McDonald notes:

> When students are shy and do not contribute to discussions, journals allow teachers to see more accurately what they understand. Journal writing also allows students to create "something to say" when students meet in small or large groups. At the intermediate level, journals allow me to see how special they are in their responses, at an age where it is embarrassing to reveal themselves in public.

Each week, journals are sent home for parent review. Parents read and sign the journals and may write a note to the student, the teacher, or both. This provides enhanced communication about school work among the student, teacher, and parent.

Fifth Grade—Emily Grady and Lee Ann Lyons, Captain School

This fifth-grade class is taught by two teachers in a time-share situation, so students keep both a morning and an afternoon journal. Mathematics and science are kept in the morning journal and writing and literature are kept in the afternoon journal. Social studies is integrated and is kept in both journals. Students use their journals to record science experiments, their work and explanations in math, and responses to literature they read. They also include current events, instructions for playing math games, responses to field trips and classroom visitors, directed skill lessons, and morning check-in items.

Student journal entries include reactions to a learning experience and reflections about what has been learned and how they feel about the experience. Students use their journals as a reference and often share reflections or responses in either small or large group discussions. At the end of the day, students write a journal entry reflecting on the day. Day-end discussions of these reflections help the teachers "get the pulse on how a student is feeling about his or her learning and interactions during the day. This dialogue helps us blend the community learners." They often look at the journals for subjects they do not teach to find aspects of an individual student that might not have been seen or appreciated. They also use the journals to look at areas of concern about a student's progress. The students' reflections provide valuable insight and afford teachers the opportunity for personal dialogue that cannot always occur in the classroom due to time constraints.

Introduction to journals and their organization occurs early in the school year:

> Early in the year we model how to expand ideas in order to get to different layers of learning. Since the students use the learning journal the entire year as a reference tool for all learning, we take time to organize the table of contents and set up a system that is easy for everyone to use. We want the students, as well as ourselves, to be able to locate a particular piece of information quickly. Therefore, all entries are given a page number, dated, and recorded in the table of contents.

The teachers note that they respond to entries and ask that parents periodically do the same. They comment on individual entries as needed, for depth of understanding, clarification, or correction. Parents respond by writing notes in the journals, encouraging their children's work, reminding them of their goals, and praising their efforts. By using the journal as an assessment tool, these fifth-grade teachers see specific measurable growth as the year progresses. Students participate in this evaluation when they are asked periodically to look over their journals, reflect on the growth they have made as learners, and then write a response. Their teachers observe that these "reflections are often impressive and exude honesty about themselves as learners."

With student permission, selected responses from journals are projected on the overhead. These responses are analyzed in terms of language used, personal connections, and what makes sense or needs clarification. As the year progresses, the teachers notice that students begin making connections between subjects, such as the unit on interdependence and a literature study of *The Island of the Blue Dolphins*. Students also increasingly relate what they are learning in school to their own experience.

IDEAS FROM OTHER SCHOOLS

Kindergarten—Claudia Loehring, Henning School, Troy, Illinois

Mrs. Loehring uses journals in conjunction with thematic units in her kindergarten class.

> For example, we study about zebras by reading both fiction and non-fiction books. Before the children write, we make a word bank (including illustrations), put up pictures of zebras and display zebra books. Before the children begin, I model an example of how a page might look. As I circulate around the room, I encourage the children to try writing their own words. Then I sit at a table and have them come to me and tell me about their journal entry. It's at this time they can dictate to me or I "underwrite" on the page to interpret their "kindergarten" spelling.

Mrs. Loehring believes that journals help her students organize their thoughts, learn sequencing skills, develop responsibility to finish a task, take pride in a finished product, and feel successful. She adds:

> Journals help me learn about the children's personalities. Sometimes a quiet child is hard to get to know. By studying his or her journal entries, I can learn what the child is actually thinking. I can see, at a glance, if children are grasping phonics, beginning and ending sounds and other elements of writing.

First Grade—Gail Nave, Tampa Palms Elementary, Tampa, Florida

Mrs. Nave's students keep journals in hanging files. In response to books read aloud and theme topics, students draw pictures and write, recording their name and dating their entry with a stamp. Students also keep math journals made from 8½" × 11" paper cut in half and stapled together with construction paper covers. In these daily math journals, students record equations for each successive day in school, then discuss how they find answers to their problems.

Second Grade—Pat Sheahan, Summerfield School, Summerfield, Illinois

Mrs. Sheahan uses several types of journals with her second-grade class. Children record a grammar or phonics skill in a notebook at the end of each day, with the assignment to find three words that are examples. Comparison words, prefixes, suffixes, rhyming words, and parts of speech are included. The next day:

> each child shares his or her word in a sentence and, if necessary, gives the definition of the word. The class often uses the Skills Notebook for alphabetizing words, writing sentences, reviewing syllabication, finding rhyming words and writing poems and stories. This exercise encourages parent involvement and increased use of the dictionary. Within a few weeks, children begin bringing in as many words as possible, far surpassing the three words required. Throughout the school year, the children call my attention to words which could go into their Skills Notebook.

Second graders in this classroom use writing journals and record responses to topics proposed by the teacher or those they select themselves. They also use the journals to express personal concerns or happiness about events in their lives. The teacher notes, "Journal writing gives me insight into the feelings of my children and allows me to evaluate their writing skills. I can also note proficiency in spelling, vocabulary and sentence structure."

Mrs. Sheahan has a personal journal that includes a professional biography, school information, personal information, articles for current reading, a list of books in her personal library, school photos of the children in her class, and a section that includes newspaper articles, journal clippings, and letters related to professional recognition.

Third Grade—Ingrid Owens, Summerfield School

Students in Mrs. Owens' class keep two journals: one for phonics, vocabulary, and skills and the other for personal reflection, narratives, creative writing, persuasive writing, and expository writing. In addition to the other values of these journals, they also help students prepare for the Illinois Goals and Progress writing test. Mrs. Owens notes:

> Journals are valuable to students because they have copies of their work and can follow their own progress. When they want to share a story or polish one for publication, they know where to find the material. Plus, the act of writing frequently improves their skills. It is always amazing to them how they have changed during the year. Journals are valuable to me as a teacher because students often tell personal things they might not want to share openly in class. I make sharing time voluntary. Sometimes just being able to write about an experience gives closure to that event. Of course, I can also tell if they need to practice spelling, capitalization or punctuation.

Fourth Grade—Pam Senjan, Sihler School, Litchfield, Illinois

Mrs. Senjan organizes instruction in her classroom around hands-on, self-instruction centers, including writing, spelling, computers, social studies, science, and reading. Students use journals to record their work for language and science. For example, at the science center, students record their observations and steps in conducting an experiment. Later, they use these notes to discuss the experiment as a class and correlate the topic with what is going on in other areas of the curriculum. Students also use their journals at the beginning of a unit to record what they already know about a topic.

Mrs. Senjan believes that journal writing provides her with information for formative assessment. A brief review of the journals lets her know more specifically which students are experiencing difficulty with understanding. If only a few are having problems, they can be drawn into a small group for review, but if most of the class is having difficulty, this indicates the need for reteaching specific concepts. Mrs. Senjan also believes that journals provide a helpful complement to testing. Not all students test well, and a review of journal entries can often better indicate a student's true level of understanding. She observes:

> I feel that journals allow students to better understand what they are doing. At the science centers, they record the processes of an experiment: the hypothesis, procedure, materials, conclusions and results. From their writing, I can tell what they have learned. Often they draw pictures, rather than write, to show me what they have learned. After reading *At the Waterworks* in Joanna Cole's *Magic Schoolbus* series, I asked the class to record interesting facts about water that they did not know before the study. An inclusion student, who has difficulty writing, drew pictures to express his ideas, and I could tell where he was experiencing difficulties in understanding.

Fourth Grade—Sue Wolf, St. Boniface School, Edwardsville, Illinois

Students in Mrs. Wolf's fourth grade use journals for a variety of purposes. Entries are dated and include creative writing, descriptions of outside of school activities and responses to social studies, extracurricular activities, and school events, such as all school assemblies and invited speakers. Combining social studies and creative writing, Mrs. Wolf might ask students to pretend that they are early American settlers and to record a description of a typical day in their journals. For specific writing assignments, students share their journal entries by reading them aloud to the rest of the class. Other kinds of entries are shared on a voluntary basis.

When asked why they enjoy writing in their journals, students eagerly responded, listing reasons such as: "I've got all these things in my head I want to write about"; "I like to look back at what I've learned or thought about"; "I can get lost in my imagination"; and "I can pretend like I'm a person in history." When asked to think of reasons why they did not like journal writing, one student replied: "It hurts my hand, because there's so much I want to write!" Wolf, who is an avid writer herself, describes how journals provide support for her teaching:

I learn children's likes and dislikes and become familiar with their writing abilities and styles. Journals help me look at children through *their* eyes. Specific writing assignments help bring closure to a topic, program or event. For example, last week the band teacher gave the entire class kazoos to take home. The next day they recorded their experiences: tunes they tried to play; sounds they made; and reactions of parents and siblings (some quite humorous). They also wrote descriptions of the instrument and recorded some music theory.... Best of all, the students wrote about a personal experience that they enjoyed.

Fifth Grade—Christine Lanning, Summerfield School

Mrs. Lanning uses research and creative writing journals during center time, while several students attend the resource room. She also meets with individual students for book conferences during this time. Students keep a research notebook to record information related to a current social studies topic, a holiday, or something else of interest. Creative writing journal entries are made in response to teacher prompts or topics chosen by the students. Mrs. Lanning observes that students seem to write with more focus in response to a specific topic. She notes:

> Even though the notebooks aren't graded, I can check them and get a view of the student's handwriting, spelling and grammar. I also am able to find what interests them. If they are interested in a topic, they may write more than the required ½ page in their research notebook. Often students will write me a personal note in one of their notebooks. These students won't always contribute to a discussion, but will share a personal item, such as a vacation to a place we've discussed.

Fifth Grade—Jackie Hogue, Marine School, Marine, Illinois

In Mrs. Hogue's fifth-grade classroom, students use literature journals to record their responses to literature and to prepare for group discussions. Each member of the literature circle performs a necessary function for the group and these jobs rotate from meeting to meeting. Group jobs include the following:

- *Secretary*—fills out the literature circle contract and records assignments.
- *Reader*—reads discussion questions.
- *Checker*—makes sure everyone has come to group prepared with necessary materials and assignments completed.
- *Encourager*—uses positive comments to support and motivate members.
- *Coordinator*—makes sure that everyone has a chance to talk; keeps the group on task.

Together, they decide on a group assignment (how many chapters or pages to read) and then they silently read the agreed on assignment. When they have finished reading, they write their responses in their journals for the next literature circle meeting. These include:

1. Responses to discussion questions.
2. Page number and paragraph of a passage to read aloud.

3. Connections with personal knowledge or experience.
4. Vocabulary words (words new to the reader), page number and paragraph where they are located, and an explanation of how they figured them out.

The group records difficult or new words from the book on individual bookmarks. When they have completed a book, they choose five words and quiz each other on the spelling and definitions. The teacher may visit the group periodically to observe individual participation and group dynamics or she may schedule a group conference when they have completed their reading and discussion. Each group completes a project related to the book, which might include a bulletin board, a report on the book, reading parts of the book aloud to a younger class, writing a story in the same genre, drawing characters, or making character wheels.

In this fifth-grade classroom, students have a journal for each subject. When they discuss sentences with grammar mistakes, they write the relevant rule in their English journals. Spelling journals are used to record specialized vocabulary words from science and social studies that are used frequently in writing. Students create sentences with the words, using information from their study in the content areas. They also create project journals, which involve topics from science or social studies. For example, when students research a key battle of the Revolutionary War, they take notes in their journals, looking for the who, what, when, where, and why. These notes are used to write newspaper articles about the battle. Reading journals are used to write summaries of what they have read, or they may write with a buddy and ask each other questions about their books. Math journals record computation and sentences that describe how students worked their problems. Mrs. Hogue says:

> Journals help me know when I need to spend more time on a concept and when to move on. I like reading their connections in literature journals, and often times, I can relate a similar story that happened to me. Because all the work is saved in the journal, there's no question about assignments that were turned in or not turned in. Parents like seeing the accumulation of work too. I don't give tests often, but when I do, I let the kids use their journals for reference. After the first time, I could see an improvement in the thoroughness of their research! When I give a grammar quiz, they scramble for their English journals. Often times kids will ask me if they can write in their journals or beg for more time to write.

Mrs. Hogue notes that she has kept her own journal, which served different purposes at different times (see chapter 4 for excerpts from this journal). She keeps a check list with responses to the questions "What are you researching now?" and "What is your goal for today?" The next day, she inquires about how much was accomplished, if the goal was reached, and any new plans. Students seem to stay on task better, because they know the teacher is aware of what they are doing. She also keeps similar notes on each student for literature study.

Sixth Grade—Susy Drake, Marine School

Mrs. Drake currently uses reading and writing journals with her sixth-grade students and has experimented with math journals. Students used their math journals to generate examples of problems, explain them, and make up their own word problems. She believes that journals are valuable to students because:

> Writing completes the process of observation and thinking, and improves both comprehension and retention. Journals help me have much better insight into student understanding, because I can detect their strengths and difficulties. For example, with math journals, if students don't understand the concept, they have difficulty explaining what they don't understand. It puts them in the position of teaching the concept themselves and if they can do that, they understand.

Mrs. Drake keeps a journal in the back of her plan book, which keeps everything together. She makes a note of successful or unsuccessful activities and uses this record as a reference for the following year.

Seventh Grade—Vivian Rohleder, Marie Shaefer Junior High, O'Fallon, Illinois

Mrs. Rohleder's class uses literature journals as part of a reading workshop. This involves sustained reading, with 5- to 10-minute minilessons each day. Students record notes on their individual reading in their journals, including their thoughts, descriptions, connections, and questions. She notes that, "Students are thinking more critically about what they read. Some have gone from summaries to analysis of character and author's style." Mrs. Rohleder believes that journals are valuable to students because they "allow students to reconstruct the literature they are reading. They are also a useful discussion tool, reminding the students what they want to question or say about the literature." She observes that journals provide her with a picture of individual students and how they think. She notes that what she learns about a student's background through the connections they make with literature helps her better understand them as persons and learners.

From experience, she notes that it is impossible to respond thoughtfully to the journal entries of 150 students on a weekly basis, and is careful to explain to her students that the journal's primary audience is themselves. Because her students have indicated that they want other audiences for their journals, she offers them the option of getting feedback either from herself or another student twice per month. Journals are also sent home twice per quarter for parents to respond to their children's writing.

References

Abbott, E. A. (1992). *Flatland: A romance of many dimensions.* Verplanck, NY: Emerson. (Original work published 1884)

Altwerger, B. & Flores, B. (1994). Theme cycles: Creating communities of learners. *Primary Voices K–6, 2*(1), 2–6.

Armstrong, T. (1994). *Multiple intelligences in the classroom.* Alexandria, VA: Association for Supervision and Curriculum Development.

Atwell, N. (1987). *In the middle: Writing, reading, and learning with adolescents.* Portsmouth, NH: Boynton/Cook.

Baratta-Lorton, M. (1994). *Mathematics their way.* Saratoga, CA: Center for Innovation in Education.

Baratta-Lorton, R. (1994). *Mathematics, a way of thinking.* Saratoga, CA: Center for Innovation in Education.

Barnes, D. (1976). *From communication to curriculum.* New York: Penguin.

Barnes, D., & Todd, F. (1977). *Communication and learning in small groups.* London: Routledge & Kegan Paul.

Beane, J. (1993). Problems and possibilities for an integrative curriculum. *Middle School Journal, 25*(1), 18–23.

Bickmore-Brand, J. (Ed.). (1993). *Language in mathematics.* Portsmouth, NH: Heinemann.

Brandt, R. (1991). Editor's note. *Educational Leadership, 48*(6), 3.

Britton, J. (1990). Talking to learn. In D. Barnes, J. Britton, & M. Torbe (Eds.), *Language, the learner and the school* (pp. 89–130). Portsmouth, NH: Heinemann.

Britton, J. (1993). *Language and learning.* Portsmouth, NH: Boynton/Cook.

Britton, J., Burgess, T., Martin, N., McLeod, A., & Rosen, H. (1975). *The development of writing abilities (11–18).* London: Macmillan.

Bromley, K. (1993). *Journaling: Engagements in reading, writing, and thinking.* New York: Scholastic.

Bromley, K., Irwin-De Vitis, L., & Modlo, M. (1995). *Graphic organizers.* New York: Scholastic.

Brown, C. S. (1994). *Connecting with the past: History workshops in middle and high schools.* Portsmouth, NH: Heinemann.

Bruner, J. (1960). *The process of education.* New York: Vintage.

Bruner, J. (1966). *Toward a theory of instruction.* Cambridge, MA: Harvard University Press.

Bruner, J. (1990). *Acts of meaning.* Cambridge, MA: Harvard University Press.

Bullock, A. (1975). *Language for life* (Report of the Committee of Inquiry appointed by the Secretary of State for Education and Science). London: Her Majesty's Stationary Office.

Burns, M. (1987). *A collection of math lessons, from grades 3 through 6.* Portsmouth, NH: Heinemann.

Burns, M. (1991–1995). *Math by all means* (Series for 2nd, 3rd, 4th grades). Portsmouth, NH: Math Solutions-Heinemann.

Burns, M. (1992). *Math and literature (K–3).* White Plains, NY: Math Solutions.

Burns, M., & Humphreys, C. (1990). *A collection of math lessons, from grades 6 through 8.* Portsmouth, NH: Heinemann.

Burns, M., & Tank, B. (1987). *A collection of math lessons, from grades 1 through 3.* Portsmouth, NH: Heinemann.

Caine, R., & Caine, G. (1994). *Making connections: Teaching and the human brain.* New York: Addison-Wesley.

Caine, R., & Caine, G. (1995). Reinventing schools through brain-based learning. *Educational Leadership, 52*(4), 43–47.

Calkins, L. M., & Harwayne, S. (1991). *Living between the lines.* Portsmouth, NH: Heinemann.

Cheyney, A. B. (1979). *The writing corner.* Glenview, IL: Scott, Foresman.

Chittenden, L. (1982). What if all the whales are gone before we become friends? In M. Barr, P. D'Arcy, & M. K. Healy (Eds.), *What's going on: Language learning episodes in British and American classrooms, grades 4–13* (pp. 36–51). Portsmouth, NH: Boynton/Cook.

Churchland, P. (1995). *The engine of reason, the seat of the soul: A philosophical journey into the brain.* Cambridge, MA: MIT Press.

Clarke, L. K. (1988). Invented versus traditional spelling in first grader's writings: Effects on learning to spell and read. *Research in the Teaching of English, 22,* 281–309.

Countryman, J. (1992). *Writing to learn mathematics.* Portsmouth, NH: Heinemann.

Crafton, L. K., & Burk, C. (1994). Inquiry-based evaluation: Teachers and students reflecting together. *Primary Voices K–6, 2*(2), 2–7.

D'Arcy, P. (1977). *Writing across the curriculum: Language for learning.* Exeter, England: Exeter University School of Education.

D'Arcy, P. (1987). Writing to learn. In T. Fulwiler (Ed.), *The journal book* (pp. 41–46). Portsmouth, NH: Boynton/Cook.

D'Arcy, P. (1989). *Making sense, shaping meaning: Writing in the context of a capacity-based approach to learning.* Portsmouth, NH: Boynton/Cook,

Dewey, J. (1964). *Democracy and education.* New York: Macmillan. (Original work published 1916)

Duckworth, E. (1987). *"The having of wonderful ideas" and other essays on teaching and learning.* New York: Teachers College Press.

Dunston, P. J. (1992). A critique of graphic organizer research. *Reading Research and Instruction, 31*(2), 57–65.

Eggers, M. (1995, Spring). As cited in Using language and literature to explore mathematics. *Lewis and Clark Reading Council Newsletter,* p. 5.

Eisner, E. (1977). Cognition and representation: A way to pursue the American dream. *Delta Kappa, 78*(5), 348–353.

Ellis, S. S., & Whalen, S. F. (1990). *Cooperative learning: Getting started.* New York: Scholastic.

Evans, C. S. (1984). Writing to learn in math. *Language Arts, 61,* 825–835.

Fiderer, A. (1993). *Teaching writing: A workshop approach.* New York: Scholastic.

Freeman, E. B., & Person, D. G. (Eds.). (1992). *Using nonfiction trade books in the elementary classroom: From ants to zeppelins.* Urbana, IL: National Council of Teachers of English.

Fulwiler, T. (1987). *The journal book.* Portsmouth, NH: Boynton/Cook.

Gallas, K. (1994). *The languages of learning: How children talk, write, dance, draw, and sing their understanding of the world.* New York: Teachers College Press.

Gardner, H. (1992). *Multiple intelligences: The theory in practice.* New York: Basic Books.

Gomez, M. L, Graue, M. E., & Bloch, M. N. (1991). Reassessing portfolio assessment: Rhetoric and reality. *Language Arts, 68,* 620–628.

Graham, A. L. (1994). Writing to learn: Placing the student center stage. *Middle School Journal, 25*(4), 7–10.

Graves, D. (1991). *Build a literate classroom.* Portsmouth, NH: Heinemann.

Griffiths, R., & Clyne, M. (1991). *Books you can count on.* Portsmouth, NH: Heinemann.

Griffiths, R., & Clyne, M. (1994). *Language in the mathematics classroom.* Portsmouth, NH: Heinemann.

Gunderson, L., & Shapiro, J. (1988). Whole language instruction: Writing in 1st grade. *The Reading Teacher, 41,* 430–437.

Hanselman, C. (1996). Using brainstorming webs in the mathematics classroom. *Mathematics Reaching in the Middle School, 1*(9), 766–770.

Hart, L. (1983). *Human brain and human learning.* New York: Longman.

Harwayne, S. (1992). *Lasting impressions: Weaving literature into the writing process.* Portsmouth, NH: Heinemann.

Healy, M. K. (1981). Purpose in learning to write: An approach to writing in three curriculum areas. In C. H. Frederiksen & J. F. Dominic (Eds.), *Writing: The nature, development and teaching of written communication* (Vol. 2, pp. 223–232). Hillsdale, NJ: Lawrence Erlbaum Associates.

Hough, D. L., & Donlan, D. (1994). Achieving independent student responses through integrated instruction. *Middle School Journal, 25*(5), 35–42.

International Reading Association (IRA) and National Council of Teachers of English (NCTE) Joint Task Force on Assessment. (1994). *Standards for the assessment of reading and writing* (IRA Publication No. 674, NCTE Publication No. 02131). Urbana, IL: National Council of Teachers of English.

International Reading Association (IRA) and National Council of Teachers of English (NCTE). (1996). *Standards for the English language arts* (IRA Publication No. 889, NCTE Publication No. 46767–3050). Urbana, IL: National Council of Teachers of English.

Irvin, L., & Rose, E. O. (1995). *Starting early with study skills: A week-by-week guide for elementary students*. Boston: Allyn & Bacon.

Isaacs, J., & Brodine, J. (1994). *Journals in the classroom: A complete guide for the classroom*. Winnipeg, Canada: Pequis.

Jaggar, A. M., Carrara, D. H., & Weiss, S. E. (1986). Research currents: The influence of reading on children's narrative writing (and vice versa). *Language Arts, 63,* 292–300.

Johnson, N., & Ebert, M. J. (1992). Time travel is possible: Historical fiction and biography—Passport to the past. *The Reading Teacher, 45*(7), 488–495.

Johnson, T. D., & Louis, D. R. (1987). *Literacy through literature*. Portsmouth, NH: Heinemann.

Jorgensen, K. (1993). *History workshop: Reconstructing the past with elementary students*. Portsmouth, NH: Heinemann.

Koblitz, D. (1995). New perspectives on teaching and learning spelling. *Mid-Missouri TAWL Newsletter* (p. 2) and *Clayton Curriculum Quarterly* (pp. 3–4).

Language and Learning Across the Curriculum Committee. (1995). *Learning through language: A call for action in all disciplines* (NCTE Publication No. 04061). Urbana, IL: National Council of Teachers of English.

Lemke, J. L. (1990). *Talking science: Language, learning and values*. Norwood, NJ: Ablex.

Lindquist, T. (1995). *Seeing the whole through social studies*. Portsmouth, NH: Heinemann.

McCallum, R., & Whitlow, R. (1994). *Linking mathematics and language: Practical classroom activities*. Markham, Ontario: Pippin.

Medway, P. (1980). *Language in science*. Hatfield, England: The Association for Science Education.

Moss, B. (1991). Children's nonfiction trade books: A complement to content area texts. *The Reading Teacher, 45*(1), 26–32.

Myers, J. (1984). *Writing to learn*. Bloomington, IN: Phi Delta Kappa.

Muschla, G. (1993). *Writing workshop survival kit*. West Nyack, NY: Center for Applied Research in Education.

O'Neill, D. K. (1996). *The Co-Vis Project*. Available by e-mail: oneill@covis.nwu.edu.

Peterson, R., & Eeds, M. (1990). *Grand conversations: Literature groups in action*. New York: Scholastic.

Peto-Ostberg, C. (1992, Spring). Stepping into the writing process. *WLSIG Newsletter: Whole Language Special Interest Group of I. R. A., 5*(2), 2–3.

Popp, M. (1995, Fall). Using learning journals to explore the elementary curriculum. *Lewis and Clark Reading Council Newsletter 8*(6), 3–4.

Popp, M. (1996). *Teaching language and literature in elementary classrooms: A guide to professional development*. Mahwah, NJ: Lawrence Erlbaum Associates.

Purves, A. C., & Monson, D. L. (1984). *Experiencing children's literature*. Glenview, IL: Scott, Foresman.

Richards, I. A. (1958). *How to read a page*. Boston: Beacon Press.

Rosenblatt, L. (1978). *The reader, the text, and the literary work*. Carbondale: Southern Illinois University Press.

Rosenblatt, L. (1983). *Literature as exploration* (4th ed.). New York: Modern Language Association.

Rosenblatt, L. (1985). Language, literature and values. In S. N. Tchudi (Ed.), *Language, schooling, and society* (pp. 64–80). Upper Montclair, NJ: Boynton/Cook.

Rosenblatt, L. (1991). Literature—S.O.S! *Language Arts, 68*(6), 444–448.

Rudell, R. (1992). A whole language and literature prospective: Creating a meaning-making instructional environment. *Language Arts, 69,* 612–619.

Salesi, R. (1992). Reading and writing connection: Supporting content-area literacy through nonfiction trade books. In E. B. Freeman & D. G. Person (Eds.), *Using nonfiction trade books in the elementary classroom: From ants to zeppelins* (pp. 86–94). Urbana, IL: National Council of Teachers of English.

Salk, J. (1995, August 1) [An interview]. *Bottom Line: Personal,* p. 13.

Saul, W., Reardon, J., Schmidt, A., Pearce, C., Blackwood, D., & Bird, M. D. (1993). *Science workshop: A whole language approach.* Portsmouth, NH: Heinemann.

Schiebelhut, C. (1994). I do and I understand, I reflect and I improve. *Teaching Children Mathematics, 1*(4), 242–246.

Scott, J. (Ed.). (1993). *Science and language links: Classroom implications.* Portsmouth, NH: Heinemann.

Sheffield, S. (1994). *Math and literature (K–3): Book two.* Portsmouth, NH: Heinemann.

Sparks-Langer, G. M., & Colton, A. B. (1991). Synthesis of research on teachers' reflective thinking. *Educational Leadership, 48*(6), 37–44.

Stice, C. F., & Bertrand, N. P. (1990). *Whole language and the emergent literacy of at-risk children: A two year comparative study.* Nashville: Center for Excellence, Basic Skills, Tennessee State University. (ERIC Document Reproduction Service No. ED 324 626)

Stillman, P. (1987). Of myself, for myself. In T. Fulwiler (Ed.), *The journal book* (pp. 77–86). Portsmouth, NH: Boynton/Cook.

Stires, S. (1993). Writing all day. *Primary Voices K–6, 1*(1), 14–19.

Stix, A. (1992). The development and field testing of a multimodal method for teaching mathematical concepts to preservice teachers by utilizing pictorial journal writing (Doctoral dissertation, Columbia University Teachers College, 1992). *Dissertation Abstracts International, 92,* 18719.

Sulzby, E. (1992). Research directions: Transitions from emergent to conventional writing. *Language Arts, 69,* 290–297.

Summerfield, G. (1987). Not in utopia: Reflections on journal-writing. In T. Fulwiler (Ed.), *The journal book* (pp. 33–40). Portsmouth, NH: Boynton/Cook.

Tchudi, S. (Ed.). (1993). *The astonishing curriculum: Integrating science and humanities through language.* Urbana, IL: National Council of Teachers of English.

Thaiss, C. (1986). *Language across the curriculum in the elementary grades.* Urbana, IL: National Council of Teachers of English.

Tomlinson, C. A. (1993). A flexible tool for encouraging academic and personal growth. *Middle School Journal, 25*(1), 55–59.

Torbe, M., & Medway, P. (1981). *The climate for learning.* London: Ward Lock Educational Press.

Trelease, J. (1995). *The new read-aloud handbook* (3rd ed.). New York: Penguin.

Tunnell, M. O., & Ammon, R. (1993). *The story of ourselves: Teaching history through children's literature.* Portsmouth, NH: Heinemann.

Vacca, R., & Vacca J. (1993). *Content area reading* (4th ed.). New York: HarperCollins.

Vygotsky, L. S. (1962). *Thought and language.* Cambridge, MA: MIT Press.

Wellington, B. (1991). The promise of reflective practice. *Educational Leadership, 48*(6), 4–5.

Whitin, D. J., & Wilde, S. (1992). *Read any good math lately? Children's books for mathematical learning, K–6.* Portsmouth, NH: Heinemann.

Whitin, D. J., & Wilde, S. (1995). *It's the story that counts: More children's books for mathematical learning, K–6.* Portsmouth, NH: Heinemann.

Willis, S., & Checkley, K. (1996, Summer). Bring mathematics to life. *Curriculum Update,* pp. 1–7.

Winship, M. (1993). Writing informational books in a first-grade classroom. *Primary Voices K–6, 1*(1), 7–13.

Wollman-Bonilla, J. E., & Werchaldo, B. (1995). Literature response journals in a first-grade classroom. *Language Arts, 72,* 562–570.

Young, K. A. (1994). *Constructing buildings, bridges, & minds.* Portsmouth, NH: Heinemann.

Zarnowski, M., & Gallagher, A. (Eds.). (1993). *Children's literature & social studies: Selecting and using notable books in the classroom.* Washington, DC: National Council for the Social Studies.

Zimmerman, B. (1992). *How to tape instant oral biographies: Recording your family's life story in sound and sight.* New York: Bantam Books.

CHILDREN'S BOOKS REFERENCED IN THE TEXT

Adler, D. (1990). *A picture book of Thomas Jefferson.* New York: Holiday House.

Avi. (1991). *Nothing but the truth.* New York: Orchard.

Avi. (1992). *The true confessions of Charlotte Doyle.* Dresdon, TN: Avon.

Base, G. (1986). *Animalia.* New York: Harry N. Abrams.

Birch, D. (1988). *The king's chessboard.* Bergenfield, NJ: Dial.

Blos, J. (1979). *A gathering of days: A New England girl's journal.* New York, Scribner.

Carle, E. (1969). *The very hungry caterpillar.* East Rutherford, NJ: G. P. Putnam.

Carle, E. (1977). *The grouchy ladybug.* New York: Harper.

Carle, E. (1987) *Rooster's off to see the world.* East Rutherford, NJ: G. P. Putnam.

Cleary, B. (1983). *Dear Mr. Henshaw.* New York: Morrow.

Conrad, P. (1991). *Pedro's journal: A voyage with Christopher Columbus, August 3, 1942–February 14, 1493.* New York: Boyds Mill.

Cushman, K. (1994). *Catherine, called Birdie.* New York: HarperCollins.

Filipovic, Z. (1994). *Zlata's diary: A child's life in Sarajevo.* New York: Scholastic.

Fitzhugh, L. (1964). *Harriet the spy.* New York: Harper.

Frank, A. (1961). *Anne Frank: The diary of a young girl.* New York: Doubleday.

Fritz, J. (1976). *Will you sign here, John Hancock?* New York: Scholastic.

George, J. (1988). *My side of the mountain.* New York: Trumpet Club.

Gurney, J. (1992). *Dinotopia: A land apart from time.* New York: Scholastic.

Gurney, J. (1995). *Dinotopia: The world beneath.* New York: Scholastic.

Heller, R. (1987). *A cache of jewels and other collective nouns.* New York: Scholastic.

Heller, R. (1988). *Kites sail high.* New York: Scholastic.

Heller, R. (1989). *Many luscious lollipops: A book about adjectives.* New York: Scholastic.

Hesse, K. (1993). *Letters from Rifka.* Westminster, MD: Crown.

Huff, D. (1954). *How to lie with statistics.* New York: Norton.

Humez, A., Humez, N., & Maguire, J. (1993). *Zero to lazy eight: The romance of numbers.* New York: Simon & Schuster.

Hutchins, P. (1986). *The doorbell rang.* Fairfield, NJ: Greenwillow.

James, E., & Barkin, C. (1978). *What do you mean by average?* New York: Lothrop, Lee & Shephard.

Johnson, S. T. (1995). *Alphabet city.* New York: Viking.

Little, J. (1986). *Hey world, here I am!* New York: Harper Row.

McGovern, A. (1970). *. . . If you sailed on the Mayflower in 1620.* New York: Scholastic.

Nichol, B. (1994). *Beethoven lives upstairs.* New York: Orchard.

Pallota, J. (1992). *The icky bug counting book.* Watertown, MA: Charlesbridge.

Sandburg, C. (1982). Arithmetic. In L. B. Hopkins (Comp.), *Rainbows are made: Poems by Carl Sandburg.* New York: Harcourt.

Sandved, K. B. (1996). *The butterfly alphabet.* New York: Scholastic.

Schwartz, D. (1985). *How much is a million?* New York: Scholastic.

Scieszka, J., & Smith, L. (1995). *Math curse.* New York: Viking.

Weiss, M. E. (1977). *Solomon Grundy, born on oneday: A finite arithmetic puzzle.* New York: Harper.

Williams, V. (1981). *Three days on a river in a red canoe.* New York: Scholastic.

Williams, V. (1988). *Stringbean's trip to the shining sea.* Fairfield, NJ: Greenwillow.

Wright, B. R. (1983). *The dollhouse murders.* New York: Holiday House.

Author Index

Subject Index

A

ACT, 5–6, 75–76
Author's chair, 110, 111

B

Book previews, 31, 61, 90
Brainstorming, 110, 127

C

Cartoons, 49, 69
Charts, 5, 19, 35, 49, 51, 66, 70, 74, 81, 94, 122,
     136, 165
Classroom activities, 37, 95, *see also* Book pre-
     views; Conferences; Discussion; Journal
     buddies; KWL activities; Learning jour-
     nals; Minilessons; Observation; Reading ac-
     tivities; Recording activities; Response
     activities; Review activities; Sharing activi-
     ties; Study; Workshops; Writing
  learning journals and, 60–61
  related to content areas, 30–31
Cognitive development, 126
Cognitive psychology, 8
Communication
  home–school, 2, 35–37
  of learning, 34–35, 137
Conferences, *see also* Individual conferences
  group, 39–40
  peer, 111
  periodic review of journals, 40, 84
  two-minute, 39, 84
Constructivism, 8–9
Content area, 105, *see also* Curriculum
  learning, 1, 2, 4, 5, 10, 21–22
  related activities, 30–31
  resources, 168–172
  study, 43, 82
CoVis program, 59
Curriculum, 19, *see also* Content area

integrated, 1, 7–9, 22, 85, 106
language across the, 4, 15–16
teaching across the, 72

D

Data banks, 48, 66, 95
Diagrams, 5, 19, 46, 49, 50, 75, 94, 109, 126,
     136, 153
Dialogue journals, 2, 5
Diaries, 2, 48, 95
Dictionaries, personal, 49, 83, 105, 109, 157
Discussion, 10, 85, 136, *see also* Group discus-
     sions
  creating resources for, 30–31
  prompts, 112
Drawing, 5, 18, 22, 42, 48, 87, 153, 299, *see also*
     Cartoons; Science journals
  kindergarten level, 109, 124–125
  language and, 26–27
  math journals and, 121, 122
  primary level, 78, 80, 91, 125–126
  as response formats, 94
  younger children, 33

E

Essays, 46, 47, 66, 80, 94
Evaluation, 4, 45, 84, 90, *see also* Conferences;
     Self-evaluation
  end of term, 37
  functions, 5
  mathematical journals and, 119, 124,
     129–130
  responses, guidelines for, 82
  science journals and, 134–135
  of student progress, 38–39, 75

G

Geography, 52, 80
Glossaries, 49, 70, 105, 137